D0928033

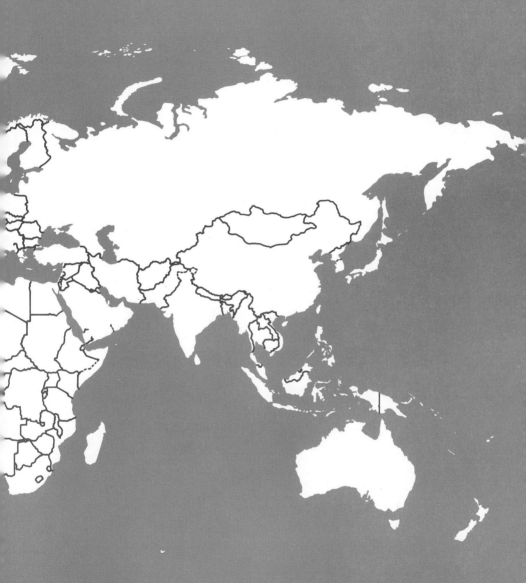

Nepal and Bhutan
country studies

Federal Research Division
Library of Congress
Edited by
Andrea Matles Savada
Research Completed
September 1991

On the cover: Mountains and monasteries are typical of both
Nepal and Bhutan.

Third Edition, First Printing, 1993.

Library of Congress Cataloging-in-Publication Data

Nepal and Bhutan : country studies / Federal Research Division, Library
of Congress ; edited by Andrea Matles Savada. — 3rd ed.
   p. cm. — (Area handbook series, ISSN 1057-5294)
(DA pam ; 550-35)
   "Supersedes the 1973 edition of Area handbook for Nepal,
Bhutan, and Sikkim written by George L. Harris, et al."—T.p.
verso.
   "Research completed September 1991."
   Includes bibliographical references (pp. 369–393) and index.
   ISBN 0-8444-0777-1
   1. Nepal. 2. Bhutan. I. Savada, Andrea Matles, 1950- . II.
Library of Congress. Federal Research Division. III. Area hand-
book for Nepal and Bhutan. IV. Series. V. Series: DA pam ;
550-35.
DS491.4.N46   1993   93-12226
954.96—dc20   CIP

Headquarters, Department of the Army
DA Pam 550-35

For sale by the Superintendent of Documents, U.S. Government Printing Office
Washington, D.C. 20402

Foreword

This volume is one in a continuing series of books prepared by the Federal Research Division of the Library of Congress under the Country Studies/Area Handbook Program sponsored by the Department of the Army. The last page of this book lists the other published studies.

Most books in the series deal with a particular foreign country, describing and analyzing its political, economic, social, and national security systems and institutions, and examining the interrelationships of those systems and the ways they are shaped by cultural factors. Each study is written by a multidisciplinary team of social scientists. The authors seek to provide a basic understanding of the observed society, striving for a dynamic rather than a static portrayal. Particular attention is devoted to the people who make up the society, their origins, dominant beliefs and values, their common interests and the issues on which they are divided, the nature and extent of their involvement with national institutions, and their attitudes toward each other and toward their social system and political order.

The books represent the analysis of the authors and should not be construed as an expression of an official United States government position, policy, or decision. The authors have sought to adhere to accepted standards of scholarly objectivity. Corrections, additions, and suggestions for changes from readers will be welcomed for use in future editions.

Louis R. Mortimer
Chief
Federal Research Division
Library of Congress
Washington, D.C. 20540

Acknowledgments

The authors wish to thank the various individuals and organizations that provided assistance in the preparation of this book. Allen W. Thrasher, Asian Division, and Lygia M. Ballantyne and the staff of the New Delhi Field Office of the Library of Congress provided useful and timely research materials from Bhutan. Karl Ryavec of the Defense Mapping Agency verified hard-to-locate Nepalese and Bhutanese place-names and spellings. Staff of the Royal Nepalese Embassy in Washington provided photographs, statistical data, and the clarification of information. Staff of the Permanent Mission to the United Nations of the Kingdom of Bhutan kindly provided maps, photographs, and documentary information on Bhutan.

Special thanks goes to Brian C. Shaw for lending his expertise on Nepal and Bhutan in serving as reader of the completed manuscript. Additionally, Thierry Mathou, a member of the staff of the Embassy of France in Washington, who is preparing his own manuscript on Bhutan, reviewed the Bhutan text and provided helpful research materials and insights. Gopal Siwkoti, then an attorney with the Washington-based International Human Rights Law Group, also provided materials and shared his insights on the development of Nepalese politics during the prodemocracy movement. Tshering Dorji, director of the Department of Telecommunications of the Kingdom of Bhutan, graciously allowed the author of the Bhutan chapter to interview him when he visited the Library of Congress and reviewed and suggested corrections to the section on Bhutan's telecommunications. Thanks are also due Ralph K. Benesch, who oversees the Country Studies/Area Handbook Program for the Department of the Army.

Thanks also go to staff members of the Federal Research Division of the Library of Congress who directly assisted with the book. Sandra W. Meditz reviewed the entire manuscript and made useful suggestions; David P. Cabitto prepared the layout and graphics; Marilyn Majeska supervised editing and managed production; Andrea Merrill provided invaluable assistance in preparing the tables; Timothy L. Merrill reviewed the maps and geography and telecommunications sections; Ly Burnham reviewed sections on demography; Alberta J. King provided secondary-source research assistance in the preparation of Chapter 6 and bibliographic assistance for other chapters; and Izella Watson and Barbara Edgerton performed word processing.

The following individuals are gratefully acknowledged as well: Harriett R. Blood for preparing the topography and drainage maps; Barbara Harrison and Beverly J. Wolpert for editing the body of the book; Catherine Schwartzstein for prepublication editorial review; Joan C. Cook for preparing the index; Joyce L. Rahim for word-processing support; and Malinda B. Neale and Linda Peterson of the Printing and Processing Section, Library of Congress, for phototypesetting, under the direction of Peggy Pixley.

Finally, the authors acknowledge the generosity of the individuals and the public and private agencies who allowed their photographs to be used in this study.

Contents

James Heitzman

Nanda R. Shrestha

Chapter 3. Nepal: The Economy 105
Vishwa S. Shukla

Chapter 4. Nepal: Government and Politics 143
Enayetur Rahim

List of Figures

Preface

This is the first edition of *Nepal and Bhutan: Country Studies*. It supersedes the 1973 *Area Handbook for Nepal, Bhutan, and Sikkim*. The material on Nepal is presented in the standard five-chapter format of the country study series. A sixth chapter, on Bhutan, covers the subjects addressed in the five Nepal chapters, but in a single chapter. The material on Sikkim has been dropped; readers should consult *India: A Country Study* for information on Sikkim.

Nepal and Bhutan: Country Studies is an effort to present an objective and concise account of the social, economic, political, and national security concerns of contemporary Nepal and Bhutan within historical frameworks. A variety of scholarly monographs and journals, official reports of government and international organizations, and foreign and domestic newspapers and periodicals were used as sources. Brief commentary on some of the more useful and readily accessible sources appears at the end of each chapter. Full references to these and other sources appear in the Bibliography. The annual editions of the *Bibliography of Asian Studies* will provide the reader with additional materials on Nepal and Bhutan.

The authors have limited the use of foreign and technical terms, which are defined when they first appear. Readers are also referred to the Glossary at the back of the volume. Spellings of contemporary place-names generally are those approved by the United States Board on Geographic Names. All measurements are given in the metric system. A conversion table is provided for those readers who may not be familiar with metric equivalents (see table 1, Appendix).

The body of the text reflects information available as of September 1991. Certain other portions of the text, however, have been updated. The Introduction discusses significant events that have occurred since the completion of research, the Country Profile includes updated information as available, and the Bibliography includes recently published sources thought to be particularly helpful to the reader.

Introduction

THE HIMALAYAN KINGDOMS of Nepal and Bhutan share a history of influence by Tibet, China, and India, and an interlude of British colonial guidance. Although the kingdoms are not contiguous, each country is bordered by China to the north and India on its other peripheries. Both kingdoms are ruled by hereditary monarchs and are traditional societies with predominantly agricultural economies; their cultures, however, differ. Nepal's Hinduism, a legacy of India's influence, defines its culture and caste-structured society. Bhutan's Buddhist practices and culture reflect India's influence by way of Tibet. The two countries' legal systems also reflect their heritage. Nepal's judicial system blends Hindu legal and English common law traditions. Bhutan's legal system is based on Buddhist law and English common law.

Nepal has existed as a kingdom centered in the Kathmandu Valley for more than 1,500 years (see fig. 1). The country is known for its majestic Himalayas and has nine of the fourteen peaks in the world over 8,000 meters, including Mount Everest and Annapurna I.

Modern Nepal began its evolution in the sixteenth century with the founding of the House of Gorkha by Dravya Shah in 1559. In the late eighteenth century, Gorkha conquests extended the kingdom through the Himalayas for almost 1,500 kilometers from the western boundary of Garhwal, India, through the territory of Sikkim in the east. In the early nineteenth century, Gorkha power came into conflict with the British East India Company. The resulting Anglo-Nepalese War (1814–16) was devastating for Nepal: the Treaty of Sagauli reduced the kingdom to the boundaries it has since occupied, less than 900 kilometers from east to west. For almost thirty years after the treaty was concluded, infighting among aristocratic factions characterized Nepal.

The next stage of Nepalese politics was the period of hereditary Rana rule—the establishment of a dictatorship of successive Rana prime ministers beginning with Jang Bahadur Kunwar in 1846. During the period of Rana rule, which lasted until the end of 1950, Nepal was governed by a landed aristocracy; parliamentary government was in name only. This period provided stability, but also inhibited political and economic development because the Ranas isolated the country and exercised total control over internal affairs. Although during this period Nepal was a constitutional monarchy with universal suffrage granted at age eighteen, political parties were not formed until the mid-twentieth century and were later banned. The longevity of the Rana dictatorship was also a result of a partnership between the rulers and the army. Patronage ensured loyal soldiers: the military supported the Rana prime ministers and, later, the Shah monarchs, who were figureheads during Rana rule.

In January 1951, the Ranas were forced to concede to the restoration of the monarchy, which then assumed charge of all executive powers: financial management, appointment of government officials, and command of the armed forces. The latter power became an increasingly useful tool for enforcing control. In 1962 King Mahendra Bir Bikram Shah Dev devised the centrally controlled partyless council system of government called *panchayat* (see Glossary). This system served as the institutional basis of the king's rule and was envisioned by the palace as a democratic administration although it functioned only at the king's behest. Incorporated into the 1962 constitution, the *panchayat* system was established at the village, district, and national levels. Successive changes in government and constitutional revisions did not weaken the powers of the absolute monarchy. In fact, a May 1980 referendum reaffirmed the status quo of the *panchayat* system and its continuation as a rubber stamp for the king. Elections in 1981 and 1986 were characterized by the lack of political programs.

Government by an absolute monarch behind a democratic façade lasted for some thirty years. Although many party members were exiled to India, opposition to the government and the *panchayat* system continued to grow, particularly in the late 1980s when the outlawed political parties announced a drive for a multiparty system. A coalition between the Nepali Congress Party and the Communist Party of Nepal was formed in late 1989. The increasing disillusionment with and unpopularity of King Birendra Bir Bikram Shah Dev's regime and the worsening economic situation caused by the trade and transit dispute with India added to the momentum of the incipient prodemocracy movement.

The dissolution of the Berlin Wall and the Soviet Union, and the successes of the prodemocracy movements in Eastern Europe in the late 1980s and early 1990s, had an impact in Nepal. In part as a result of the participatory experiences of Nepalese in India, movements arose to effect changes in Nepal's government and society. Nepal's longstanding history of continuity of rule and relative stability was challenged when the Movement for the Restoration of Democracy, or prodemocracy movement, was formally established on February 18, 1990, almost forty years after the end of Rana control. Demonstrations and rallies—accompanied by violence, arrests, and even deaths—were held throughout the country. Political unrest became widespread. Ethnic groups agitated for official recognition of their cultural heritage and linguistic tradition and demonstrated against the monarchy. The goal of the prodemocracy movement, however, was to establish a more representative democracy and to end the *panchayat* system.

The demonstrations and protests characterizing the prodemocracy movement gained momentum when the ban on political parties and activities was lifted in April 1990. That same month, the prime minister resigned, the Council of Ministers and the Rashtriya Panchayat (National Panchayat, or Parliament) were dissolved, and talks with the opposition were begun. A multiparty interim government replaced the *panchayat* system. The king nominated a four-member council, established a Constitution Recommendation Commission, and announced that he would begin an official inquiry into the deaths that had resulted from the prodemocracy demonstrations. In mid-May, a general amnesty was declared for all political prisoners. A draft constitution was announced in the summer of 1990. King Birendra wanted the draft amended to give him more leverage, but subsequent negotiations did not yield as much as he desired. In November 1990, the king finally approved and promulgated a new, more democratic constitution that vested sovereignty in the people.

The *panchayat* system finally ended in May 1991, when general elections, deemed "generally fair, free, and open" by an international election inspection team, were held. Approximately 65 percent of the populace voted. Although more than forty political parties registered with the election commission, only twenty political parties—mostly small, communist splinter groups—were on the ballot. The Nepali Congress Party won 110 of the 205 seats in the House of Representatives, and the Communist Party of Nepal (United Marxist-Leninist) won 69 seats. Previously operating in exile and behind the scenes, the various communist and other parties and coalitions became a powerful presence in the newly constituted bicameral Parliament. Nepal continued its gradual move toward a multiparty democracy.

Prodemocracy protests continued unabated. Demonstrations were held on February 18, 1992, the second anniversary of the founding of the prodemocracy movement. In early April 1992, rival student groups clashed, and communist and leftist opposition groups called for a general strike as a response to double-digit inflation and a more than 60 percent increase in water and electricity rates. As a result of skirmishes between the police and demonstrators, a curfew was imposed. In addition, the government banned primary and secondary schoolteachers from political activities and from joining or campaigning for political parties.

Elections to the village development committees and municipalities were held in late May 1992; the elections pitted the various communist factions and other parties against the Nepali Congress Party administration of Prime Minister Girija Prasad (G.P.) Koirala. More than 90,000 civilian and security personnel were assigned to safeguard the elections. In contrast to the May 1991 parliamentary election, the Nepali Congress Party routed the communists in the urban areas and even made some gains in the rural areas. The Nepali Congress Party won 331 positions, or 56 percent of the seats, in the municipalities; the Communist Party of Nepal (United Marxist-Leninist) won 119 seats, or 20 percent of the seats; and other lesser parties won the remainder of the seats. In newly established village development committees, the Nepali Congress Party won 21,461 positions; the Communist Party of Nepal (United Marxist-Leninist) won 11,175 seats.

The Nepalese army has long been intertwined with the monarchy; the 1990 constitution, however, changed the relationship between the military and the king. For the first time, the military no longer was solely an instrument of the king; it was also subordinate to the authority of Parliament. Although under the constitution the king retains his title as the supreme commander of the army, the functional commander in chief is appointed on the recommendation of the prime minister. Although both the king and the government are responsible for implementing national security and military policy, the king's power to declare a state of national emergency and to conduct foreign affairs has national security implications.

Nepal is noted for its famed Gurkha soldiers. Gurkhas served both at home and abroad in the British, Indian, Singapore, and Brunei armies. Their remittances to Nepal were of primary importance to the economy and served as an important source of foreign exchange. By 1997, however, the number of Gurkhas serving in the British army is expected to be reduced from 8,000 to 2,500 persons, and the Gurkha garrison in Hong Kong is scheduled to be withdrawn gradually in the period up to 1995. As of April 1992, a token number of Gurkhas were serving in a United Nations peacekeeping force in the former Yugoslavia.

The difficulty of replacing Nepal's long tradition of autocracy with a democracy, coupled with the economic challenges posed by physical geography and location, was daunting. As of 1992, many of the prescribed changes had only just been instituted, or were still to come. Many observers expected that the populist experiment of a multiparty democracy would meet with eventual failure and that the monarchy and the army would return to some type of power-sharing formula.

Nepal's population, estimated in 1990 as approximately 19.1 million, is very diverse. The country is home to more than a dozen ethnic groups, which originate from three major ethnic divisions: Indo-Nepalese, Tibeto-Nepalese, and indigenous Nepalese. Ethnic identity—distinguished primarily by language and dress—constrains the selection of a spouse, friendships, and career, and is evident in social organization, occupation, and religious observances. Hinduism is the official religion of Nepal, although, in fact, the religion practiced by the majority of Nepalese is a synthesis of Hinduism and Buddhism and the practices have intermingled over time. The socioeconomic ramifications of the country's diversity have proven problematic for Nepal in the late twentieth century.

Considered a least-developed country, Nepal depends heavily on farming, which accounts for most of the country's gross domestic product. The work force is largely unskilled and mostly illiterate. Nepal's industrial base was established in the 1930s, but little progress has been made in improving economic performance. In the early 1990s, tourism was one of the largest sources of foreign exchange; visitors from the United States were the most numerous.

Social status in Nepal is measured by economic standing. Landownership is both a measure of status and a source of income. Women occupy a secondary position, particularly in business and the civil service, although the constitution guarantees equality between men and women. Nepalese tribal and communal customs dictate women's lesser role in society, but their status differs from one ethnic group to another and is usually determined by caste.

As of 1992, education was free and compulsory for five years; however males had literacy rates about three times higher than the rates for females and higher school enrollment levels. There were relatively few other social services in the country. The absence of modern medical care, clean drinking water, and adequate sanitation resulted in the prevalence of gastrointestinal diseases. Malnutrition was also a problem, particularly in rural areas. A period of drought in 1992 was expected to cause further food shortages, especially of grain. The country has consistently had high morbidity and death rates.

Economic assistance from other countries, especially India, has been vital to Nepal. Since the 1980s, however, bilateral aid and multilateral assistance programs from countries other than India have been an increasingly important part of development planning.

Nepal has received aid from both the United States and communist countries.

In the late twentieth century, Nepal's foreign policy continued to be affected by its geostrategic location between China and India and its attempt to maintain a balance between these powerful neighbors. Nepal's relationship with India is governed by the 1950 Treaty of Peace and Friendship and its accompanying letters, which established an informal military alliance whereby both countries are required to consult and "devise effective countermeasures" in case the security of either is threatened. Since the 1970s, however, Nepal has exhibited greater independence in its foreign policy, establishing bilateral diplomatic relations with other countries and joining various multilateral and regional organizations.

Nepal, for example, belongs to the United Nations and its affiliated agencies such as the Group of 77, as well as the Nonaligned Movement and the Asian Development Bank. It is also a member of the South Asian Association for Regional Cooperation (SAARC), founded in 1983, initially under a slightly different name, as an institutionalized framework for regional cooperation; its permanent secretariat was established in 1987 in Kathmandu. Nepal does not accept compulsory United Nations International Court of Justice jurisdiction.

One of India's longstanding sources of power over Nepal has been India's control of access to raw materials and supply routes. The effect of this control was especially evident during the 1989 trade and transit dispute—and its aftermath—when the foreign trade balance was negatively affected and the economy took a downturn.

In early 1992, Nepal's relations with India were clouded by controversy over the December 1991 agreement for cooperation on a hydroelectric and irrigation project at Tanakpur, near the southwestern Nepalese-Indian border. The Communist Party of Nepal (United Marxist-Leninist) and other leftist parties opposed the project, which they regarded as against Nepal's national interest because the site, on Nepalese territory, was not covered by a formal treaty. The constitution stipulates that treaties need parliamentary assent if exploitation of the nation's natural resources is involved. Prime Minister G.P. Koirala said he had signed a memorandum of understanding, not a treaty. The opposition took its case to the Supreme Court.

Military relations between Kathmandu and New Delhi were cordial. In March 1992, the Indian chief of army staff visited Nepal and was made an honorary general of the Royal Nepal Army, an uncommon occurrence.

Nepal's relations with China were low-key and an exercise in caution. Nonetheless, India interpreted sales of air defense weapons by China to Nepal in 1988 as interfering with its treaty arrangements with Nepal. Nepal and China, however, signed technical and economic cooperation agreements in March 1992.

Bhutan has its own distinct history, although it shares Nepal's Himalayan geography and neighbors (see fig. 2). Only one-third the size of Nepal, Bhutan also has a much smaller population: estimated at about 600,000 persons in 1990 as compared to a population of over 19 million in Nepal.

The precursor of Bhutan, the state of Lhomon or Monyul, was said to have existed between 500 B.C. and A.D. 600. At the end of that period, Buddhism was introduced into the country; a branch of Mahayana Buddhism is the state religion of Bhutan. Bhutan was subject to both Indian and Tibetan influences, and small independent monarchies began to develop in the country by the early ninth century. Religious rivalry among various Buddhist subsects also influenced political development; the rivalry began in the tenth century and continued through the seventeenth century, when a theocratic government independent of Tibetan political influence united the country. From that time until 1907, the Kingdom of Bhutan, or Drukyul (literally land of the Thunder Dragon), had a dual system of shared civil and spiritual (Buddhist) rule. In 1907 the absolute monarchy was established, and the hereditary position of Druk Gyalpo, or Dragon King, was awarded to the powerful Wangchuck family. Since 1972, Jigme Singye Wangchuck has held the position of Druk Gyalpo.

The Druk Gyalpo controls the executive, legislative, and judicial branches of the government. The monarchy is absolute, but the king is admired and respected and is referred to by the people as "our King." The Council of Ministers and Royal Advisory Council are part of the executive branch of government. The legislative branch is made up of the unicameral National Assembly, or Tshogdu, whose members are either indirectly elected or appointed by the Druk Gyalpo. Bhutan has neither a written constitution nor organic laws. The 1953 royal decree on the Constitution of the National Assembly is the primary legal, or constitutional, basis for that body and sets forth its rules and procedures. The Supreme Court of Appeal, in effect the Druk Gyalpo, is the highest level court; judges are appointed by the Druk Gyalpo. There are no lawyers. The civil code and criminal code are based on seventeenth-century concepts.

Under Jigme Singye Wangchuck, Bhutan's centrally controlled government system has been instrumental in initiating greater political participation. In the early 1990s, however, there were still no legal political parties—although there were elite political factions—and no national elections. There was no overt communist presence. Each family was allowed one vote in village-level elections. Local government was divided into zones, districts, subdistricts, and village groups, and meetings were regularly held at the village and block (*gewog*) levels, where issues were decided by public debate. The complex administrative network of consultation and decisionmaking by consensus obscured the need for national elections. At the 1992 session of the National Assembly, support for the hereditary monarchy was unanimously reaffirmed.

Like Nepal, Bhutan has a diverse population. It is home to four ethnic groups: Ngalop—of Tibetan origin; Sharchop—of Indo-Mongoloid origin; aboriginal, or indigenous, tribal peoples; and Nepalese. In the early 1990s, the first three groups made up about 72 percent of the population. According to this estimate, the Nepalese constituted approximately 28 percent of the population; other estimates suggested that 30 to 40 percent might be Nepalese. The Nepalese constituted a majority in southern Bhutan, where, in an effort to maintain traditional culture and control, the government has tried to confine their immigration and restrict their residence and employment. In the early 1990s, only approximately 15 percent of the Nepalese in Bhutan were considered legal permanent residents; only those immigrants who had resided in Bhutan for fifteen or twenty years—the number of years depended on their occupational status and other criteria—were considered for citizenship. Nepalese immigrants who were asked to leave because their claims to citizenship did not conform to the 1985 Citizenship Act openly voiced their discontent with the government. Illegal immigrants often were militant antinationals.

In the 1980s, the Bhutanese, believing their identity threatened by absorption of a growing Nepalese minority and the specter of annexation by India, promulgated a policy of *driglam namzha,* "national customs and etiquette." This policy sought to preserve and enhance Bhutanese cultural identity and bolster Bhutanese nationalism. The policy mandated the wearing of national dress for formal occasions and the use of the official language, Dzongkha, in schools. In 1989, it was decreed that Nepali, which had been offered as an optional language, was no longer to be taught in the schools. Subsequent government decrees contributed to a growing conflict with ethnic Nepalese, who sought to maintain their own identity and viewed these edicts as restrictive. Ethnic strife increased as the aftereffects of Nepal's prodemocracy movement spread to Bhutan, where Nepalese communities demonstrated against the government in an effort to protect their rights from the *driglam namzha* policy. Expatriate Nepalese political groups in Nepal and India supported these antigovernment activities, further alienating the Bhutanese.

Bhutan's military force, the Royal Bhutan Army, is very small; in 1990 it numbered only 6,000 persons. The Druk Gyalpo is the supreme commander of the army, but daily operations are the responsibility of the chief operations officer. The army's primary mission is border defense although it also assists the Royal Bhutan Police in internal security matters.

Bhutan, like Nepal, is considered a least-developed country. Its work force is largely unskilled, and a wide gap exists between the rich and the poor. Farming is the mainstay of the economy and accounts for most of the gross domestic product. Although Bhutan did not begin to establish its industrial base until the 1950s, careful economic planning and use of foreign aid have resulted in measurable improvements in economic efficiency and performance over the last four decades. As is the case in Nepal, tourists bring in a major portion of the country's foreign exchange.

Social status in Bhutan, as in Nepal, depends primarily on economic standing in the community. Specifically, it depends on land-ownership, occupation, and perceived religious authority. The society is male dominated. Although as of 1992 the government officially encouraged increased participation of women in political and administrative life, women remained in a secondary position, particularly in business and the civil service. Bhutanese women, however, do have a dominant social position, and land often passes to daughters, not to sons. Bhutan's traditional society is both matriarchal and patriarchal; the head of the family is the member in highest esteem. However, men predominate in government and have more opportunities for higher education than do women.

As of 1992, education in Bhutan is free for eleven years but not compulsory. Men have literacy rates about three times higher than those for women, and school enrollment levels are higher for males. As is the case in Nepal, social services are not widespread. Modern medical care is lacking, as are clean drinking water and adequate sanitation. Not surprisingly, gastrointestinal diseases are widespread. Nutrional deficiencies are also prevalent; serious malnutrition, however, does not appear to be a problem. Like Nepal, the country had high morbidity and death rates in the early 1990s.

Foreign aid, grants, and concessionary loans constituted a large percentage of Bhutan's budget in the early 1990s. Like Nepal, Bhutan received foreign assistance from the United Nations, the Colombo Plan (see Glossary), the Asian Development Bank, the World Bank (see Glossary), and the Organization of the Petroleum Exporting

Countries, as well as official development assistance and other official flows. Because Bhutan had no formal diplomatic relations with the United States as of 1992, no official aid was forthcoming from Washington.

As has been the case in Nepal, Bhutan's foreign policy has been affected by its geostrategic location. From the seventh century until 1860, the country's foreign policy was influenced by Tibet; next followed a period of British guidance over foreign affairs. After India received independence from Britain in 1947, Bhutan came under India's influence. Thimphu and New Delhi's relationship is governed by the 1949 Treaty of Friendship between the Government of India and the Government of Bhutan—in force in perpetuity—which calls for peace and noninterference in internal affairs and New Delhi's guidance and advice in external relations. Like Nepal, however, Bhutan has been exhibiting greater independence in its foreign policy, and by the early 1990s was, in effect, autonomous in its foreign relations. Thimphu has established bilateral diplomatic relations with other countries and has joined various multilateral and regional organizations. Bhutan belongs to the United Nations, as well as to organizations such as SAARC, the Nonaligned Movement, and the Asian Development Bank. It does not accept compulsory United Nations International Court of Justice jurisdiction.

Both Nepal and Bhutan were facing refugee problems in the early 1990s; statistics on the number of refugees come from diverse sources and are discrepant. In April 1992, the United Nations High Commissioner for Refugees (UNHCR) estimated that since 1986 more than 30,000 ethnic Nepalese had left Bhutan because of political discontent, poor employment prospects, or because they were considered illegal immigrants. A much higher figure is projected by G.P. Koirala, Nepal's prime minister, who has estimated that in the early 1990s Nepalese from Bhutan seeking to escape the sanctions imposed by *driglam namzha* arrived in Nepal at the rate of 200 persons daily.

Antinationals in Bhutan used the growing number of southern Bhutanese-Nepalese in the refugee camps within Nepal as a means to publicize and internationalize their plight. To this end, they encouraged Nepalese to leave Bhutan and also encouraged Nepalese from India to enter the camps. For Bhutan, the departure of the Nepalese often meant the loss of skilled laborers; however, it also resulted in the exodus of unwanted agitators. For Nepal, the refugees were an added economic burden—more people needing housing, food, clothing, education, and other social services. Living conditions in the refugee camps within Nepal were reported to be poor. As of mid-1992, the camps were filled with people holding Nepalese citizenship cards, Bhutanese citizenship cards, and UNHCR certificates attesting they were "Bhutanese refugees." However, because each party seeks to present its own case, all statistics and statements related to the Nepalese refugee situation must be viewed cautiously.

The refugee problem presented a challenge to India, which needed to balance its interests in maintaining Bhutan's stability with the necessity of not inflaming nationalist passions among its own ethnic Nepalese population and not upsetting its relations with either Nepal or Bhutan. India would not allow its territory to be used as a staging ground for protests by Bhutanese residents of Nepalese origin. The situation was further complicated by the fact that Indian laborers who entered Nepal in search of work displaced underemployed and unemployed Nepalese workers.

September 10, 1992

*　　*　　*

Since the Introduction was written, the events taking place in Nepal and Bhutan in late 1992 and early 1993 have continued to reflect the issues that have faced the two countries in the past few years. The refugee issue has continued to be problematic. The leaders of both Nepal and Bhutan met with India's leaders in late 1992 and early 1993; all the parties reaffirmed that the issue was an internal matter that should be resolved through bilateral talks between Nepal and Bhutan. In spite of the agitation and activities of antinationals in the south, Bhutan's National Assembly passed a National Security Act in late 1992 that abolished the death penalty for crimes of treason as stipulated in a 1957 law, providing instead for life imprisonment.

In December 1992, the Supreme Court of Nepal ruled against Prime Minister G.P. Koirala's signing of a December 1991 accord for hydroelectric power cooperation with India at Tanakpur. After their victory, Koirala's opponents in the Communist Party of Nepal (United Marxist-Leninist) pressed him to step down, but he refused. As a result of the court's decision, however, Kathmandu said the Koirala government would present the Tanakpur accord and its relevant documents to the next parliamentary session for ratification—a step that would have otherwise been bypassed.

In November 1992, the Nepal Investment Forum, jointly organized by the government, the United Nations Development Programme, and the United Nations Industrial Development Organization, held its inaugural meeting. The forum of investors and industrialists aimed to increase investment in the industrial sector; Nepal said it would even simplify some economic procedures to ensure a favorable investment climate. In December 1992, Nepal passed laws to encourage foreign (and local) investment by creating a more favorable investment environment. Foreigners would be allowed to repatriate earnings and hold total equity in new projects.

In March 1993, communist factions demonstrated against the government, protesting the Tanakpur accord as well as power cuts, despite an almost 100 percent increase in electricity rates. The communists also rallied to show their support for an upcoming general strike in the Kathmandu Valley. More than 6,000 persons participated in the strike, which idled markets, schools, and factories. That same month, the Nepal Electricity Authority said power cuts could continue until July 1995 because of the water shortage in reservoirs. In addition, other dams had technical problems and needed refurbishing.

Also in March, Nepal estimated 100,000 Bhutanese refugees in UNHCR-run camps in Nepal and elsewhere. The World Food Programme announced in April that it would supply 8,000 tons of food until September 1993 to ethnic Nepalese refugees from Bhutan in southeastern Nepal. Talks between Nepal's foreign minister and Bhutan's king at the SAARC summit meeting in April failed to resolve the refugee problem.

In April 1993, King Birendra suspended the fourth session of Parliament a day after the House of Representatives agreed by unanimous decision to establish an all-party special parliamentary committee to evaluate the Tanakpur accord. That same month, the government arrested three journalists for allegedly offending members of the royal family.

In mid-May 1993, two senior leaders of the Communist Party of Nepal (United Marxist-Leninist) died in an automobile accident, which subsequently was being investigated. It was expected that a void in the communist leadership would result from the deaths of the two leaders.

Late 1992 and early 1993 brought a number of published reports on Bhutan's ethnic problems. The reports were a mix of investigation, condemnation, explanation, and defense. Prominent among these reports was Amnesty International's *Bhutan: Human Rights Violations Against the Nepali-Speaking Population in the South.* Published in New York in December 1992, the report was based on Amnesty International's investigations of reports of human rights violations since late 1990 as well as its delegations' visits to Nepal in November 1991 to interview Nepali-speaking refugees from Bhutan and to Bhutan in January 1992 at the invitation of the Druk Gyalpo to discuss the earlier human rights findings and measures to be taken to improve the human rights situation. Information provided by refugees included charges of arbitrary arrest, detention without charge or trial, unfair trials, ill treatment, torture, rape, deaths in custody, and inadequate prison conditions. The report also outlined measures taken by the Bhutanese government during and after the January 1992 visit to Bhutan: more than 1,500 political prisoners, including some identified by Amnesty International as prisoners of conscience, were granted amnesty; others still imprisoned were allowed regular access to their relatives and had their living conditions improved, including the elimination of the use of shackles. Other steps taken included punishment of members of security forces involved in human rights violations and the introduction of legislation that would eliminate a mandatory death penalty for acts of treason.

Both the Amnesty International report and another written investigative report by British academic Michael Hutton, following his visits to Bhutan and Nepal and published in the April 1993 issue of *Index on Censorship,* attributed the rise of ethnic unrest to Bhutan's Citizenship Act of 1985, which retroactively reclassified citizenship qualifications; the 1988 census, which revealed the presence of some 100,000 illegal residents in southern Bhutan and led to mass deportations; and the series of government decisions and directives between 1987 and 1989 designed to enforce *driglam namzha.* While Hutton concluded that "journalists are easily misled by both sides" on the human rights issue, he noted the contrast of the "well-produced" reports written in flawless English by Bhutan's official press with the "injudiciously emotive" but sometimes "extraordinarily thorough" reports coming from Kathmandu-based organizations.

In early May 1993, the *Nation* [Bangkok] published a revealing interview given by Bhutan's minister of foreign affairs, Dawa Tsering. While strongly denying charges of "ethnic cleansing," Tsering insisted that "there is no violence" and that the majority of people leaving or who have left Bhutan were illegal residents. At the encouragement of Amnesty International, he said, the government had agreed to give illegal residents work permits, the same as had been granted to outsiders working in Bhutan. He added that the government was dismayed that "a big chunk of genuine"

Bhutanese nationals, that is, legal emigrants, had left the country because of fear and insecurity caused not only by antigovernment terrorist attacks but also by fear of Bhutanese security forces who were "functioning under lots of tension . . . and might sometimes be a bit rough on the common people." To reverse this trend, he said that the government had exempted legal southern Bhutanese citizens from paying land taxes in order to convince them not to emigrate. Countering a common misperception, Tsering said that Nepali had not been banned and that in National Assembly sessions both Dzongkha and Nepali, with the Druk Gyalpo's blessing, were still being spoken—with simultaneous translations. However, he defended the government's right to insist that all citizens should adopt the national dress and learn the Dzongkha language. (Hutton's investigation revealed that many native Dzongkha speakers easily used Nepali in their daily dealings with Nepali-speaking residents.) Queried about the number of dissidents, he admitted that there were approximately 180 people in detention, some of whom had been convicted during trial but all of whom had been given access to the International Committee of the Red Cross starting in January 1993.

As the mid-1990s approached, Bhutan, like Nepal, was experiencing a sometimes painful transition to more democratic forms of government. Dawa Tsering concluded his interview by offering the observation that Bhutan, from its own perspective, "is being highly democratized" and that the monarchy "is a contractual monarchy and is very conscious of its responsibilities" of "keep[ing] in step with the changing times."

June 1, 1993   Andrea Matles Savada

Table A. Nepal: Chronology of Important Events

Period	Description
ca. 563 B.C.	The Buddha born in Lumbini, in Tarai Region of Nepal.
268-31 B.C.	Ashoka establishes empire in north India.
ca. A.D. 353-73	Samudragupta establishes empire in north India.
400-750	Licchavi kingdom in power in Kathmandu Valley.
750-1200	"Transitional" kingdom in power in Kathmandu Valley.
1100-1484	Khasa Malla kings rule in western Nepal.
1200-16	Arimalla, first monarch of the Malla Dynasty, rules in Kathmandu Valley.
1312	Khasa king Ripumalla leads raid in Kathmandu Valley.
1345-46	Sultan Shams ud-din Ilyas of Bengal leads raid in Kathmandu Valley.
1382-95	Jayasthitimalla rules as king of united Malla kingdom in Kathmandu Valley.
1428-82	Yakshamalla reigns—height of united Malla kingdom.
1484	Malla kingdom divided; three kingdoms of Kathmandu, Bhadgaon, and Patan expand.
1526	Mughal Empire established in north India.
1559	Gorkha kingdom established.
1606-33	Ram Shah of Gorkha reigns; Gorkha kingdom experiences first expansion.
1728	Chinese influence established in Tibet.
1743	Prithvi Narayan Shah ascends to throne of Gorkha.
1764	British East India Company gains control of Bengal.
1768-90	Gorkha conquers Kathmandu and Patan, Bhaddgaon, eastern Nepal, and western Nepal.

Table A. —Continued

Period	Description
1775	Prithvi Narayan Shah dies, first king of united Nepal.
1982	B.P. Koirala, Nepali Congress Party leader, dies.
1986	Second elections held to National Panchayat.
1989	Failure to renegotiate trade and transit treaties with India disrupts economy.
1990	New constitution promulgated as result of agitations and successes of Movement for the Restoration of Democracy.
1991	Elections held to Parliament; first session of first multiparty Parliament held in thirty-two years.

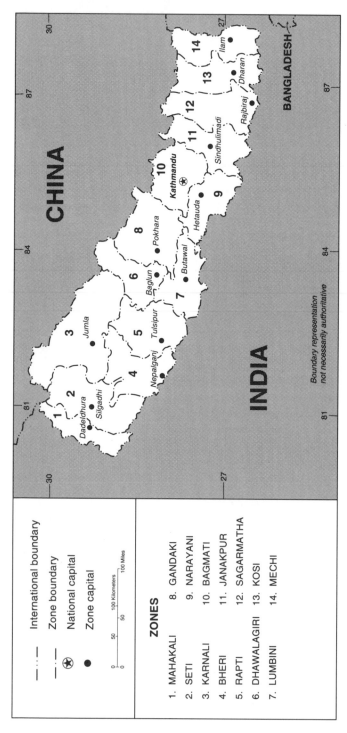

Figure 1. Nepal: Zonal Administrative Divisions, 1991

Nepal: Country Profile

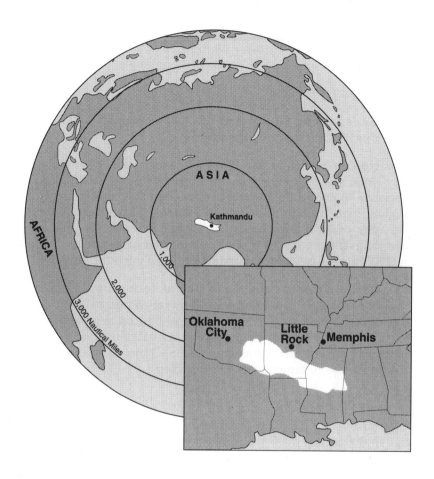

Country

Formal Name: Kingdom of Nepal.

Short Form: Nepal.

Term for Citizens: Nepalese.

Capital: Kathmandu.

NOTE: The Country Profile contains updated information as available.

Date of Independence: 1768, when a number of independent hill states were unified by Prithvi Narayan Shah as the Kingdom of Gorkha.

National Holiday: December 28, birthday of King Birendra Bir Bikram Shah Dev.

Geography

Location and Size: Landlocked between China and India; total land area 147,181 square kilometers.

Topography: Mountainous and hilly, although with physical diversity. Three broad physiographic areas run laterally—lowland Tarai Region in south; central lower mountains and hills constituting Hill Region; high Himalayas, with 8,796-meters-high Mount Everest and other peaks forming Mountain Region in north. Of total land area, only 20 percent cultivatable. Deforestation severe problem; by 1988 forests covered approximately 30 percent of land area.

Climate: Five climatic zones based on altitude range from subtropical in south, to cool summers and severe winters in north. Annual rainfall with seasonal variations depending on monsoon cycle, which provides 60 to 80 percent of total annual rainfall; 2,500 millimeters in eastern part of country; 1,420 millimeters around Kathmandu; 1,000 millimeters in western Nepal.

Society

Population: 15,022,839 at time of 1981 census; estimated 19,145,800 in July 1990 (July 1991 estimate 19,611,900). Growth rate in 1980s 2.6 percent; birth rate 44 per 1,000 in 1985 (39 per 1,000 in 1991); crude death rate 14 per 1,000 in 1985 (15 per 1,000 in 1991—increase from steady decline). Nearly 44 percent of population resides in Tarai Region; about 48 percent in Hill Region, nearly 9 percent in Mountain Region. Population density per square kilometer total land 102 persons; 61 persons per hectare of cultivatable land. Only 6.3 percent total population in urban areas in 1981. Sex ratio 105 males to 100 females in 1981. Life expectancy at birth close to fifty years in 1985; in 1991, fifty-one years male, fifty years female.

Ethnic Groups: Three major ethnic groups in terms of origin: Indo-Nepalese, Tibeto-Nepalese, and indigenous Nepalese, composed of Newar, Bhote, Rai, Limbu, Sherpa, Gurung, Tamang, Magar, Thakali, Brahman, and other smaller ethnic groups.

Languages: Nepali, written in Devanagari script, official, national language; spoken by almost 60 percent of population. More than twelve other languages with numerous dialects, although rarely spoken outside ethnic enclaves.

Religion: Only official Hindu state in world although intermingling and synthesis of Hindu and Buddhist beliefs in practice. About 89.5 percent of population Hindu, approximately 5.3 percent and 2.7 percent, Buddhist and Muslim, respectively; remainder, other religions, including Christianity.

Education: Literacy rate in 1990 estimated at 33 percent; higher percentage males literate; also higher literacy rates in urban areas. Free, compulsory primary education, five years; total school enrollment approximately 52 percent school-age children (70 percent male, 30 percent female) in 1984. In 1987 primary and secondary education included 12,491 primary schools (15,834 in 1989), 3,824 lower-secondary schools (3,941 in 1989), 1,501 higher-secondary schools (1,791 in 1989); apparent primary school enrollment ratio 85 percent in 1987. In 1989 there were 63,945 primary school teachers, 12,245 lower-secondary school teachers, 33,779 higher-secondary school teachers. In 1989 students numbered 2,536,147 at the primary school level, 325,237 in lower-secondary school, and 338,779 in higher-secondary school. National Education Plan set framework for universal education; national development goals stressed through curriculum. Tribhuvan University sole doctoral-granting institution; sixty-nine public colleges under Tribhuvan University; sixty-three private colleges. In 1987, almost 83,000 students, mostly male, enrolled in higher education institutions. Longstanding prejudice against education of women gradually diminishing, but social class and geography continue to bias educational attainment.

Health: Infant mortality 98 per 1,000 in 1991. Poor nutrition, sanitation, general absence of modern medical care and other social services, especially in rural areas. Goiter, leprosy, intestinal parasites, diarrhea, gastrointestinal disorders, and tuberculosis prevalent although latter somewhat reduced since 1970s. Three types health-care practices—popular folk medical care, Ayurvedic treatment, and modern medicine, sometimes intertwined. Limited health-care delivery system; public and private health-care facilities. Hospitals, mostly confined to urban areas, provide wider range of services than predominantly rural health centers and health posts. In 1990 only 123 hospitals, 16 health centers, 816 health posts, and

153 Ayurvedic dispensaries; 951 physicians, or 1 physician for approximately 19,000 persons.

Economy

Salient Features: Underdeveloped with economy tied to India as result of geographic position and historical relationship. Predominantly agricultural; limited industrial activity; services—particularly related to tourism, growing part of economy. In FY 1989, tourism provided more than 3.5 percent of GDP and about 25 percent of total foreign exchange earnings. Services, remittances of Nepalese working outside the country, and foreign loans and grants finance the deficit. Economic prospects poor—projected population growth expected to outpace growth rate of agricultural production. Underemployment estimated at 25–40 percent in 1987; unemployment averaged 5 percent. Foreign aid averaged 64 percent of development from 1956–90; 44.4 percent of FY 1991 budget from foreign loans or grants. Real growth averaged 4 percent annually in early 1980s, almost 5 percent in late 1980s, but plummeted to between 1.5 percent and 2.3 percent in FY 1989 and FY 1990 because of trade and transit dispute with India. No labor laws as of 1991; limited activity of labor unions, but trade unions legalized following prodemocracy movement.

Gross National Product: Per capita income for 1988 US$158–180 range.

Gross Domestic Product (GDP): US$3 billion in FY 1990. GDP increase at constant prices averaged 3.7 percent annually FY 1975–86; increased 2.1 percent in FY 1990. Foreign aid as percentage of GDP increased from less than 8 percent in 1984 to almost 13 percent in 1987. Major share of GDP from FY 1979 to FY 1987 from agricultural sector.

Agriculture: Dominated economy; livelihood for more than 90 percent of population; approximately 60 percent GDP and 75 percent of exports in late 1980s. Some parts of country food deficit areas although enough generally produced to feed population; production dependent on weather conditions—particularly monsoons, distribution of inputs, scarcity of new lands, and continued environmental degradation. Tarai Region main agricultural belt. Paddy (rice) and corn major food crops, also wheat and millet; potatoes, oilseed, sugarcane, jute, and tobacco major cash crops.

Industry: Limited industrial base—less than 20 percent of total GDP in 1980s; 7 percent in FY 1990—established with foreign aid.

Industries used agricultural products and/or dependent on various imported inputs, particularly from India. Traditional cottage industries such as basket-weaving and production of cotton fabrics approximately 60 percent of output.

Manufacturing: Larger plants generally in public sector. Major industries include jute, sugar, cigarettes, beer, matches, shoes, chemicals, cement, and bricks. Small mineral industry; most commodities used for domestic construction; cement, clay, limestone, garnet, magnesite, and talc most important mineral resources.

Energy: As of late 1980s, about 95 percent of energy consumed from traditional sources—fuelwood, 76 percent (hence deforestation). Tremendous potential for hydroelectric power inhibited by terrain, lack of infrastructure, and insufficient capital investment.

Foreign Trade: Traditionally predominantly with India although decreased from more than 70 percent in 1975 to 37 percent of total trade in 1989. Also unrecorded border trade with India. As a result of trade and transit dispute, India's share of exports, 25 percent in FY 1989, dropped to approximately 9 percent in FY 1990; imports fell to only 25 percent FY 1990. Persistent and growing trade deficit with India. Other primary trading partners the United States, Bangladesh, China, Britain, former Soviet Union, West Germany, South Korea, Japan, Singapore, Thailand, Hong Kong, and Pakistan. Major exports clothing, carpets, grain, and leather goods. Major imports petroleum products, fertilizer, and machinery.

Balance of Payments: Improvement in 1980s as a result of foreign loans and assistance although increasing foreign debt. Mid-1989, official foreign debt outstanding and disbursed about US$1.3 billion. In FY 1988, exports US$187 million; imports US$630 million.

Currency/Exchange Rate: 1 Nepalese rupee (NR) or rupee (R) = 100 paisa. Coins issued in denominations of 1, 5, 10, 25, 50 paisa, and 1 rupee; notes issued in denominations of 1, 5, 10, 100, 500, and 1,000 rupees. In 1989, Rs per US$1 = 27.19; in 1990, 29.37; in January 1991, 30.8. Linked to Indian rupee.

Fiscal Year: 16 July–15 July.

Transportation and Communications

Roads: Many built with foreign assistance. By mid-July 1989, approximately 2,900 kilometers paved roads, 1,600 kilometers gravel roads, 2,500 kilometers earthen roads. Main roads east-west and north-south highways. Terrain and weather, particularly monsoons, factors in building and maintaining roads.

Railroads: Average 1.5 million passengers annually between FY 1985–89; goods transported between 15,000 and 19,000 tons (only 13,000 tons in FY 1990). Limited service, from commercial centers in Tarai to railheads near Indian border; two separate rail tracks with total length of 101 kilometers; lines south of the border through India.

Airports: Main airport Tribhuvan International Airport outside Kathmandu; more than thirty airfields. Domestic service and international flights to and from Asian and European cities. Government-owned Royal Nepal Airlines in 1990 carried 291,208 domestic passengers, 317,095 passengers on international flights.

Other Modes of Transportation: Forty-two kilometer ropeway from Hetauda into Kathmandu valley transports food, construction materials, and heavy goods. Local transportation—bus service—common only in Kathmandu Valley.

Telecommunications: Postal service improved, but still inaccessible for many Nepalese; 2,232 post offices in FY 1990. Public telephone services in most urban areas; forty-two exchanges, seventy-six public call offices, fifty-five wireless stations in FY 1990. Rudimentary radio relay network. Radio programming approximately 100 hours weekly. International telephone, telex, and facsimile services available but limited. AM radio broadcast stations, but no FM. Limited television programming.

Government and Politics

Government: Constitutional monarchy. Multiparty democracy established with November 1990 constitution; replaced *panchayat* system. First elections to bicameral legislature, Parliament, made up of House of Representatives and National Council, held May 1991. Executive powers vested in king and Council of Ministers. Prime minister appointed by king leader of political party with majority in House of Representatives.

Administrative Divisions: Fourteen zones and seventy-five districts grouped into five development zones. Following prodemocracy movement, former village *panchayat* renamed Village Development Committee and town *panchayat* renamed Municipal Development Committee. Each district headed by a chief district officer responsible for maintaining law and order and coordinating works of field agencies of different ministries.

Judiciary: Blend of Hindu and Western legal traditions. New judicial system established with 1990 constitution. Supreme Court at apex of system; fifty-four appellate courts, numerous district courts. Judicial Council monitored court system's performance, advised king and government on judicial matters and appointments.

Foreign Relations: Foreign policy focused on maintaining equidistant and friendly relations with India and China. Founding member of non-aligned movement; proposed as zone of peace in 1975; active member of South Asian Association for Regional Cooperation (SAARC—see Glossary) and international organizations.

Media: Approximately 400 Nepalese newspapers and periodicals in 1991. Freedom of expression constitutional right. Radio and television programming controlled by government

National Security

Armed Forces: Royal Nepal Army, of about 35,000 volunteers. Enlistment for initial period of ten years; former Gurkhas for three years. Primary mission to back up local police and maintain security in Kathmandu Valley—the seat of government. No personnel mobilization plan in event of war or declared national emergency; no contingency plan to draft during or in anticipation of emergency.

Military Units and Equipment: Fourteen infantry brigades in Royal Nepal Army; one air wing in Royal Nepal Army Air Service. Shortages of virtually all categories of weapons and equipment. Obsolete weapons in inventory.

Military Budget: In 1989 US$33 million, or approximately 1.2 percent of GNP and 6.2 percent of total central government expenditures.

Foreign Military Relations: Royal Nepal Army personnel serve in United Nations Interim Force in Lebanon; Gurkhas also serve in British Brigade of Gurkhas, in Hong Kong, India, Singapore, and Brunei.

Police Force: Nepalese Police Force of 28,000 personnel under central administration of Ministry of Home Affairs. Overseen by king and advisers with little or nor public accountability.

Chapter 1. Nepal: Historical Setting

The all-seeing eyes of the Buddha, a detail from the great stupa of Svayambhunath, a Buddhist shrine west of Kathmandu

NEPAL HAS BEEN A KINGDOM for at least 1,500 years. During most of that period, the Kathmandu Valley has been Nepal's political, economic, and cultural center. The valley's fertile soil supported thriving village farming communities, and its location along trans-Himalayan trade routes allowed merchants and rulers alike to profit. Since the fourth century, the people of the Kathmandu Valley have developed a unique variant of South Asian civilization based on Buddhism and Hinduism but influenced as well by the cultures of local Newar citizens and neighboring Tibetans. One of the major themes in the history of Nepal has been the transmission of influences from both the north and the south into an original culture. During its entire history, Nepal has been able to continue this process while remaining independent.

The long-term trend in Nepal has been the gradual development of multiple centers of power and civilization and their progressive incorporation into a varied but eventually united nation. The Licchavi (fourth to eighth centuries) and Malla (twelfth to eighteenth centuries) kings may have claimed that they were overlords of the area that is present-day Nepal, but rarely did their effective influence extend far beyond the Kathmandu Valley. By the sixteenth century, there were dozens of kingdoms in the smaller valleys and hills throughout the Himalayan region. It was the destiny of Gorkha, one of these small kingdoms, to conquer its neighbors and finally unite the entire nation in the late eighteenth century. The energy generated from this union drove the armies of Nepal to conquer territories far to the west and to the east, as well as to challenge the Chinese in Tibet and the British in India. Wars with these huge empires checked Nepalese ambitions, however, and fixed the boundaries of the mountain kingdom. Nepal in the late twentieth century was still surrounded by giants and still in the process of integrating its many localized economies and cultures into a nation state based on the ancient center of the Kathmandu Valley.

Nepal took a fateful turn in the mid-nineteenth century when its prime ministers, theoretically administrators in service to the king, usurped complete control of the government and reduced the kings to puppets. By the 1850s, a dynasty of prime ministers called Rana (see Glossary) had imposed upon the country a dictatorship that would last about 100 years. The Ranas distrusted both their own people and foreigners—in short, anyone who could challenge their own power and change their position. As the rest of the world

3

underwent modernization, Nepal remained a medieval nation, based on the exploitation of peasants and some trade revenues and dominated by a tradition-bound aristocracy that had little interest in modern science or technology.

After the revolt against the Ranas in 1950, Nepal struggled to overcome its long legacy of underdevelopment and to incorporate its varied population into a single nation. One of the early casualties of this process was party-based democracy. Although political parties were crucial in the revolution that overthrew Rana rule, their constant wrangling conflicted with the monarchy's views of its own dignity and with the interests of the army. Instead of condoning or encouraging a multiparty democracy, King Mahendra Bir Bikram Shah Dev launched a coup in late 1960 against Bishweshwar Prasad (B.P.) Koirala's popularly elected government and set up a system of indirect elections that created a consultative democracy. The system served as a sounding board for public opinion and as a tool for economic development without exercising effective political power. Nepal remained until 1990 one of the few nations in the world where the king, wielding absolute authority and embodying sacred tradition, attempted to lead his country towards the twenty-first century.

Ancient Nepal, ca. 500 B.C.–A.D. 700

Early Influences on Nepal

Neolithic tools found in the Kathmandu Valley indicate that people were living in the Himalayan region in the distant past, although their culture and artifacts are only slowly being explored. Written references to this region appeared only by the first millennium B.C. During that period, political or social groupings in Nepal became known in north India. The Mahabharata and other legendary Indian histories mention the Kiratas (see Glossary), who still inhabited eastern Nepal in 1991. Some legendary sources from the Kathmandu Valley also describe the Kiratas as early rulers there, taking over from earlier Gopals or Abhiras, both of whom may have been cowherding tribes. These sources agree that an original population, probably of Tibeto-Burman ethnicity, lived in Nepal 2,500 years ago, inhabiting small settlements with a relatively low degree of political centralization.

Monumental changes occurred when groups of tribes calling themselves the Arya migrated into northwest India between 2000 B.C. and 1500 B.C. By the first millennium B.C., their culture had spread throughout northern India. Their many small kingdoms were constantly at war amid the dynamic religious and cultural environment of early Hinduism (see Hinduism, ch. 2). By 500 B.C., a cosmopolitan society was growing around urban sites linked by trade routes that stretched throughout South Asia and beyond. On the edges of the Gangetic Plain, in the Tarai Region, smaller kingdoms or confederations of tribes grew up, responding to dangers from larger kingdoms and opportunities for trade. It is probable that slow and steady migration of Khasa (see Glossary) peoples speaking Indo-Aryan languages was occurring in western Nepal during this period; this movement of peoples would continue, in fact, until modern times and expand to include the eastern Tarai as well (see Geography, ch. 2).

One of the early confederations of the Tarai was the Sakya clan, whose seat apparently was Kapilavastu, near Nepal's present-day border with India. The clan's most renowned son was Siddhartha Gautama (ca. 563–483 B.C.), a prince who rejected the world to search for the meaning of existence and became known as the Buddha, or the Enlightened One. The earliest stories of his life recount his wanderings in the area stretching from the Tarai to Banaras on the Ganges River and into modern Bihar State in India, where he found enlightenment at Gaya—still the site of one of the greatest Buddhist shrines. After his death and cremation, his ashes were distributed among some of the major kingdoms and confederations and were enshrined under mounds of earth or stone called stupas. Certainly, his religion was known at a very early date in Nepal through the Buddha's ministry and the activities of his disciples (see Buddhism, ch. 2).

The political struggles and urbanization of north India culminated in the great Mauryan Empire, which at its height under Ashoka (reigned 268–31 B.C.) covered almost all of South Asia and stretched into Afghanistan in the west. There is no proof that Nepal was ever included in the empire, although records of Ashoka are located at Lumbini, the Buddha's birthplace, in the Tarai. But the empire had important cultural and political consequences for Nepal. First, Ashoka himself embraced Buddhism, and during his time the religion must have become established in the Kathmandu Valley and throughout much of Nepal. Ashoka was known as a great builder of stupas, and his archaic style is preserved in four mounds on the outskirts of Patan (now often referred to as Lalitpur), which were locally called Ashok stupas, and possibly in the Svayambhunath (or Swayambhunath) stupa. Second, along with religion came an entire cultural style centered on the king as the upholder of dharma, or the cosmic law of the universe. This political concept of the king as the righteous center of the political system had a powerful impact on all later South Asian governments and continued to play a major role in modern Nepal.

The Mauryan Empire declined after the second century B.C., and north India entered a period of political disunity. The extended urban and commercial systems expanded to include much of Inner Asia, however, and close contacts were maintained with European merchants. Nepal was apparently a distant part of this commercial network because even Ptolemy and other Greek writers of the second century knew of the Kiratas as a people who lived near China. North India was united by the Gupta emperors again in the fourth century. Their capital was the old Mauryan center of Pataliputra (present-day Patna in Bihar State), during what Indian writers often describe as a golden age of artistic and cultural creativity. The greatest conqueror of this dynasty was Samudragupta (reigned ca. 353–73), who claimed that the "lord of Nepal" paid him taxes and tribute and obeyed his commands. It still is impossible to tell who this lord may have been, what area he ruled, and if he was really a subordinate of the Guptas. Some of the earliest examples of Nepalese art show that the culture of north India during Gupta times exercised a decisive influence on Nepali language, religion, and artistic expression.

The Early Kingdom of the Licchavis, 400–750

In the late fifth century, rulers calling themselves Licchavis began to record details on politics, society, and economy in Nepal. The Licchavis were known from early Buddhist legends as a ruling family during the Buddha's time in India, and the founder of the Gupta Dynasty claimed that he had married a Licchavi princess. Perhaps some members of this Licchavi family married members of a local royal family in the Kathmandu Valley, or perhaps the illustrious history of the name prompted early Nepalese notables to identify themselves with it. In any case, the Licchavis of Nepal were a strictly local dynasty based in the Kathmandu Valley and oversaw the growth of the first truly Nepalese state.

The earliest known Licchavi record, an inscription of Manadeva I, dates from 464, and mentions three preceding rulers, suggesting that the dynasty began in the late fourth century. The last Licchavi inscription was in A.D. 733. All of the Licchavi records are deeds reporting donations to religious foundations, predominantly Hindu temples. The language of the inscriptions is Sanskrit, the language of the court in north India, and the script is closely related to official Gupta scripts. There is little doubt that India exerted a powerful cultural influence, especially through the area called Mithila, the northern part of present-day Bihar State.

*Svayambhunath stupa,
decked with multicolored
Buddhist prayer flags
Courtesy Harvey Follender*

Politically, however, India again was divided for most of the Licchavi period.

To the north, Tibet grew into an expansive military power through the seventh century, declining only by 843. Some early historians, such as the French scholar Sylvain Lévi, thought that Nepal may have become subordinate to Tibet for some time, but more recent Nepalese historians, including Dilli Raman Regmi, deny this interpretation. In any case, from the seventh century onward a recurring pattern of foreign relations emerged for rulers in Nepal: more intensive cultural contacts with the south, potential political threats from both India and Tibet, and continuing trade contacts in both directions.

The Licchavi political system closely resembled that of northern India. At the top was the "great king" (maharaja), who in theory exercised absolute power but in reality interfered little in the social lives of his subjects. Their behavior was regulated in accordance with dharma through their own village and caste councils. The king was aided by royal officers led by a prime minister, who also served as a military commander. As the preserver of righteous moral order, the king had no set limit for his domain, whose borders were determined only by the power of his army and statecraft—an ideology that supported almost unceasing warfare throughout South Asia. In Nepal's case, the geographic realities of the hills limited the Licchavi kingdom to the Kathmandu Valley and neighboring valleys and to the more symbolic submission of less hierarchical societies to the east and west. Within the Licchavi system, there was ample room for powerful notables (*samanta*) to keep their own private armies, run their own landholdings, and influence the court. There was thus a variety of forces struggling for power. During the seventh century, a family known as the Abhira Guptas accumulated enough influence to take over the government. The prime minister, Amsuvarman, assumed the throne between approximately 605 and 641, after which the Licchavis regained power. The later history of Nepal offers similar examples, but behind these struggles was growing a long tradition of kingship.

The economy of the Kathmandu Valley already was based on agriculture during the Licchavi period. Artworks and place-names mentioned in inscriptions show that settlements had filled the entire valley and moved east toward Banepa, west toward Tisting, and northwest toward present-day Gorkha. Peasants lived in villages (*grama*) that were administratively grouped into larger units (*dranga*). They grew rice and other grains as staples on lands owned by the royal family, other major families, Buddhist monastic orders (*sangha*), or groups of Brahmans (*agrahara*). Land taxes due in theory to the king were often allocated to religious or charitable foundations, and additional labor dues (*vishti*) were required from the peasantry in order to keep up irrigation works, roads, and shrines. The village head (usually known as *pradhan*, meaning a leader in family or society), and leading families handled most local administrative issues, forming the village assembly of leaders (*panchalika* or *grama pancha*). This ancient history of localized decision making served as a model for late twentieth-century development efforts.

One of the most striking features of present-day Kathmandu Valley is its vibrant urbanism, notably at Kathmandu, Patan, and Bhadgaon (also called Bhaktapur), which apparently goes back to ancient times. During the Licchavi period, however, the settlement pattern seems to have been much more diffuse and sparse. In the present-day city of Kathmandu, there existed two early villages— Koligrama ("Village of the Kolis," or Yambu in Newari), and Dakshinakoligrama ("South Koli Village," or Yangala in Newari)— that grew up around the valley's main trade route. Bhadgaon was simply a small village then called Khoprn (Khoprngrama in Sanskrit) along the same trade route. The site of Patan was known as Yala ("Village of the Sacrificial Post," or Yupagrama in Sanskrit). In view of the four archaic stupas on its outskirts and its very old tradition of Buddhism, Patan probably can claim to be the oldest true center in the nation. Licchavi palaces or public buildings, however, have not survived. The truly important public sites in those days were religious foundations, including the original stupas at Svayambhunath, Bodhnath, and Chabahil, as well as the shrine of Shiva at Deopatan, and the shrine of Vishnu at Hadigaon.

There was a close relationship between the Licchavi settlements and trade. The Kolis of present-day Kathmandu and the Vrijis of present-day Hadigaon were known even in the Buddha's time as commercial and political confederations in north India. By the time of the Licchavi kingdom, trade had long been intimately connected with the spread of Buddhism and religious pilgrimage. One of the main contributions of Nepal during this period was the transmission of Buddhist culture to Tibet and all of central Asia, through merchants, pilgrims, and missionaries. In return, Nepal gained money from customs duties and goods that helped to support the Licchavi state, as well as the artistic heritage that made the valley famous.

Medieval Nepal, 750–1750

Transition to the Medieval Kingdom, 750–1000

The period following the decline of the Licchavi Dynasty witnessed little growth in the geographical or administrative power of the Nepalese state. In fact, it is the least understood time in Nepal's history, with only a very few inscriptional sources supplemented by some dated religious manuscripts. It appears that the Kathmandu Valley and surrounding valleys officially remained part of a single political unit, although there were struggles for the throne among different royal lineages and notable families. Donations to religious foundations were dated by a new Newari era beginning in 879, a development suggesting the founding of a new dynasty. Surviving records show a movement away from Sanskrit and admixtures of early Newari, the language of the Newar people in the valley.

The main influences on Nepal continued to come from Mithila or Tirhut to the south. This area came intermittently under the domination of warriors allied to the Chalukya Dynasty from Karnataka in southern India. One of their lieutenants proclaimed himself king in 1097 and founded a capital at Simraongarh in the Tarai. From there he launched raids that allowed the Chalukyas to later claim domination over Nepal without exerting a perceptible impact on Nepalese history. By the late twelfth century, however, the king in Nepal was called Somesvaradeva (or Someswaradeva, reigned ca. 1178–85), a name of Chalukya kings, indicating some degree of political contact with Indian rulers. By the end of Somesvaradeva's reign, there was evidence of mounting political chaos and fighting for the throne.

Profound changes were occurring in the religious system of Nepal. The early patronage of Buddhism by the kings gave way to a more strictly Hindu devotion, based on the worship of a variety of deities but ultimately relying on Pashupatinath, the site of one of Hinduism's most sacred Shiva shrines. Within the Buddhist community, the role of the monks and monasteries changed slowly but radically. Early Buddhism had rested on the celibacy and meditation of monks and nuns who had withdrawn from the world in their own living complexes (*vihara*). As a more ritualistic *vajrayana* Buddhism expanded, a division grew up between the "teachers of the thunderbolt" (*vajracharya*) and ordinary monks (*bhikshu*), leading to caste-like divisions and the marriage of religious teachers. The higher-ranking teachers monopolized the worship in the monasteries and controlled the revenues brought in from monastic estates. Monasteries became social and economic centers, serving as workshops and apartments as well as shrines. These roles were kept intact well into the twentieth century.

The Malla Kings

Beginning in the early twelfth century, leading notables in Nepal began to appear with names ending in the term *malla*, (wrestler in Sanskrit), indicating a person of great strength and power. Arimalla (reigned 1200-16) was the first king to be so called, and the practice of adopting such a name was followed regularly by rulers in Nepal until the eighteenth century. (The names of the Malla kings were also represented as, for example, Ari Malla.) This long Malla period witnessed the continued importance of the Kathmandu Valley as a political, cultural, and economic center of Nepal. Other areas also began to emerge as significant centers in their own right, increasingly connected to the Kathmandu Valley.

The time of the earlier Malla kings was not one of consolidation but was instead a period of upheaval in and around Nepal. In the twelfth century, Muslim Turks set up a powerful kingdom in India at Delhi, and in the thirteenth century they expanded their control over most of northern India. During this process, all of the regional kingdoms in India underwent a major reshuffling and considerable fighting before they eventually fell under Delhi's control. This process resulted in an increasing militarization of Nepal's neighbors and sections of Nepal as well. For example, in western Nepal, around Dullu in the Jumla Valley, an alternative seat of

Majestic view, Shipton Pass, in the Makulu region
Courtesy Linda Galantin

political and military power grew up around a separate dynasty
of Mallas (who were not related to the Mallas of the Kathmandu
Valley), who reigned until the fourteenth century. These Khasa
kings expanded into parts of western Tibet and sent raiding expeditions into the Kathmandu Valley between 1275 and 1335. In 1312
the Khasa king, Ripumalla, visited Lumbini and had his own inscription carved on Ashoka's pillar. He then entered the Kathmandu Valley to worship publicly at Matsyendranath, Pashupatinath,
and Svayambhunath. These acts were all public announcements
of his overlordship in Nepal and signified the temporary breakdown of royal power within the valley. At the same time, the rulers in Tirhut to the south led raids into the valley until they were
in turn overrun by agents of the Delhi Sultanate. The worst blow
came in 1345–46, when Sultan Shams ud-din Ilyas of Bengal led
a major pillaging expedition into the Kathmandu Valley, resulting
in the devastation of all major shrines. In fact, none of the existing buildings in the valley proper dates from before this raid.

The early Malla period, a time of continuing trade and the rein-
troduction of Nepalese coinage, saw the steady growth of the small
towns that became Kathmandu, Patan, and Bhadgaon. Royal
pretenders in Patan and Bhadgaon struggled with their main rivals,
the lords of Banepa in the east, relying on the populations of their

towns as their power bases. The citizens of Bhadgaon viewed Devaladevi as the legitimate, independent queen. The betrothal in 1354 of her granddaughter to Jayasthitimalla, a man of obscure but apparently high birth, eventually led to the reunification of the land and a lessening of strife among the towns.

By 1370 Jayasthitimalla controlled Patan, and in 1374 his forces defeated those in Banepa and Pharping. He then took full control of the country from 1382 until 1395, reigning in Bhadgaon as the husband of the queen and in Patan with full regal titles. His authority was not absolute because the lords of Banepa were able to pass themselves off as kings to ambassadors of the Chinese Ming emperor who traveled to Nepal during this time. Nevertheless, Jayasthitimalla united the entire valley and its environs under his sole rule, an accomplishment still remembered with pride by Nepalese, particularly Newars. The first comprehensive codification of law in Nepal, based on the dharma of ancient religious textbooks, is ascribed to Jayasthitimalla. This legendary compilation of traditions was seen as the source of legal reforms during the nineteenth and twentieth centuries.

After the death of Jayasthitimalla, his sons divided the kingdom and ruled collegially, until Jayajyotirmalla, the last surviving son, ruled on his own from 1408 to 1428. His son, Yakshamalla (reigned ca. 1428–82), represented the high point of the Mallas as rulers of a united Nepal. Under his rule, a military raid was launched against the plains to the south, a very rare event in Nepalese history. Yakshamalla built the Mul Chok in 1455, which remains the oldest palace section in Bhadgaon. The struggles among the landed aristocracy and leading town families (*pradhan*), especially acute in Patan, were controlled during his reign. Outlying areas such as Banepa and Pharping were semi-independent but acknowledged the leadership of the king. Newari appeared more often as the language of choice in official documents. The royal family began to accept Manesvari (also known as Taleju), a manifestation of Shiva's consort, as their personal deity.

The Three Kingdoms

After 1482, a crucial date in Nepalese history, the kingdom became divided. At first, the six sons of Yakshamalla attempted to reign collegially, in their grandfathers' pattern. Ratnamalla was the first to rebel against this system of joint rule, seizing Kathmandu in 1484 and ruling there alone until his death in 1520. Rayamalla, the eldest brother, ruled Bhadgaon with the other brothers until his death, when the crown there passed into the hands of his descendants. Banepa broke away under Ramamalla until its reincorporation into the Bhadgaon kingdom in 1649. Patan remained aloof, dominated by factions of its local nobility, until Sivasimhamalla, a descendant of Ratnamalla, conquered it in 1597 and united it with Kathmandu. On his death, however, Kathmandu and Patan were given to different grandsons and again separated. The center of Nepal thus remained split into three competing kingdoms, roughly based on Bhadgaon, Kathmandu, and Patan. The influence of these petty kingdoms outside the valley varied over time. Bhadgaon extended its feeble power as far as the Dudh Kosi in the east, Kathmandu controlled areas to the north and as far west as Nuwakot, and Patan included territories to the south as far as Makwanpur. The relationships among the kingdoms within the valley became quite convoluted. Although all three ruling houses were related and periodically intermarried, their squabbles over minuscule territorial gains or ritual slights repeatedly led to warfare. The kings attended coronation rituals or marriages at each other's capitals and then plotted the downfalls of their relatives.

The period of the three kingdoms—the time of the later Mallas—lasted until the mid-eighteenth century. The complete flowering of the unique culture of the Kathmandu Valley occurred during this period, and it was also during this time that the old palace complexes in the three main towns achieved much of their present-day forms. The kings still based their legitimate rule on their role as protectors of dharma, and often they were devout donors to religious shrines. Kings built many of the older temples in the valley, gems of late medieval art and architecture, during this late Malla period. Buddhism remained a vital force for much of the population, especially in its old seat of Patan. Religious endowments called *guthi* arranged for long-term support of traditional forms of worship or ritual by allowing temple or *vihara* lands to pass down through generations of the same families; this support resulted in the preservation of a conservative art, architecture, and religious literature that had disappeared in other areas of South Asia. Newari was in regular use as a literary language by the fourteenth century and was the main language in urban areas and trading circles based in the Kathmandu Valley. Maithili, the language of the Tirhut area to the south, became a popular court language during the seventeenth century and still was spoken by many people in the Tarai in the late twentieth century. In the west, Khas bhasha, or the language of the Khasa, was slowly expanding, only later to evolve into present-day Nepali.

The final centuries of Malla rule were a time of great political change outside the Kathmandu Valley. In India overlordship in Delhi fell to the powerful Mughal Dynasty (1526–1858). Although the Mughals never exercised direct lordship over Nepal, their empire had a major indirect impact on its institutional life. During the sixteenth century, when the Mughals were spreading their rule over almost all of South Asia, many dispossessed princes from the plains of northern India found shelter in the hills to the north.

Legends indicated that many small principalities in western Nepal originated in migration and conquest by exiled warriors, who added to the slow spread of the Khasa language and culture in the west. Along with these exiles came Mughal military technology, including firearms and artillery, and administrative techniques based on land grants in return for military service. The influence of the Mughals is reflected in the weapons and dress of Malla rulers in contemporary paintings and in the adoption of Persian terminology for administrative offices and procedures throughout Nepal.

Meanwhile, in Tibet domestic struggles during the 1720s led to decisive intervention by the powerful Qing rulers of China (1644–1911). A Chinese force installed the sixth Dalai Lama (the highest ranking Tibetan religious leader) in Lhasa in 1728, and thereafter the Chinese stationed military governors (*amban*) in Lhasa to monitor local events. In 1729 representatives of the three Nepalese kingdoms sent greetings and presents to the Chinese emperor in Beijing, after which the Qing viewed Nepal as an outlying tributary kingdom (a perception not shared within Nepal). The expansion of big empires in both the north and south thus took place during a time when Nepal was experiencing considerable weakness in its traditional center. The three kingdoms lived a charmed life—isolated, independent, and quarreling in their mountain valley—as the systems around them became larger and more centralized.

By the seventeenth century, the mountain areas to the north of the valley and the Kiranti region to the east were the only areas that maintained traditional tribal communal systems, influenced to various degrees by Hindu ideas and practices. In the west and the south of the three kingdoms, there were many petty states ruled by dynasties of warrior (Kshatriya) status, many claiming an origin among princely, or Rajput, dynasties to the south. In the near west, around the Narayani River system (the Narayani was one of the seven Gandak rivers), there was a loose confederation of principalities called the Chaubisi (the Twenty-four), including Makwanpur and Palpa. In the far west, around the Karnali River system, there was a separate confederation called the Baisi (the Twenty-two), headed by the raja of Jumla. The confederations were in constant conflict, and their member states were constantly quarreling with each other. The kingdoms of Kathmandu, Patan, and Bhadgaon periodically allied themselves with princes among these confederations. All of these small, increasingly militarized states were operating individually at a higher level of centralized organization than ever before in the hills, but they were expending their resources in an almost anarchic struggle for survival. There was an awareness of the distinct culture of the Himalayan area but no real concept of Nepal as a nation.

The first contacts between the people of Nepal and Europeans also occurred during the period of the later Mallas. The Portuguese missionaries John Cabral and Stephen Cacella visited Lhasa in 1628, after which Cabral traveled to Nepal. The first Capuchin mission was founded in Kathmandu in 1715. These contacts, however, affected only a minuscule number of people. Of far greater importance was the growth of British power in India, notably in Bengal to the southeast of Nepal, during the eighteenth century. By 1764 the British East India Company, officially a private trading corporation with its own army, had obtained from a decaying Mughal Empire the right to govern all of Bengal, at that time one of the most prosperous areas in Asia. The company explored possibilities for expanding its trade or authority into Nepal, Bhutan, and toward Tibet, where the Nepalese had their own trading agencies in important settlements (see fig. 2). The increasingly powerful company was emerging as a wild card that could in theory be played by one or more of the kingdoms in Nepal during local struggles, potentially opening the entire Himalayan region to British penetration.

The Making of Modern Nepal

The Expansion of Gorkha

Among the small hill states struggling for power during the later Malla period was Gorkha (see Glossary), founded in 1559 by Dravya Shah in an area chiefly inhabited by Magars. Legends trace his dynasty to warrior princes who immigrated from Rajputana in India during the fifteenth century. During its early fight for existence, the House of Gorkha stayed out of the two major confederations in western Nepal. No major expansion of the kingdom occurred until the reign of Ram Shah, from 1606 to 1633, who extended his territories slightly in all directions. During the seventeenth and early eighteenth centuries, Gorkha continued a slow expansion and appeared increasingly often as an ally of one or more of the three kingdoms in their quarrels with each other, giving the rulers of the hill state experience in the affairs of the Kathmandu

15

Figure 2. Nepal and Bhutan, 1991

Valley. Nar Bhupal Shah (reigned 1716–42) extended his lands toward the Kairang Pass in the north and Nuwakot in the east. He attempted to take Nuwakot and failed, but he did arrange the marriage of his son to the daughter of the raja of Makwanpur.

This son, Prithvi Narayan Shah (reigned 1743–75), made full use of his position to achieve supreme power and was one of the great figures in Nepalese history. Following in his father's footsteps, he apparently dedicated himself at an early age to the conquest of the valley and the creation of a single state. Before going on the offensive, he traveled to Banaras, or Varanasi, to seek financial assistance and purchase armaments, thus obtaining a personal view of conditions in the outside world, especially the position of the British East India Company. On his return to Gorkha, he established a number of arsenals and trained his troops to use the more modern weapons he had obtained in India. He arranged alliances with, or bought the neutrality of, neighboring states.

When King Ranajit of Bhadgaon (reigned 1722–69) quarreled with King Jayaprakasa of Kathmandu (reigned 1735–68), Prithvi Narayan Shah took Nuwakot and laid siege to Kirtipur, which was controlled by the king of Patan, Tej Narasimha (reigned 1765–68). During the fighting, Prithvi Narayan Shah was almost killed, and when his troops failed to take the town, he withdrew. At this point, he changed direction, as the Gorkhas were to do effectively time and again. The Gorkhas instituted a blockade of the entire valley, closed off all trade routes, and began executing blockade runners. Gorkha agents remained active in the towns, and the army attempted to starve the valley into submission.

When a second siege of Kirtipur also was unsuccessful, Prithvi Narayan Shah turned his attention toward Lamji, one of the Chaubisi principalities, and overran it after several bloody battles. The Gorkha army reappeared at Kirtipur. After a siege of six months, the town was treacherously delivered to the Gorkhas, and its inhabitants were deliberately mutilated. The Gorkhas moved on to Patan in 1767, but their attention was diverted by the appearance of a 2,400-man expeditionary force sent by the British East India Company to aid the traditional kings of the valley. The British column, ravaged by malaria contracted in the Tarai, had to withdraw quickly without accomplishing anything other than delaying the Gorkhas. This token opposition by the British, however, was not forgotten by Prithvi Narayan Shah and his successors. With the field again clear, on September 29, 1768, Gorkha troops infiltrated Kathmandu while the population was celebrating a religious festival and took the town without a fight. Jayaprakasa fled to Bhadgaon with Tej Narasimha, and Prithvi Narayan Shah was crowned king of Kathmandu. He soon entered Patan unopposed and then moved against villages east of Bhadgaon, arriving before the town the next year. His troops were admitted into Bhadgaon by nobles who had been bought off. Ranajit retired to Banaras, Jayaprakasa retired to die at the shrine of Pashupatinath, and Tej Narasimha died in prison. For the first time, the hill ruler, the raja of Gorkha, had become sole ruler in the Kathmandu Valley. One of his first acts in 1769 was to expel permanently from his territories all foreigners, including traders, Roman Catholic missionaries, and even musicians or artists influenced by northern India's style.

The conquest of the three kingdoms was only the beginning of a remarkable explosion of Gorkha military power throughout the Himalayan region. Prithvi Narayan Shah quickly made a movement toward the Chaubisi states in the west, but after encountering resistance in Tanahu, the Gorkha armies drove east into the Kirata country, overrunning all of eastern Nepal by 1773. They were poised for the invasion of Sikkim, but because its rulers came from Tibet, Sikkim was viewed as a client of Tibet (and thus of the Chinese). A warning from Tibet and the death of Prithvi Narayan Shah in 1775 stalled hostilities, but a full-scale invasion began in 1779. Resistance was encountered until 1788, when Gorkha forces drove the ruler of Sikkim into exile in Tibet and occupied all of western Sikkim. Guerrilla warfare continued as the Gorkhas constructed a base near Vijaypur to administer the eastern conquests. In the west, a marriage alliance with the rajas of Palpa kept them quiet while General Ram Krishna Rana conquered Tanahu and Lamjung (Gorkha's traditional rival) and advanced to Kaski by 1785. By 1790 all rulers as far as the Kali River had submitted to the Gorkhas or had been replaced. Even farther to the west lay Kumaon, in the throes of civil strife between two coalitions of *zamindar* (large landowners responsible for tax collection in their jurisdictions), who struggled to control the monarchy. One group invited the intervention of the Gorkhas, who defeated local forces in two battles and occupied the capital, Almora, in 1790. The Gorkhas were poised for greater adventures, but by then they were irritating bigger players and began to encounter resistance to their ambitions.

The Struggle for Power at Court

The premature death of Pratap Singh Shah (reigned 1775–77), the eldest son of Prithvi Narayan Shah, left a huge power vacuum that remained unfilled for decades, seriously debilitating the emerging Nepalese state. Pratap Singh Shah's successor was his son, Rana Bahadur Shah (reigned 1777–99), aged two and one-half years at his accession. The acting regent until 1785 was Queen Rajendralakshmi, followed by Bahadur Shah (reigned 1785–94), the second son of Prithvi Narayan Shah. Court life was consumed by rivalry centered on alignments with these two regents rather than on issues of national administration. In 1794 the king came of age, and in 1797 he began to exercise power on his own. Rana Bahadur's youth had been spent in pampered luxury amid deadly intrigue and had made him incapable of running either his own life or the country. He became infatuated with a Maithili Brahman widow, Kantavati, and cleared the way to the throne for their illegitimate son, Girvan Yuddha Shah. Disconsolate after the death of his mistress in 1799, Rana Bahadur began to engage in such irrational behavior that leading citizens demanded his abdication. He was forced to turn his throne over to Girvan Yuddha Shah, aged one and one-half years, and retired to Banaras.

During the minority of the king, Damodar Pande took over the administration as *mukhtiyar,* or prime minister (1799–1804), with complete control over administration and the power to conduct foreign affairs. He set a significant precedent for later Nepalese history, which has seen a recurring struggle for effective power between king and prime minister. The main policy of Damodar Pande was to protect the young king by keeping his unpredictable father in Banaras and to play off against each other the schemes of the retired king's wives. By 1804 this policy had failed. The former king engineered his return and took over as *mukhtiyar.* Damodar Pande was executed and replaced by Bhimsen Thapa as chief administrator (*kaji*). In a bizarre turn of events on April 25, 1806, Rana Bahadur Shah quarreled in open court with his half-brother, Sher Bahadur. The latter drew his sword and killed Rana Bahadur Shah before being cut down by a nearby courtier. Taking advantage of this opportunity, Bhimsen Thapa became prime minister (1806–37), and the junior queen, Tripurasundari, became regent (1806–32). They cooperated to liquidate ninety-three of their enemies. The death of Girvan Yuddha Shah in 1816 and the accession of his infant son meant the retention of the regency.

The struggle for power at the court had unfortunate consequences for both foreign affairs and for internal administration. All parties tried to satisfy the army in order to avoid interference in court affairs by leading commanders, and the military was given a free hand to pursue ever larger conquests. As long as the Gorkhas were invading disunited hill states, this policy—or lack of policy—was adequate. Inevitably, continued aggression led Nepal into disastrous collisions with the Chinese and then with the British (see The Enclosing of Nepal, this ch.). At home, because power struggles centered on control of the king, there was little progress in sorting out procedures for sharing power or expanding representative institutions. A consultative body of nobles, a royal court called the Assembly of Lords (Bharadari Sabha), was in place after 1770 and it had substantial involvement in mayor policy issues. The assembly consisted of high government officials and leading courtiers, all heads of important Gorkha families. In the intense atmosphere surrounding the monarch, however, the Assembly of Lords broke into factions that fought for access to the prime minister or regent, and alliances developed around patron/client relationships.

Five leading families contended for power during this period—the Shahs, Choutariyas, Thapas, Basnyats, and Pandes. Working for these families and their factions were hill Brahmans, who acted as religious preceptors or astrologers, and Newars, who occupied secondary administrative positions. No one else in the country had any influence on the central government. When a family or faction achieved power, it killed, exiled, or demoted members of opposing alliances. Under these circumstances, there was little opportunity for either public political life or coordinated economic development.

The Enclosing of Nepal

The Gorkha state had its greatest success in expanding to the east and west, but it also pressed northward toward Tibet. There was a longstanding dispute with the government of Tibet over trade issues, notably the status of Nepalese merchants in Lhasa and other settlements and the increasing debasement of coinage used in Tibet. There also was a dispute over control of the mountain passes into Tibet, including the Kuti and Kairang passes north of Kathmandu. In the 1780s, Nepal demanded that Tibet surrender territory around the passes. When the Tibetans refused, the Nepalese closed trade routes between Lhasa and Kathmandu. In 1788 the Nepalese overran Sikkim, sent a punitive raid into Tibet, and threatened Shigatse, seat of the Panchen Lama, the second highest-ranking lama in Tibet. They received secret assurances of an annual payment from the Tibetan and local Chinese authorities, but when the agreement was not honored they invaded again in 1791, pillaging the monastery at Shigatse before withdrawing to Nepal. These acts finally moved the emperor in Beijing to send a huge army to Tibet. Alarmed, the government in Kathmandu concluded a trade agreement with the British East India Company, hoping for aid in their struggle. They were to be disappointed because the British had no intention of confronting China, where there were so many potential trading opportunities.

In 1792 the Chinese forces easily forced the Nepalese out of Tibet and pursued them to within thirty-five kilometers of Kathmandu. The Nepalese were forced to sign a humiliating treaty that took away their trading privileges in Tibet. It made them subordinate to the Qing Empire and required them to pay tribute to Beijing every five years. Thus, Nepal was enclosed on the north, and the British had again shown themselves to be untrustworthy.

The kingdom of Garhwal to the west was mostly hill country but included the rich vale of Dehra Dun. During the late eighteenth century, the kingdom had been devastated by conquerors as varied as Afghans, Sikhs from the Punjab, and Marathas from western India. The armies of Nepal were poised to attack Garhwal in 1790, but the affair with Tibet shifted their attention. In 1803 after Garhwal was devastated by an earthquake, the Nepalese armies moved in, defeated and killed the raja of Garhwal in battle, and annexed a ruined land. General Amar Singh Thapa moved farther west and during a three-year campaign defeated or bought off local princes as far as Kangra, the strongest fort in the hills. The Nepalese laid siege to Kangra until 1809, when Ranjit Singh, ruler of the Sikh state in the Punjab, intervened and drove the Nepalese army east of the Sutlej River. Amar Singh Thapa spent several years putting down rebellions in Garhwal and Kumaon, towns that submitted to military occupations but were never fully integrated into Gorkha. The Nepalese were being checked in the west.

There had been little direct contact with the lands controlled by the British East India Company or its clients, but by the early 1800s a confrontation was becoming more likely. Just as Nepal had been expanding toward the west throughout the late eighteenth century, so the company had steadily added to its annexed or dependent territories all the way to the Punjab. Amar Singh Thapa claimed lowland areas of Kumaon and Garhwal as part of his conquests, but David Ochterlony, the British East India Company's representative in the west, kept up constant diplomatic resistance against such claims, which were not pressed. In 1804 Palpa was finally annexed by Gorkha and along with it came claims to parts of the Butawal area in the Tarai. As Nepalese troops slowly occupied those tracts, local landlords complained to the company that their rights were being violated. Similar claims to Saran District led to armed clashes between Nepalese troops and the forces of local landlords. During these proceedings, there was constant diplomatic intercourse between the government of Nepal and the British East India Company and little desire on either side for open hostilities. The Gorkha generals, however, were quite confident in their ability to wage warfare in the mountains, and the company, with its far greater resources, had little reason to give in to this aggressive state, which blocked commerce in the hills. After retreating before a reoccupation by company troops, Nepalese forces counterattacked against police outposts in Butawal, killing eighteen police officers on April 22, 1814. The fragile state of Nepal was at war with the British Empire.

At this stage in its history, Nepal's single major unifying force was the Gorkha-led army and its supply system. Prithvi Narayan Shah and his successors had done the best they could to borrow military techniques used by the British in India, including modern ordnance, command structures, and even uniforms. An entire munitions and armaments industry had been created in the hills, based on locally mined and processed raw materials, and supported by a system of forced labor to transport commodities. The soldiers in the army were renowned for their ability to move relatively fast with their supplies and to fight with discipline under tough conditions. They also knew their terrain better than the British, who had little experience there. Although the Nepalese army of an estimated 16,000 regulars would have to fight on a wide front, it had great logistical advantages and a large reservoir of labor to support it.

The initial British campaign was an attack on two fronts. In the eastern theater, two columns totaling about 10,000 troops were supposed to coordinate their attacks in the Makwanpur-Palpa area, but poor leadership and unfamiliarity with hill warfare caused the early collapse of these campaigns. In the west, another 10,000 troops in two columns were to converge on the forces of Amar Singh Thapa. One of the western columns failed miserably, but the main force under Ochterlony outmaneuvered the Nepalese army and defeated General Thapa on May 9, 1815, leading to the complete loss of Kumaon by Nepal (see fig. 3). The Nepalese forces had already proved their abilities, so the British East India Company took no chances the next year, marshalling 35,000 men and more than 100 artillery pieces under Ochterlony for a thrust toward Makwanpur. Simultaneous operations by the *chogyal,* or king, of Sikkim were driving the Nepalese army from the east. Major battles before Makwanpur in late February 1816 resulted in the final defeat of Nepalese forces by early March. Diplomats had already begun preparing a peace treaty, which reached Ochterlony on March 5.

The Anglo-Nepalese War (1814–16) was a total disaster for Nepal. According to the Treaty of Sagauli, signed in 1816, Nepal lost Sikkim, the territories west of the Kali River (Kumaon and Garhwal), and most of its lands in the Tarai. The British East India Company was to pay 200,000 rupees (for value of the rupee—

see Glossary) annually to Nepal to make up for the loss of revenues from the Tarai. Kathmandu was also forced to accept a British resident, which was extremely disturbing to the government of Nepal because the presence of a resident had typically preceded outright British conquest throughout India. In effect, the treaty proved to be less damaging, for the company soon found the Tarai lands difficult to govern and returned some of them to Nepal later in 1816, simultaneously abolishing the annual payments. The return of Tarai territory was important for the survival of Nepal because the government relied on the area as a source of land grants, and it is doubtful that the country as it was then run could have survived without this source of endowments. The presence of the resident, too, turned out to be less difficult than first imagined because all later governments in Kathmandu took stringent measures to isolate him by restricting his movements and keeping a close eye on the people he met. Nevertheless, the glory days of conquest were over, and Nepal had been squeezed into the boundaries it still had in the early 1990s.

Infighting among Aristocratic Factions

The Gorkha aristocracy had led Nepal into disaster on the international front but preserved the political unity of the country, which at the end of the Anglo-Nepalese War in 1816 had been a unified nation only about twenty-five years. The success of the central government rested in part on its ability to appoint and control regional administrators, who also were high officers in the army. In theory these officials had great local powers; in practice they spent little energy on the daily affairs of their subjects, interfering only when communities could not cope with problems or conflicts. Another reason for Gorkha success in uniting the country was the willingness to placate local leaders by preserving areas where former kings and communal assemblies continued to rule under the loose supervision of Kathmandu. This approach left substantial parts of the country out of the control of regional administrators. Even within the areas directly administered by the central government, agricultural lands were given away as *jagir* (see Glossary) to the armed services and as *birta* (see Glossary) to court favorites and retired servicemen. The holder of such grants in effect became the lord of the peasants working there, with little if any state interference. From the standpoint of the average cultivator, the government remained a distant force, and the main authority figure was the landlord, who took part of the harvest, or (especially in the Tarai) the tax collector, who was often a private individual contracted to extort money or crops in return for a share. For the leaders

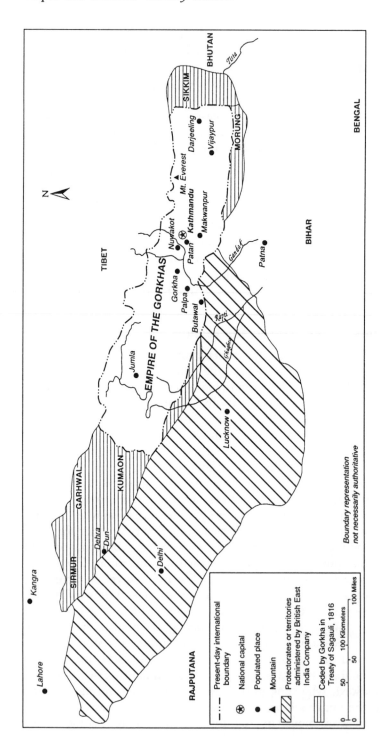

Figure 3. Nepal, 1815

in the administration and the army, as military options became limited and alternative sources of employment grew very slowly, career advancement depended less on attention to local conditions than on loyalty to factions fighting at court.

Prime Minister Bhimsen Thapa, in collusion with the queen regent, Tripurasundari, remained in power despite the defeat of Nepal. He faced constant opposition at court from factions centered around leading members of other families, notably the Pandes, who decried what they felt was his craven submission to the British. Bhimsen Thapa managed to keep his opposition under control by maintaining a large army and modernizing its equipment and by convincing the suspicious British that he had no intention of using the army. During the minority of King Rajendra Bikram Shah (reigned 1816–47), the prime minister kept the king in isolation—he did not even have the freedom to leave the palace without permission. Bhimsen Thapa appointed members of his own family to the highest positions at court and in the army, giving his brother, Ranbir Singh Thapa, control over the western provinces and his nephew, Mathbar Singh Thapa, control over the eastern provinces. The Pandes and other opponents were frozen out of power. Aside from the army and some attention to increasing trade, little effort could be expended on issues of national development.

The power balance began to change after the king came of age and Queen Tripurasundari died in 1832. The prime minister lost his main support at a time when the young ruler was coming under greater influence from the Pande faction at court. In 1833 Brian Hodgson became British resident and began a more aggressive campaign to increase British influence and trading opportunities; because Bhimsen Thapa opposed him, Hodgson openly favored Bhimsen Thapa's opponents. In 1837 the king announced his intention to rule independently, deprived both Bhimsen Thapa and Mathbar Singh of their military powers, and promoted some members of the Pande faction. Shortly afterward the youngest son of the elder queen died, and Bhimsen Thapa was arrested on a trumped up charge of poisoning the prince. All the property of the Thapas was confiscated. An eight-month trial led to an acquittal, but the Thapas were in disarray. When Rana Jang Pande, head of his family, became prime minister, he reimprisoned Bhimsen Thapa. The man who had ruled the country with an iron hand committed suicide in prison in August 1839. This series of events marked the end of the longest stable period in the early history of the Shah Dynasty of Nepal, dominated by the prime minister in the name of the king.

The fall of Bhimsen Thapa did nothing to solve the factional fight-ing at court. The Pandes were dismissed, and Fateh Jang Chau-taria was appointed prime minister in November 1840. His ministry was unable to control renewed competition between a resurgent Thapa coalition and the disgraced Pandes, who preferred the ab-dication of the king in favor of the heir apparent. The king be-came increasingly attentive to the advice of his wives. Under intense pressure from the aristocracy, the king decreed in January 1843 that he would rule the country only with advice and agreement of his junior queen, Lakshmidevi, and commanded his subjects to obey her even over his own son, Surendra. The queen, seeking support of her own son's claims to the throne over those of Suren-dra, invited back from exile Mathbar Singh Thapa, who was popu-lar in army circles. Upon his arrival in Kathmandu, an investigation of his uncle's death took place, and a number of his Pande ene-mies were executed. By December 1843, Mathbar Singh was ap-pointed prime minister, but he proved no more capable of extinguishing court intrigues than had his predecessors. Against the wishes of the queen, he supported heir apparent Surendra. Once Mathbar Singh had alienated the person who officially wielded state authority, his days were numbered. On May 17, 1845, he was killed, most likely on the queen's orders. The assassin apparently was Jang Bahadur Kunwar, his nephew, then a minor but rising star in court politics.

Rana Rule

The death of Mathbar Singh set the stage for one of the crucial sequences of events in modern Nepalese history—the destruction of the old aristocracy and the establishment of a dictatorship of the prime minister. These events provided the long period of stability the country needed but at the cost of political and economic de-velopment.

The Kot Massacre

After three months of squabbling, a coalition ministry was formed in September 1845, again headed by Fateh Jang Chautaria. The real power behind the throne was the favorite of Queen Lakshmi-devi, Gagan Singh, who controlled seven regiments in the army compared to the three under the prime minister. Abhiman Singh and Jang Bahadur also served as commanders, each with three regi-ments. Plots and counterplots continued until Gagan Singh was found murdered during the night of September 14, 1846. The queen was beside herself at the death of her favorite, whom she had hoped to use to elevate her own son to the monarchy. She commanded

Abhiman Singh to assemble the entire military and administrative establishment of Kathmandu immediately at the courtyard of the palace armory (*kot*).

Emotions ran high among the assembled bands of notables and their followers, who listened to the queen give an emotional harangue blaming the Pandes and demanding that the prime minister execute the Pande leader whom she suspected of the murder. While Abhiman Singh hesitated, fighting broke out in the crowd, and he was wounded. During the free-for-all that followed, swords and knives were used on all sides to dispatch opponents. Through some scheme that has never been explained adequately, the only leader with organized bodies of troops in the *kot* area was Jang Bahadur, whose troops suppressed the fighting, killing many of his opponents in the process. When the struggle subsided, the courtyard was strewn with the bodies of dozens of leading nobles and an unknown number of their followers—the cream of the Nepalese aristocracy. The Pande and Thapa families in particular were devastated during this slaughter.

Why the Kot Massacre took place has never been established, although the queen herself was obviously at fault for calling the assembly and whipping it into a frenzy. It has always seemed suspicious that the king was notably absent when the fighting began and that Jang Bahadur was the only leader who was ready for trouble. The extent of the carnage was apparently unexpected. Jang Bahadur was the only true beneficiary of the massacre and became the only military leader in a position of strength in the capital. The next day, he became prime minister and immediately launched a purge that killed many of his aristocratic competitors and drove 6,000 people into exile in India.

The Dictatorship of Jang Bahadur

History has not been kind to Jang Bahadur during the twentieth century. He was blamed for setting up a dictatorship that repressed the entire nation for more than 100 years and left it in a primitive economic condition. From the standpoint of the nineteenth century during which he lived, however, he was a pillar of strength who eliminated the useless factional fighting at court, introduced innovations into the bureaucracy and the judiciary, and made efforts to "modernize" Nepal. In this sense, he remains one of the most important figures in Nepalese history.

Jang Bahadur Kunwar's early career paralleled that of many members of the lower aristocracy in Nepal, despite the Kunwar family's claims of descent from Indian princes. Jang Bahadur's great-grandfather was an important military leader under Prithvi

Narayan Shah in the eighteenth century, and during the war with China (1791–92) his grandfather was also a military leader, who became one of the four chief administrators (*kaji*) of the Gorkha-Nepalese state. His father, Bala Narasimha Kunwar, was in court the day Rana Bahadur Shah was murdered and killed the murderer on the spot. For this action, he was rewarded with the position of *kaji*, which was made hereditary in his family. Jang Bahadur joined the military service in 1832–33 at the age of sixteen. As maternal grandson of Bhimsen Thapa, he lost his job and his property when the latter fell. After wandering in northern India for several years, he returned to Nepal as a captain in the artillery in 1840. In November 1841, he was asked by the king to join his bodyguard, and in January 1842 he began work as *kaji* in the palace. When Mathbar Singh returned to power, Jang Bahadur rose with him but Mathbar Singh disliked his ambition and had him removed to a lesser position on the staff of the heir apparent. When Fateh Jang Chautaria came to power, Jang Bahadur became fourth in the hierarchy of the coalition government and took pains to flatter the queen while showing no signs of ambition to Gagan Singh. A career opportunist, he was ready and waiting when the time came to act at the Kot Massacre.

Queen Rajendralakshmi was not pleased by the new prime minister. She conspired to eliminate Jang Bahadur and elevate her son to the throne. The Basnyat Conspiracy, so called because many of its participants belonged to one of the last leading noble families, the Basnyats, was betrayed, and its ringleaders were rounded up and executed in 1846. A meeting of leading notables packed with Rana supporters found the queen guilty of complicity in the plot, stripped her of her powers, and sent her into exile in Banaras along with King Rajendra. The king still had illusions of grandeur and began plotting his return from India. In 1847 Jang Bahadur informed the troops of the exiled king's treasonous activities, announced his dethronement, and elevated Rajendra's son to the throne as Surendra Bikram Shah (1847–81). Rajendra was captured later that year in the Tarai and brought back as a prisoner to Bhadgaon, where he spent the rest of his life under house arrest.

By 1850 Jang Bahadur had eliminated or overawed all of his major rivals, installed his own candidate on the throne, appointed his brothers and cronies to all the important posts, and ensured that major administrative decisions were made by himself as prime minister. At this point, he took the unprecedented step of traveling to Britain, leaving from Calcutta in April 1850 and returning to Kathmandu in February 1851. Although he unsuccessfully tried to deal directly with the British government while he was there,

Kathmandu Valley
Courtesy Elsa Martz

the main result of the tour was a great increase in goodwill between the British and Nepal. Recognizing the extent of the world and the power of industrialized Europe, he became convinced that close cooperation with the British was the best way to guarantee Nepal's independence. From then on, European architecture, fashion, and furnishings became more prevalent in Kathmandu and among the Nepalese aristocracy in general.

As part of his modernization plans, Jang Bahadur commissioned leading administrators and interpreters of texts on dharma to revise and codify the legal system of the nation into a single body of laws, a process that had not been carried out since the seventeenth century under Ram Shah of Gorkha. The result was the 1,400-page Muluki Ain of 1854, a collection of administrative procedures and legal frameworks for interpreting civil and criminal matters, revenue collection, landlord and peasant relations, intercaste disputes, and marriage and family law. In contrast to the older system, which had allowed execution or bodily mutilation for a wide range of offenses, the Muluki Ain severely limited—without abolishing—corporal punishment. For example, the old system gave wide scope for blood vengeance by aggrieved parties, such as cuckolded husbands, but the Muluki Ain restricted such opportunities. Substitutions included confiscation of property or prison terms.

29

Torture to obtain confessions was abolished. Strict penalties were set down for the abusers of judicial positions and also for persons maliciously accusing judges of corruption. There were statutes of limitations for judicial actions. Caste-based differences in the degree of punishments remained throughout, with higher castes (for example, Brahmans) exempt from the corporal punishments and heavy fines that lower-caste members incurred for the same crimes. This distinction was in keeping with the traditional approach of the *dharma shastras,* or ancient legal treatises (see The Judicial System, ch. 5).

After his return from Europe, Jang Bahadur took steps to increase his hold over the country. He reduced the king to a prisoner in his own palace, surrounded by agents of the prime minister and restricted and supervised at all times. No one outside the king's immediate family could see the king without permission from the prime minister. All communications in the name of the king were censored, and he was allowed to read only approved literature. In 1856 the king issued a royal decree (*sanad*) that formalized the dominance of the Kunwar family. There were three main provisions in this crucial document. First, the prime minister had complete authority over all internal administration, including civil, military, and judicial affairs, and all foreign relations, including the powers to make war and peace. Second, Jang Bahadur was made great king (maharajah) of Kaski and Lamjung districts, in effect serving as their independent ruler. The Shah king retained the title of *maharajadhiraja* (supreme king) and the right to use the honorific term *shri* five times with his name. The prime minister could use *shri* three times with his name. In this way, Jang Bahadur stopped short of taking the throne outright but elevated his family to a level second only to the royal house, which remained as a symbol of the nation. Finally, provisions were established for hereditary succession to the post of prime minister. Brothers and then sons would inherit the position in order of seniority. These provisions meant that the dictatorship of the Kunwar family, a virtual monarchy within the monarchy, would be passed down in the family for generations, with no legal mechanism for changing the government. Later, Jang Bahadur established official Rolls of Succession that ranked all his descendants in relation to their hereditary rights to the office of prime minister.

Jang Bahadur sealed the arrangement with the Shah Dynasty by arranging marriages between his heirs and the royal house. In 1854 his eldest son, Jagat Jang (aged eight), married the eldest daughter (aged six) of Surendra Bikram Shah. In 1855 his second son married the second daughter of the king. The ultimate test was passed in 1857, when heir apparent Trilokya Bir Bikram married two daughters of Jang Bahadur. A son of this union ascended to the throne in 1881.

Nepal began to experience some successes in international affairs during the tenure of Jang Bahadur. To the north, relations with Tibet had been mediated through China since Nepal's defeat in 1792, and during the early nineteenth century embassies had to make the arduous journey to Beijing every five years with local products as tribute to the Qing emperor. By 1854, however, China was in decline and had fallen into a protracted period of disturbances, including the Taiping Rebellion (1851–64), revolts by Muslim ethnic groups north of Tibet, and war with European powers. The Nepalese mission to Beijing in 1852, just after the death of the sixth Panchen Lama, was allegedly mistreated in Tibet. Because of this slight, the Nepalese government sent a protest letter to Beijing and Lhasa outlining several grievances, including excessive customs duties on Nepalese trade. In 1855 Nepalese troops overran the Kuti and Kairang areas. Hostilities lasted for about a year, with successes and failures on both sides, until a treaty negotiated by the Chinese resident and ratified in March 1856 gave Nepalese merchants duty-free trade privileges, forced Tibet to pay an annual tribute of 10,000 rupees to Nepal, and allowed a Nepalese resident in Lhasa. In return, Nepal gave up territorial gains and agreed that it, as well as Tibet, would remain a tributary state subject to China. As the Qing Empire disintegrated later in the century, this tributary status was allowed to lapse, and even Tibet began to shake off its subordination.

The outbreak of disorder to the south also allowed the Nepalese army to take a more active role in international affairs. Beginning in May 1857, a series of related uprisings throughout north India— known as the Sepoy Rebellion—threatened to topple the power of the British East India Company. The uprisings began with widespread mutinies in the company's army and spread to include peasant revolts and alliances of the old Mughal aristocracy against the foreigners. Most of the major cities west of Bengal fell into rebel hands, and the aged Mughal emperor was proclaimed the leader of a national revolution. Initially there was some fear in British circles that Nepal would side with the rebels and turn the tide irrevocably against the British East India Company, but Jang Bahadur proved to be a loyal and reliable ally. At that point, immediately following hostilities in Tibet, the army of Nepal had grown to around 25,000 troops. Jang Bahadur sent several columns ahead and then marched with 9,000 troops into northern India in December 1857. Heading an army of 15,000 troops, he fought several hard battles and aided the British in their campaigns around Gorakhpur and Lucknow. The prime minister returned to Nepal triumphantly in March 1858 and continued to aid the British in rooting out "rebels" who had been dislocated during the chaos and sought refuge in the Tarai.

After the Sepoy Rebellion had been crushed and Britain had abolished the British East India Company and taken direct control of India in 1858, Nepal received a reward for its loyalty. Western sections of the Tarai that had been ceded through the Treaty of Sagauli in 1816 were returned. Henceforth, the British were firm supporters of Jang Bahadur's government, and Nepal later became an important source of military recruits for the British army (see From the Anglo-Nepalese War to World War II, ch. 5).

In 1858 King Surendra bestowed upon Jang Bahadur Kunwar the honorific title of Rana, an old title denoting martial glory used by Rajput princes in northern India. He then became Jang Bahadur Rana, and the later prime ministers descended from his family added his name to their own in honor of his accomplishments. Thus they all became "Jang Bahadur Ranas," and their line became known as the house of the Ranas. Jang Bahadur remained prime minister until 1877, suppressing conspiracies and local revolts and enjoying the fruits of his early successes. He exercised almost unlimited power over internal affairs, taking for his own use whatever funds were available in the treasury. He lived in the high style of an Anglicized native prince in the British Raj, although unlike the Indian princes he was the ruler of a truly independent nation, an ally rather than a subordinate of the British. He died as he had lived, a man of action, during a hunting expedition in the Tarai.

The Rana Oligarchy

After the death of Jang Bahadur, his eldest surviving brother, Ranoddip Singh, became prime minister (1877–85). Because he was childless, his term in office was full of plots by Jang Bahadur's sons and nephews over succession. These plots were complicated by the death of King Surendra Bikram Shah in 1881 and the royal accession of Prithvi Bir Bikram Shah (reigned 1881–1911) at the age of six. Finally, the doddering Ranoddip Singh was assassinated, and Bir Shamsher, son of Jang Bahadur's youngest and closest brother, became prime minister (1885–1901). Bir Shamsher immediately launched a purge of his opponents. While in power, he brought piped water to the Kathmandu Valley, built a suspension bridge at Kulekhani, and set up a palace school where English was taught. His successor for three months was the progressive Dev

Shamsher, who emancipated all female slaves, established a network of Nepali-language schools called Bhasa Pathsalas, and started the first Nepali-language newspaper, *Gorkhapatra* (Gorkha Newsletter). A coalition of his brothers, upset with his radical tendencies, forced Dev Shamsher's resignation and retirement to India.

Chandra Shamsher took over (1901–29) and attempted to resolve the unending family feuds over succession rights by amending the Rolls of Succession that had originally been set up by Jang Bahadur. The modified Rolls of Succession contained three schedules: "A" class Ranas were the direct, legitimate offspring of Ranas, who could dine with any high-caste Chhetri family; "B" class Ranas usually were born of second wives and could take part in all forms of social interaction with high-caste Chhetris except the sharing of boiled rice; and "C" class Ranas were the offspring of wives and concubines of lower status with whom interdining was forbidden. The "A" class Ranas could fill the highest positions in the army or civil administration, but "B" or "C" class Ranas at that time could only reach the level of colonels in the army and could never become prime ministers. At the time, this plan seemed adequate for finalizing everyone's position in the state and stopping conspiracy. In the long run, however, the rigid Rolls of Succession alienated large numbers of aristocrats who saw little room for advancement in the Rana system, lost interest in preserving it, and even began opposing it. The alienation increased when Juddha Shamsher (in power 1932–45) removed all "C" class Ranas, including some of his own sons, from the swollen Rolls of Succession and appointed many of them to administrative positions in districts far from the capital. In this way, the Rana dictatorship slowly created opposition within its own ranks.

Prithvi Narayan Shah and his successors had used the older administrative systems of Gorkha and the kingdoms of the Kathmandu Valley to run the central government of a united Nepal that was in theory accountable to the king. Jang Bahadur had inherited control over these systems and proceeded to undercut their power by packing them with his own officials or by establishing parallel offices that duplicated functions and, in effect, took over the work of older offices. There had always been an Assembly of Lords filled by leading aristocrats, military leaders, administrators, or head priests. In the past, this assembly had met periodically to advise the king and make important decisions. Under Jang Bahadur and his successors, it was full of Ranas and their henchmen. Aside from the codification of the Muluki Ain, the assembly functioned as a rubber stamp for Rana decisions. Accounting procedures and records had been kept by an Office of Accounts, a State Treasury, and a Land Revenue Office. Under Jang Bahadur, separate offices staffed by his appointees kept records of military grants, religious endowments, land revenue, treasury correspondence, and military correspondence—in other words, the most important components of the older royal administration. Special offices for the investigation of corruption and for police matters (staffed by army personnel) formed the core of a police state. There were few avenues open for government personnel to work outside of a network dominated by Rana interests; those who did could be detected and were either punished or coopted into the Rana system. The government of late nineteenth-century Nepal thus stripped the monarchy of any real power and maintained a late medieval administrative framework.

Because their power was ultimately illegitimate, resting on the abdication of responsibilities by the king and his virtual incarceration, the Ranas became expert at preventing any kind of challenge. In the process, they succeeded in isolating Nepal from many of the changes happening throughout the world and even in nearby India.

The Ranas were not totally inactive during the period of dictatorship, however. On the legal front, suttee, or the suicide of a wife by throwing herself onto her husband's funeral pyre, was abolished in 1920, and slavery was abolished in 1929. Tri-Chandra College was established in 1918, and by the 1940s there were several high schools in the country and two Nepali literary magazines (see Education, ch. 2). The Ranas also attended to economic development by founding the Pharping Hydroelectric Company in 1911 and establishing the Nepal Industrial Board, a jute mill, a match factory, two cotton mills, the Nepal Plywood and Bobbin Company, and several rice mills during the 1930s (see Industry, ch. 3). As for public health, the first tuberculosis clinic was set up in 1934. In view of the population of approximately 6 million in the 1930s, these accomplishments seem pitiful. Almost all Nepalese remained illiterate and uninformed about any part of the world outside their villages or, at best, their valleys. Public health and economic infrastructure had not advanced past medieval levels in most areas, and doing anything about it was proving impossible. Under Bhim Shamsher (reigned 1929–32), fifty people were arrested and fined for setting up a public library.

Because the Ranas relied on the goodwill of the army and the British government to support their dictatorship, the army served as a legitimate—and perhaps the most viable—means for Nepalese citizens to achieve upward mobility or to see the world. During World War I (1914–18), the government of Nepal loaned more than 16,000 troops to the British, and 26,000 Nepalese citizens who

The gilded copper Sun Dhoka gate, built in 1753, in Durbar Square, at the medieval city of Bhaktapur. The gate, which is the entrance to the main courtyard palace and the Taleju Bhavani Temple, is flanked by a small shrine of the Rana period.

Hanuman Dhoka Palace, the old royal palace, Kathmandu Courtesy Harvey Follender

were part of British Indian regiments fought in France and the Middle East. In gratitude the British government in 1919 bestowed on Nepal an annual payment of 1 million Indian rupees (US$476,000) in perpetuity and in 1920 transformed the British resident in Kathmandu into an envoy. A Treaty of Perpetual Peace and Friendship signed in 1923 confirmed the independence of Nepal and its special relationship with British India. As long as British rule remained stable in India and the army offered a safety valve to release social pressures in Nepal, the Ranas were able to use their total control over internal affairs to isolate their country, a situation that could not long endure.

The Growth of Political Parties

The earliest opposition to the Rana regime that departed from the conspiratorial politics of the palace began during the rule of Chandra Shamsher, a conservative who was not interested in modern political participation, even though large numbers of Nepalese soldiers had been exposed to new ideas during and after World War I. Just after the war, Thakur Chandan Singh, a retired army officer, started two weekly newspapers in Kumaon, *Tarun Gorkha* (Young Gorkha) and *Gorkha Samsar* (Gorkha World). At the same time, Devi Prasad Sapkota, a former officer in the Foreign Department, founded the weekly *Gorkhali* in Banaras. These journals were forums where Nepalese exiles could criticize the backwardness and repression of the Rana regime. During the 1930s, a debating society called Nagrik Adhikar Samiti (Citizen's Rights Committee) was founded in Kathmandu to discuss religious issues, but its discussions veered into politics. When one of its meetings featured a political speech denouncing the Rana regime, the government banned the debating society. By 1935 the first Nepalese political party, the Praja Parishad (People's Council), began among Nepalese exiles and set up cells within the country. In Bihar it published a periodical, *Janata* (The People), advocating a multicaste, democratic government and the overthrow of the Ranas. The Rana police managed to infiltrate the organization and arrested 500 persons in Kathmandu. Four leaders were executed (they continued to be commemorated as martyrs in 1991), and others received long prison terms, but the survivors escaped to India to carry on their political agitation.

In India the British were having their own problems with an independence movement headed by the Indian National Congress, led by Mohandas K. Gandhi and Jawaharlal Nehru. Under Gandhi's leadership, the Indian National Congress pursued nonviolent campaigns of civil disobedience that mobilized millions, including members of all castes and women, into agitations for reform and the end of foreign rule. Simultaneously, there was a growth in terrorism and police repression that seriously destabilized all of South Asia. Lacking a British promise of independence, the Indian National Congress opposed participation in World War II (1939–45), but even with many of its leaders in jail during the war there was continuing public disorder and police violence. After the war ended, the British realized that their position in South Asia had become untenable, and they prepared to leave. With China in the middle of a communist revolution, their old allies the British preparing to leave India, and thousands of soldiers returning from abroad, the Rana government could no longer avoid making radical changes in Nepal.

Many of the Nepalese exiles in India had worked closely with the Indian National Congress during its struggles with the British, realizing that only after the elimination of its colonial support would the Rana regime fall. In Banaras in October 1946, a group of middle-class Nepalese exiles formed the All-India Nepali National Congress (Akhil Bharatiya Nepali Rashtriya Congress). Many of its members were students who had agitated and subsequently had been jailed during movements in India. During its council in Calcutta in January 1947, the new organization dropped its "All-India" prefix and merged with two other groups, the Nepali Sangh (Nepalese Society) of Banaras and the Gorkha Congress of Calcutta, which had closer connections with lower-class Ranas. The Nepali National Congress (Nepali Rashtriya Congress) was officially dedicated to the ouster of the Rana dictatorship by peaceful means and to the establishment of democratic socialism. One of its first mass actions was participation in a labor strike in the jute mills of Biratnagar in the Tarai; the strike disrupted traffic at the Indian railhead in Jogbani and required army intervention. Although this action garnered much publicity for the party and brought thousands of protesters into the streets even in Kathmandu, the strike was suppressed, and its leaders, including Bishweshwar Prasad (B.P.) Koirala, were imprisoned.

B.P. Koirala (1914–82) became the leader most closely identified with the Nepali National Congress. His father, a Brahman businessman, spent a good deal of time in Bihar and Bengal. He had become involved with political activists and progressive ideas, especially those of Gandhi, and participated in anti-Rana agitations including the publication of *Gorkhali* at Banaras. B.P. Koirala thus grew up in an atmosphere oriented toward radical Gandhian action. By 1937 he was studying law in Calcutta and had started working for the Congress Socialist Party. He was arrested in India a number of times and spent 1942 to 1945 in jail after instigating Nepalese soldiers to rebel against the government. His views during his early years, influenced by Gandhi, tended toward radical democratic decentralization and included cottage industries instead of large factories as models for economic development. His wing of the Nepali National Congress stressed nonviolent confrontation and general strikes, but he was not opposed to force should all other paths prove ineffective. He advocated a constitutional monarchy as a transitional political form for Nepal.

The strong-willed, conservative Juddha Shamsher resigned as prime minister in November 1945, passing on his job to Padma Shamsher, who announced that he was a servant of the nation who would liberalize the Rana regime. Padma Shamsher's repression of the Biratnagar strike, however, showed that he was not interested in the kind of political and labor reforms advocated by the Congress. In the aftermath of the repression, on May 16, 1947, he delivered a speech outlining important reforms, including the establishment of an independent judiciary, elections for municipality and district boards, expansion of education, publication of the national budget, and the formation of a special committee to consider plans for further liberalization. The Nepali National Congress called off its continuing agitations, and B.P. Koirala and other top leaders were released from detention in August. In January 1948, the prime minister announced the first constitution of Nepal, which set up a bicameral Parliament, a separate High Court, and an executive power vested in the prime minister who was to be assisted by a five-member Council of Ministers. Although this constitution reserved almost all powers for the executive branch and kept the same rules of succession as before for both king and prime minister, the Nepali National Congress agreed to function within its framework. Beset by conflicting forces from all sides, however, Padma Shamsher resigned his position in early 1948.

The Return of the King

When the arch-conservative Mohan Shamsher took over as prime minister in 1948, he quickly outlawed the Nepali National Congress and showed no interest in implementing the new constitution that was scheduled to take effect in April. He rejected the more progressive wing among the Rana aristocracy, leading several well-known opponents to found the Nepal Democratic Congress (Nepal Prajatantrik Congress) in Calcutta in August 1948. This group was well funded and publicly advocated the overthrow of the Ranas by any means, including armed insurrection. It tried to foment army coups in January 1949 and January 1950 but failed. When

Ruins of the Thyangboche Monastery, Khumbu,
destroyed by fire in January 1989
Courtesy Janet MacDonald

the Rana government arrested B.P. Koirala and other organizers
in October 1948 and subjected regime opponents to harsh conditions and even torture in jail, its democratic opponents turned
against it again. Even the release of B.P. Koirala in June at the
insistence of Indian political leaders did little to help the negative
political climate. When Mohan Shamsher convened Parliament in
September 1950, supposedly in keeping with the constitution, it
was so full of Rana appointees that no one in the opposition took
the legislature seriously. The Nepali National Congress absorbed
the Nepal Democratic Congress in March 1950 and became the
Nepali Congress Party, and it formally decided to wage an armed
struggle against the Rana regime. On November 6, King Tribhuvan Bir Bikram Shah, who had long been making anti-Rana
statements, escaped from the palace and sought asylum in the Indian embassy in Kathmandu. Armed attacks by 300 members of
the Nepali Congress Party's Liberation Army (Mukti Sena) began in the Tarai on November 11, initiating revolution in Nepal.
    Mohan Shamsher found himself in a very unfavorable interna-
tional climate. The British had left India in 1947, and in their place
was a democratic government dominated by the Indian National
Congress, led by Jawaharlal Nehru. The government of India had

39

no interest in preserving the autocratic rule of native princes and had forcibly taken over the lands of the few princes who had opposed union with the new India. Furthermore, members of the underground Nepalese opposition had helped their Indian colleagues during the struggle against the British. B.P. Koirala had met with Nehru and with Gandhi as well. Changes in the north added an element of power politics to the situation. The Chinese revolution had ended in 1949 with the victory of the Chinese Communist Party, ending 100 years of weakness. Tibet again came under China's control in 1950. India, faced with an expansive military power operating under a radically different political philosophy on its long northern borders, could not afford a destabilized Nepal. Thus, the king was assured of asylum in the Indian embassy, and the Liberation Army of the Nepali Congress Party was able to operate freely from bases along the Indian border with Nepal.

The revolution consisted of scattered fighting, mostly in the Tarai, and growing demonstrations in the towns of the hills. The initial strategy of the insurgents was to capture the rich Tarai area, which produced much of the country's grain. Rebels were able to capture several towns there but never were able to hold them against counterattacks by the army. Armed struggles did not develop in the Kathmandu Valley, but demonstrations of up to 50,000 people demanding the return of the king occurred in late November. Meanwhile, insurgents were infiltrating hill areas in the west and the east, where army operations were more difficult. After several weeks of growing demonstrations and dissension in the ranks of local commanders, Palpa fell from government control on January 6, 1951. Rebels took over in Pokhara for a day on January 9–10 and occupied Gorkha for part of January 10. Sporadic fighting in western Nepal led to the fall of many towns in mid-January. By this time, some "C" class Rana officers had resigned their commissions in protest, and troops were beginning to surrender to the rebels.

Negotiations between the Indian government and the Ranas had begun on December 24, 1950, in Delhi, finally leading to a proclamation on January 8, 1951, by Mohan Shamsher, who promised restoration of the king, amnesty for all political prisoners, and elections based on adult suffrage no later than 1952. The king formally agreed two days later, and a cease-fire went into effect on January 16. Further negotiations among the Ranas, the king, and the Nepali Congress Party produced an interim ministry headed by Mohan Shamsher with five Ranas and five Nepali Congress Party members. The king returned to Kathmandu, and the new ministry was sworn in during February 1951.

The coalition ministry was a mixture of ultra-conservatives who believed that they were born to rule and radical reformers who had almost no administrative experience. It was able to enact a new interim constitution in March 1951, set up a separate judicial branch, transfer all executive powers back to the king (including supreme command of the armed forces and power to appoint government officials and manage finances), call for a welfare state, set forth a Bill of Rights, and start procedures for the formation of local-level assemblies, or *panchayat* (see Glossary). The ministry started plans to abolish *birta* lands used by Ranas to reward their own family members, eliminated bonded labor, and established a women's college and a radio station. The ministry was beset by law and order problems caused by loose bands of Liberation Army fighters who had refused to stop fighting, bands of robbers who were victimizing the Tarai, and ultra-conservative conspiracies that instigated a mob attack on the house of B.P. Koirala, who had become the minister of home affairs in April. The final embarrassment occurred when police fired on a student demonstration and killed a student. The entire bloc of Nepali Congress Party ministers resigned in November, which allowed the king to appoint a new government for the first time since the nineteenth century. The king used the opportunity to exclude for good the conservative Rana power bloc. A royal proclamation on November 16, 1951, established a new government led by Matrika Prasad (M.P.) Koirala, the half-brother of B.P. Koirala, who had run the Nepali Congress Party during the revolutionary struggle.

The Democratic Experiment

In the early 1950s, a political style appeared that characterized much of the era after the overthrow of the Ranas. On one side stood the king, who controlled the most powerful force in the nation— the army—and found it an increasingly useful tool with which to wield his prestige and constitutional authority. On the other side stood the political parties. First there was the Nepali Congress Party, which claimed to stand for the democratic will of the people. Then there were a multitude of breakaway factions or other small parties representing a wide range of interests. The Communist Party of Nepal, for example, was established in Calcutta in 1949 but had refused to take part in the armed struggle and condemned it as a "bourgeois" revolution; despite its own difficulties with factional disputes, this party was destined to grow in a country riddled with problems. In the Kathmandu Valley, other leaders who had been locked out of high positions in the first coalition government formed a revitalized Praja Parishad. Opponents of the "antidemocratic" character of the Nepali Congress leadership and their pro-India stance, which they claimed went against the interests of Nepal, broke away to form a revitalized Nepali National Congress. In 1951 a united front of the communists and the Praja Parishad formed to oppose the Nepali Congress ministers. The political themes in the early 1950s—class, opposition to authoritarian trends within party leadership, and nationalistic propaganda, combined with agitational united front tactics—have remained standard features of party politics in Nepal. As the various political parties slashed at each other and the king maneuvered for greater power, the country began experimenting with a limping democracy.

Nepal faced an enormous task. When the Ranas fell, only 2 percent of the adult population was literate, the infant mortality rate was more than 60 percent, and average life expectancy was thirty-five years. Less than 1 percent of the population was engaged in modern industrial occupations, and 85 percent of employment and income came from agriculture, mostly performed by tenants using archaic methods and working under uncertain contracts. There were only approximately 100 kilometers of railroad tracks and a few kilometers of paved roads in the entire nation. Telephones, electricity, and postal services combined served only 1 percent of the population and only in certain pockets. Nepalese currency circulated only in and around the Kathmandu Valley. Government expenditures went almost entirely for salaries and benefits for army, police, and civil servants, with any savings going to the prime minister. Health and education received less than 1 percent of the government's expenditures. The nation still contained autonomous principalities (*rajya*) based on deals with former local kings, and landlords acted as small dictators on their own lands. Caste, ethnic, and linguistic differences abounded, but only three groups— Chhetris, Brahmans, and some Newars—had any say in the national government. The Tarai, the richest area in the nation, had been systematically ignored by the government and exploited for 200 years, and many of its people felt more at home in India than Nepal. National integration was a major problem.

Between November 1951 and February 1959, there was a succession of short-lived governments ruling under terms of the interim constitution or under the direct command of the king, attempting to fashion an environment favorable for the calling of a constituent assembly that would frame a permanent constitution. As soon as the king found a ministry uncooperative or so beset by contradictions that it could not function, he replaced it with members who had smaller bases of support. At no time during this period did the faction of the Nepali Congress Party headed by B.P.

Koirala, which commanded the widest allegiance, have any chance of forming a government because the king continued to postpone elections for an assembly.

When King Tribhuvan died, his son Mahendra Bir Bikram Shah Dev (reigned 1955–72) carried on as before, experimenting with types of councils or ministries that would do his will behind a democratic façade. Under pressure from large-scale civil disobedience campaigns, the king announced that elections for a representative assembly would take place on February 18, 1959. As political parties of all persuasions were busily preparing for the elections, the king had his own commission draw up a new constitution. He presented it as a gift to the nation on February 12, 1959, with the elections only one week away. In the first national elections in the history of the nation, the Nepali Congress won a clear victory, taking 74 out of 109 seats. B.P. Koirala at last became prime minister.

Under the terms of the new constitution, there were two legislative houses: an Upper House (Maha Sabha) of 36 members, half elected by the lower house and half nominated by the king; and a Lower House (Pratinidhi Sabha) of 109 members, all elected by universal adult suffrage. The leader of the majority party in the Lower House became prime minister and governed with a cabinet of ministers. The king could act without consulting the prime minister, and even could dismiss him. The king also had control over the army and foreign affairs and could invoke emergency powers suspending all or part of the constitution.

Against this background of formidable royal rights, the Koirala government was able to accomplish some major tasks. It finally abolished *birta* tenure in October 1959 and the autonomy of principalities (*rajya*) in the western hills. In 1960 the government revised a crucial Trade and Transit Treaty with India. It also negotiated another agreement with India on the Gandak River Project, guaranteeing territorial jurisdiction and free provision of water to Nepal (see Relations with India, ch. 4). Diplomatic relations were established with the United States, the Soviet Union, China, France, and Pakistan. Koirala himself addressed the United Nations, visited China, and presided over the signing of a Treaty of Peace and Friendship with China in 1960. In the economic sphere, the First Five-Year Plan (1956–61) had been poorly conceived and executed, but the Koirala government took steps to plan effectively for the Second Plan (1962–65).

The king initially was on good terms with the Koirala government, even taking the unprecedented step of playing soccer with his brothers at the National Stadium against a team that included the prime minister and his associates. At the same time, he was publicly opposed to democracy in principle and would not tolerate any official interference in the divine powers believed to be conferred on him as king. The army, the former aristocracy, conservative landowning groups, and the king all were uneasy about the reforms of the Koirala government and the negative propaganda of opposition groups inside Parliament, including the Gorkha Parishad and the Communist Party of Nepal. When destabilizing the Nepali Congress ministry proved difficult, the king used the nation's chronic violence—widely believed to be orchestrated by the monarch himself—as a reason to act directly. On December 15, 1960, with the army's support and with little warning, the king used his emergency powers to dismiss the cabinet and arrest its leaders on the charge that they had failed to provide national leadership or maintain law and order. B.P. Koirala spent the next eight years in prison and another eight years in exile. The experiments in liberal socialism and democracy, at least as defined by the Nepali Congress, were at an end.

The Panchayat System under King Mahendra

On December 26, 1961, King Mahendra appointed a council of five ministers to help run the administration. Several weeks later, political parties were declared illegal. At first the Nepali Congress leadership propounded a nonviolent struggle against the new order and formed alliances with several political parties, including the Gorkha Parishad and the United Democratic Party, which had been strong critics of the Nepali Congress when it ran the government. Early in 1961, however, the king had set up a committee of four officials from the Central Secretariat to recommend changes in the constitution that would abolish political parties and substitute a "National Guidance" system based on local *panchayat* led directly by the king. By late 1961, violent actions organized by the Nepali Congress in exile began along the Indian border, increasing in size and number during early 1962.

The political situation changed completely when war broke out between India and China on October 20, 1962. In a series of rapid movements, Chinese troops occupied mountain areas east and west of Nepal in an attempt to resolve border disputes with India by simply occupying disputed territories. The reversal suffered by Indian forces took the leadership in India by surprise and forced it to reevaluate the strategic situation in the Himalayas. Because India needed strong friends rather than insurrections in the region, it withdrew support from insurgents along the border with Nepal and established closer relations with the king's government. In Nepal, King Mahendra extended the state of emergency indefinitely. The

The twelve-armed Black Bhairav at Kathmandu is admired and revered as a form of Shiva.
Courtesy Harvey Follender

army trained by India during the 1950s proved itself capable of handling guerrilla warfare. In the midst of increasing desertions from his cause, the leader of the Nepali Congress, Subarna Shamsher, called off the armed struggle.

Adopted on the second anniversary of the royal coup, the new constitution of December 16, 1962, created a four-tier *panchayat* system. At the local level, there were 4,000 village assemblies (*gaun sabha*) electing nine members of the village *panchayat,* who in turn elected a mayor (*sabhapati*). Each village *panchayat* sent a member to sit on one of seventy-five district (*zilla*) *panchayat,* representing from forty to seventy villages; one-third of the members of these assemblies were chosen by the town *panchayat.* Members of the district *panchayat* elected representatives to fourteen zone assemblies (*anchal sabha*) functioning as electoral colleges for the National Panchayat, or Rashtriya Panchayat, in Kathmandu. In addition, there were class organizations at village, district, and zonal levels for peasants, youth, women, elders, laborers, and ex-soldiers, who elected their own representatives to assemblies. The National Panchayat of about ninety members could not criticize the royal government, debate the principles of partyless democracy, introduce budgetary bills without royal approval, or enact bills without approval of the king. Mahendra was supreme commander of the armed forces, appointed (and had the power to remove) members of the Supreme Court, appointed the Public Service Commission to oversee the civil service, and could change any judicial decision or amend the constitution at any time. To many of the unlettered citizens of the country, the king was a spiritual force as well, representing the god Vishnu upholding dharma on earth. Within a span of ten years, the king had, in effect, reclaimed the unlimited power exercised by Prithvi Narayan Shah in the eighteenth century.

The first elections to the National Panchayat took place in March and April 1963. Although political parties officially were banned and the major opposition parties publicly refused to participate, about one-third of the members of the legislative were associated with the Nepali Congress. Support of the king by the army and the government bureaucracy prevented opposition to his rule from developing within the *panchayat* system. Real power came from the king's secretariat, and in the countryside influence rested in the offices of zonal commissioners and their official staffs or the parallel system of development officers. The Nepali Congress leadership made increasingly conciliatory statements and began to announce its faith in democratic ideals under the leadership of the king. In 1968 the king began to release political prisoners, including B.P.

Koirala, who was freed on October 30. At this point, a three-way split developed in the Nepali Congress. B.P. Koirala went to India, where he headed a wing committed to democratic revolution and violent overthrow of the *panchayat* system. He was a symbol for youth but powerless politically. Subarna Shamsher's wing continued to advocate local cooperation with the king outside the *panchayat* system. A third wing tried to work within the *panchayat* system in the expectation that it would evolve into a democratic system. The disunity of the political opposition left King Mahendra to do as he wished.

Under the direct leadership of the king, the government implemented some of the major projects that were initiated under the previous democratic regime and oversaw further steps toward the development of the country (see Constitutional Development, ch. 4). Land reforms led to the confiscation of large Rana estates. *Rajya* reform abolished special privileges of some aristocratic elites in western Nepal. A new legal code promulgated in 1963 replaced the Muluki Ain of 1854. A major land reform program launched in 1964 essentially was a failure. The new *panchayat* system managed to bring 50,000 to 60,000 people into a single system of representative government in a way that had been rendered impossible for the elite-based political parties. Nepal was able to carry out its second plan (1962–65) and third plan (1965–70), and to begin the Fourth Five-Year Plan (1970–75). Eradication of malaria, construction of the Mahendra Highway, or East-West Highway, along the southern foot of the hills, and land settlement programs contributed to a massive movement of population from the hills into the Tarai, resulting in a large increase in the area devoted to agriculture (see Population, ch. 2; Agriculture, ch. 3).

The death of Mahendra in January 1972 and the accession of Birendra Bir Bikram Shah Dev allowed the possibility of turmoil. The new king was associated with young, educated, administrative experts who were dedicated to economic development, but not to sharing power with political parties. Students at Tribhuvan University went on an indefinite strike in August to support a ten-point charter of demands. That month, 100 armed men attacked an eastern Tarai village and killed a constable in a revolutionary action supposedly linked to the policies of B.P. Koirala. In June 1973, terrorists hijacked a Royal Nepal Airlines airplane to India and escaped with 30 million Indian rupees (approximately US$4.6 million). Other armed attacks and assassination attempts occurred into 1974. These isolated incidents had relatively little impact on a government that the army and the bureaucracy supported and that monopolized the allocation of all resources to local development projects.

In 1975 the king appointed a seven-member Reform Commission to investigate making changes in the *panchayat* system, but during that year Indian prime minister Indira Gandhi declared a state of emergency in her country, jailing members of the opposition and curtailing democracy there. In this climate, the recommendations of the Reform Commission in Nepal led to a 1975 constitutional amendment that made cosmetic changes in the *panchayat* system but only increased its rigidity. The changes included the establishment of five development regions to promote planning and the increase in membership of the National Panchayat from 90 to 134 persons. The king was to nominate 20 percent of its members.

Modernization under King Birendra

When it became apparent that the *panchayat* system was going to endure, B.P. Koirala and other political exiles began to tone down their revolutionary rhetoric and advocate a reconciliation with the king. On December 30, 1976, Koirala and his close associate, Ganeshman Singh, flew to Kathmandu hoping to "make a fresh attempt." They were arrested for antinational activities and violence, and a tribunal was set up for a trial. After considerable agitation, Koirala was released in June 1977 because of ill health. He met briefly with the king and then went to the United States for treatment. When he returned to Nepal in November 1977, he was again arrested at the airport. After further public agitations on his behalf, he underwent five treason trials in early 1978 and was ultimately acquitted. Thereafter, despite factional splits, the Nepali Congress resembled other opposition parties in its acceptance of the king's power. Thus, the pattern of modern Nepalese politics was established—loyalty to the king and opposition to his government. In practice, there were continuing student demonstrations against the *panchayat* system and for human rights in 1977 and 1978.

On May 24, 1979, King Birendra announced on Radio Nepal that there would be a national referendum in the near future, during which the people could decide to support or reject the *panchayat* system of government. This referendum represented the first time in modern history that the monarch had publicly consulted his subjects. Political freedom was allowed to all citizens during the period of preparation for the referendum, and there was intense realignment of political factions inside and outside the *panchayat* system. Finally, on May 2, 1980, out of a potential 7.2 million voters, 4.8 million cast their ballots. The outcome supported the *panchayat* system, with 54.7 percent for and 45.3 percent against

Ghats along the Hanumante River in Bhaktapur, a place to bathe and wash
Courtesy Ann Matles

it. Koirala and the Nepali Congress accepted the results. Although the referendum was a victory for the king, its narrow margin clearly indicated the need for change. Accordingly, the king quickly confirmed freedom of speech and political activity and announced the formation of an eleven-member Constitution Reforms Commission. The result, in December 1980, was the Third Amendment of the 1962 constitution, setting up direct elections to the National Panchayat, which would then submit a single candidate for prime minister to the king for approval. A Council of Ministers would thenceforth be responsible to the National Panchayat, not to the king.

In March 1981, the Constitution Reforms Commission announced that elections to the National Panchayat would take place on May 9, 1981. Aside from pro-Moscow factions of the Communist Party of Nepal and a "Group of 38" from the Nepali Congress, political parties rejected the amended constitution and refused to participate in the elections. The Nepali Congress led by Koirala observed an "election boycott week" from May 1 to 8, but on election day a 52 percent turnout of voters chose 111 representatives to the National Panchayat. Surya Bahadur Thapa was returned as prime minister, and the king formed a twenty-eight-member Council of Ministers in June 1981.

Opposition politics were in a state of disarray, dominated by the terminal illness of Koirala, who died in July 1982. The victory of the king was not complete, however. During the elections, more than 70 percent of the candidates favored by the king lost. The *panchayat* system, a major source for local patronage, was becoming the stage for factional fights and shuffling coalitions. On many college campuses, elections for student unions went to communists after violent clashes.

The trend toward factionalism in the National Panchayat intensified in 1983, when a serious food crisis and charges of corruption caused the fall of Surya Bahadur Thapa's government. Lokendra Bahadur Chand took over as prime minister, but two blocs, or *samuha* (see Glossary), had emerged in the National Panchayat around Thapa and Chand. The factional fighting did not prevent the celebration in 1986 of the *panchayat* system's twenty-fifth anniversary, which created an opportunity for the second general election to the National Panchayat. The Nepali Congress and most other opposition parties again boycotted the elections, although the communists and a few other small parties did participate. The elections drew 60 percent of the voters, and 60 percent of the members of the National Panchayat supported Marich Man Singh Shrestha as prime minister.

Before elections to the local *panchayat* the following year, the Nepali Congress announced that it would continue its boycott but then changed its strategy and allowed its members to run for local seats, claiming that it could "capture the outposts" of the system and politicize the people. The poor showing of the Nepali Congress candidates embarrassed the party, however, and revealed its isolation from many rural voters.

Despite low growth figures, throughout the 1980s Nepal at least had made some progress in economic development, but it remained in any case one of the poorest countries in the world (see Economic Setting, ch. 3). The king was achieving a higher profile in international affairs, canvassing widespread support for the declaration of Nepal as a zone of peace and participating in the South Asian Association for Regional Cooperation (SAARC—see Glossary; International and Regional Organizations, ch. 4). These modest trends encountered a sudden interruption in 1989 when a major international incident with India occurred. On March 1, the Indian embassy announced that trade and transit treaties with Nepal, renewed regularly since the 1950s, would expire twenty-two days later. Both the Indian and Nepalese governments accused each other of delaying negotiations. When March 23 arrived, India declared the treaties had expired and closed all but two border entry points into Nepal. These closures caused huge backups on the border and delayed or halted the bulk of foreign trade, including crucial shipments of oil and gasoline, and the tourist trade, a major source of foreign exchange carefully cultivated under King Birendra. Agricultural production declined, layoffs in factories increased, and the inflation rate in 1987–88 rose to 11 percent. The growth rate of the economy, a healthy 9.7 percent in 1987–88, declined to 1.5 percent in 1988–89.

The Nepali Congress, early in its history accused of bowing to Indian opinion, in September organized a National Awakening Week during which 3,500 party members committed nonviolent civil disobedience. Student demonstrations against India began to take on antigovernment tones, and all campuses in Kathmandu closed for two months. The crisis demonstrated the fragility of the political and economic system in Nepal—an old culture but a young nation—landlocked between two giants and directed by a medieval monarchy.

* * *

The most complete and readable account of ancient and medieval Nepalese history in English is Mary Shephers Slusser's *Nepal Mandala,* which also contains an excellent bibliography of the considerable work available only in Nepali. Luciano Petech's *Medieval History of Nepal (ca. 750–1480)* contains interesting details and summarizes information in a quite readable manner. Dilli Raman Regmi's *Ancient Nepal* and *Medieval Nepal* are exhaustive accounts with large amounts of original material.

Ludwig Stiller describes the period of the Gorkha conquests and the consolidation of the Nepalese state in the early eighteenth century in *The Rise of the House of Gorkha* and *The Silent Cry.* John Pemble presents a straightforward analysis of the Anglo-Nepalese War in *The Invasion of Nepal.*

For relations between the British and Nepal later in the nineteenth century, see Ravuri Dhanalaxmi's *British Attitude to Nepal's Relations with Tibet and China, 1814–1914,* Sushila Tyagi's *Indo-Nepalese Relations (1858–1914),* or Kanchanmoy Mojumdar's *Anglo-Nepalese Relations in the Nineteenth Century.* Affairs of the Ranas in the late nineteenth century are covered in M.S. Jain's *Emergence of a New Aristocracy in Nepal (1837–58),* Krishna Kant Adhikari's *Nepal under Jang Bahadur, 1846–1877,* and Satish Kumar's *Rana Polity in Nepal.*

There is no shortage of books on the fall of the Rana regime and the political changes that led to the king's dominance by 1980.

Leo E. Rose has written books on his own, including *Nepal: Strategy for Survival,* as well as those with other authors, including the introductory *Nepal: Profile of a Himalayan Kingdom* (with John T. Scholz), *The Politics of Nepal* (with Margaret W. Fisher), and *Democratic Innovations in Nepal* (with Bhuwan Lal Joshi).

There also are a number of works that describe recent developments from several Nepalese perspectives, including Shashi P. Misra's *B.P. Koirala: A Case Study in Third World Democratic Leadership* and Parmanand's *The Nepali Congress since Its Inception.* Hem Narayan Agrawal gives a straightforward presentation of the modern constitutions in *Nepal: A Study in Constitutional Change.* For current events, the short annual country profiles of Nepal in February issues of *Asian Survey* can keep the reader up to date. (For further information and complete citations, see Bibliography.)

Chapter 2. Nepal: The Society and Its Environment

Hanuman, the monkey god of the Ramayana, *the Hindu epic. Hanuman, aided by monkeys, assists Rama in recovering his wife, Sita, from Ravana by bridging the straits between India and Sri Lanka with boulders brought from the Himalayas.*

NEPAL IS OFTEN CHARACTERIZED as a country caught in two different worlds, having one leg in the sixteenth century and another in the twentieth century. Entrenched in a feudalistic social structure, the deeply tradition-bound society increasingly was experiencing the pervasive influence of Western material culture. Most affected were the parts of the population that came in regular contact with Westerners. Nowhere was this juxtaposition of local traditional values and Western material culture more pronounced than in the Kathmandu Valley—the country's most urbanized region.

In the Kathmandu Valley in 1991, hordes of people took ritual baths in the highly polluted Baghmati River, especially near the temple of Pashupatinath, and walked to temples that dotted the valley's landscape. Numerous peasants carried their produce to the market on bicycles or on what is locally called a *kharpan,* a device that resembles a large weighing balance and is carried on the shoulder. Yet, young boys wore T-shirts emblazoned with Michael Jackson or other Hollywood celebrities and watched ''Miami Vice'' or other American television shows. The skyline of urban areas such as Kathmandu, Siddhartha Nagar, and Pokhara was interrupted by television antennas. Copying Western popular culture and values had become the thing to do. Nepalese youth even took drugs, and the number of drug addicts had increased significantly in the 1980s.

The adoption of Western popular cultural values has not, however, translated into much-needed technological and economic progress and a consequent reduction in pervasive poverty. Although youths, especially those living in and around urban centers, readily adopted Western consumer habits, they appeared to have little knowledge about more productive habits that the West exemplifies. Entranced by the tide of consumerism, Nepalese youths seemed poorly prepared or unwilling to do hard work and make sacrifices that were imperative for establishing dynamic economic production and development. As a result, consumerism outpaced productive capacity—a process that was clearly contrary to sustained socioeconomic progress—and the country remained in a state of economic backwardness.

Despite Nepal's increasing contact with the West since liberation from Rana rule in 1951, the feudalistic yoke has not been broken (see Modernization under King Mahendra, ch. 1). Even after thirty-five years of economic development planning, poverty remained throughout the country. Government intervention in economic development under the rubric of planning has led to a breakdown in the traditional patron-client relations. In the past, this relationship provided some security of survival—or what Karl Polyani termed in 1957 "the absence of the threat of individual starvation"—for the clients, although they were placed in a subservient position. In 1991 such patron-client relations had been replaced by wage relations, but planned development had not been able to create enough employment opportunities to gainfully absorb the clients who no longer could rely on their patrons.

There was no doubt among observers that only an increasing flow of foreign aid and loans had kept Nepal from bankruptcy. Yet there seemed to be little evidence suggesting that the aid had, despite good intentions, alleviated mass poverty and uplifted the society as a whole. Unemployment among the educated was partially addressed through the continued expansion of government jobs, but such expansion resulted in bureaucratic redundancy and, in fact, hindered economic development. Furthermore, such a strategy had only a limited ability to reduce the mass unemployment and underemployment that typified Nepal's society. Widespread unemployment and underemployment, which fueled poverty, were further exacerbated by continued rapid population growth. Despite a long-term and vigorous family planning program, the population had been growing at an increasing rate. Such population growth contributed to increasing environmental deterioration, given the frailty of the country's mountainous environment.

Geography

The Land

Sandwiched between two Asian giants—China and India—Nepal traditionally has been characterized as "a yam caught between two rocks." Noted for its majestic Himalayas, which in Sanskrit means the abode of snow, Nepal is very mountainous and hilly. Its shape is roughly rectangular, about 650 kilometers long and about 200 kilometers wide, and comprises a total of 147,181 square kilometers of land. It is slightly larger than Bangladesh or the state of Arkansas. Nepal is a landlocked country, surrounded by India on three sides and by China's Xizang Autonomous Region (Tibet) to the north. It is separated from Bangladesh by an approximately fifteen-kilometer-wide strip of India's state of West Bengal, and from Bhutan by the eighty-eight-kilometer-wide Sikkim, also an Indian state. Such a confined geographical position is hardly enviable.

Nepal is almost totally dependent on India for transit facilities and access to the sea—that is, the Bay of Bengal—even for most of the goods coming from China.

For a small country, Nepal has great physical diversity, ranging from the Tarai Plain—the northern rim of the Gangetic Plain situated at about 300 meters above sea level in the south—to the almost 8,800-meter-high Mount Everest, locally known as Sagarmatha (its Nepali name), in the north. From the lowland Tarai belt, landforms rise in successive hill and mountain ranges, including the stupendous rampart of the towering Himalayas, ultimately reaching the Tibetan Plateau beyond the Inner Himalayas. This rise in elevation is punctuated by valleys situated between mountain ranges. Within this maze of mountains, hills, ridges, and low valleys, elevational (altitudinal) changes resulted in ecological variations.

Nepal commonly is divided into three broad physiographic areas: the Mountain Region, the Hill Region, and the Tarai Region (see fig. 4). All three parallel each other, from east to west, as continuous ecological belts, occasionally bisected by the country's river systems. These ecological regions were divided by the government into development sectors within the framework of regional development planning.

The rhythm of life in Nepal, as in most other parts of monsoonal Asia, is intricately yet intrinsically intertwined with its physical environment. As scholar Barry Bishop learned from his field research in the Karnali region in the northwest, the livelihood patterns of Nepal are inseparable from the environment.

The Mountain Region

The Mountain Region (called Parbat in Nepali) is situated at 4,000 meters or more above sea level to the north of the Hill Region. The Mountain Region constitutes the central portion of the Himalayan range originating in the Pamirs, a high altitude region of Central Asia. Its natural landscape includes Mount Everest and seven other of the world's ten highest peaks, which are the legendary habitat of the mythical creature, the yeti, or abominable snowman. In general, the snow line occurs between 5,000 and 5,500 meters. The region is characterized by inclement climatic and rugged topographic conditions, and human habitation and economic activities are extremely limited and arduous. Indeed, the region is sparsely populated, and whatever farming activity exists is mostly confined to the low-lying valleys and the river basins, such as the upper Kali Gandaki Valley.

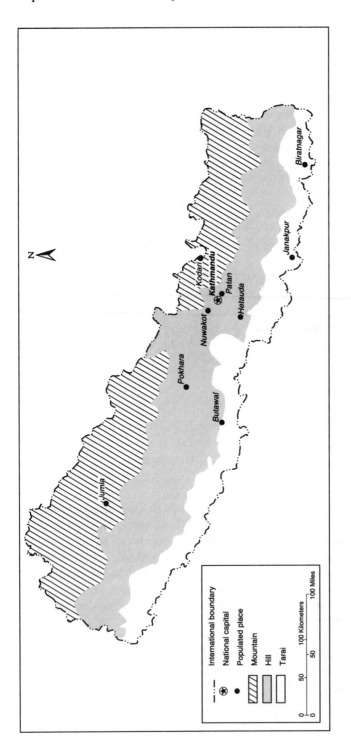

Source: Based on information from Leo E. Rose and John T. Scholz, *Nepal: Profile of a Himalayan Kingdom*, Boulder, 1980, 4; Nanda R. Shreshtha, *Landlessness and Migration in Nepal*, Boulder, 1990, 6; and Pitamber Sharma, *Urbanization in Nepal*, Honolulu, May 1989, 132.

Figure 4. Nepal: Geographic Regions

In the early 1990s, pastoralism and trading were common economic activities among mountain dwellers. Because of their heavy dependence on herding and trading, transhumance was widely practiced. Herders moved their *goths* (temporary animal shelters) in accordance with the seasonal climatic rhythms, and traders also migrated seasonally between highlands and lowlands, buying and selling goods and commodities in order to generate much-needed income and to secure food supplies.

The Hill Region

Situated south of the Mountain Region, the Hill Region (called Pahar in Nepali) is mostly between 1,000 and 4,000 meters in altitude. It includes the Kathmandu Valley, the country's most fertile and urbanized area. Two major ranges of hills, commonly known as the Mahabharat Lekh and Siwalik Range (or Churia Range), occupy the region. In addition, there are several intermontane valleys. Despite its geographical isolation and limited economic potential, the region always has been the political and cultural center of Nepal, with decision-making power centralized in Kathmandu, the nation's capital. Because of immigration from Tibet and India, the hill ranges historically have been the most heavily populated area. Despite heavy out-migration, the Hill Region comprised the largest share of the total population in 1991.

Although the higher elevations (above 2,500 meters) in the region were sparsely populated because of physiographic and climatic difficulties, the lower hills and valleys were densely settled. The hill landscape was both a natural and cultural mosaic, shaped by geological forces and human activity. The hills, sculpted by human hands into a massive complex of terraces, were extensively cultivated.

Like the Mountain Region, the Hill Region was a food-deficit area in the early 1990s, although agriculture was the predominant economic activity supplemented by livestock raising, foraging, and seasonal migrating of laborers. The vast majority of the households living in the hills were land-hungry and owned largely *pakho* (hilly) land. The poor economic situation caused by lack of sufficient land was aggravated by the relatively short growing season, a phenomenon directly attributable to the climatic impact of the region's higher altitude. As a result, a hill farmer's ability to grow multiple crops was limited. The families were forced to adapt to the marginality, as well as the seasonality, of their environment, cultivating their land whenever they could and growing whatever would survive. Bishop has noted that "as crop productivity decreases with elevation, the importance of livestock in livelihood pursuits . . . increases. For many Bhotia [or Bhote] living in the highlands . . . animal husbandry supplants agriculture in importance.'' During the slack season, when the weather did not permit cropping, hill dwellers generally became seasonal migrants, who engaged in wage labor wherever they could find it to supplement their meager farm output. Dependence on nonagricultural activities was even more necessary in the mountain ecological belt.

The Tarai Region

In complete topographic contrast to the Mountain and Hill regions, the Tarai Region is a lowland tropical and subtropical belt of flat, alluvial land stretching along the Nepal-India border, and paralleling the Hill Region. It is the northern extension of the Gangetic Plain in India, commencing at about 300 meters above sea level and rising to about 1,000 meters at the foot of the Siwalik Range. The Tarai includes several valleys (*dun*), such as the Surkhet and Dang valleys in western Nepal, and the Rapti Valley (Chitwan) in central Nepal.

The word *tarai*, a term presumed to be derived from Persian, means "damp," and it appropriately describes the region's humid and hot climate. The region was formed and is fed by three major rivers: the Kosi, the Narayani (India's Gandak River), and the Karnali. A region that in the past contained malaria-infested, thick forests, commonly known as *char kose jhari* (dense forests approximately twelve kilometers wide), the Tarai was used as a defensive frontier by Nepalese rulers during the period of the British Raj (1858–1947) in India. In 1991 the Tarai served as the country's granary and land resettlement frontier; it became the most coveted internal destination for land-hungry hill peasants.

In terms of both farm and forest lands, the Tarai was becoming Nepal's richest economic region. Overall, Tarai residents enjoyed a greater availability of agricultural land than did other Nepalese because of the area's generally flat terrain, which is drained and nourished by several rivers. Additionally, it has the largest commercially exploitable forests. In the early 1990s, however, the forests were being increasingly destroyed because of growing demands for timber and agricultural land.

Climate

Nepal has a great deal of variation in climate. Its latitude is about the same as that of Florida, and a tropical and subtropical climate exists in the Tarai Region. Outside the Tarai, however, the climate is completely different. The remarkable differences in climatic conditions are primarily related to the enormous range of altitude within such a short north-south distance. The presence of the east-west-trending Himalayan massifs to the north and the monsoonal alteration of wet and dry seasons also greatly contribute to local variations in climate. Scholar Sharad Singh Negi identifies five climatic zones in Nepal based on altitude: the tropical and subtropical zone of below 1,200 meters in altitude; the cool, temperate zone of 1,200 to 2,400 meters in altitude; the cold zone of 2,400 to 3,600 meters in altitude; the subarctic climatic zone of 3,600 to 4,400 meters in altitude; and the arctic zone above 4,400 meters in altitude. In terms of natural vegetational regimes or distribution patterns, altitude again plays a significant role. Below 1,200 meters, the dominant form of vegetation consists of tropical and subtropical rain forests.

Altitude also affects annual rainfall or precipitation patterns. Up to about 3,000 meters, annual rainfall totals increase as the altitude increases; thereafter, annual totals diminish with increasing altitude and latitude. In addition to this latitudinal differentiation in rainfall, two other patterns can be discerned. First, given the northwestward movement of the moisture-laden summer monsoon (June to September), the amount of annual rainfall generally decreases from east to west. However, there are certain pockets with heavy annual rainfall totals, for example, the Pokhara Valley in central Nepal. Second, the horizontal extension of hill and mountain ranges creates a moist condition on south-and east-facing slopes whereas it produces a major rain shadow on the northern sides of the slopes. The aridity increases with altitude and latitude, especially on the northern slopes, and reaches its climax in the inner Himalayan region and on the Tibetan Plateau. Eastern Nepal receives approximately 2,500 millimeters of rain annually, the Kathmandu area about 1,420 millimeters, and western Nepal about 1,000 millimeters.

The towering Himalayas play a critical role, blocking the northwesterly advances of moist, tropical air from the Bay of Bengal, and ultimately leading to its conversion to rain in the summer. In the winter, this range prevents the outbursts of cold air from Inner Asia from reaching southern Nepal and northern India, thus ensuring warmer winters in these regions than otherwise would be the case.

In addition, there are seasonal variations in the amount of rainfall, depending on the monsoon cycle. Bishop divides the monsoon cycle into four seasons: premonsoon, summer monsoon, postmonsoon, and winter monsoon. The premonsoon season generally occurs during April and May; it is characterized by the highest temperatures, reaching 40°C during the day in the Tarai Region and other lowlands. The hills and mountains, however, remain cool.

The summer monsoon, a strong flow of moist air from the south-west, follows the premonsoon season. For the vast majority of southern Asians, including Nepalese, the term *monsoon* is synonymous with the summer rainy season, which makes or breaks the lives of hundreds of millions of farmers on the subcontinent. Even though the arrival of the summer monsoon can vary by as much as a month, in Nepal it generally arrives in early June, is preceded by violent lightning and thunderstorms, and lasts through September, when it begins to recede. The plains and lower Himalayas receive more than 70 percent of their annual precipitation during the summer monsoon. The amount of summer monsoon rain generally declines from southeast to northwest as the maritime wedge of air gradually becomes thinner and dryer. Although the success of farming is almost totally dependent on the timely arrival of the summer monsoon, it periodically causes landslides; subsequent losses of human lives, farmlands, and other properties (not to mention great difficulty in the movement of goods and people); and heavy flooding in the plains. Conversely, when prolonged breaks in the summer monsoon occur, severe drought and famine often result.

The postmonsoon season begins with a slow withdrawal of the monsoon. This retreat leads to an almost complete disappearance of moist air by mid-October, thus ushering in generally cool, clear, and dry weather, as well as the most relaxed and jovial period in Nepal. By this time the harvest is completed and people are in a festive mood. The two biggest and most important Hindu festivals—Dashain and Tihar (Dipawali)—arrive during this period, about one month apart (see Religion, this ch.). The postmonsoon season lasts until about December.

After the postmonsoon, comes the winter monsoon, a strong northeasterly flow, which is marked by occasional, short rainfalls in the lowlands and plains and snowfalls in the high-altitude areas. The amount of precipitation resulting from the northeast land trade winds varies considerably but increases markedly with elevation. The secondary winter precipitation in the form of snowfalls in the Himalayas is important for generating a sufficient volume of spring and summer meltwaters, which are critical for irrigation in the lower hills and valleys where agriculture predominates. Winter precipitation is also indispensable for the success of winter crops, such as wheat, barley, and numerous vegetables.

The River System

Nepal can be divided into three major river systems from east to west: the Kosi River, the Narayani River (India's Gandak

River), and the Karnali River (see fig. 5). All ultimately become major tributaries of the Ganges River in northern India. After plunging through deep gorges, these rivers deposit their heavy sediments and debris on the plains, thereby nurturing them and renewing their alluvial soil fertility. Once they reach the Tarai Region, they often overflow their banks onto wide floodplains during the summer monsoon season, periodically shifting their courses. Besides providing fertile alluvial soil, the backbone of the agrarian economy, these rivers present great possibilities for hydroelectric and irrigation development. India managed to exploit this resource by building massive dams on the Kosi and Narayani rivers inside the Nepal border, known, respectively, as the Kosi and Gandak projects (see Energy, ch. 3). None of these river systems, however, support any significant commercial navigation facility. Rather, the deep gorges formed by the rivers represent immense obstacles to establishing the broad transport and communication networks needed to develop an integrated national economy. As a result, the economy in Nepal has remained fragmented. Because Nepal's rivers have not been harnessed for transportation, most settlements in the Hill and Mountain regions remain isolated from each other. As of 1991, trails remained the primary transportation routes in the hills.

The eastern part of the country is drained by the Kosi River, which has seven tributaries. It is locally known as the Sapt Kosi, which means seven Kosi rivers (Tamur, Likhu Khola, Dudh, Sun, Indrawati, Tama, and Arun). The principal tributary is the Arun, which rises about 150 kilometers inside the Tibetan Plateau. The Narayani River drains the central part of Nepal and also has seven major tributaries (Daraudi, Seti, Madi, Kali, Marsyandi, Budhi, and Trisuli). The Kali, which flows between the Dhaulagiri Himal and the Annapurna Himal (Himal is the Nepali variation of the Sanskrit word *Himalaya*), is the main river of this drainage system. The river system draining the western part of Nepal is the Karnali. Its three immediate tributaries are the Bheri, Seti, and Karnali rivers, the latter being the major one. The Maha Kali, which also is known as the Kali and which flows along the Nepal-India border on the west side, and the Rapti River also are considered tributaries of the Karnali.

Population

Population Structure and Settlement Patterns

At the time of the 1981 census, the total population of Nepal was 15,022,839, the average family was made up of 5.8 persons, and life expectancy at birth was close to fifty years. As of July 1990, the population was estimated at 19,145,800 persons. The annual population growth rate increased from less than 2 percent during the 1950s to more than 2.6 percent in 1990, suggesting that despite a trend toward increasing acceptance of family planning, the program did not have much influence on reducing the population growth rate. The Central Bureau of Statistics forecast that the total population would increase to 23.6 million by 2001 (see table 2, Appendix).

The 1981 census reveals a significant variation in regional growth rates. Although the Tarai Region's annual growth rate of 4.2 percent was much higher than the national average, the Hill and Mountain regions, respectively, posted growth rates of 1.7 and 1.4 percent. In terms of regional distribution, 43.6 percent (6,556,828 persons) of the country's population resided in the Tarai, whereas the shares of the Hill and Mountain regions totaled 7,163,115 (47.7 percent) and 1,302,896 (8.7 percent), respectively.

About 70 percent of the total population was of working age, or between the ages of fifteen and fifty-nine years. More than 65 percent of this segment of the population was considered economically active in 1981 (see Labor, ch. 3). In terms of employment structure, more than 91 percent of the economically active population was engaged in agriculture and allied activities, and the rest in the secondary (industrial) and tertiary (service) sectors, including government employment. In 1981 males and females who were widowed or separated constituted only a tiny fragment of the population—0.4 percent for each sex.

Dependency and Sex Ratios

The dependency ratio is defined as the ratio of the population in the birth to fourteen age-group, and those sixty years and older, to the population in the productive age-group, that is, fifteen to fifty-nine years of age. In 1981 this ratio stood at eighty to nine. The temporal increase in the number of those in the young population group has depressed the median age of the population from 21.1 years in the mid-1950s to 19.9 years in 1981. The sex ratio in 1981, defined as the number of males to 100 females, was 105 males to every 100 females (see fig. 6).

Fertility and Mortality

According to the estimates made by the Central Bureau of Statistics in 1985, the crude birthrate was 44 per 1,000, and the crude death rate was almost 14 per 1,000. The total fertility rate, defined as the average number of children a woman might bear, was 6.3

children, with a variation between rural and urban fertility rates. The rural total fertility rate was 6.4, compared with 5.8 for urban areas. Both the crude birthrate and the total fertility rate have remained high and fairly constant for the past several decades, whereas the crude death rate has been declining consistently, thereby contributing to rapid population growth.

The most significant category of deaths was the infant mortality rate. Varying techniques for calculating infant mortality, however, have led to discrepant estimations. They ranged from more than 147 deaths per 1,000 in 1985 to between 101 and 128 per 1,000 in 1989. Infant mortality rates also varied widely among the three geographic regions, which may have been partly because of differing rates of migration and the expectancy that higher mortality rates are found in migrant families. Nonetheless, infant mortality was almost twice as high in rural areas as urban areas, a clear indication of the lack of health services in rural areas, and was high compared to many other Asian countries (see Health Care Facilities, this ch.).

Population Density

One of the major consequences of rapid population growth was the progressive deterioration of the ratio of people to land. This land shortage greatly affected Nepal's predominantly agrarian society, where land was the most important source of livelihood and social status, and it was most evident in terms of population density. In 1981 the population density was 102 persons per square kilometer of total land. Although the ratio appears to suggest a fairly low density, the figures are misleading. When density is measured in terms of persons per hectare of cultivatable land (that is, agricultural density), the true nature of the human-land ratio emerges. The agricultural density in 1981 was 6.1 persons per hectare (or almost 0.2 hectare per person), which represents a very high density, especially given that the country's production technology remains in a backward state (see table 3, Appendix). Nepal's ability to reclaim more land in order to accommodate a rapidly growing population already had reached a maximum threshold.

Urbanization

Urbanization, defined as the percentage of total population living in settlements designated as urban areas, generally was viewed as closely related to economic development. If the correlation between urbanization and economic development—historically based on the experience of the industrialized nations—is accepted, then Nepal has a long way to go before it becomes economically advanced.

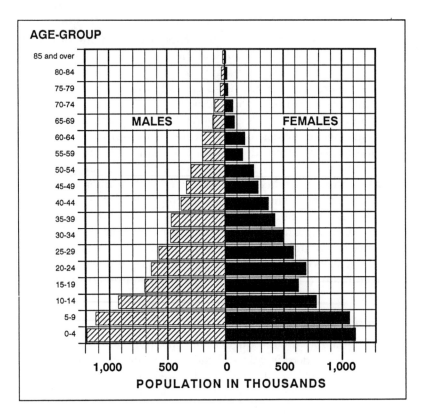

AGE-GROUP

85 and over	
80-84	
75-79	
70-74	
65-69	MALES / FEMALES
60-64	
55-59	
50-54	
45-49	
40-44	
35-39	
30-34	
25-29	
20-24	
15-19	
10-14	
5-9	
0-4	

1,000   500   0   500   1,000

POPULATION IN THOUSANDS

Source: Based on information from Nepal, National Planning Commission Secretariat, Central Bureau of Statistics, *Statistical Pocket Book: Nepal,* 1988, Kathmandu, 1988, 26.

Figure 6. Nepal: Population Distribution by Age and Sex, 1988

Nepal was one of the least urbanized countries in the world, with only 6.3 percent of its total population residing in urban areas in 1981. Yet it appears that the 1971-81 decade experienced a major growth spurt in urban population, increasing by approximately 108 percent, at an annual rate of more than 8.4 percent. The urbanization rate in the early 1990s was around 8 percent. Nevertheless, only twenty-three settlements were designated as urban areas, and only one of these settlements—the capital city of Kathmandu—had a population above 100,000. Kathmandu had a total population of slightly more than 235,000. Together with the other two major urban settlements—Patan (also called Lalitpur), which had about 79,800 people, and Bhadgaon (also called Bhaktapur), with about 48,500 people—the Kathmandu Valley in the Hill Region had the largest concentration of the total urban population—almost 40 percent.

In terms of the regional distribution of these urban settlements, the pattern was skewed in favor of the Tarai. Fourteen of the twenty-three settlements were found there, the majority located in eastern and central Tarai. The Mountain Region had no urban settlements. This situation clearly demonstrated that Nepal not only remained predominantly rural, but also that the existing urban areas were neither well developed nor well connected in terms of their geographical distribution. The only real urban network was found in the central section—the quadrangle consisting of Kathmandu, Pokhara, Butawal (and Siddhartha Nagar), and Hetauda.

Migration

Nepal was once a sanctuary for waves of migrants from north and south of its borders. The early migration from the north was largely of nomadic Mongoloid people from Tibet (the Bhote groups), followed by waves of Indo-Aryans from India. Some of the migrants from the south, especially the Brahmans and Rajputs, were fleeing the religious crusades of invading Mughals (or Indian Muslims) and their suppression of Hindus; others (especially those from Bihar and West Bengal) were lured by the possibilities of the Tarai land. As of 1991, a large number of Indians from Bihar and other neighboring areas still crossed the border into Nepal. Most of those recent migrants were found in towns and cities, where they were engaged in semiskilled labor and mercantile activities.

Since at least the late nineteenth century, the migration trend has reversed its course. In the early 1990s, there was a massive and persistent outflow of people from the hills, the areas that had once served as a refuge for migrants. In addition, the volume of migration has been increasing over time. There have been two major types of migration. Permanent or lifetime migration occurred primarily within the national boundary, particularly from the highlands to the Tarai Region; it was motivated by the search for land. Circular migration included seasonal migrants, who moved to wage-labor sites, such as urban centers and construction areas, during the agricultural slack season (November to February). These circular or absentee migrants included long-term (but not permanent) migrants, who moved in search of long-term salaried employment, such as army, government, *chaukidar* (doorman or guard) services, or factory jobs. Once these migrants succeeded in landing a relatively permanent job, they normally visited their families and villages once every two to three years; if they did not secure such a

69

job, they might return in a few months. Unlike permanent migration, circular migration was both internal (within the country) as well as external (outside the country). Although internal circular migrants ultimately might become permanent migrants, the vast majority of external circular migrants, most of whom went to India, returned to Nepal upon their retirement and discharge from service. Increasing numbers of these external migrants settled in the Indian states of West Bengal and Assam, and they have been filtering into Bhutan since the late nineteenth century (see Population, ch. 6).

Lifetime Regional Migration

Until the mid-1950s, the volume of permanent migration within the country was very small. Since then, however, there has been increased permanent internal migration, mainly because of population pressures, paucity of land resources in the hills, and the implementation of land resettlement programs in the Tarai Region. This form of migration was identified in the 1981 census as lifetime internal migration.

The total volume of lifetime internal migration in 1981 was close to 1,272,300 persons, a figure that represented 8.5 percent of the total population. The vast majority of lifetime internal migrants originated in the Hill and Mountain regions and moved to the Tarai Region in search of land in a movement that can be called frontier migration (see table 4, Appendix). These findings confirmed that the north-south (highland-lowland) flows of migration have made a substantial contribution—both directly and indirectly—to the rapid population growth of the Tarai Region.

One of the major variables responsible for this trend was the Hill residents' quest for land. About half of the male Hill migrants to the Tarai mentioned "agriculture" as their reason for migrating (see table 5, Appendix). The "not stated and others" category also constituted a high percentage, probably because most family members who moved with their parents or household heads had no specific reason for their migration.

A high score for trade and commerce among the mountain migrants might reflect the fact that they historically were deeply engaged in interregional as well as cross-border trade with Tibet as their principal economic activity. Because their traditional trade and commercial relations with Tibet had been largely cut off because of political changes after 1950, they might have moved to the Tarai, where such opportunities were expanding, particularly in urban areas.

Namche Bazar, the gateway to Khumbu, on the route to Mount Everest
Courtesy Janet MacDonald

The pattern for female migrants was generally consistent with the pattern for male migrants. The exception was female migrants for whom marriage as a reason for geographical mobility ranked quite high. This pattern generally reflected the commonly observed reality that female mobility in Nepal was largely tied to family mobility (that is, husbands or parents). Although individual (unmarried) female migration seemed to be gradually on the rise, it still was quite limited.

Circular Migration

Circular migrants, both internal and external, were classified as absentee population in the 1981 census. The major difference between the two groups was that the internal absentee population generally consisted of short-term or seasonal migrants. Such migrants left the hills in search of temporary jobs in nearby towns or at construction sites and generally returned to their villages after the winter season to resume farming. On the other hand, the external absentee population was largely composed of long-term migrants. In the cases of both types, most migrants were adult males although some husbands periodically took their wives with them after they were well established in their jobs.

The volume of circular migration, or absentee population, has been rising. In the mid-1950s, such migration totaled almost 217,000 persons, most coming from the hills. More than 90 percent, or more than 198,000 people, were external migrants; the vast majority went to India. In 1981 the absentee population totaled almost 591,000 people. Of these, 188,000 people, or 32 percent, were internal migrants, and approximately 403,000 people, or 68 percent, were external migrants. Even though the percentage of external migrants in the total absentee population had declined from 90 percent in the mid-1950s to 68 percent in 1981, their absolute number had increased by 205,000 people. Whereas the increasing number of absentee population from the hills was an unmistakable indicator of the region's deteriorating economic and environmental conditions, the decreasing percentage of external migration in the total volume was largely the result of the emergence of the Tarai as an alternative, internal destination.

The vast majority of migrants came from the Hill and Mountain regions. Together, they made up 141,200 (85 percent) of the total of internal migrants and about 365,000 (91 percent) of total external migrants. Unlike in the Hill and Mountain regions, the majority of the Tarai's 82,650 absentees were found within the country.

An analysis of reasons for absence from home revealed quite a contrast between lifetime internal migration and circular migration. Service, which included a variety of jobs, surfaced as the most dominant reason for being absent from home in both internal and external cases of circular migration. On the average, 64 percent of external migrants mentioned service as their reason for migration, the highest rate being posted by the Hill migrants; 28 percent gave no reasons, or other reasons (see table 6, Appendix).

Population Planning

Although Nepal's population continued to grow at a rapid pace in the face of deteriorating per capita land availability, the country's economy as a whole remained underdeveloped. Economic growth barely kept pace with population growth. Given this reality, many viewed effective family planning as a national imperative. The need for family planning was recognized as early as 1958, when a private organization, the Nepal Family Planning Association, was established in Kathmandu. Although the government formally adopted a national family planning policy in 1965, its availability was limited to the Kathmandu Valley until 1968, when a semiautonomous board was established. This Nepal Family Planning and Maternal Child Health Board was authorized to formulate and to implement family planning policy and programs for the entire country. Under the auspices of the board, attempts have been made to provide family planning and maternal-child health services outside the Kathmandu Valley, with the help of paramedics and health-care workers who have some basic training. As of 1989, the board offered family planning services in fifty-two of Nepal's seventy-five districts. Despite these efforts, the rural population generally lacked access to family planning services.

Such services were provided by three means: stationary offices, mobile facilities, and door-to-door campaigns. The stationary offices generally were attached to a health-care institution, such as health posts, health centers, or hospitals. As an addition to the staff at these institutions, the board assigned a minimum of two full-time workers to deliver family planning and maternal-child health services. However, it has been reported that most health and family planning workers in rural health posts rarely were found in their assigned units. As a result, the availability of such services in rural areas remained poor.

The mobile facilities were a product of necessity, given the remoteness of much of the population and the lack of local family planning facilities, or easy accessibility to such a facility. They reached a large part of the country and almost exclusively stressed permanent family limitation, that is, sterilization. Mobile sterilization camps moved around the country; local residents were notified of their scheduled arrival in advance and asked to take advantage of the service. A few days or even weeks prior to the arrival of the camp, a campaign was launched to motivate and to educate people about the benefits and needs of family planning. The camp generally lasted only a few days, rarely more than a week. Because most villagers were unwilling to come to family planning centers to obtain services, the Nepal Family Planning and Maternal Child Health Board launched a door-to-door campaign to educate villagers about family planning and to distribute oral contraceptives and condoms on a periodic basis.

The government's direct expenditure on family planning in fiscal year (FY—see Glossary) 1985 was about 1 percent, or Rs54.7 million (for value of the rupee—see Glossary), of the national budget. In the same year, the government spent almost 16.5 percent of its total budget on health services. It was difficult to determine what percentage of the health budget was channeled to provide family planning services. Although the expenditure on family planning appeared to be relatively low given the gravity of the issue, the absolute budget amount had gone up significantly in the 1970s and 1980s: from Rs2 million in FY 1969, when the board was set up, to almost Rs55 million in FY 1985. In FY 1981, more than 60 percent of the board's budget was borne by foreign agencies.

In terms of absolute numbers, the diffusion of family planning increased significantly over two decades. In FY 1969, only 7,774 persons had adopted family planning; by FY 1985, the number who had adopted family planning had climbed to almost 340,000 persons.

Caste and Ethnicity

Ethnic Groups

Nepalese society was ethnically diverse and complex in the early 1990s, ranging in phenotype (physical characteristics) and culture from the Indian to the Tibetan. Except for the sizable population of those of Indian birth or ancestry concentrated in the Tarai bordering India, the varied ethnic groups had evolved into distinct patterns over time.

Political scientists Joshi and Rose broadly classify the Nepalese population into three major ethnic groups in terms of their origin: Indo-Nepalese, Tibeto-Nepalese, and indigenous Nepalese. In the case of the first two groups, the direction of their migration and Nepal's landscapes appeared to have led to their vertical distribution; most ethnic groups were found at particular altitudes. The first group, comprising those of Indo-Nepalese origin, inhabited the more fertile lower hills, river valleys, and Tarai plains. The second major group consisted of communities of Tibeto-Mongol origin occupying the higher hills from the west to the east. The third and much smaller group comprised a number of tribal communities, such as the Tharus and the Dhimals of the Tarai; they may be remnants of indigenous communities whose habitation predates the advent of Indo-Nepalese and Tibeto-Mongol elements.

Even though Indo-Nepalese migrants were latecomers to Nepal relative to the migrants from the north, they have come to dominate the country not only numerically, but also socially, politically, and economically. They managed to achieve early dominance over the native and northern migrant populations, largely because of the superior formal educational and technological systems they brought with them. Consequently, their overall domination has had tremendous significance in terms of ethnic power structure.

Within the Indo-Nepalese group, at least two distinct categories can be discerned. The first category includes those who fled India and moved to the safe sanctuaries of the Nepal hills several hundred years ago, in the wake of the Muslim invasions of northern India.

Terracing in the Rapti Valley, between Tulsipur and Salyan Courtesy John N. Gunning

The hill group of Indian origin primarily was composed of descendants of high-caste Hindu families. According to Joshi and Rose, "These families, mostly of Brahman and Kshatriya status, have spread through the whole of Nepal with the exception of the areas immediately adjacent to the northern border. They usually constitute a significant portion of the local elites and are frequently the largest landowners in an area." This segment of the Indo-Nepalese population, at the apex of which stands the nation's royal family, has played the most dominant role in the country. Other ethnic groups, including those of Indian origin that settled in the Tarai, have been peripheral to the political power structure.

The second group of Indo-Nepalese migrants includes the inhabitants of the Tarai. Many of them are relatively recent migrants, who were encouraged by the government of Nepal or its agents to move into the Tarai for settlement during the nineteenth and early twentieth centuries. In the early 1990s, this group mostly consisted of landless tenants and peasants from northern India's border states of Bihar and Bengal. Some of these Indian migrants later became large landowners.

The north Indian antecedents of a number of caste groups in the hills (that is, the first group of Indo-Nepalese migrants), which, in the early 1990s, made up more than 50 percent of the total population, are evident in their language, religion, social organization, and physical appearance. All of these features, however, have been modified in the Nepalese environment. These groups—several castes of Brahmans, the high-ranking Thakuri and Chhetri (the Nepalese derivative of the Kshatriya) castes, and an untouchable category—generally are classified as Pahari, or Parbate. However, in most parts of Nepal (except in the Tarai), the term *pahari* has only a limited use in that the Paharis generally are known by their individual caste names (see Caste and Ethnicity, this ch.).

Nepali, the native tongue of the Paharis and the national language of Nepal, is closely related to, but by no means identical with, Hindi. Both are rooted in Sanskrit. The Hinduism of the Pahari has been influenced by Buddhism and indigenous folk belief. The Paharis' caste system was neither as elaborately graded nor as all embracing in its sanctions as that of the Indians; physically, many of the Paharis showed the results of racial intermixture with the various Mongoloid groups of the region. Similarly, the Bhote or Bhotia groups inhabiting the foothills of the Himalayas—among whom the Sherpas have attracted the most attention in the mountaineering world—have developed regional distinctions among themselves, although clearly related physically as well as culturally to the Tibetans. The term *Bhote* literally means inhabitant of Bhot, a Sanskrit term for the trans-Himalayan region of Nepal, or the Tibetan region. However, *Bhote* is also a generic term, often applied to people of Tibetan culture or Mongoloid phenotype. As used by the Paharis and the Newars, it often had a pejorative connotation and could be applied to any non-Hindu of Mongoloid appearance.

An extraordinarily complex terrain also affected the geographic distribution and interaction among various ethnic groups (see fig. 7). Within the general latitudinal sorting of Indo-Nepalese (lower hills) and Tibeto-Nepalese (higher hills and mountains) groups, there was a lateral (longitudinal) pattern, in which various ethnic populations were concentrated in specific geographic pockets. The deeply cut valleys and high ridges tended to divide ethnic groups into many small, relatively isolated, and more or less self-contained communities. This pattern was especially prominent among the Tibeto-Nepalese population. For example, the Bhote group was found in the far north, trans-Himalayan section of the Mountain Region, close to the Tibetan border. The Sherpas, a subgroup within the Bhote, were concentrated in the northeast, around the Mount Everest area. To the south of their areas were other Tibeto-Nepalese ethnic groups—the Gurung in the west-central hills and the Tamang and Rai in the east-central hills—particularly close to and east of the Kathmandu Valley. The Magar group, found largely in the central hills, was much more widely distributed than the Gurung, Tamang, and Rai. In the areas occupied by the Limbu and Rai peoples, the Limbu domain was located farther east in the hills, just beyond the Rai zone. The Tharu group was found in the Tarai, and the Paharis were scattered throughout Nepal. Newars largely were concentrated in the Kathmandu Valley. However, because of their past migration as traders and merchants, they also were found in virtually all the market centers, especially in the hills, and as far away as Lhasa in Tibet.

This geographically concentrated ethnic distribution pattern generally remained in effect in the early 1990s, despite a trend toward increasing spatial mobility and relocating ethnic populations. For example, a large number of Bhotes (also called Mananges from the Manang District) in the central section of the Mountain Region, Tamangs, and Sherpas have moved to the Kathmandu Valley. Similarly, Thakalis from the Mustang District adjacent to Manang have moved to Pokhara, a major urban center in the hills about 160 kilometers west of Kathmandu, and to Butawal and Siddhartha Nagar, two important urban areas in the central part of the Tarai, directly south of Pokhara. Gurungs, Magars, and Rais also have become increasingly dispersed.

Most of the Indo-Nepalese peoples—both Paharis and Tarai dwellers (commonly known among the Paharis as *madhesis,* meaning midlanders)—were primarily agriculturalists, although a majority of them also relied on other activities to produce supplementary income. They generally raised some farm animals, particularly water buffalo, cows, goats, and sheep, for domestic purposes. The Paharis traditionally have occupied the vast majority of civil service positions. As a result, they have managed to dominate and to control Nepal's bureaucracy to their advantage. It was not until the 1980s that a prime minister came from the non-Pahari segment of the population. Despite some loosening of the total Pahari domination of the bureaucracy in recent years, a 1991 newspaper report, summarized in the *Nepal Press Digest,* revealed that 80 percent of the posts in the civil service, the army, and the police still were held by the Brahmans and Chhetris of the hills, who comprised less than 50 percent of the population; 13 percent were held by Kathmandu Valley Newars, whose share of the total population was merely 3 percent. The report added that even in 1991, the eleven-member Council of Ministers had six Brahmans and three Newars. Furthermore, six of the nine-member Constitution Recommendation Commission, which drafted the new constitution in 1990, were hill Brahmans (see The Constitution of 1990, ch. 4). In spite of the increasing number of Newars holding government jobs, they traditionally were recognized as a commercial merchant

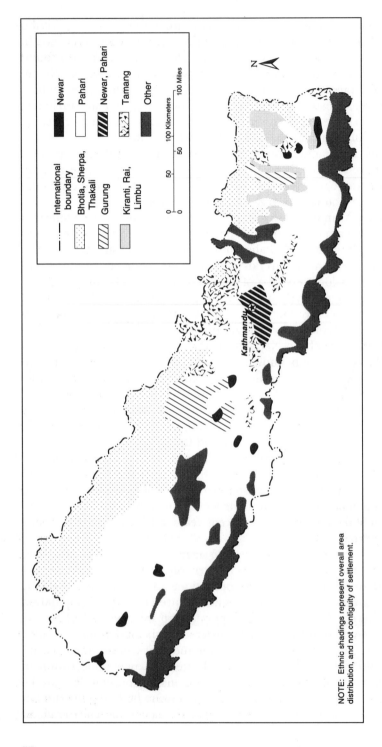

NOTE: Ethnic shadings represent overall area distribution, and not contiguity of settlement.

Figure 7. Nepal: Distribution of Principal Ethnic Groups, 1990

and handicraft class. It was no exaggeration that they historically have been the prime agents of Nepalese culture and art. A significant number of them also were engaged in farming. In that sense, they can be described as agro-commercialists.

Most of the Tibeto-Nepalese groups traditionally could be considered agro-pastoralists. Because their physical environment offered only limited land and agricultural possibilities, the Tibeto-Nepalese groups who occupied the high mountainous areas, such as the Bhote and particularly the Sherpa, were almost forced to rely more on herding and pastoral activities than on crop farming. They also participated in seasonal trading activity to supplement their income and food supply. However, those peoples inhabiting the medium and low hills south of the high mountains—particularly the Gurung, Magar, Tamang, Rai, and Limbu groups—depended on farming and herding in relatively equal amounts because their environment was relatively more suitable for agriculture. Among these groups, the Gurung, Magar, and Rai historically have supplied the bulk of the famous Gurkha (see Glossary) contingents to the British and Indian armies, although their ranks have been augmented from the Thakuri and Chhetri castes of the Indo-Nepalese Paharis (see Origins of the Legendary Gurkha, ch. 5). The term *Gurkha* was derived from the name of the former principality of Gorkha, about seventy kilometers west of Kathmandu, and was not an ethnic designation.

The Caste System

One integral aspect of Nepalese society is the existence of the Hindu caste system, modeled after the ancient and orthodox Brahmanic system of the Indian plains. The caste system did not exist prior to the arrival of Indo-Aryans. Its establishment became the basis of the emergence of the feudalistic economic structure of Nepal: the high-caste Hindus began to appropriate lands—particularly lowlands that were more easily accessible, more cultivable, and more productive—including those belonging to the existing tribal people, and introduced the system of individual ownership. Even though the cultural and religious rigidity of the caste system slowly has been eroding, its introduction into Nepal was one of the most significant influences stemming from the migration of the Indo-Aryan people into the hills. The migrants from the north later were incorporated into the Hindu caste system, as defined by Indo-Aryan migrants, who quickly controlled the positions of power and authority. Tibetan migrants did not practice private ownership; their system was based on communal ownership.

79

No single, widely acceptable definition can be advanced for the caste system. Bishop and others, however, view caste as a multi-faceted status hierarchy composed of all members of society, with each individual ranked within the broad, fourfold Hindu class (*varna*, or color) divisions, or within the fifth class of untouchables— outcastes and the socially polluted. The fourfold caste divisions are Brahman (priests and scholars), Kshatriya or Chhetri (rulers and warriors), Vaisya (or Vaisaya, merchants and traders), and Sudra (farmers, artisans, and laborers). These Paḥari caste divisions based on the Hindu system are not strictly upheld by the Newars. They have their own caste hierarchy, which, they claim, is parallel in caste divisions to the Pahari Hindu system. In each system, each caste (*jati*) is ideally an endogamous group in which membership is both hereditary and permanent. The only way to change caste status is to undergo Sanskritization. Sanskritization can be achieved by migrating to a new area and by changing one's caste status and/or marrying across the caste line, which can lead to the upgrading or downgrading of caste, depending on the spouse's caste. However, given the rigidity of the caste system, intercaste marriage carries a social stigma, especially when it takes place between two castes at the extreme ends of the social spectrum.

As Bishop further asserts, at the core of the caste structure is a rank order of values bound up in concepts of ritual status, purity, and pollution. Furthermore, caste determines an individual's behavior, obligations, and expectations. All the social, economic, religious, legal, and political activities of a caste society are prescribed by sanctions that determine and limit access to land, position of political power, and command of human labor. Within such a constrictive system, wealth, political power, high rank, and privilege converge; hereditary occupational specialization is a common feature. Nevertheless, caste is functionally significant only when viewed in a regional or local context and at a particular time. The assumed correlation between the caste hierarchy and the socioeconomic class hierarchy does not always hold. Because of numerous institutional changes over the years and increased dilution (or expansion) of the caste hierarchy stemming from intercaste marriages, many poor high-caste and rich low-caste households could be found in the society in 1991.

Although Paharis, especially those in rural areas, were generally quite conscious of their caste status, the question of caste did not usually arise for Tibeto-Nepalese communities unless they were aware of the Hindu caste status arbitrarily assigned to them. Insofar as they accepted caste-based notions of social rank, the Tibeto-Nepalese tended not only to see themselves at a higher level than did the Hindu Pahari and Newar, but also differed as to ranking among themselves. Thus, it was doubtful that the reported Rai caste's assumption of rank superiority over the Magar and Gurung castes was accepted by the two latter groups. Moreover, the status of a particular group was apt to vary from place to place, depending on its relative demographic size, wealth, and local power.

Language

Even though Nepali (written in Devanagari script, the same as Sanskrit and Hindi) was the national language and was mentioned as the mother tongue by approximately 58 percent of the population, there were several other languages and dialects. Other languages included Maithili, Bhojpuri, Tharu, Tamang, Newari, and Abadhi. Non-Nepali languages and dialects rarely were spoken outside their ethnic enclaves. In order to estimate the numerical distribution of different ethnic groups, the census data indicating various mother tongues spoken in the country must be used (see table 7, Appendix).

In terms of linguistic roots, Nepali, Maithili, and Bhojpuri belonged to the Indo-European family; the mother tongues of the Tibeto-Nepalese groups, including Newari, belonged predominantly to the Tibeto-Burman family. The Pahari, whose mother tongue was Nepali, was the largest ethnic group. If the Maithili- and Bhojpuri-speaking populations of the Tarai were included, more than 75 percent of the population belonged to the Indo-Nepalese ethnic group. Only three other ethnic groups—the Tamang, the Tharu, and the Newar—approached or slightly exceeded the one-half million population mark. Most of those non-Nepali linguistic and ethnic population groups were closely knit by bonds of nationalism and cultural harmony, and they were concentrated in certain areas.

Social System and Values

In the mid-twentieth century, Nepal remained gripped in a feudalistic socioeconomic structure despite the influence of Western popular culture, growing commercialization, and some penetration of capitalism. The first challenge to this feudalistic power structure came in 1950–51, when the Rana autocracy was overthrown by the popular democratic movement that restored the authority of the monarchy (see Rana Rule, ch. 1).

There was no popularly elected government until 1959. During his reign, King Mahendra Bir Bikram Shah Dev frequently changed the government, pitting one ruling clan against another in a manner clearly reminiscent of Shah politics prior to the rise of Rana

rule (see The Democratic Experiment, ch. 1). He also reconstitut-
ed the system of palace patronage, replacing the system of Rana
patronage. The Ranas, however, firmly controlled the armed forces
(see Armed forces and Society, ch. 5).

In December 1960, King Mahendra launched a palace coup
against the popularly elected government of Prime Minister Bishweshwar Prasad (B.P.) Koirala and reestablished his absolute
monarchical rule under the banner of the partyless *panchayat* (see
Glossary) system (see Political Dynamics, ch. 4). Until early 1990,
the *panchayat* system, strictly controlled by the palace, remained
firmly in place. The transition to a new social order was stymied;
society remained entrenched in a feudalistic structure.

There was, however, a tide of Western popular culture and commercialization sweeping over Nepal. In the 1960s and 1970s, many
Westerners, so-called hippies, were attracted to Nepal, looking for
inexpensive marijuana and hashish. Nepal suddenly emerged as
a "hippie Shangri-la." There were no laws or legal restrictions on
the sale and purchase of such drugs, and they could be used openly.
In fact, some Westerners thought the Nepalese were generally happy
and content because they were always high. Although this view
was a distortion, nonetheless it was very common to see elderly
Nepalese men smoking marijuana, invariably mixed with tobacco, in public. Marijuana plants grew almost everywhere; sometimes they were found growing even along main streets. Locally
produced hashish also was widely consumed, particularly during
festivals celebrated by some ethnic groups and tribes. It was,
however, very unusual for a Nepalese to develop a marijuana or
hashish habit until reaching about forty years of age.

By the late 1980s, the situation had changed dramatically. There
was an emerging drug subculture in the urban areas, and a number of youths, including college and high school students, sold and
consumed drugs. Many of these youths had gone beyond using
marijuana and hashish to more potent drugs, such as "crack" and
cocaine—drugs unheard of in the past. In the 1960s, Westerners
had sought release from the overbearing materialism of developed
countries; they copied the Nepalese (and other Easterners) who
smoked marijuana and hashish. Ironically, in the 1980s and 1990s,
it was Nepalese youths who were enchanted by the North American material and drug culture. There were an estimated 20,000
heroin addicts in 1989. In response to the drug situation in the country, in the late 1980s the government initiated antinarcotics measures and narcotics training, and King Birendra Bir Bikram Shah
Dev directed extensive media attention to narcotics abuse. The

effectiveness of the battle against narcotics, however, was limited by the lack of an official government body to target drug abuse.

Rural Society and Kinship

Nepal in the early 1990s was predominantly a rural-agricultural society, where more than 90 percent of the people lived in rural areas and depended on farming as a source of livelihood. Even in settlements designated as urban areas, the rural-urban distinction easily was blurred; approximately 50 percent of urbanites outside the three cities in the Kathmandu Valley were engaged in farming for their livelihood. Even in the Kathmandu Valley cities, 30 to 40 percent of city dwellers were agriculturalists. In this sense, most urban areas were economic extensions of rural areas, but with an urban manifestation and a commercial component. Farming was the dominant order of society and the mainstay of the economy, a situation that was unlikely to change, given the extremely sluggish pace of economic transformation.

The basic social unit in a village was the family, or *paribar,* consisting of a patrilineally extended household. The extended family system should not, however, be construed as a necessarily harmonious form of village life. Many extended families broke apart as sons separated from parents and brothers from each other. At the time of separation, the family property was equally divided among the sons. If parents were alive, they each received a share. Family separation generally occurred in cases where the head of the household was less assertive and domineering, when the father died, or when all the sons married. Unmarried sons normally did not separate from their parents; if the parents were deceased, unmarried sons usually stayed with their older brothers. Because family separation always resulted in a division of family landholdings, landholdings were extremely fragmented, both geographically and socially. Sometimes, family separation and resulting land fragmentation turned into a bitter feud and led to legal disputes.

Beyond the immediate family, there existed a larger kinship network that occasionally involved sharing food. This network also was an important means of meeting farm labor needs, especially during the planting and harvesting seasons, when labor shortages were common.

Above the kinship network was the village, which functioned as a broader unit of social existence. Some villages were no more than hamlets made up of just a few houses; others were sizable communities of several neighboring hamlets. In more populous villages, the caste groups contained occupational low (untouchable) caste groups, such as the Kami (ironsmiths who make tools), the Sarki

(leathersmiths), and the Damai (tailors and musicians), who fulfilled the vital basic needs of the village as a fairly self-contained
production unit.

Villagers occasionally pooled their resources and labored together
to implement village-level projects, such as building irrigation
ditches, or channels, or facilities for drinking water. If a household could afford to hire farm labor, it usually relied on the mutual
labor-sharing system called *parma,* which allowed villagers to exchange labor for labor at times of need.

Although farming traditionally ranked among the most desirable
occupations, villagers frequently encouraged some of their children
to leave in search of civil service, army, and other employment
opportunities. Individual migration was often the result of a family
decision and an important economic strategy; it not only served
as a safety valve for growing population pressures but also generated cash incomes, thereby averting any undue economic crises
in the family. Well-to-do village families usually pushed their children to obtain civil service jobs as a means of climbing the
bureaucratic ladder and of developing valuable connections with
the elite political structure.

Farming was the most important source of livelihood in rural
areas, but the scarcity of land placed severe constraints on agricultural development. Landholding was the most important basis for,
or criterion of, socioeconomic stratification. The 1981 agricultural census data identifies five classes of peasantry: landless and nearly
landless, people with no land or less than half a hectare; subsistence,
those with half a hectare to one hectare; small, holders of one to
three hectares; medium, people with three to five hectares; and
large, farmers of more than five hectares (see table 8, Appendix).

In terms of production relations, the first two classes were dependent on large landowners for survival. Small landowners, on
the other hand, were relatively independent; they did not have to
depend on the large landowning class for survival, especially if they
were involved in circular migration as a source of supplementary
cash income. Nor did they regularly employ members of the first
two classes. Landowners of medium-sized plots were independent
of large landowners. Their engagement in wage laboring or tenancy
farming was sporadic, if present at all. In some cases, they employed others during peak farming seasons. The large landowning class regularly employed farm workers and benefited from the
existence of excess labor, which kept wages low. In general, the
situation of landholders was exacerbated by the archaic nature of
farming technology and the absence of other resources. It therefore was not surprising that rural poverty was widespread.

A deforested area,
a typical scene in Nepal

Demands for fuelwood
and fodder contribute to
the deforestation problem.
Courtesy United States
Agency for International
Development

Women's Status and Role in Society

The United Nations has defined the status of women in the context of their access to knowledge, economic resources, and political power, as well as their personal autonomy in the process of decision making. When Nepalese women's status is analyzed in this light, the picture is generally bleak. In the early 1990s, Nepal was a rigidly patriarchical society. In virtually every aspect of life, women were generally subordinate to men.

Women's relative status, however, varied from one ethnic group to another. The status of women in Tibeto-Nepalese communities generally was relatively better than that of Pahari and Newari women. Women from the low caste groups also enjoyed relatively more autonomy and freedom than Pahari and Newari women.

The senior female member played a commanding role within the family by controlling resources, making crucial planting and harvesting decisions, and determining the expenses and budget allocations. Yet women's lives remained centered on their traditional roles—taking care of most household chores, fetching water and animal fodder, and doing farm work. Their standing in society was mostly contingent on their husbands' and parents' social and economic positions. They had limited access to markets, productive services, education, health care, and local government. Malnutrition and poverty hit women hardest. Female children usually were given less food than male children, especially when the family experienced food shortages. Women usually worked harder and longer than men. By contrast, women from high-class families had maids to take care of most household chores and other menial work and thus worked far less than men or women in lower socioeconomic groups.

The economic contribution of women was substantial, but largely unnoticed because their traditional role was taken for granted. When employed, their wages normally were 25 percent less than those paid to men. In most rural areas, their employment outside the household generally was limited to planting, weeding, and harvesting. In urban areas, they were employed in domestic and traditional jobs, as well as in the government sector, mostly in low-level positions.

One tangible measure of women's status was their educational attainment. Although the constitution offers women equal educational opportunities, many social, economic, and cultural factors contributed to lower enrollment and higher dropout rates for girls. Illiteracy imposed the greatest hindrance to enhancing equal opportunity and status for women. They were caught in a vicious circle imposed by the patriarchical society. Their lower status hindered their education, and the lack of education, in turn, constricted their status and position (see Education since 1951, this ch.). Although the female literacy rate has improved noticeably over the years, the level in the early 1990s fell far short of the male level.

The level of educational attainment among female children of wealthy and educated families was much higher than that among female children of poor families. This class disparity in educational attainment was also true for boys. In Nepal, as in many societies, education was heavily class-biased (see Education, this ch.).

In the early 1990s, a direct correlation existed between the level of education and status. Educated women had access to relatively high-status positions in the government and private service sectors, and they had a much higher status than uneducated women. This general rule was more applicable at the societal level than at the household level. Within the family, an educated woman did not necessarily hold a higher status than her uneducated counterpart. Also within the family, a woman's status, especially a daughter-in-law's status, was more closely tied to her husband's authority and to her parental family's wealth and status than anything else.

Social Classes and Stratification

In terms of differences in wealth and access to political power, Nepalese society could be divided into a small ruling elite; a growing, intermediate-sized group of government officials, large landholders, and merchants; and the vast majority of the population, consisting of a peasant base. These divisions are descriptive, functional class categories rather than social class entities based on the Marxian concept of the social relations of production. In a way, all three classes were a long continuum in Nepal's social structure because most members of the ruling elite and government functionaries had their direct roots in the rural landed class, which was one stratum of the farming population.

Even though the agricultural sector as a whole faced similar economic and technological circumstances, it was diverse and contained several strata in landholding, relative economic dependence, and independence (see Rural Society and Kinship, this ch.). The numerically small intermediate stratum of the farmers was only slightly less diverse than the rest of the rural population in terms of members' ethnic and geographical backgrounds. The relative economic and educational advantages of this group and its occupational activities, however, made its members relatively homogeneous in terms of shared interest. They generally aspired to achieve a middle- or elite-class status.

The smallest and least diverse of the three categories was the ruling elite, largely composed of high-caste, educated Paharis, namely different strata of Brahmans and Chhetris. At the zenith of this class was the monarch, whose authority was derived from the orthodox Hindu contention that the king was the reincarnation of Vishnu, whose assigned role in the Hindu trinity is protection. The monarch's authority was not based on electoral support.

The continued expansion of the bureaucracy was a direct response to a consistent increase in the educated population. Because of the lack of development, a large number of educated people failed to find gainful employment upon graduation. Because they constituted the most potent revolutionary force, and happened to be geographically concentrated in urban centers, the ruling class was almost compelled to absorb them into an already bloated bureaucracy in order to neutralize any sociopolitical disturbance they might cause.

In the 1980s, a significant number of college- and university-educated people residing in Kathmandu Valley cities discovered a second employment outlet. Development consultant firms and associated services have emerged throughout Kathmandu. Because of the growing pressure on foreign donors to hire Nepalese consultants for development feasibility and evaluation projects, these firms were able to tap into the large pool of foreign aid money and have generated a significant number of jobs. This opportunity has allowed many of the more educated to attain middle class status.

Religion

Religion and Society

Religion occupies an integral position in Nepalese life and society. In the early 1990s, Nepal was the only constitutionally declared Hindu state in the world; there was, however, a great deal of intermingling of Hindu and Buddhist beliefs. Many of the people regarded as Hindus in the 1981 census could, with as much justification, be called Buddhists. The fact that Hindus worshipped at Buddhist temples and Buddhists worshipped at Hindu temples has been one of the principal reasons adherents of the two dominant groups in Nepal have never engaged in any overt religious conflicts. Because of such dual faith practices (or mutual respect), the differences between Hindus and Buddhists have been in general very subtle and academic in nature. However, in 1991, approximately 89.5 percent of the Nepalese people identified themselves as Hindus. Buddhists and Muslims comprised only 5.3 and 2.7 percent, respectively. The remainder followed other religions, including Christianity.

Bridge crossing over the Arun River
Courtesy Linda Galantin

The geographical distribution of religious groups revealed a preponderance of Hindus, accounting for at least 87 percent of the population in every region. The largest concentrations of Buddhists were found in the eastern hills, the Kathmandu Valley, and the central Tarai; in each area about 10 percent of the people were Buddhist. Buddhism was relatively more common among the Newar and Tibeto-Nepalese groups. Among the Tibeto-Nepalese, those most influenced by Hinduism were the Magar, Sunwar, and Rai peoples. Hindu influence was less prominent among the Gurung, Limbu, Bhote, and Thakali groups, who continued to employ Buddhist monks for their religious ceremonies.

Hinduism

Hinduism generally is regarded as the oldest formal religion in the world. The origins of Hinduism go back to the pastoral Aryan tribes, spilling over the Hindu Kush from Inner Asia, and mixing with the urban civilization of the Indus Valley and with the tribal cultures of hunting and gathering peoples in the area. Unlike other world religions, Hinduism had no single founder and has never been missionary in orientation. It is believed that about 1200 B.C., or even earlier by some accounts, the Vedas, a body of hymns originating in northern India were produced; these texts form the theological and philosophical precepts of Hinduism.

Hindus believe that the absolute (the totality of existence, including God, man, and universe) is too vast to be contained within a single set of beliefs. A highly diverse and complex religion, Hinduism embraces six philosophical doctrines (*darshanas*). From these doctrines, individuals select one that is congenial, or conduct their worship simply on a convenient level of morality and observance. Religious practices differ from group to group. The average Hindu does not need any systematic formal creed in order to practice his or her religion. Hindus need only to comply with the customs of their family and social groups.

One basic concept in Hinduism is that of dharma, natural law and the social and religious obligations it imposes. It holds that individuals should play their proper role in society as determined or prescribed by their dharma. The caste system, although not essential to philosophical Hinduism, has become an integral part of its social or dharmic expression. Under this system, each person is born into a particular caste, whose traditional occupation—although members do not necessarily practice it—is graded according to the degree of purity and impurity inherent in it.

Other fundamental ideas common to all Hindus concern the nature and destiny of the soul, and the basic forces of the universe.

The souls of human beings are seen as separated portions of an all-embracing world soul (*brahma*); man's ultimate goal is reunion with this absolute.

Karma (universal justice) is the belief that the consequence of every good or bad action must be fully realized. Another basic concept is that of *samsara,* the transmigration of souls; rebirth is required by karma in order that the consequences of action be fulfilled. The role an individual must play throughout his or her life is fixed by his or her good and evil actions in previous existences. It is only when the individual soul sees beyond the veil of *maya* (illusion or earthly desires)—the forces leading to belief in the appearances of things—that it is able to realize its identity with the impersonal, transcendental reality (world soul) and to escape from the otherwise endless cycle of rebirth to be absorbed into the world soul. This release is known as *moksha.*

Veneration for the cow has come to be intimately associated with all orthodox Hindu sects. Because the cow is regarded as the symbol of motherhood and fruitfulness, the killing of a cow, even accidentally, is regarded as one of the most serious of religious transgressions.

Hinduism is polytheistic. It incorporates many gods and goddesses with different functions and powers; but in the most important and widely held doctrine, the Vedanta, gods and goddesses are considered merely different manifestations or aspects of a single underlying divinity. This single divinity is expressed as a Hindu triad comprising the religion's three major gods: Brahma, Vishnu, and Shiva, personifying creation, preservation, and destruction, respectively. Vishnu and Shiva, or some of their numerous avatars (incarnations), are most widely followed.

Buddha, the founder of Buddhism, is regarded as the ninth avatar of Vishnu. Some Hindus identify Christ as the tenth avatar; others regard Kalki as the final avatar who is yet to come. These avatars are believed to descend upon earth to restore peace, order, and justice, or to save humanity from injustice. The *Mahabharata* (compiled by the sage Vyasa, probably before A.D. 400), describes the great civil war between the Pandavas (the good) and the Kauravas (the bad)—two factions of the same clan. It is believed that the war was created by Krishna. Perhaps the flashiest and craftiest avatar of Vishnu, Krishna, as a part of his *lila* (sport or act), is believed motivated to restore justice—the good over the bad.

Buddhism

Buddhism had its origin in the teachings of Siddhartha Gautama, a Kshatriya caste prince of the Sakya clan; he was born in

Lumbini, in the central Tarai Region, about 563 B.C. His father was the ruler of a minor principality in the region. Born a Hindu and educated in the Hindu tradition, Siddhartha Gautama renounced worldly life at about the age of twenty-nine and spent the next six years in meditation. At the end of this time, he attained enlightenment; thereafter, known as the Buddha, or the Enlightened One, he devoted the remainder of his life to preaching his doctrine.

The Buddha accepted or reinterpreted the basic concepts of Hinduism, such as karma, *samsara,* dharma, and *moksha,* but he generally refused to commit himself to specific metaphysical theories. He said they were essentially irrelevant to his teachings and could only distract attention from them. He was interested in restoring a concern with morality to religious life, which he believed had become stifled in details of ritual, external observances, and legalisms.

The Four Noble Truths summarize the Buddha's analysis of the human situation and the solution he found for the problems of life. The first truth is that life, in a world of unceasing change, is inherently imperfect and sorrowful, and that misery is not merely a result of occasional frustration of desire or misfortune, but is a quality permeating all experience. The second truth is that the cause of sorrow is desire, the emotional involvement with existence that led from rebirth to rebirth through the operation of karma. The third truth is that the sorrow can be ended by eliminating desire. The fourth truth sets forth the Eightfold Path leading to elimination of desire, rebirth, and sorrow, and to the attainment of nirvana or *nibbana* (see Glossary), a state of bliss and selfless enlightenment. It rejoins right or perfect understanding, aspiration, speech, action, livelihood, effort, thought, and contemplation.

Education

Education under Rana Rule

The Rana rulers, who placed Nepal under their feudal yoke for about 100 years until the beginning of the 1950s, feared an educated public. This fear also was held by Prime Minister Chandra Shamsher Rana, who established Tri-Chandra College in 1918 and named it after himself. During the inauguration of the college, Chandra Shamsher lamented that its opening was the ultimate death knell to Rana rule. He personally felt responsible for the downfall of Rana rule, and his words became prophetic for the crumbling of Rana political power in 1950–51.

The privileged access of members of the higher castes and wealthier economic strata to education was for centuries a distinguishing

feature of society. The Ranas kept education the exclusive prerogative of the ruling elite; the rest of the population remained largely
illiterate. The Ranas were opposed to any form of public schooling
for the people, although they emphasized formal instruction for
their own children to prepare them for a place in the government.

The founder of the Rana regime, Jang Bahadur Kunwar, later
known as Jang Bahadur Rana, decided to give his children an English education rather than the traditional religiously oriented training. In 1854 Jang Bahadur engaged an English tutor to hold classes
for his children in the Rana palace. This act tipped the balance
in favor of English education and established its supremacy over
the traditional type of Sanskrit-based education. In 1991 English
education still carried a higher status and prestige than did traditional education.

Jang Bahadur's successor opened these classes to all Rana children and formally organized them into Durbar High School. A
brief shift in government education policy came in 1901, when
Prime Minister Dev Shamsher Rana took office and called for
sweeping education reforms. He proposed a system of universal
public primary education, using Nepali as the language of instruction and opening Durbar High School to children who were not
members of the Rana clan. Dev Shamsher's policies were so un-
popular that he was deposed within a few months. His call for reforms did not entirely disappear, however. A few Nepali-language
primary schools in the Kathmandu Valley, the Hill Region, and
the Tarai remained open, and the practice of admitting a few
middle- and low-caste children to Durbar High School continued.

Before World War II (1939–45), several new English middle and
high schools were founded in Patan, Biratnagar, and elsewhere,
and a girls' high school was opened in Kathmandu. In the villages,
public respect for education was increasing, largely as a result of
the influence of returning Gurkha soldiers, many of whom had
learned to read and write while serving in the British army. Some
retired soldiers began giving rudimentary education to children in
their villages. Some members of the high-caste, elite families sent
their children to Patna University, Banaras Hindu University, or
other universities in India for higher academic or technical training. It was in fact, some of these students, having realized how
oppressive the policies of Rana rule were, who initiated anti-Rana
movements, provided revolutionary cadres, and finally began the
revolution that ultimately led to the overthrow of Rana rule in 1951.

Before the 1950–51 revolution, Nepal had 310 primary and middle schools, eleven high schools, two colleges, one normal school,
and one special technical school. In the early 1950s, the average

literacy rate was 5 percent. Literacy among males was 10 percent and among females less than 1 percent. Only 1 child in 100 attended school.

Education since 1951

After the 1951 revolution, efforts were made to establish an education system. The National Education Planning Commission was founded in 1954, the All Round National Education Committee in 1961, and the National Education Advisory Board in 1968 in order to implement and to refine the education system. In 1971 the New Education System came into operation as an integral part of the Fourth Five-Year Plan (1970–75); it was designed to address individual, as well as societal, needs in concert with the goals of national development (see The Five-Year Plans, ch. 3).

Formal schooling in modern times was still constrained by the economy and culture. Children were generally needed to work in the fields and at home. Many students began school late (at ages nine or ten); more than half left school after completing only one year. Educating females was viewed as unnecessary; as a consequence, their enrollment levels were far lower than those of males. Regional variations often hindered the effectiveness of uniform text materials and teacher training. Although the government was relatively successful in establishing new schools, the quality of education remained low, particularly in remote regions where the majority of the population lived. Terrain further inhibited management and supervision of schools.

Most schools operated for ten months of the year, five and one-half days a week. In the warmer regions, June and July were vacation months; in the northern regions, mid-December through mid-February were vacation months. All schools in Kathmandu closed for winter vacation.

In 1975 primary education was made free, and the government became responsible for providing school facilities, teachers, and educational materials. Primary schooling was compulsory; it began at age six and lasted for five years. Secondary education began at age eleven and lasted another five years in two cycles—two years (lower) and three years (higher). Total school enrollment was approximately 52 percent of school-age children (approximately 70 percent of school-age boys, 30 percent of school-age girls) in 1984. Secondary school enrollment was only 18 percent of the relevant age-group (27 percent of the total boys, 9 percent of the total girls). About 72 percent of all students were male. The Ministry of Education supervised the finance, administration, staffing, and

A house in the Makalu area of the Mountain Region, near Khandbari
An open dwelling in Thumlingtar
Courtesy Linda Galantin

95

inspection of government schools. It also inspected private schools that received government subsidies.

As of 1987, Nepal had 12,491 primary schools, 3,824 lower-secondary schools, and 1,501 higher-secondary schools. There were 55,207 primary, 11,744 lower-secondary, and 8,918 higher-secondary school teachers. Primary school enrollments totaled 1,952,504 persons; lower-secondary and higher-secondary enrollment figures stood at 289,594 and 289,923 persons, respectively.

Curriculum was greatly influenced by United States models, and it was developed with assistance from the United Nations Educational, Scientific, and Cultural Organization. The National Education Plan established a framework for universal education. The goal of primary education was to teach reading, writing, and arithmetic, and to instill discipline and hygiene. Lower-secondary education emphasized character formation, a positive attitude toward manual labor, and perseverance. Higher-secondary education stressed manpower requirements and preparation for higher education. National development goals were emphasized through the curriculum.

The School Leaving Certificate examination, a nationally administered and monitored high-school-matriculation examination, was given after completion of the higher-secondary level. Those who passed this examination were eligible for college. In addition, some communities had adult education schools.

In the early 1980s, approximately 60 percent of the primary school teachers and 35 percent of secondary school teachers were untrained, despite the institution of a uniform method of training in 1951. The Institute of Education, part of Tribhuvan University, was responsible for inservice and preservice teacher training programs. Beginning in 1976, the institute organized a distance-learning program—electronic links between distant locations—for prospective teachers. Developments in telecommunications will provide new educational options.

At the higher education level, there was only one doctoral degree-granting institution in Nepal, Tribhuvan University. It was named after King Tribhuvan Bir Bikram Shah, the grandfather of King Birendra, and was chartered in 1959. All public colleges fell under Tribhuvan University. Private colleges were operated independently, although they also were required to meet the requirements and standards set by Tribhuvan University. The total number of colleges increased significantly, from 8 in 1958 to 132 in 1988 (69 under Tribhuvan University and 63 private colleges). In terms of subjects, these colleges covered a wide range of disciplines, such as social sciences; humanities; commerce (business); physical sciences, including some medical sciences; engineering; education; forestry; law; and Sanskrit. The number of students enrolled in higher education institutions totaled almost 83,000 in 1987; the largest percentage was in humanities and social sciences (40 percent), followed by commerce (31 percent), science and technology (11 percent), and education (6 percent). Approximately 20 percent of the students enrolled in Tribhuvan University were females.

The 1981 census found 24 percent of the population to be literate; as of 1990, the literacy rate was estimated to be 33 percent. There still was a big gap between male and female literacy rates. About 35 percent of the male population was literate in 1981, but only 11.5 percent of the female population was. A gulf also existed in literacy rates between rural and urban areas. In rural areas, the literacy rates for males and females were 33 percent and 9 percent, respectively; in urban areas, they were significantly higher, 62 percent and 37 percent, respectively. The higher literacy rates in urban areas were largely attributed to the availability of more and better educational opportunities, a greater awareness of the need for education for employment and socioeconomic mobility, and the exodus of educated people from rural to urban areas. Nepal launched a twelve-year literacy program in 1990, targeting 8 million people between the ages of six and forty-five.

There was little doubt among observers that the historical monopoly of educational opportunity by members of the wealthier and higher caste groups gradually was diminishing. Schools and colleges were open to all, and enrollment figures were rising rapidly. The long-standing prejudice against the education of women seemed to be very slowly breaking down, as attested to by increasing enrollments of girls in schools and colleges. Yet two distinct biases—social class and geography—remained pronounced in educational attainment.

Despite general accessibility, education still nonetheless primarily served children of landlords, businessmen, government leaders, or other elite members of the society, for they were the only ones who could easily afford to continue beyond primary school. They also were far more able to afford, and likely to continue, education beyond the high school level. Many students in the general population dropped out before they took the School Leaving Certificate examination. There was an even more important ingredient for success after leaving school: if the quality of available higher education was considered inadequate or inferior, higher caste families could afford to send their children overseas to obtain necessary degrees. Foreign educational degrees, especially those obtained from United States and West European institutions, carried greater prestige than degrees from Nepal. Higher caste families also had the necessary connections to receive government scholorships to study abroad.

Further, education remained largely urban-biased. The majority of education institutions, particularly better quality institutions, were found in urban areas. In rural areas where schools were set up, the quality of instruction was inferior, facilities were very poor, and educational materials were either difficult to find or virtually unavailable. Consequently, if rural families were serious about the education of their children, they were forced to send them to urban areas, a very expensive proposition that the vast majority of rural households could not afford.

Although there has been a remarkable numerical growth in the literacy rates, as well as the number of education institutions over the years, the quality of education has not necessarily improved. There were few top-notch teachers and professors, and their morale was low. At the higher educational level, the research focus or tradition was virtually absent, largely because there were few research facilities available for professors. There were some excellent private schools, mostly located in the Kathmandu Valley, but many appeared to be merely money-making ventures rather than serious, devoted educational enterprises. The large majority of schools and colleges were run by poorly prepared and poorly trained teachers and professors. Schools and colleges frequently were closed because of strikes. Students had little respect for teachers and professors and were concerned with obtaining a certificate rather than a quality education. Cheating was rampant during examinations at all levels.

Health

Health-care problems were varied and enormous. Health and health-care facilities were generally poor and directly reflected the mode of life. The majority of people lived in mass poverty and deprivation, while the nation's small wealth was concentrated in the hands of a few. Deprivation was apparent in the pervasiveness of poor nutrition and sanitation, inadequate housing for most families, and the general absence of modern medical care and other social services, especially in rural areas. The rich lived comparatively well but also shared such common problems as the lack of an abundant and clean water supply, and the prevalence of disease.

Diseases and Disease Control

Poor health conditions were evident in the high rate of infant mortality and a short life expectancy. In the mid-1960s, a national

Stone sculpture of Ugrachandi Durga, with eighteen arms,
Bhaktapur Durbar Square
Courtesy Linda Galantin

health survey was conducted. In 1991 that survey was still considered the major comprehensive published source of information on the national public health situation.

A number of diseases and chronic infections were prevalent. Goiter, a disease directly associated with iodine deficiency, was endemic in certain villages in the hills and mountains. In most of the villages surveyed, more than half of the population had goiter, and in these same villages the incidence of deafness and mental retardation was much higher than in other villages. Leprosy also was a serious problem. Foreign assistance, specifically through Christian missions, was responsible for setting up leprosy treatment centers in different parts of the country. Tuberculosis has been a chronic problem and was more common in urban areas. During the 1970s, the Tuberculosis Control Project was established to provide immunizations to all children younger than fifteen, and it is likely that this project has reduced tuberculosis. Other chronic, widespread problems were intestinal parasites, diarrhea, and gastrointestinal disorders. Some polio and typhoid infections were common but not severe.

Malnutrition was a chronic problem, especially in rural areas. More than 50 percent of the children surveyed were reported to have stunted growth. "Wasting," defined as a condition in which a child has very low weight for his or her height, was also evident. These conditions were particularly bad in the Hill and Mountain regions, both of which suffered from food shortages. The country's public health program, however, has essentially eliminated smallpox and has been able to control malaria, which used to be endemic to the Tarai Region and other lowlands.

Health-Care Facilities

The health-care delivery network in Nepal was poorly developed. Health-care practices in the country could be classified into three major categories: popular folk medical care, which relied on a *jhankri* (medicine man or shaman); Ayurvedic treatment; and allopathic (modern) medicine. These practices were not necessarily exclusive; most people used all three, sometimes even simultaneously, depending on the type of illness and the availability of services.

Popular folk medicine derived from a large body of commonly held assumptions about magical and supernatural causes of illness. Sickness and death often were attributed to ghosts, demons, and evil spirits, or they were thought to result from the evil eye, planetary influences, or the displeasures of ancestors. Many precautions against these dangers were taken, including the wearing of charms or certain ornaments, the avoidance of certain foods and sights, and the propitiation of ghosts and gods with sacrificial gifts. When illness struck or an epidemic threatened, people went to see a *jhankri* for treatment. Such pseudomedical practices were ubiquitous; in many parts of Nepal, a *jhankri* was the only source of medical care available. Nepalese also regularly saw *jotishi* (Brahman astrologers) for counseling because they believed in planetary influence on their lives, resulting from disalignments of certain planetary signs. *Jotishi* were commonly relied on even in urban areas, and even by those who were well educated and frequently used modern medicine. And, virtually no arranged marital union was proposed and concluded without first consulting a *jotishi*.

The Ayurvedic system of medicine was believed to have evolved among the Hindus about 2,000 years ago. It originally was based on the *Ayur-Veda* (the Veda of Long Life), but a vast literature since has accumulated around this original text. According to the Ayurvedic theory, the body, like the universe, consists of three forces—phlegm, bile, and wind—and physical and spiritual well-being rests on maintaining the proper balance among these three internal forces. A harmonious existence between body and mind results. Ayurvedic pharmacopoeia—based on medicinal plants, plant roots, and herbs—remained a major source of medical treatment in Nepal. This school of medical practice also applies the hot-and-cold concept of foods and diets. In the late 1980s, there were nearly 280 practicing Ayurvedic physicians, popularly known as *vaidhya;* 145 Ayurvedic dispensaries; and a national college of Ayurvedic medicine in Kathmandu.

In 1991 the most commonly used form of medical treatment, especially for major health problems, was modern medicine whenever and wherever accessible. Within the domain of modern medicine, providing public health-care facilities was largely the responsibility of the government. Private facilities also existed in various regions. Modern medical service generally was provided by trained doctors, paramedics, nurses, and other community health workers. The government-operated health-care delivery system consisted of hospitals and health centers, including health posts in rural areas.

Hospitals were located mostly in urban areas and provided a much wider range of medical services than health centers. They were attended by doctors, as well as by nurses, and equipped with basic laboratory facilities. Small health centers and posts in rural areas—most of them staffed by paramedical personnel, health aides, and other minimally trained community health workers—served the needs of the scattered population. Even though these rural facilities were more accessible than urban hospitals, they generally failed to provide necessary services on a regular and consistent basis. The majority of them were barely functional because of such problems as inadequate funding; lack of trained staff; absenteeism; and chronic shortages of equipment, medicines, and vaccines.

Nepal had a total of 123 hospitals, eighteen health centers, and 816 health posts in 1990. There was one hospital bed for every 4,283 persons, an improvement since 1977, when there was one hospital bed for every 6,489 persons. The number of doctors totaled 879 in 1988, or one physician available for about 20,000 people. For the same period, other medical personnel included 601 nurses, 2,062 assistant nurses and midwives, 2,790 senior and assistant auxiliary health workers and health assistants, and 6,808 village-based health workers.

There was no doubt in the late 1980s that considerable progress had been made in health care, but the available facilities were still inadequate to meet the growing medical needs of the population. The majority of people lacked easy access to modern medical centers, partly because of the absence of such facilities in nearby locations and partly because of the physical barrier posed by the country's rugged terrain. Because there were very few modern means of transportation in rural areas, particularly in the hills and mountains, people had to walk on average about half a day to get to health posts. Such a long walk was not only difficult (especially when the patient needed medical attention), but also meant economic hardship for the majority who rarely could afford to be absent for the whole day from their daily work. As a result, many minor illnesses went untreated, and some of them later developed into major illnesses.

In the early 1990s, Nepal's geographical limitations continued to play a large part in the country's social and economic problems. Moreover, despite twenty-five years of family planning programs, the population growth rate continued to outpace agricultural production and parts of the country continued to be food deficit areas. The educational base was also limited; only one-third of the population was literate. The generally poor health of the population and a lack of adequate health-care facilities also hindered social and economic improvements.

*   *   *

A good source of information on cultural and physical geography, although outdated, is Pradyumna P. Karan's *Nepal: A Cultural and Physical Geography*. Barry C. Bishop's *Karnali under Stress* not only provides a good geographic and climatic description of

Nepal, but also covers ethnic history and analyzes the economic strategies practiced by the mountain and hill peoples. Although Bishop's surveys were conducted in the Karnali region, they apply to the entire upland region—hills and mountains—of Nepal. Jack D. Ives's and Bruno Messerli's *The Himalayan Dilemma* is another good source of physical geographic information on Nepal; sections concerning environmental degradation are particularly useful.

The *Population Monograph of Nepal,* prepared by the National Planning Commission, is a good source of statistics on demographic, social, and economic issues. Another publication by the commission, *The Statistical Year Book of Nepal, 1989,* supplies fairly extensive and up-to-date data on various social and economic variables and indicators. Pitamber Sharma's *Urbanization in Nepal* uses census data from 1952 to 1981 to examine the various aspects of urbanization.

Badri Prasad Shrestha's *An Introduction to Nepalese Economy* is somewhat outdated, but has good background material on the contemporary economic situation. Mahesh Chandra Regmi's *An Economic History of Nepal, 1846-1901* is an excellent historical treatment of the economy, and his *Landownership in Nepal* is a classic study of land tenure. Nanda R. Shrestha's *Landlessness and Migration in Nepal* and Vidya Bir Singh Kansakar's *Effectiveness of Planned Resettlement Programme in Nepal* supply detailed analyses of internal migration and land resettlement in the Tarai. (For further information and complete citations, see Bibliography.)

Chapter 3. Nepal: The Economy

A Nepalese porter carrying supplies for a trek

NEPAL IS ONE OF THE POOREST COUNTRIES in the world; it was listed as the eleventh poorest among 121 countries in 1989. Estimates of its per capita income for 1988 ranged from US$158 to US$180. Various factors contributed to the economic underdevelopment—including terrain, lack of resource endowment, landlocked position, lack of institutions for modernization, weak infrastructure, and a lack of policies conducive to development.

Until 1951 Nepal had very little contact with countries other than India, Tibet, and Britain. Movement of goods or people from one part of the country to another usually required passage through India, making Nepal dependent on trade with or via India. The mountains to the north and the lack of economic growth in Tibet (China's Xizang Autonomous Region after 1959) meant very little trade was possible with this northern neighbor.

Prior to 1951, few all-weather roads existed, and the transportation of goods was difficult. Goods were able to reach Kathmandu by railroad, trucks, and ropeways, but for other parts of the country such facilities remained almost non-existent. The lack of infrastructure made it hard to expand markets and pursue economic growth. Since 1951 Nepal has tried to expand its contacts with other countries and to improve its infrastructure, although the lack of significant progress was still evident in the early 1990s.

The effects of being landlocked and of having to transit goods through India continued to be reflected in the early 1990s. As a result of the lapse of the trade and transit treaties with India in March 1989, Nepal faced shortages of certain consumer goods, raw materials, and other industrial inputs, a situation that led to a decline in industrial production.

Economic Setting

Nepal's economy is irrevocably tied to India. Nepal's geographical position and the scarcity of natural resources used in the production of industrial goods meant that its economy was subject to fluctuations resulting from changes in its relationship with India. Trade and transit rights affected the movement of goods and increased transportation costs, although Nepal also engaged in unrecorded border trade with India. Real economic growth averaged 4 percent annually in the 1980s, but the 1989 trade and transit dispute with India adversely affected economic progress, and economic growth declined to only 1.5 percent that year as the availability of imported raw materials for export industries was disrupted.

The Nepalese rupee (Rs or NRs; for value of the rupee—see Glossary) was linked to the Indian rupee. Since the late 1960s, the universal currency has been Nepalese, although as of 1991 Indian currency still was used as convertible currency. During the trade and transit dispute of 1989, however, Kathmandu made convertibility of the Indian rupee more difficult.

Agricultural domination of the economy had not changed by 1991. What little industrial activity there was largely involved the processing of agricultural products. Since the 1960s, investment in the agricultural sector has not had a parallel effect in productivity per unit of land. Agricultural production continued to be influenced by weather conditions and the lack of arable land and has not always kept pace with population growth (see table 9, Appendix).

Nepal suffered from an underdeveloped infrastructure. This problem was exacerbated by a weak public investment program and ineffective administrative services. Economic development plans sought to improve the infrastructure but were implemented at the expense of investment in direct production and resulted in a slow growth rate. Further, economic growth did not keep pace with population growth. Largely dependent on agriculture, economic growth also was undermined by poor harvests. The growth of public expenditures during the first half of the 1980s doubled the current account deficit of the balance of payments and caused a serious decline in international reserves.

Role of Government

Government participation (or interference) in the economy was very strong, beginning with the Rana period, which lasted from the mid-nineteenth century until the mid-twentieth century (see Rana Rule, ch. 1). During Rana rule, there were very few industries other than the cottage type, and they were under strict government supervision. After the fall of the Ranas in 1950–51, economic planning as an approach to development was discussed. Finally, in 1956 the First Five-Year Plan (1956–61) was announced.

The Five-Year Plans

Economic plans generally strove to increase output and employment; develop the infrastructure; attain economic stability; promote industry, commerce, and international trade; establish administrative and public service institutions to support economic development; and introduce labor-intensive production techniques to alleviate underemployment. The social goals of the plans were improving health and education as well as encouraging equitable income distribution. Although each plan had different development priorities, the allocation of resources did not always reflect these priorities. The first four plans concentrated on infrastructure—to make it possible to facilitate the movement of goods and services—and to increase the size of the market. Each of the five-year plans depended heavily on foreign assistance in the forms of grants and loans (see Foreign Aid, this ch.).

The First Five-Year Plan (1956–61) allocated about Rs576 million for development expenditures. Transportation and communications received top priority with over 36 percent of the budget allocations. Agriculture, including village development and irrigation, took second priority with about 20 percent of budget expenditures. The plan, which also focused on collecting statistics, was not well conceived, however, and resulted in actual expenditures of about Rs382.9 million—two-thirds the budgeted amount. In most cases, targets were missed by a wide margin. For example, although approximately 1,450 kilometers of highways were targeted for construction, only about 565 kilometers were built.

After Parliament, which had been established under the 1959 constitution, was suspended in 1960, the Second Plan failed to materialize on schedule. A new plan was not introduced until 1962 and covered only three years, 1962–65. The Second Plan had expenditures of almost Rs615 million. Transportation and communication again received top priority with about 39 percent of budget expenditures. Industry, tourism, and social services were the second priority. Although targets again were missed, there were improvements in industrial production, road construction, telephone installations, irrigation, and education. However, only the organizational improvement area of the target was met.

The first two plans were developed with very little research and a minimal data base. Neither plan was detailed, and both contained only general terms. The administrative machinery with which to execute these plans also was inadequate. The National Planning Commission, which formulated the second plan, noted the difficulty of preparing plans in the absence of statistical data. Further, as was the case with the first plan, the bulk of the development budget depended on foreign aid—mostly in the form of grants. The failure of these plans was indicated by the government's inability to spend the budgeted amounts.

The Third Five-Year Plan (1965–70) increased the involvement of local *panchayat* (see Glossary). It also focused on transport, communications, and industrial and agricultural development. Total planned expenditures were more than Rs1.6 billion.

The Fourth Five-Year Plan (1970–75) increased proposed expenditures to more than Rs3.3 billion. Transportation and communications again were the top priority, receiving 41.2 percent of expenditures, followed by agriculture, which was allocated 26 percent of the budget. Although the third and fourth plans increased the involvement of the *panchayat* in the development process, the central government continued to carry most of the responsibilities.

The Fifth Five-Year Plan (1975–80) proposed expenditures of more than Rs8.8 billion. For the first time, the problem of poverty was addressed in a five-year plan, although no specific goals were mentioned. Top priority was given to agricultural development, and emphasis was placed on increasing food production and cash crops such as sugar cane and tobacco. Increased industrial production and social services also were targeted. Controlling population growth was considered a priority.

The Sixth Five-Year Plan (1980–85) proposed an outlay of more than Rs22 billion. Agriculture remained the top priority; increased social services were second. The budget share allocated to transportation and communication was less than that allocated in the previous plan; it was felt that the transportation network had reached a point where it was more beneficial to increase spending on agriculture and industry.

The Seventh Five-Year Plan (1985–90) proposed expenditures of Rs29 billion. It encouraged private sector participation in the economy (less than Rs22 billion) and local government participation (Rs2 billion). The plan targeted increasing productivity of all sectors, expanding opportunity for productive employment, and fulfilling the minimum basic needs of the people. For the first time since the plans were devised, specific goals were set for meeting basic needs. The availability of food, clothing, fuelwood, drinking water, primary health care, sanitation, primary and skill-based education, and minimum rural transport facilities was emphasized.

Because of the political upheavals in mid-1990, the new government postponed formulating the next plan. The July 1990 budget speech of the minister of finance, however, implied that for the interim, the goals of the seventh plan were being followed.

Foreign aid as a percentage of development averaged around 66 percent (see table 10, Appendix). The government continually failed to use all committed foreign aid, however, probably as a result of inefficiency. In the Rs26.6 billion budget presented in July 1991, approximately Rs11.8 billion, or 44.4 percent of the budget, was expected to be derived from foreign loans or grants.

Market scenes in Durbar Square, Kathmandu, showing merchandise for sale and flowers sold as offerings for Hindu rituals Courtesy Linda Galantin

Other Development Programs

The government launched the Structural Adjustment Program and the Basic Needs Program in 1985. These programs stressed self-reliance, financial discipline, and austerity as goals through the year 2000. The Structural Adjustment Program sought to confront some of the longer-term constraints to economic growth. Its measures included increasing domestic resource mobilization, reducing the growth of expenditures and domestic bank borrowings, and strengthening the commercial banking and public enterprise sectors.

The Structural Adjustment Program initiative focused on sustainable growth through balance in different sectors of the economy. Rural development in particular was targeted in order to raise the standard of living and increase agricultural production. Funds for education and health services, electricity and power, irrigation, and transportation and communications were provided. Government subsidies were supposed to be removed, new and improved standards of government efficiency were issued, and privatization of government enterprises was increased. Further, domestic resources were more fully used, and domestic bank borrowings and the growth of expenditures were decreased. The initial response to the Structural Adjustment Program was good, as gross domestic product (GDP—see Glossary), exports, and agriculture showed growth.

The objective of the Basic Needs Program was also to improve the standard of living by increasing food production, as well as to provide clothing, health services, and education. Six goals were to be achieved by the year 2000. Daily food consumption was to be raised to 2,250 calories per capita. Each person was to have the equivalent of eleven meters of clothing and a pair of shoes per year. Housing requirements were estimated at thirty square meters per urban household and at forty to sixty square meters per rural household. Essential utilities and sanitation were to be furnished by the government. Universal primary education for all children between five and ten years of age also was to be provided. The government was responsible for supplying teachers, classrooms, and educational materials, although villagers pitched in with labor and supplies to build schoolhouses (see Education, ch. 2). The population growth rate was targeted at 1.9 percent by 2000 (down from 2.6 percent in the 1980s), and life expectancy was to increase to 65 years of age by 2000 (up from almost 51 years in the late 1980s). The infant mortality rate was to be reduced to 45 deaths per 1,000 by the year 2000; World Bank (see Glossary) figures placed infant mortality at 171 per 1,000 in 1965 and at 126 per 1,000 in 1988. Universal primary health services also were to be ensured, primarily by the government, improved social services provided to handicapped people, law and order maintained, and an environment conducive to development established (see Population, ch. 2).

Budgeting Process

Prior to 1951, there was no budgeting process. Since the political changes in 1951, the government has presented a budget every fiscal year (FY—see Glossary). Until 1959 the budget was published in the *Nepal Raj Patra*, the government gazette. Since 1959 the budget has first been presented to a legislative body whenever one existed and then published.

Regular and Development Budget

After the First Five-Year Plan was introduced in 1955–56, the budget was divided into two parts—regular and development (see table 11, Appendix). In a speech delivered on July 13, 1990, the minister of finance presented a budget with four major objectives: to direct the development programs by eliminating the existing anomalies and by making them more realistic and productive, as well as overseeing their consistency in directly benefiting the deprived community; to rationalize the role of the private sector and the facilities provided by the government; to minimize the increasing hardship faced by the common people; and to start a process of repaying the accumulated financial liabilities of the government. Because the planned expenditures for development were rarely met, the 1990 budget lowered development expenditures to make the plan more realistic.

The 1990 budget allowed for total expenditures of Rs19.8 billion. Revenue was estimated to be just over Rs10.1 billion. The deficit was to be met through foreign grants (Rs2.5 billion), foreign loans (Rs5.5 billion), and domestic borrowing. The budget was not unique in terms of the size of the deficit or its dependence on foreign grants and loans, as this pattern had existed for more than three decades.

Taxation

Until the late 1950s, the two major sources of revenues were a land tax and a tariff on foreign trade. After 1959, however, income, sales, and property taxes, as well as several other minor taxes, were introduced. An import-export tax and various business taxes, such as a sales tax, were the dominant sources of revenue. A land tax, which accounted for a considerable portion of revenue prior to 1960, no longer provided an important source of revenue. Income tax on individual incomes accounted for less than 7 percent of revenues. Most of the other taxes were progressive in nature. In the late 1980s, the total tax burden was about 10 percent of gross national product (GNP—see Glossary)—lower than in the neighboring countries of India, Pakistan, and Sri Lanka, which taxed at rates of 11 to 13 percent.

Money and Banking

Nepal's first commercial bank, the Nepal Bank Limited, was established in 1937. The government owned 51 percent of the shares in the bank and controlled its operations to a large extent. Nepal Bank Limited was headquartered in Kathmandu and had branches in other parts of the country.

There were other government banking institutions. Rastriya Banijya Bank (National Commercial Bank), a state-owned commercial bank, was established in 1966. The Land Reform Savings Corporation was established in 1966 to deal with finances related to land reforms.

Nepal had two other specialized financial institutions. Nepal Industrial Development Corporation, a state-owned development finance organization headquartered in Kathmandu, was established in 1959 with United States assistance to offer financial and technical assistance to private industry. Although the government invested in the corporation, representatives from the private business sector also sat on the board of directors. The Co-operative Bank, which became the Agricultural Development Bank in 1967, was the main source of financing for small agribusinesses and cooperatives. Almost 75 percent of the bank was state-owned; 21 percent was owned by the Nepal Rastra Bank, and 5 percent by cooperatives and private individuals. The Agricultural Development Bank also served as the government's implementing agency for small farmers' group development projects assisted by the Asian Development Bank (see Glossary) and financed by the United Nations Development Programme. The Ministry of Finance reported in 1990 that the Agricultural Development Bank, which is vested with the leading role in agricultural loan investment, had granted loans to only 9 percent of the total number of farming families since 1965.

Since the 1960s, both commercial and specialized banks have expanded. As a result, more businesses and households had better access to the credit market although the credit market had not expanded.

In the mid-1980s, three foreign commercial banks opened branches in Nepal. The Nepal Arab Bank was co-owned by the

Emirates Bank International Limited (Dubai), the Nepalese government, and the Nepalese public. The Nepal Indosuez Bank was jointly owned by the Banque Indosuez (a French institution), Rastriya Banijya Bank, Rastriya Beema Sansthan (National Insurance Corporation), and the Nepalese public. Nepal Grindlays Bank was co-owned by a British firm called Grindlays Bank, local financial interests, and the Nepalese public.

Nepal Rastra Bank was created in 1956 as the central bank. Its function was to supervise commercial banks and to guide the basic monetary policy of the nation. Its major aims were to regulate the issue of paper money; secure countrywide circulation of Nepalese currency and achieve stability in its exchange rates; mobilize capital for economic development and for trade and industry growth; develop the banking system in the country, thereby ensuring the existence of banking facilities; and maintain the economic interests of the general public. Nepal Rastra Bank also was to oversee foreign exchange rates and foreign exchange reserves.

Prior to the establishment of Nepal Rastra Bank, Kathmandu had little control over its foreign currency holdings. Indian rupees were the prevalent medium of exchange in most parts of the country. Nepalese currency was used mostly in the Kathmandu Valley and the surrounding hill areas. The existence of a dual currency system made it hard for the government to know the status of Indian currency holdings in Nepal. The exchange rates between Indian and Nepalese rupees were determined in the marketplace. Between 1932 and 1955, the value of 100 Indian rupees varied between Rs71 and Rs177. The government entered the currency market with a form of fixed exchange rate between the two currencies in 1958. An act passed in 1960 sought to regulate foreign exchange transactions. Beginning in the 1960s, the government made special efforts to use Nepalese currency inside the country as a medium of exchange.

It was only after the signing of the 1960 Trade and Transit Treaty with India that Nepal had full access to foreign currencies other than the Indian rupee. Prior to the treaty, all foreign exchange earnings went to the Central Bank of India, and all foreign currency needs were provided by the Indian government. After 1960 Nepal had full access to all foreign currency transactions and directly controlled its exports and imports with countries other than India.

As a result of the treaty, the government had to separate Indian currency (convertible currency because of free convertibility) from other currencies (nonconvertible currency because it was directly controlled by Nepal Rastra Bank). In 1991 government statistics still separated trade with India from trade with other countries.

Tables showing international reserves listed convertible and non-convertible foreign exchange reserves separately.

Foreign Trade

Nepal's traditional trade was with India (see table 12, Appendix). In the 1950s, over 90 percent of its foreign trade was conducted with India. Most of Nepal's basic consumer goods were imported from India, and most of its agricultural exports went to India. India also supplied Nepal's industries with coal, cement, machines, trucks, and spare parts.

Because goods moved by land for at least a few hundred kilometers through India, a good relationship with India was essential for the smooth transport of goods to and from foreign countries (see Relations with India; ch. 4; India, ch. 5). The March 1989 impasse in negotiations for trade and transit treaties with India hence seriously damaged Nepal's economy (see table 13, Appendix). The transit treaty had allowed goods from third countries entering at Calcutta to pass through to Nepal and exempted them from customs and transit duties. The treaty allowed trade to transit at twenty-one border points, and primary commodities were essentially duty-free in both directions. Imports from India had no quantitative restrictions and low tariffs.

As a result of the breakdown in negotiations, only two trade and transit points remained open—both in eastern Nepal. Nepal's exports to India were subjected to high tariffs, and imports from India also carried increased costs. The dispute was not solved until June 1990, when Kathmandu and New Delhi agreed to restore economic relations to the status quo ante of April 1, 1987.

Although India remained an important trade partner in 1991, foreign trade with India has been on the decline vis-à-vis other countries since 1960. Trade with India decreased from more than 70 percent in 1975 to about 27 percent of total trade in 1989. However, the trade deficit with India in this period increased at an annual rate of about 11 percent.

To increase exports, Kathmandu introduced some fiscal and monetary measures, including the Export Entitlement Program and the Dual Foreign Exchange rate, along with cash grants, income tax rebates, and low tariffs. Until the trade and transit dispute of 1989, exports had increased by 11 percent or more per year since 1975. Nepal's major exports were clothing, carpets, grain, and leather goods. In 1989–90 the carpet industry was responsible for producing 54 percent of Nepal's exports. In FY 1988, India received 38 percent of Nepal's exports, the United States 23 percent, Britain

Newari architecture in Durbar Square, Patan
Bustling Bhotahiti Square, Kathmandu
Courtesy Harvey Follender

6 percent, and other European countries 9 percent (see table 14; table 15, Appendix).

Imports increased at a faster rate than exports. Since the 1970s, the foreign trade deficit had increased in most years. Nepal's primary imports were petroleum products, fertilizer, and machinery; the other chief imports were boots and shoes, cement, cigarettes, iron and steel, medicines, salt, sugar, tea, and textiles. India supplied 36 percent of imports, Japan 13 percent, European countries 4 percent, and the United States 1 percent in FY 1988. Receipts from service and transfer payments were insufficient to finance trade deficits. This imbalance has resulted in an increase in the current account deficit (see table 16; table 17, Appendix).

In March 1989, the government introduced the Open General License as a step to support the Structural Adjustment Program. It included inputs for existing industries—raw wool, cotton yarn, and cotton fabrics. The program also allowed supports for petroleum products, coal, tractors, buses, and trucks, as well as for some household items, such as ovens and toasters. In May 1990, however, Kathmandu deleted all goods except raw wool, cotton yarn, petroleum products, coal, and newsprint from Open General License imports.

The government also introduced an auction system for the import of goods. The goods were classified in three categories: industrial raw materials, semiluxury items, and luxury items. Premiums were assigned and foreign exchange quotas allocated for each category. The premium for raw materials was lower than that for luxury items.

Balance of Payments

The balance of payments in the 1980s improved, despite a continued trade deficit. This improvement was achieved through foreign loans and assistance. Nonetheless, foreign debt was increasing. Because foreign debt and the balance of payments were intrinsically linked, an improvement in one area was at the expense of the other. Between 1986 and 1990, the debt service ratio increased from an average of under 7 percent to about 12 percent. In 1989 the debt service ratio skyrocketed to 17 percent. This increase was the result of the acquisition of two commercial aircraft and a decline in exports caused by trade and transit difficulties. According to World Bank figures, by mid-1989 official foreign debt outstanding and disbursed was approximately US$1.3 billion. There also was a deficit in the balance of payments of convertible Indian currency.

The Structural Adjustment Program addressed the trade deficit and sought to increase the speed of economic development.

Although exports increased in FY 1988 by 34 percent over the previous year, Nepal still imported much more than it exported. In FY 1988, exports were US$187 million (up from US$139 million the previous year), but imports were US$630 million, up from US$507 the previous year. Nonetheless, more efficient use of foreign aid, increased earnings from exports, tourism, and other services improved the balance of payments situation and increased the international reserves through FY 1989. Foreign exchange reserves also had increased, mostly because of loans from the World Bank and the International Monetary Fund (IMF—see Glossary) for the Structural Adjustment Program, as well as loans from the Asian Development Bank. Both Kuwait and Saudi Arabia had made loans that alleviated the balance of trade deficit. The trade and transit problems with India that began in March 1989, however, erased those gains and resulted in tremendous financial hardships.

Foreign Aid

Nepal has been a recipient of foreign assistance since 1952 when it joined the Colombo Plan for Cooperative, Economic, and Social Development in Asia and the Pacific (Colombo Plan—see Glossary). The plan was established, under a slightly different name, by the British Commonwealth countries in 1951. During the 1950s, many Nepalese received scholarships through the Colombo Plan to go to various countries for studies in technical and professional areas.

During the 1950s, all other aid was in the form of grants. The bulk of assistance was directed toward developing agriculture, transportation infrastructure, and power generation. Other areas targeted for assistance were communications, industry, education, and health. India and the United States each were responsible for more than one-third of all grants. Both countries established aid missions to Nepal and directed aid to special projects. Other major donors during the 1950s were China and the Soviet Union. Britain, Switzerland, Australia, Japan, and New Zealand also were involved in lesser assistance programs. The United Nations (UN) provided some technical assistance.

Until the mid-1960s, Nepal depended mostly, if not totally, on foreign grants for all its development projects. Most of these grants were on a bilateral basis. Grants from India helped to build the airport in Kathmandu, the Kosi Dam, and various irrigation projects. The Soviet Union helped to build cigarette and sugar factories, a hydroelectric plant, and part of the East-West Highway. Grants from China helped to construct roads; a trolley bus line in Kathmandu; and leather and shoe, brick, and tile factories.

United States grants supported village development, agriculture, education, and public health. The United States also helped to start the Nepal Industrial Development Corporation, which granted loans to several industries (see Money and Banking, this ch.).

Beginning in the 1960s, some bilateral assistance was in the form of loans. The loan share of foreign aid increased from under 4 percent between 1965 and 1970 to more than 25 percent by the 1985–88 period (see table 18, Appendix).

In the 1970s, multilateral assistance programs started to play an important role in development planning and accounted for more than 70 percent of funding for development planning. By the end of the 1980s, the great majority of foreign aid was in the form of multilateral assistance programs. The major sources of borrowing or grants for these programs were the International Development Association of the World Bank and the Asian Development Bank. Most of these loans could be characterized as soft loans (see Glossary).

Sources of foreign aid were numerous. Eleven UN agencies, seven multilateral lending agencies (such as the World Bank), and eight private agencies (for example, the Ford Foundation) had participated in aid programs. At least seventeen countries offered bilateral assistance. Under the auspices of the World Bank, the Nepal Aid Group was created in 1976. By 1987 sixteen countries and six international agencies participated in the group. The level of commitment from the Nepal Aid Group had increased from Rs1.5 billion in 1976–77 to Rs5.6 billion in 1987–88. The bulk of foreign aid contributions after 1976 came from this group.

Most economic development projects were funded with external assistance on concessional terms. In the mid- to late 1980s, recorded aid disbursements averaged more than US$200 million annually—about 7 percent of GDP. More than 70 percent of the aid was in the form of grants; the remainder was in the form of concessional loans. A high percentage of technical assistance and direct aid payments was not documented. Much of the aid granted was underused (see table 19, Appendix).

As of 1991, Nepal was receiving external assistance in the form of project aid, commodity aid, technical assistance, and program aid. Project aid funded irrigation programs, hydroelectric plants, and roads. Commodity assistance targets included fertilizers, improved seeds, and construction materials provided by donor aid agencies. Technical assistance covered services of experts to advise the government in training indigenous personnel to perform research in technological fields and resulted in the development of skilled labor. Program aid supported various projects, in particular the agricultural and health fields.

Dependence on foreign aid was increasing. Between 1984 and 1987, foreign aid as a percentage of GNP increased from under 8 percent to almost 13 percent. Debt service as a percentage of GDP increased from less than 0.1 percent in 1974–75 to almost 1 percent in 1987–88. Outstanding debt in this period increased from Rs346 million to almost Rs21 billion.

From FY 1970 through FY 1988, United States commitments, including United States Export-Import Bank (Eximbank—see Glossary) funds, totaled US$285 million. In the 1980s, bilateral United States economic assistance channelled through the Agency for International Development averaged US$15 million annually. The United States also contributed to various international institutions and private voluntary organizations that serviced Nepal for a total contribution to multilateral aid in excess of US$250 million in the 1980s. Other Western countries and official development assistance (ODA—see Glossary) and bilateral commitments for the 1980–87 period totaled US$1.8 billion. The Organization of the Petroleum Exporting Countries (OPEC) provided US$30 million in bilateral aid from 1979 to 1989. Communist countries provided US$273 million in aid from 1970 to 1988. From 1981 until 1988, Japan was the premier source of bilateral ODA for Nepal, accounting for more than one-third of all funds. The second biggest donor during that period was the Federal Republic of Germany (West Germany).

Labor

Workers' rights and organized labor were in transition in mid-1991. During the late 1940s and early 1950s, some labor disputes led to strikes and lockouts, and labor unions sprang up in various factories. In 1957 the government announced the Industrial Policy of Nepal, under which it undertook the responsibility of promoting, assisting, and regulating industries.

The Factories and Factory Workers' Act of 1959 established rules and regulations to govern labor-management relationships and working conditions in factories. The 1977 amended version of the act provided for a six-day, forty-eight-hour work week, thirty days annually for holidays and fifteen days annually for sick leave, and some health and safety standards and benefits. Implementation of the act, a responsibility of the Ministry of Labor and Social Services, was not always forthcoming, however, and was only somewhat affected by the success of the prodemocracy movement.

A revision of the body of labor laws was pending in mid-1991; it was to include a code that defined and regulated workers' rights.

Labor unions, restricted prior to the July 1991 repeal of the Organization and Control Act of 1963, still were limited. Estimates suggested that only approximately 3 percent of the economically active population, or 30 percent of nonagricultural workers, were union members.

Because of limited industrialization, unemployment and particularly underemployment were quite high. In 1977 the National Planning Commission undertook a survey, which determined unemployment to be 5.6 percent in rural areas and almost 6 percent in urban areas. Underemployment was estimated to be about 63 percent in rural areas and about 45 percent in urban areas. In 1981 the Asian Regional Team for Employment Production estimated the unemployment and underemployment rates to range from 21 to 28 percent in the Tarai Region and from 37 to 47 percent in the Hill Region. The availability of nonagricultural employment opportunities in the labor force was reported at approximately 600,000 positions in 1981. Underemployment for all of Nepal was reported to range from 25 to 40 percent in 1987; unemployment nationally stood at 5 percent.

Agriculture

Agriculture dominated the economy. In the late 1980s, it was the livelihood for more than 90 percent of the population, although only approximately 20 percent of the total land area was cultivable. Agriculture accounted for, on average, about 60 percent of the GDP and approximately 75 percent of exports. Since the formulation of the Fifth Five-Year Plan (1975–80), agriculture has been the highest priority because economic growth was dependent on both increasing the productivity of existing crops and diversifying the agricultural base for use as industrial inputs.

In trying to increase agricultural production and diversify the agricultural base, the government focused on irrigation, the use of fertilizers and insecticides, the introduction of new implements and new seeds of high-yield varieties, and the provision of credit. The lack of distribution of these inputs, as well as problems in obtaining supplies, however, inhibited progress. Although land reclamation and settlement were occurring in the Tarai Region, environmental degradation—ecological imbalance resulting from deforestation—also prevented progress (see The Land, ch. 2).

Although new agricultural technologies helped increase food production, there still was room for further growth. Past experience indicated bottlenecks, however, in using modern technology to achieve a healthy growth. The conflicting goals of producing cash crops both for food and for industrial inputs also were problematic.

Oxen in fields, Tulsipur area, Rapti Zone in the Tarai Region
Courtesy John N. Gunning

The production of crops fluctuated widely as a result of these factors as well as weather conditions. Although agricultural production grew at an average annual rate of 2.4 percent from 1974 to 1989, it did not keep pace with population growth, which increased at an average annual rate of 2.6 percent over the same period. Further, the annual average growth rate of food grain production was only 1.2 percent during the same period.

There were some successes. Fertile lands in the Tarai Region and hardworking peasants in the Hill Region provided greater supplies of food staples (mostly rice and corn), increasing the daily caloric intake of the population locally to over 2,000 calories per capita in 1988 from about 1,900 per capita in 1965. Moreover, areas with access to irrigation facilities increased from approximately 6,200 hectares in 1956 to nearly 583,000 hectares by 1990 (see table 20, Appendix).

Rice was the most important cereal crop. In 1966 total rice production amounted to a little more than 1 million tons; by 1989 more than 3 million tons were produced. Fluctuation in rice production was very common because of changes in rainfall; overall, however, rice production had increased following the introduction of new cultivation techniques as well as increases in cultivated land. By 1988 approximately 3.9 million hectares of land were under paddy cultivation. In 1966 approximately 500,000 tons of corn, the second major food crop, were produced. By 1989 corn production had increased to over 1 million tons.

Other food crops included wheat, millet, and barley, but their contribution to the agricultural sector was small (see table 21, Appendix). Increased production of cash crops—used as input to new industries—dominated in the early 1970s. Sugarcane and tobacco also showed considerable increases in production from the 1970s to the 1980s. Potatoes and oilseed production had shown moderate growth since 1980. Medicinal herbs were grown in the north on the slopes of the Himalayas, but increases in production were limited by continued environmental degradation. According to government statistics, production of milk, meat, and fruit had improved but as of the late 1980s still had not reached a point where nutritionally balanced food was available to most people. Additionally, as of 1989 the increases in meat and milk production had not met the desired level of output.

Food grains contributed 76 percent of total crop production in 1988–89. In 1989–90 despite poor weather conditions and a lack of agricultural inputs—particularly fertilizer—production increased by 5 percent. In fact, severe weather fluctuations often affected production levels. Some of the gains in production through the 1980s were due to increased productivity of the work force (about 7 percent over fifteen years); other gains were due to increased land use and favorable weather conditions.

Land Reform

Nepal long had been under a feudal system where a small number of landlords held most of the agricultural land (see Infighting among Aristocratic Factions, ch. 1). The state extended its control over the land by the administrative device of making land grants and assignments and raising revenues. Most of the landlords who were granted state lands were not directly involved in farming but contracted with tenant farmers on a customary, and hereditary, basis. The basic purpose of land reform was to protect the tenant farmers, take away excess holdings from landlords, and distribute property to farmers with small landholdings (holding one to three hectares) and landless agrarian households.

Efforts at land reform began with the enactment of the Land and Cultivation Record Complilation Act in 1956 and continued with the Lands Act in 1957 when the government began to compile tenants' records. Although these acts facilitated land reform, the lot of the small farmer did not improve, and further efforts were made. The Agricultural Reorganization Act, passed in 1963, and the Land Reform Act, passed in 1964, emphasized security for tenant farmers and put a ceiling on landholdings. There were several loopholes in the acts, however, and large landholders continued to control most of the lands. There was some success in protecting the rights of tenant farmers, but not much was achieved in land redistribution. As of 1990, average landholdings remained small (see table 8, Appendix).

Forests

From 1950 to 1980, Nepal lost half of its forest cover. The first scientific measurement of forest resources was done in a 1964 survey, which estimated about 6.5 million hectares of forest area. Later studies indicated that as of 1987 the forest area in the hills had remained the same but that elsewhere forests had been degraded. By 1988 forests covered only approximately 30 percent of the land area. Deforestation was typical of much of the country and was linked to increased demands for grazing land, farmland, and fodder as the animal and human populations grew. Further, most of the population's energy needs were met by firewood. All these factors exacerbated deforestation.

Fuelwood needs of the population mainly resulted from the lack of alternative sources of energy. This fact was particularly evident during the 1989 trade and transit impasse with India because the dispute resulted in a shortage of domestic cooking fuel. As a result of the decreased availability of kerosene during this period, the demand for fuelwood rose sharply in the Kathmandu Valley, and fuelwood consumption increased by an estimated 415 percent.

Deforestation caused erosion and complicated cultivation, affecting the future productivity of agricultural lands. Although several laws to counter degradation had been enacted, the results were modest, and government plans for afforestation had not met their targets. The government also established the Timber Corporation of Nepal, the Fuelwood Corporation, and the Forest Products Development Board to harvest the forests in such a way that their degradation would be retarded. In 1988–89 the Fuelwood Corporation merged with the Timber Corporation of Nepal, but forest management through these and other government agencies had made very little progress. In FY 1989, more than 28,000 hectares were targeted for afforestation, but only approximately 23,000 hectares were afforested that year.

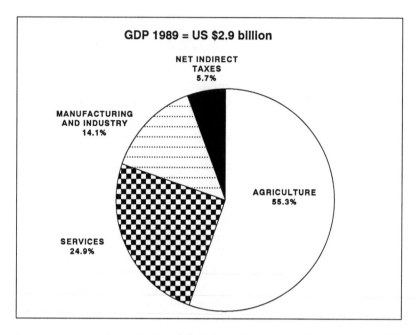

Source: Based on information from World Bank, *Trends in Developing Economies, 1990,*
Washington, 1990, 386.

Figure 8. Nepal: Shares of Gross Domestic Product, 1989

A twenty-one-year forestry master plan was devised in FY 1989
to stem deforestation. Implemented with the help of the Asian Development Bank, the program targeted reforestation and education. It sought to maintain the forestation level at 37 percent of
land area.

Industry

During the 1950s and 1960s, Kathmandu received aid commitments from Moscow and Beijing. During the 1960s, Soviet and
Chinese aid also supported development of a few government-
owned industries. Most of the industries established used agricultural products such as jute, sugar, and tea as raw materials. Other
industries were dependent on various inputs imported from other
countries, mainly India.

As a result of the 1989–90 trade dispute with India, many inputs were unavailable, causing lower capacity utilization in some
industries. During the same period, Nepal also lost India as its traditional market for certain goods. The lack of industrial materials

such as coal, furnace oil, machinery, and spare parts adversely affected industrial production.

Industry accounted for less than 20 percent of total GDP in the 1980s (see fig. 8). Relatively small by international standards, most of the industries established in the 1950s and 1960s were developed with government protection. Traditional cottage industries, including basket-weaving as well as cotton fabric and edible oil production, comprised approximately 60 percent of industrial output; there also were attempts to develop cottage industries to produce furniture, soap, and textiles. The remainder of industrial output came from modern industries, such as jute mills, cigarette factories, and cement plants.

Manufacturing

Among the modern industries were large manufacturing plants, including many public sector operations. The major manufacturing industries produced jute, sugar, cigarettes, beer, matches, shoes, chemicals, cement, and bricks. The garment and carpet industries, targeted at export production, have grown rapidly since the mid-1980s whereas jute production has declined. Industrial estates were located in Patan (also called Lalitpur), Balaju, Hetauda, Pokhara, Dharan, Butawal, and Nepalganj. The government provided the land and buildings for the industrial estates, but the industries themselves were mostly privately owned.

The 1986–87 Nepal Standard Industrial Classification counted 2,054 manufacturing establishments of 10 or more persons from 51 major industry groups, employing about 125,000 workers. That same year the total output from these industries amounted to about Rs10 billion; value added was estimated at almost Rs3.6 billion. It was nearly Rs5.1 billion in FY 1989. By FY 1989, 2,334 such establishments were recorded, employing about 141,000 persons.

Private Industry

The history of incorporated private firms in Nepal is short. The Nepal Companies Act of 1936 provided for the incorporation of industrial enterprises on joint stock principle with limited liability. The first such firm, Biratnagar Jute Mills, was a collaborative venture of Indian and Nepalese entrepreneurs. It was formed in 1936 with initial capital of 160,000 Indian rupees.

In response to shortages of some consumer goods during World War II (1939–45), fourteen private companies emerged in such diverse fields as mining, electrical generation, and paper and soap production. The initial capital invested in each of these industries was small. In 1942 two paper mills emerged as joint ventures of

Nepalese and Indian entrepreneurs. Industrial growth gained momentum after 1945, although the end of World War II had reduced the scarcity of goods and caused many of these companies to incur losses.

Under the Nepal Companies Act, there was no provision for private limited companies. In 1951, however, a new act was implemented that had such a provision. This act encouraged the establishment of ninety-two new private joint stock companies between 1952 and 1964. Most of these companies were much smaller than existing companies. Under the provisions of the 1951 act, public disclosure of the activities of the firms was not required, whereas the 1936 act allowed substantial government intervention. The Industrial Enterprises Act of 1974 and its frequent amendments shifted the government's emphasis on growth from the public to the private sector. However, discrepancies between policy and practice were evident, and the public sector continued to be favored.

Public Companies

Public companies also had varied success. Between 1936 and 1939, twenty public companies were formed, of which three failed. Between 1945 and 1951, thirty-five public firms were incorporated, six of which went out of business. Between 1936 and 1963, fifty-four firms were incorporated, but at the end of 1963 only thirty-four remained in operation. The success of public companies continued to be erratic.

Minerals

Because only a few minerals were available in small quantities for commercial utilization, the mineral industry's contribution to the economy was small. Most mineral commodities were used for domestic construction. The principal mineral agency was the Department of Mines and Geology. Geological surveys conducted in the past had indicated the possibility of major metallic and industrial mineral deposits, but a poor infrastructure and lack of a skilled work force inhibited further development of the mineral industry.

The most important mineral resources exploited were limestone for cement, clay, garnet, magnetite, and talc. Crude magnetite production declined from a high of approximately 63,200 tons in 1986 to approximately 28,000 tons in 1989; it was projected to decline further to 25,000 tons in 1990.

In 1990 mineral production decreased significantly, largely because of political unrest. Production of cement fell approximately 51 percent over 1989—from approximately 218,000 tons to about

107,200 tons. Production of clays for cement manufacture dropped from 7,206 tons to 824 tons. Lignite production decreased 19 percent, and talc production fell 73 percent. Ornamental marble production, however, increased in 1989—by 100 percent in cut marble and 1,560 percent in marble chips.

Nonetheless, the mining industry had the potential to become a more important part of the economy, as new mines were being planned or were being developed. Two cement plants already were in operation, and a third one was being planned. It was expected that with full production in the three plants, Nepal might become self-sufficient in cement. A magnetite mine and pressuring plant east of Kathmandu had completed its construction phase and began production of chalk powder (talcum powder) on a trial basis in 1990. A high-grade lead and zinc mine was being developed north of Kathmandu in the region of Ganesh Himal and was expected to become operational in the 1990s, although raising enough capital for the project was problematic. Production of agricultural lime in 1989 doubled that of the previous year, suggesting that progress was being made towards meeting requirements of the agricultural sector.

Energy

According to government reports for 1988-89, approximately 95 percent of energy used was from traditional sources: fuelwood (76 percent), agricultural products (11 percent), and animal waste (8 percent). The remaining resources consisted of petroleum products (over 3 percent), coal (over 1 percent), and electricity (under 1 percent). Alternative sources, including steam, solar, and wind power, also were used on a very small scale.

Despite the great potential for hydroelectric power, most of the energy used by the Nepalese came from its forests (see Forests, this ch.). The terrain, lack of a transportation network, and the need for large amounts of capital investment for hydroelectric plants and electric facilities hindered the development of these sources of energy. The uneven distribution of resources, however, indicated the importance of moving away from excessive dependence on fuelwood as a source of energy. Nepal's forests were rapidly being degraded.

In the early 1980s, more than half the electric energy generated was used by households, and only one-third was used by the industrial sector. The share of electricity use by the household sector was declining in the late 1980s. In 1985 about 6 percent of the population had access to electricity, and by 1991 electricity was accessible to more than 8 percent of the population. There were

Various modes of transportation on New Road, Kathmandu
Courtesy Harvey Follender

no regional power grids, and electricity was available regularly only in the capital and a few of the larger population centers. Approximately 15 percent of the electricity was generated by diesel plants.

Some estimates indicated Nepal's hydroelectric power potential at 80 million kilowatts—2.6 percent of the world's capacity. Only a tiny fraction of this potential energy had been utilized until 1960, and by 1964 less than 3,000 kilowatts of electricity was generated by hydropower. By 1989, however, in excess of 230,000 kilowatts of electricity—more than 80 percent of the country's installed electric power—was generated by hydroelectric power. Although there were difficulties, the output of electricity had grown. For example, a 60-megawatt hydroelectric project known as Kulekhani I, funded by the World Bank, Kuwait, and Japan, became operational in 1982. Kulekhani II, an additional 32-megawatt project, was completed in 1987. Kulekhani III, in the planning stages in 1990, projected an additional 17-megawatt capacity. It was estimated that by late 1990, generating capacity would be at least 237 megawatts.

Feasibility studies and engineering designs were planned for several hydroelectric projects and rural electric facilities. Nepal and India had joint irrigation-hydroelectric projects on the Narayani (India's Gandak River), Kosi, and Trisuli rivers. A feasibility study was being conducted for a dam project to harness the hydropower potential of the Karnali River. Inasmuch as Nepal could not use as much energy as it could produce, the potential for selling excess energy to neighboring countries (especially India) existed. The expansion of electric power, however, had to be accompanied by the construction of transmission lines across the country, a project requiring considerable capital.

The Asian Development Bank committed funds to establish a national electricity grid with hydroelectric power plants on the Arun and Marsyandi rivers. The Marsyandi site, a US$325 million project with a 69-megawatt capacity, was commissioned in 1990 with major financing provided by Germany, Japan, Kuwait, Saudi Arabia, the Asian Development Bank, and the World Bank. A 404-megawatt Arun III Project was planned, but construction was not scheduled to begin until 1992, and completion was not expected until 1997.

The government also encouraged establishing biogas plants with help from the Agriculture Development Bank. More than 1,000 plants were erected in 1988 and 1989. Although these plants were small, they were capable of slowing deforestation—at least for the short term.

To meet energy needs, petroleum products were imported. In the late 1980s, more than 40 percent of Nepal's foreign exchange earnings were spent on petroleum imports—particularly during the trade and transit dispute with India. In 1988–89, the government contracted with two foreign companies to do exploratory drilling for oil and gas. A joint venture of Royal Dutch Shell and Triton Energy received a concession to explore for petroleum in southeastern Nepal, but the companies relinquished their contract in May 1990 upon drilling dry wells. Nonetheless, further analysis of the area was being carried on, and other exploration blocks were being evaluated and traded among various companies.

Transportation

The inadequacy of the transportation system assured its high priority in all development plans. Nonetheless, budget allocations for transport and communications declined by more than half from the Fifth Five-Year Plan (1975–80) to the Seventh Five-Year Plan (1985–90). Before 1960 the bulk of goods transported used human labor and animals. Although the infrastructure remained underdeveloped, since 1960 the building of paved roads has helped make the transportation of both goods and people more accessible (see fig. 9). By the early 1990s, the major modes of transportation were by road or by air; however, trails still were used to transport goods.

The 1989 trade and transit dispute with India in also affected the transportation system. There were acute shortages of coal and petroleum products as well as spare parts supplied by India. These shortages hampered the domestic transport system; the shortages in turn affected service industries and tourism.

Roads

Nepal's first paved road was built with aid from India in the early 1950s. It connected Kathmandu with Raxaul on the Indian border. As of 1991, additional roads were being built, primarily with the cooperation of India but also the United States, including an East-West Highway through southern portions of the country. Other roads, in various stages of planning, construction, or already completed, were built with assistance from Saudi Arabia, India, Britain, the Soviet Union, Switzerland, China, the United States, the World Bank, and the Asian Development Bank.

Prior to the First Five-Year Plan, Nepal had approximately 600 kilometers of roads, including fair weather roads. Although targets were rarely met on time, road construction has increased. By mid-July 1989, approximately 2,900 kilometers of paved roads, 1,600 kilometers of gravel roads, and 2,500 kilometers of earthen (fair weather) roads were in existence. Most goods and passengers

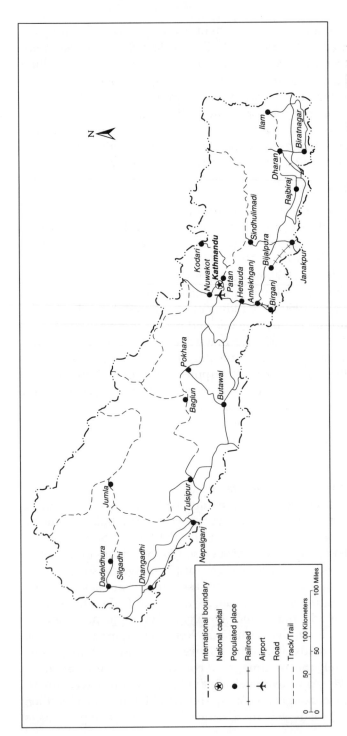

Source: Based on information from Frederick H. Gaige, *Regionalism and National Unity in Nepal*, Berkeley, 1975, 36; and Pitamber Sharma, *Urbanization in Nepal*, Honolulu, 1989, 132.

Figure 9. Nepal: Transportation System, 1991

utilized these roads, and transit no longer was exclusively through India.

The main roads consisted of east-west and north-south highways. The longest highway was the Mahendra Highway, or East-West Highway. Its total proposed length was approximately 1,050 kilometers, of which 850 kilometers were completed as of 1989. The 114-kilometer Arniko Highway, which connected Kathmandu with Kodari on the Chinese border, was constructed with Chinese assistance. The Siddhartha Highway was constructed with India's help and connected the Pokhara Valley with Sonauli in India's Uttar Pradesh state. Some of the other completed highways (*rajmarg*) running east-west were the Tribhuvan-Rajpath, Prithvi, and Kodari highways. Among north-south highways, Gorkha-Narayangadh, Kohalpur-Surkhet, Sindhuli-Bargachi, and Dhangadhi-Dadeldhura roads were mostly completed in the early 1990s. A number of north-south roads were being constructed to connect with the east-west Mahendra Highway.

Because of the terrain, building and maintaining roads were very expensive. Landslides in hilly areas during monsoon season were very common. Nepal also had several rivers and creeks running from north to south whose levels during monsoon season were difficult to predict. All these factors caused periodic slowdowns in the movement of trucks and buses. Nevertheless, as a result of road expansion, several private firms ran passenger buses and trucks to transport goods. From 1980 to 1990, the number of passenger vehicles increased by more than 100 percent. During FY 1990, new vehicle registrations included 723 buses and minibuses, 240 trucks, and 1,831 jeeps, cars, and pickup vans.

Railroads

The railroad system was used by an average of 1.5 million passengers annually from 1985 to 1989. Goods transported averaged between 15,000 and 19,000 tons annually during that same period.

Railroad service was initiated in 1928 and generally connected the commercial centers of the Tarai with Indian railheads near the southern border. The Janakpur Railway, headquartered in Jaynagar, India, was a fifty-three-kilometer narrow-gauge railroad between Jaynagar and Janakpur and Bijalpura in Nepal. As of the late 1980s, its equipment consisted of ten steam locomotives, twenty-five passenger coaches and vans, and fifty-two freight wagons. The Nepal Government Railway consisted of forty-eight kilometers linking Amlekhganj to the railhead in Raxaul, India, and was equipped with seven steam locomotives, twelve coaches, and eighty-two wagons. The opening of a north-south highway, however, made the railroad service from Raxaul to Amlekhganj somewhat obsolete. The Sixth Five-Year Plan provided for construction of a rail line between Udaipur Garhi in eastern Nepal and Calcutta.

Ropeways

Ropeways using cables to transport freight were constructed as part of an effort to provide transport facilities for the populace and to replace human and animal power as a means to traverse the difficult terrain. The first ropeway was initiated in 1922 and was extended twice.

In the early 1950s, many goods were transported to Kathmandu using ropeways. Ropeways have become less important with the development and extension of roads. Nonetheless, the forty-two-kilometer ropeway that traverses Hetauda into the Kathmandu Valley still was operational in 1991. The transport of food, construction materials, and heavy goods on that ropeway could be accomplished at the rate of twenty-two and a half tons of freight per hour. During the 1985 to 1989 period, the ropeway carried approximately 12,000 tons of freight per year.

Civil Aviation

Air transportation to Kathmandu from India started around 1950. Although the primary airport is Tribhuvan International Airport outside Kathmandu, more than thirty airfields have been added since the 1950s. The primary domestic air routes from Kathmandu in 1991 were to Jumla, Bhairahwa, Biratnagar, Nepalganj, Gorkha, and Pokhara. There also were international flights from West European cities, such as London and Frankfurt, and Asian cities, including Karachi, Paro (in Bhutan), New Delhi, Hong Kong, and Bangkok, to Kathmandu. Several airlines, including Royal Nepal Airlines (owned by the government), connected Kathmandu with cities in other parts of the world. These flights have facilitated international traffic considerably. Royal Nepal Airlines reported approximately 452,000 passengers in FY 1986, approximately 569,200 passengers in FY 1988, and approximately 608,300 passengers in FY 1990. The carrier transported almost 3,900 tons of freight in FY 1986, approximately 6,000 tons in FY 1988, and about 7,260 tons in FY 1990. The Royal Nepal Airlines fleet, which was to be increased by two Boeing 757 aircraft in 1991, was often disabled by poor maintenance and lack of spare parts and aircraft. In the absence of Nepalese operations, the Soviet Union's Aeroflot, Bhutan's Druk-Air, and Hong Kong's Dragonair began servicing Kathmandu during 1990.

Airplane at an unpaved landing strip at Lukla, en route to the Khumbu region, gateway to the Everest area
Courtesy
Janet MacDonald

Other Modes of Transportation

Local public transportation was not common except in the Kathmandu Valley. A trolley bus serviced the eastern part of the valley between Kathmandu and Bhadgaon (or Bhaktapur), carrying about 500,000 passengers annually during the late 1980s. Sajha (Cooperative Union) buses provided passenger service in Kathmandu and to other locations in the eastern and western parts of the country.

There was discussion in Kathmandu of developing a water transportation system to utilize the rivers passing through Nepal. The combined length of rivers was about 3,500 kilometers (see The River System, ch. 2). The government pursued feasibility studies with the help of consultants, mostly foreign; however, studies conducted as of 1991 were not encouraging.

Communications

Postal services have been in existence, although extremely slow and with limited service, since the Shah and Rana periods. With the advancement in transportation systems, however, postal service also had improved. In FY 1985, there were 1,868 post offices. By FY 1990, the number of post offices had increased to 2,232, but even the government admitted that access to postal service for many Nepalese still was far from satisfactory.

137

Public telephone services also became available during Rana rule, but service was limited. Beginning in the early 1950s, a few hundred telephones were installed, mostly for government offices and military officers' homes. As of 1989, the number of private telephones had increased to over 45,000, and most of the urban areas had telephone service. In 1986 there were twenty-six telephone exchanges; by 1990 there were forty-two such exchanges. The number of public call offices during this same period increased from twenty-one to seventy-six. International telephone and telex services were available, as were facsimile (fax) services. There was also a rudimentary radio relay network with fifty-eight channels nationwide in 1989. In addition, there were fifty-five point-to-point shortwave stations for telephone transmission in 1990.

Radio Nepal, transmitting by shortwave, has been in existence since the early 1950s. In 1991 Nepal had six AM broadcast stations. Radio was a good source of news and entertainment for many Nepalese; Radio Nepal, for example, provided about 100 hours of programming every week. Estimates of the total number of radio sets ranged from 600,000 to 2 million in 1989.

In late 1985, television programming began on a small scale in Kathmandu. In 1991 total programming was only three hours daily, with an additional two hours on Saturday mornings. The single station, Nepal Television had a transmitter outside Kathmandu and transmitting stations in Pokhara, Biratnagar, and Hetauda. The programs of foreign television organizations, such as the Cable News Network, also could be received by a satellite dish in Nepal. There were approximately 200,000 television sets in 1991, and in some areas the government provided television sets for community viewing.

Tourism

Tourism was a major source of foreign exchange earnings. Especially since Mount Everest (Sagarmatha in Nepali) was first climbed by Sir Edmund Hillary and Tensing Sherpa in 1953, the Himalayas have attracted foreigners to Nepal. Mountaineering and hiking were of considerable interest as were rafting, canoeing, and hang gliding. Tourism was facilitated with the opening of airways to Kathmandu and other parts of the country and the easing of travel restrictions.

In the 1950s, there was a shortage of hotels. Beginning in the 1960s, the government encouraged the building of hotels and other tourist facilities through loans. According to government statistics, between 1985 and 1988 the number of hotel rooms increased from under 22,000 to more than 27,000.

Porters at a rest stop along the route to Sedua
Courtesy Linda Galantin

Prior to the trade impasse with India that began in March 1989, tourism had grown by more than 10 percent per year for most of the 1980s. Between 1985 and 1988, the number of tourists increased from approximately 181,000 to about 266,000. More than 80 percent of the tourists arrived in the country by air.

In FY 1985, more than US$40 million worth of foreign exchange was earned through tourism. By FY 1988, this amount had increased to more than US$64 million. In FY 1989, tourism accounted for more than 3.5 percent of GDP and about 25 percent of total foreign exchange earnings. The 1989 trade and transit impasse with India negatively affected tourism because the transport and service sectors of the economy lacked supplies. Beginning in FY 1990, however, Kathmandu initiated a policy to allocate fuel on a priority basis to tour operators and hotels.

Problems and Prospects

Nepal was a resource poor country. Although it had made some progress since the 1950s, it still was well behind most countries in the world as of 1991. Among the issues it needed to address were changes in economic policy, international debt, low labor productivity, income distribution, and population growth.

In the economic policy area, the performance of public enterprises needed improvement. Most of the country's large-scale firms were in the public sector, and many of these enterprises either were protected or subsidized, which inhibited their efficiency. Most public enterprises also lacked a sound financial footing. More than fifty public enterprises dominated major sectors of the economy. These enterprises included energy, basic utilities, oil, telecommunications, water supply, cement, jute, tobacco, and sugar. Some of these enterprises, for example, the Agricultural Inputs Corporation and the Nepal Food Corporation, incurred losses year after year.

Foreign indebtedness was also problematic. Compared with many less-developed countries, Nepal's foreign debts were not very high. However, these debts were increasing. At the end of the 1980s, the value of merchandise imports was more than three times that of merchandise exports, a situation that could create future problems in the balance of payments. Many analysts believed that domestic borrowing for development expenditures would better serve development.

Labor productivity needed to increase to improve the well-being of the people. Nepal suffered, however, from technology deficits, as well as from shortfalls in its literacy rate, basic science education, and technical training. Although there had been some progress in raising the literacy rate, properly trained technicians remained in short supply.

Income distribution data on a large scale were not available. Nonetheless, some sample studies had been done. In 1990 Dr. B.P. Shreshtha found that 75 percent of the families accounted for less than 35 percent of income. A 1983 study by Blaikie et al. noted that more than 50 percent of the family landholdings in the Hill Region amounted to less than half a hectare. Only in the western Tarai Region were landholdings generally much bigger. In a country where 90 percent of the population was largely dependent on agriculture, few families had landholdings exceeding four hectares, largely because of the shortage of land.

The need for greater agricultural and labor productivity, as well as employment opportunities, to offset the demands of a growing populace was paramount. Of equal importance, however, were increased efforts at controlling population growth. With an annual population growth rate of 2.6 percent, per capita resources were reduced—another obstacle to further economic development.

*　　*　　*

For general background material on the state of the economy

prior to 1970, Yadav Prasad Pant's *Problems in Fiscal and Monetary Policy,* Rishikesh Shaha's *Nepali Politics,* and Badri Prasad Shreshtha's *The Economy of Nepal* provide useful information. Pierce M. Blaikie et al.'s *Nepal in Crisis* details the status of the economy in the 1970s, although it focuses on the western and central parts of the country. Mahesh Chandra Regmi's books on Nepal's economic history are valuable for their perspective and insight into continuing problems. For more recent assessments of the economy, Badri Prasad Shreshtha's *Nepalese Economy in Retrospect and Prospect,* Babu Ram Shrestha's *Managing External Assistance in Nepal,* and the Far Eastern Economic Review's annual *Asia Yearbook* are helpful. Shrestha's book also details the extent of foreign assistance in Nepal and provides some data on expenditures in some of the development plans. *Economic Survey, 1987–88* and *Economic Survey, 1989–90,* published by Nepal's Ministry of Finance, and *Statistical Pocketbook, 1988* and *Statistical Pocketbook, 1990,* published by Nepal's Central Bureau of Statistics, provide the most current statistical data.

Yadav Prasad Pant and Badri Prasad Shreshtha, professional economists from Nepal, have held several posts in the government and have also written extensively about Nepal's economy. Although the aforementioned texts by Shreshtha and Pant's *Problems in Fiscal and Monetary Policy* are difficult to obtain in the United States, they provide useful information. (For further information and complete citations, see Bibliography.)

Chapter 4. Nepal: Government and Politics

Jang Bahadur Rana, founder of the Rana line of prime ministers, who reigned from 1846 to 1877

THE DRAMATIC EVENTS of the beginning months of 1990 marked a watershed in Nepal's political system. The quest for a multiparty, representative form of government had begun on December 15, 1960, when an unprecedented royal coup d'état dismissed the constitutionally elected government of Bishweshwar Prasad (B.P.) Koirala. King Mahendra Bir Bikram Shah Dev abrogated the constitution and suspended all guarantees of fundamental rights and political activities. The traditional partyless *panchayat* (see Glossary) system of local and national assemblies imposed by fiat was found unsatisfactory in the face of the Nepalese desire to secure legitimate political and human rights and establish accountability in government.

Monarchical opposition toward political parties or groups had been so vigorous that the centrist Nepali Congress Party, the oldest political party, carried on its activities from exile in India. Other political parties, including the splintered leftist groups, either operated from abroad or were disbanded. Although political parties were banned and at times their leaders were incarcerated or forced to go underground, they remained a vital force in sensitizing and mobilizing public opinion against government authoritarianism.

The Movement for the Restoration of Democracy (MRD), popularly known as the prodemocracy movement, finally succeeded in early 1990 in restoring democratic rights denied for decades by the powerful palace clique. In April 1990, tens of thousands of Nepalese marched on the royal palace in Kathmandu, demonstrating against King Birendra Bir Bikram Shah Dev, who was traditionally revered as an incarnation of the Hindu god Vishnu. Police and troops shot and killed many of the marchers. As shock waves reverberated through Nepal, long an oasis of civil order in South Asia, the king quickly scrapped the *panchayat* system, lifted the ban on political parties, and formed an interim government from among the ranks of the veteran opposition leaders under the premiership of Nepali Congress leader Krishna Prasad (K.P.) Bhattarai.

The interim government, which represented the spectrum of public opinion, was directed to conduct fair and free elections within a stipulated period under a new constitution framed by an independent constitutional commission appointed by the Council of Ministers—the Constitution Recommendation Commission. Although the constitution was proclaimed from the throne, its development, unlike past constitutional edicts, was through a democratic process

145

in which the interim Council of Ministers served as a legislature. Nepal's human rights records—poor before the success of the prodemocracy movement—also improved.

During the prodemocracy movement, a range of political parties acted in concert and rapidly commanded the loyalty and imagination of the overwhelming majority of the urban population. This unprecedented expression of national unity and the government's subsequent attempts to suppress the movement triggered the reactions of major and regional world powers including the United States, Japan, and India, and international financial institutions, such as the World Bank (see Glossary) and Asian Development Bank (see Glossary). Their timely expressions of concern and threats to reevaluate their commitments of economic and technical assistance both bolstered the movement and served as a damper against the monarchy's continued use of excessive force to contain it.

Strategically wedged between China and India, Nepal has always been fearful of foreign intervention and has tried to maintain equal distance from these two powerful neighbors in a continuing effort to protect its sovereignty. Nepal's choice not to align with any superpower facilitated grants of economic assistance from diverse sources, including the United States, the Soviet Union, India, China, and Japan. Nepal maintained a high profile in various international organizations and activities and was a charter member of the South Asian Association for Regional Cooperation (SAARC—see Glossary).

Although the vast majority of the Nepalese population was illiterate, Nepal's printed media have been influential as well as strident. Before the introduction of the 1990 constitution, which guarantees freedom of expression, several stringent publication and censorship laws limited freedom of expression.

Constitutional Development

The Rana System

Beginning in 1856, the center of power in Nepal rested with the Rana prime ministers, who retained sovereign power until the revolution of 1950–51 (see The Rana Oligarchy, ch. 1). Many of the nobles who participated in the consultative court called the Assembly of Lords, or Bharadari Sabha, had been slaughtered at the Kot Massacre in 1846. Following his official visit to Britain and Europe in 1851, Jang Bahadur Kunwar (later called Jang Bahadur Rana) began to use the Bharadari Sabha as deliberative body for state affairs. For almost 100 years, this council served as a rubber stamp for the Rana autocracy. The next major effort at institutional development was initiated in 1947 by Padma Shamsher Rana, a liberal prime minister, who appointed a Constitutional Reform Committee to draft the first constitution. Known as the Government of Nepal Constitution Act, 1948, this constitution, written with the help of Indian advisers, superficially changed the Rana system. It established a bicameral legislative body. The entire membership of one house and a majority of the other was selected by the prime minister, who could reject any measure that the legislature might pass. There was a cabinet of at least five members, of whom at least two were chosen from among the few elected members of the legislature.

The act also specified that a *panchayat* system of local self-government would be inaugurated in the villages, towns, and districts. It enumerated certain fundamental rights and duties, which included freedoms of speech, the press, assembly, and worship; equality before the law; free elementary education for all; and equal and universal suffrage. Despite the appearance of reform, the alterations made in the Rana system by the constitution were slight. The more conservative Ranas perceived the constitution as a dangerous precedent, forced Padma Shamsher to resign, and suspended promulgation of the constitution. The constitution became effective in September 1950 but remained in force only until February 1951, when the Rana monopoly was broken and the creation of a new constitutional system began.

The Interim Constitution, 1951

The revolution of 1950–51 resulted in the overthrow of the Rana system (see The Growth of Political Parties; The Return of the King, ch. 1). In 1951 King Tribhuvan Bir Bikram Shah announced by royal proclamation an interim government and an interim constitution until a new Constituent Assembly could be elected. The interim constitution, based on principles in India's constitution and entitled the Interim Government of Nepal Act, 1951, ratified the end of the authority of the prime minister and the system surrounding that office. It also reasserted the king's supreme executive, legislative, and judicial powers. The king exercised his executive authority through, and was aided and advised by, a Council of Ministers, which he appointed and which served at his pleasure.

The king also appointed an Advising Assembly to sit until the Constituent Assembly was elected. The king retained sovereign and plenary legislative powers. The Advising Assembly was, with certain exceptions, authorized only to discuss matters and to recommend

147

measures to the king for enactment into law. The final authority to approve any legislative measure lay with the king. The constitution also established a Supreme Court, made the king supreme commander of the armed forces, reiterated and enlarged upon the fundamental rights included in the Rana constitution, and proclaimed numerous social and economic objectives of the government. These objectives were to promote the welfare of the people by securing a social order in which social, economic, and political justice pervaded all the institutions of national life. King Mahendra (reigned 1955–72) vigorously sought to broaden the monarch's political base, but the Nepali National Congress succeeded in gaining some democratic reforms. Although the constitution was expected to be temporary pending the election of a Constituent Assembly and the preparation of a permanent organic law, King Mahendra was unable to resist the increasingly well-orchestrated political demands by the Nepali National Congress for a more democratic and representative government, and was forced to promulgate a new constitution.

The Royal Constitution of 1959

The most significant aspect of the constitution of 1959 was that it was granted by the king rather than drawn up by elected representatives of the people as had been specified in the 1951 constitution. Although the constitution formally brought into being a democratically elected parliamentary system under a constitutional monarchy, the king retained ultimate sovereignty, even though the document itself did not explicitly grant this power.

The 1959 constitution, modeled on British and Indian constitutional custom, vested executive power in the king, who was advised and assisted by a Council of State (Raj Sabha) and a Council of Ministers (cabinet). The Council of State, which consisted of officers of Parliament, ministers ex officio, former ministers, and royal appointees, advised the monarch on legislation and handled the details of regency and succession in the event of his death or disability. The general direction and control of the government were entrusted to the Council of Ministers, headed by a prime minister required to command a majority in the lower house of Parliament, to which the council was collectively responsible.

The king was an integral part of the legislative arm of the government. Parliament was defined as consisting of the king; the House of Representatives, composed of 109 popularly elected members; and the Senate, composed of 36 members of whom half were elected by the house and half were nominated by the king. All bills approved by the two houses required the assent of the king to become law. The constitution granted the king wide latitude to nullify the parliamentary system. The king could suspend the operation of the cabinet and perform its functions himself if he determined that no person could command a majority in the house as prime minister. In the event of a breakdown of the parliamentary system or of any one of a number of emergency conditions, the king could suspend either or both houses of Parliament, assume their powers, and suspend the constitution in whole or part. In December 1960, King Mahendra invoked these emergency powers to dissolve the Nepali Congress Party government. The constitutional system that had prevailed before 1959 was then returned to operation (see The Democratic Experiment, ch. 1).

The Panchayat Constitution, 1962

By royal proclamation on December 16, 1962, King Mahendra announced a new constitution that radically reformed the 1959 constitution but also adopted many features of the Rana system (see The Panchayat System under King Mahehdra, ch. 1; The Administrative System, this ch.). Known as the Panchayat Constitution, it was the fourth constitution in fifteen years.

The *panchayat* system was an institution of great antiquity. Historically, each caste group system of Nepal formed its own *panchayat,* or council of elders, a sociopolitical organization operational on a village level that could expand to include neighboring districts, or even function on a zonal basis. Although it could be argued that the *panchayat* system was adopted from India, King Mahendra had argued for its incorporation at the national level as an exponent of Nepalese culture—a worthy and historically correct representation of cultural expression.

The 1962 constitution was based on some elements from other "guided democracy" constitutional experiments—notably "Basic Democracy" in Pakistan, "Guided Democracy" in Indonesia, and the "Dominant Party System" in Egypt. The Panchayat Constitution not only codified the irrelevance of political parties, but also declared them illegal.

The 1962 constitution contained a stronger and more explicit statement of royal authority than did previous constitutions. Real power remained with the king, who was the sole source of authority and had the power not only to amend the constitution but also to suspend it by royal proclamation during emergencies. The Council of Ministers, selected from the members of the legislative (Rashtriya Panchayat, or National Panchayat), served as an advisory body to the king. Members of the Rashtriya Panchayat were elected indirectly by the members of local *panchayat* as well as by the members of professional and class organizations such as the Nepal Workers' Organization, the Nepal Ex-servicemen's Organization, and the Nepal Youth Organization. The constitution abolished all political parties.

Constitutional Amendments

The Panchayat Constitution was amended several times, primarily to increase the power and prerogatives of the monarchy against the increasing popular demand for liberalization of the political institutions and processes. In view of the mounting criticism against the Panchayat Constitution, King Birendra, who had succeeded his father in 1972, pursuant to recommendations of a specially created Constitutional Reform Commission, announced in 1975 that the constitution would be amended to include provisions governing the amending procedure itself. Previously the king could not amend the constitution unless two-thirds of the Rashtriya Panchayat ratified the proposed amendment. Under the proposed amendment, the king would have to consult a special committee of the Rastriya Panchayat before amending the constitution. In addition, the term of a delegate to the Rashtriya Panchayat was reduced from six years to four years.

The Referendum of 1980

In May 1979, concerned by the unabated political demonstrations and considerable general unrest, King Birendra called for a nationwide referendum to determine the future form of government. The referendum offered two choices: a continuation of the partyless *panchayat* system, with prospects for further reform; or a multiparty system. Although no clear definition of a multiparty system was provided, the implication was that it stood for a parliamentary system of government run on a party basis. The referendum, the first nationwide vote in twenty-two years, was held on May 2, 1980, and 67 percent of the eligible voters participated. The *panchayat* system was chosen with a majority of 54.7 percent of the votes. On May 21, 1980, the king appointed an eleven-member Constitution Reforms Commission to be chaired by the acting chief justice of the Supreme Court (see The Judiciary, this ch.). On December 15, the king promulgated three constitutional amendments: direct elections to the Rashtriya Panchayat would be held every five years for 112 seats, with 28 additional seats filled by the king's personal nomination; the prime minister would be elected by the Rashtriya Panchayat; the cabinet would be appointed by the king on the recommendation of the prime minister and would be accountable to the Rashtriya Panchayat; and Nepal would

King Birendra
Bir Bikram Shah Dev

Queen Aishwarya Rajya
Laxmi Devi Rana
Courtesy
Royal Nepalese Embassy

151

commit to the Nonaligned Movement as a zone of peace. These provisions, with a few minor modifications, remained in operation until early 1990, when the prodemocracy movement successfully agitated for a multiparty democratic system.

The Constitution of 1990

Widespread prodemocracy protests toppled the *panchayat* system in April 1990. The king appointed an independent Constitution Recommendation Commission to represent the main opposition factions and to prepare a new constitution to accommodate their demands for political reform. On September 10, 1990, the commission presented King Birendra with the draft of a new constitution, which would preserve the king's status as chief of state under a constitutional monarchy but establish a multiparty democracy with separation of powers and human rights. As agreed upon earlier, the king turned the draft constitution over to Prime Minister K.P. Bhattarai and his cabinet for review and recommendations. The draft was discussed extensively and approved by the interim cabinet. A major obstacle to approval was avoided when the commission removed a disputed provision under which both the constitutional monarchy and multiparty system could have been eliminated by a three-quarters majority vote of Parliament.

On November 9, 1990, King Birendra promulgated the new constitution and abrogated the constitution of 1962. The 1990 constitution ended almost thirty years of absolute monarchy in which the palace had dominated every aspect of political life and political parties were banned.

The constitution, broadly based on British practice, is the fundamental law of Nepal. It vests sovereignty in the people and declares Nepal a multiethnic, multilingual, democratic, independent, indivisible, sovereign, and constitutional monarchical kingdom. The national and official language of Nepal is Nepali in the Devanagari script. All other languages spoken as the mother tongue in the various parts of Nepal are recognized as languages of the nation (see Caste and Ethnicity, ch. 2). Although Nepal still is officially regarded as a Hindu kingdom, the constitution also gives religious and cultural freedom to other religious groups, such as Buddhists, Muslims, and Christians. The preamble of the constitution recognizes the desire of the Nepalese people to bring about constitutional changes with the objective of obtaining social, political, and economic justice. It envisages the guarantee of basic human rights to every citizen, a parliamentary system of government, and a multiparty democracy. It also aims to establish an independent and competent system of justice with a view to transforming the concept of the rule of law into reality.

Other safeguards include the right to property; the right to conserve and promote one's language, script, and culture; the right to education in the student's mother tongue; freedom of religion; and the right to manage and protect religious places and trusts. Traffic in human slavery, serfdom, forced labor, or child labor in any form is prohibited. The right to receive information about matters of public importance and the right to secrecy and inviolability of one's person, residence, property, documents, letters, and other information also are guaranteed.

Part three of the constitution provides for the fundamental rights of citizens. Although some elements of fundamental rights guaranteed in the 1962 constitution are reflected in the 1990 constitution, the latter provides new safeguards in unequivocal language and does not encumber the fundamental rights with duties or restrictions purported to uphold public good. All citizens are equal before the law, and no discrimination can be made on the basis of religion, race, sex, caste, tribe, or ideology. No person shall, on the basis of caste, be discriminated against as an untouchable, be denied access to any public place, or be deprived from the use of public utilities. No discrimination will be allowed in regard to remuneration for men and women for the same work. No citizen can be exiled or be deprived of liberty except in accordance with the law; and capital punishment is disallowed.

In addition, sections on fundamental rights provide for freedom of thought and expression; freedom to assemble peacefully and without arms; freedom to form unions and associations; freedom to move and reside in any part of Nepal; and freedom to carry out any profession, occupation, trade, or industry. Similarly, prior censorship of publications is prohibited, and free press and printing are guaranteed. Unfettered cultural and educational rights also are guaranteed. Articles 23 and 88 provide for a citizen's right to constitutional remedy. Any citizen can petition the Supreme Court to declare any law or part thereof as void if it infringes on the fundamental rights conferred by the constitution.

Rights regarding criminal justice include the guarantee that no person will be punished for an act unpunishable by law or subjected to a punishment greater than that prescribed by the laws in existence at the time of commission of the offense; no person will be prosecuted more than once in any offense; and no one will be compelled to bear witness against himself or herself (see The Judicial System, ch. 5). Inflicting cruelty on a person in detention is prohibited, as is detaining a person without giving information about the grounds for such detention. Further, the person in detention must be produced within twenty-four hours of such arrest before the judicial authorities. Any person wrongly detained will be compensated.

The constitution lays down various directives in matters of political, economic, and social development, and foreign policy. These lofty policies are guidelines to promote conditions of welfare on the basis of the principles of an open society. One objective is to transform the national economy into an independent and self-reliant system by making arrangements for the equitable distribution of the economic gains on the basis of social justice. The constitution stresses the creation of conditions for the enjoyment of the fruits of democracy through the maximum participation of the people in governance of the country. Other aims include the pursuit of a policy in international relations that will enhance the dignity of the nation and ensure sovereignty, integrity, and national independence and the protection of the environment from further ecological damage.

Other Features of the Constitution

The constitution guarantees the citizens' unfettered rights to political pluralism and a multiparty democracy. All legitimate political organizations or parties that register with the Election Commission are allowed to publicize and broadcast for the purpose of securing support and cooperation of the general public toward their objectives and programs. Any law, arrangement, or decision that restricts any of these activities is inconsistent with the constitution and void. Any law, arrangement, or decision to impose a one-party system is also inconsistent with the constitution and void. Under the section on political organization, any political party is not eligible for registration if it discriminates, if at least 5 percent of its candidates are not women, or if it fails to obtain at least 3 percent of the total votes cast in the previous election to the House of Representatives.

The constitution may be amended or repealed by a majority of two-thirds in each house of Parliament. However, such amendment or repeals may not be designed to frustrate the spirit of the preamble of the constitution, which recognizes the Nepalese people as the source of sovereign authority. After passage in both houses, any bill to repeal or amend the constitution must receive royal assent.

The Executive

Executive powers are vested in the king and the Council of Ministers—a prime minister, deputy prime minister, and other ministers as required. The direction, supervision, and conduct of the general administration of the country are the responsibility of the Council of Ministers. All transactions made in the name of the king, except those within his exclusive domain, are authenticated by the Council of Ministers (see fig. 10).

The king appoints the leader of the political party commanding a majority in the House of Representatives as prime minister. If a single party does not have a majority in the house, the member commanding a majority on the basis of two or more parties is asked to form the government. When this alternative also is not possible, the king may ask the leader of a party holding the largest number of seats in the house to form the government. In this case, the leader forming the government must obtain a vote of confidence in the house within thirty days. If a vote of no confidence is obtained, the king will dissolve the house and order new elections within six months. Other ministers are appointed by the king from members of Parliament on the recommendation of the prime minister.

The constitution declares the king the symbol of the nation and the unity of its people. Expenditures and privileges of the king and royal family are determined by law. The king is obliged to obey and protect the constitution. Although, as in previous constitutions the monarch remains the supreme commander of the Royal Nepal Army, a three-member National Defence Council, headed by the prime minister, commands the military (see Legal Basis Under the 1990 Constitution, ch. 5). Nonetheless, the king retains his power over the army because if there were a threat to sovereignty, indivisibility, or security because of war, foreign aggression, armed revolt, or extreme economic depression, he could declare a state of emergency. During the period of emergency—which would have to be approved by the House of Representatives within three months and which would remain in effect for six months from the date of its announcement, renewable for six months—fundamental rights, with the exception of the right of habeas corpus, could be suspended. Additional prerogatives of the king include the power to grant pardons; suspend, commute, or remit any sentence passed by any court; confer titles, honors, or decorations of the kingdom; appoint all ambassadors and emissaries for the kingdom; and remove any barriers to enforcing the constitution. The king also nominates the members of the Raj Parishad (King's Council), the body that determines the accession to the throne of the heir apparent.

The Legislature

The constitution provides for a bicameral legislature, the Parliament. This body consists of the king and two houses, the House

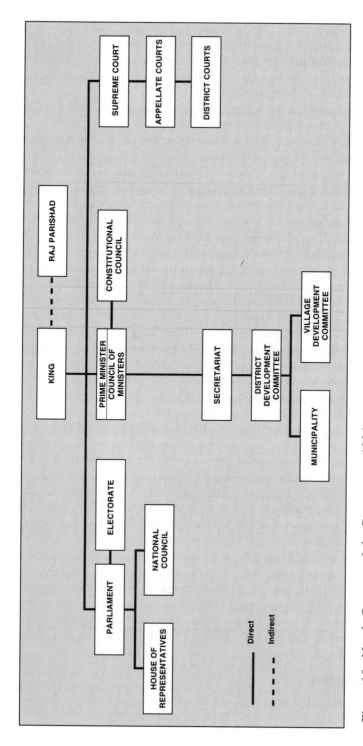

Figure 10. Nepal: Structure of the Government, 1991

of Representatives (Pratinidhi Sabha) and the National Council (Rashtriya Sabha). The House of Representatives has 205 directly elected members. The term for the House of Representatives is five years unless it dissolves earlier, pursuant to the provisions of the constitution. On the recommendation of the prime minister, the king may dissolve the house, but new elections must be held within six months. Administrative districts are the election districts; and each district's allocation of seats is proportional to its population. All persons eighteen years or older are enfranchised.

The National Council has sixty members consisting of ten nominees of the king; thirty-five members, including at least three women, to be elected by the House of Representatives by means of a single transferable vote, pursuant to the system of proportional representation; and fifteen members to be elected by the electoral college comprising the voters, including the chair and deputy chair of the village and town and district committees of various development regions. The National Council is a permanent body; one-third of its members must retire every two years. Council members serve six-year terms.

With the exception of finance bills, introduced only in the House of Representatives, bills may be introduced in either house. All bills, however, must be passed by both houses before receiving royal assent. When a bill is rejected by the National Council, the House of Representatives has the overriding authority. If the joint session of Parliament receives and passes a bill that the king returned for reconsideration, it receives royal assent within thirty days. The king may, when both the Houses of Parliament are not in session, promulgate ordinances, which are not effective unless approved by both the houses when reconvened. Financial procedures are outlined in part ten of the constitution, which states that taxes cannot be levied or loans raised except in accordance with the law.

The Judiciary

An independent judiciary, unencumbered by the executive branch of the government and palace interference, was a stated goal of all political parties. Of the many changes which have taken place since the fall of the Ranas in 1951, among the most striking have been the growing autonomy of the courts and the gradual liberalization of many basic judicial principles. Despite major improvements, however, the judicial system has suffered from serious impediments in providing speedy, expeditious, and equal justice. The independence and integrity of the judiciary were repeatedly questioned in the press; intervention of political figures and government officials in the judicial process was a frequent occurrence;

157

and caste and economic status were important determinants of the availability of justice.

The court system formerly was one of many instruments used by the prime minister to maintain the authoritarian rule of the Rana family, and the concepts of law it applied were arbitrary, punitive, and oppressive. After an initial attempt to keep the judiciary subordinate when the monarchy was restored, it was allowed to become a relatively independent branch of government. Reforms in the legal system rendered both substantive and procedural law progressively more systematic.

Never clearly demarcated, the jurisdiction of the courts became further complicated with the introduction of the *panchayat* system, which at the local level exercised some quasijudicial functions. Therefore, the fundamental role of the judiciary and its position within the government became a subject of national focus during the prodemocracy movement.

According to the constitution, the courts comprise three tiers: the Supreme Court, appellate courts, and district courts. In addition, courts or tribunals may be constituted for the purpose of hearing special types of cases (see The Police System, ch. 5).

The Supreme Court is the highest court. All other courts and institutions exercising judicial powers, except the military courts, are under its jurisdiction. The Supreme Court has the authority to inspect, supervise, and give directives to all subordinate courts and all other institutions that exercise judicial powers. The Supreme Court has both original and appellate jurisdiction and consists of a chief justice and fourteen other judges.

The chief justice is appointed on the recommendation of the Constitutional Council. Other judges of the Supreme Court, appellate courts, and district courts are appointed on the recommendation of the Judicial Council. All appointments are made by the king. The tenure of office of the chief justice is limited to seven years from the date of appointment. Supreme Court justices can be impeached in the House of Representatives for reasons of incapacity, misbehavior, or malafide acts while in office. The Judicial Council, presided over by the chief justice of the Supreme Court, makes recommendations and advises on appointments, transfers, and disciplinary actions of the judges and other matters relating to judicial administration.

All appointments, promotions, transfers, and disciplinary actions of the judges of the appellate and district courts are under the jurisdiction of the Judicial Council. An independent Judicial Service Commission, appointed by the king, and with the chief justice of the Supreme Court serving as ex-officio chairman, appoints, transfers, promotes, and provides departmental punishment of the gazetted officers of the civil service.

An Abuse of Authority Investigating Commission is empowered to investigate the misuse of authority or corruption by public officials. Members of the commission have no specific party affiliation and are appointed by the king on the recommendation of the Constitutional Council.

The Supreme Court is the supreme judicial authority of the nation. All orders and decisions made by the court are binding. Any interpretation of a law or any legal principle laid down by the court is binding on all, including the king.

As a guarantor of personal liberty and fundamental rights conferred by the constitution, the Supreme Court has the authority to declare a law as void ab initio if it finds that the impugned law contravenes the provisions of the constitution. The Supreme Court also has the power to issue appropriate orders and writs, including habeas corpus, mandamus, certiorari, prohibition, and quo warranto.

The Civil Service

The Nepal Civil Service Act, passed in 1956, classified all civil employees of the government into two categories—gazetted services and nongazetted services. Gazetted services included all services prescribed by the government by notification in the *Nepal Raj Patra,* the government gazette. In 1991 categories of the gazetted services were education, judicial, health, administrative, engineering, forest, agricultural, and miscellaneous services. The gazetted posts were further grouped into classes I, II, and III. Nongazetted posts also had several class echelons. As of 1990, there were approximately 80,000 civil service employees in all ranks.

According to the 1990 constitution, all members of the civil service are recruited through an open competitive examination conducted by the Public Service Commission. Police and military officers are excluded from the jurisdiction of the commission. The chairman and other members of the commission are appointed by the king on the recommendation of the Constitutional Council. The commission must be consulted in all matters concerning laws relating to the civil service—such as appointment, promotion, transfer, or departmental punishment. Tenure, benefits, and postings were regulated by the Nepal Civil Service Act of 1956.

The Administrative System

The *panchayat* system represented "democracy at the grassroots," and until April 1990 it included four integrated levels: local or village, district, zonal, and national—the Rashtriya Panchayat. Only the village *panchayat* was directly elected by the people. Championing *panchayat* rule as a political system, King Mahendra was able to tap into nascent Nepalese nationalism and also to outmaneuver the evolving political parties which had posed a challenge to the monarchy's vested power.

The country was divided into fourteen zones and seventy-five districts in support of the complex hierarchy of the *panchayat* system. The lowest unit of government was the *gaun panchayat* (village committee or council), of which there were 3,524. A locality with a population of more than 10,000 persons was organized as a *nagar panchayat* (town committee or council). The number of *nagar panchayat* varied from zone to zone. Above the *gaun panchayat* and *nagar panchayat* was the district *panchayat,* of which there were seventy-five. At the apex of the *panchayat* system was the Rashtriya Panchayat, which served as the unicameral national legislature from 1962 until 1990.

The district *panchayat* had broad powers for supervising and coordinating the development programs of the village and carried out development projects through the district development boards and centers. Each of the seventy-five districts was headed by a chief district officer, who was an elected official, responsible for maintaining law and order, and for coordinating the work of the field agencies of the various ministries.

The zonal *panchayat* was responsible for implementing development plans forwarded by the central government, formulating and executing programs of its own, and planning, supervising, and coordinating district development programs within its jurisdiction. Zonal commissioners exercised full administrative and quasijudicial powers. Each zone was administered by a zonal commissioner and one or two assistant zonal commissioners, all directly appointed by the king. Zones and districts were further regrouped into five development zones in 1971–72, an administrative division that remained in effect in 1991.

A drive for political liberalization, which had begun shortly after the 1959 constitution was abrogated and all political activities were banned in 1960, did not climax until the prodemocracy movement of 1990. At that point, ongoing debilitating interparty conflicts and halting demands for reforms of the political system ended, and national energy focused on a movement to achieve democratic rights. During the prodemocracy movement, some of the *pancha* (*panchayat* members) loyalists even were openly friendly with their former adversaries.

Royal palace, Kathmandu
Courtesy Janet MacDonald

The interim government that was installed in April 1990 consisted of strange bedfellows, who, however, succeeded in steering the nation to its first free and fair elections in thirty-two years. In April 1990, the *nagar panchayat* was renamed *nagar polika* (municipal development committee), and the *gaun panchayat* became *gaun bikas samiti,* or village development committee. The Ministry of Local Development posted an officer to each district to help with the various programs of the development committees. In mid-1991, a Nepali Congress Party government was in power, and a conglomerate of communist parties was playing the role of constitutional opposition. At that time, there were 4,015 village development committees and thirty-three municipal development committees. Elections for the heads of the development committees were scheduled for June 1992.

Political Dynamics

The Panchayat System

For centuries the government had been run by a number of interrelated aristocratic families. Despite the limitations of a royal ban on political parties and other impediments, political parties did exist and operated clandestinely. To escape harassment or

161

imprisonment, many political leaders went to India, where they also received logistical and other support.

Under the *panchayat* system, there were six government-sponsored class and professional organizations for peasants, laborers, students, women, former military personnel, and college graduates. These organizations were substitutes for the prohibited political parties and provided alternate channels for the articulation of group or class—rather than national—interests. The professional and class organizations were warned repeatedly against engaging in political activity; nevertheless, they offered the only political forum open to many Nepalese, and even some Nepali Congress Party and communist partisans considered them worthy of infiltration.

The king also launched an independent national student association, the National Independent Student Council (Rashtriya Swatantra Vidyarthi Parishad), to control the political activities of the students. The association failed to gain support, and successful student agitation in 1979 forced the king not only to abolish it but also to initiate constitutional reforms leading to the national referendum of 1980. Also in 1980, a group of dissident *pancha* brought a no-confidence motion against Prime Minister Surya Bahadur Thapa on charges of bureaucratic corruption, food shortages, and lack of economic discipline. Surya Bahadur, however, was a perennial political survivor and was returned to office in 1981.

King Birendra devised the Back-to-the-Village National Campaign (BVNC) in 1975. The BVNC was intended to circumvent the possibility of opposition within the *panchayat* and to create a loyal core of elites to select and endorse candidates for political office, thereby neutralizing the influence of underground political party organizers in the rural areas. Although it was envisioned as a means to mobilize the people for the implementation of development plans and projects, the shortlived BVNC—it was suspended in 1979—was in reality an ideological campaign to reinforce the importance of the partyless system. The campaign stressed that the partyless system was appropriate to the ways of the Nepalese people; the party system was a divisive and culturally alien institution.

Each zonal committee had a BVNC structure, with a secretary nominated by the king. The BVNC network was extended to the district and village levels so as to reinforce a national communication system. However inasmuch as the government paid the BVNC central and zonal committee members and restricted chances for popular participation, the committees carried out the same activities as the *panchayat*. In actuality, the BVNC was created by the king to ensure a loyal organization and circumvent active party members from gaining seats in the *panchayat* elections. The BVNC became an organization of centrally controlled loyal *panchayat* elites and an insurance policy for palace initiatives.

The only significant opposition to the monarchy came from the Nepali Congress Party, which operated from exile in India. Other parties either accepted and operated within the *panchayat* system on a supposedly nonpartisan basis or merged with the exiled Nepali Congress Party, polarizing politics over the issue of monarchical rule. Even the Communist Party of Nepal, divided on the tactical question of whether to seek the direct and immediate overthrow of the monarchical system or to work within it, had split into factions—a radical wing operated in India and a moderate wing underground in Nepal. Some party members, to gain tactical advantage over the Nepali Congress Party, entered the *panchayat* system with the tacit approval of the palace.

Ethnic plurality, income disparity, linguistic diversity, pervading regional loyalties, underdeveloped communications, and a paucity of written and electronic media also hindered party organization. The dominant high-caste political leaders were more interested in sharing or gaining access to power than in developing lasting foundations for party politics.

Reportedly, before political organizations were banned, there were sixty-nine political parties, most of which were characteristically fluid in their membership and inconsistent in their loyalties. Personalities rather than ideologies brought individuals and groups under the nominal canopy of a party. Fragmentation, recombination, and alliances for convenience were the outstanding aspects of party behavior.

In the polarized political climate, the monarchy looked at the *panchayat* system as its only dependable support base. The *panchayat* apparatus provided access for politically motivated individuals to form a new elite. Although the political leadership and following of the Nepali Congress Party initially stayed away from the *panchayat* system, over time, and in the absence of an outlet for political activities, some defections took place. Nevertheless, the lateral entry of some pro-Nepali Congress Party elements did not substantially change the character of the *panchayat* leadership, which was dominated by rural elites of the Hill Region rather than the urban Kathmandu and Tarai Region elites who had been in the forefront of political activities. The system was designed so that the established parties would gradually shrink and lose their influence and control. Once the new *panchayat* leadership matured, however, some members became restive under the excessive control of the palace. This group of the *panchayat* elite opposed the system from within and overtly joined the prodemocracy movement.

In the last four decades, there has been significant progress towards democracy in Nepal's traditionally authoritarian political system. The first national elections in Nepal took place in 1959—some eight years after the overthrow of the Rana system. The Nepali Congress Party-dominated government, victorious in the 1959 parliamentary elections, was overthrown by King Mahendra within two years—resulting in the ban on political parties. The pattern that developed over the following decades was that of a monarchy reinforcing its power through the traditional institution of the *panchayat*. The *panchayat* system, co-opted and easily manipulated by the monarchy to suit its political ends, nevertheless was slowly but steadily subjected to pressures to change. Over time the monarchy was forced by necessity to expand the role of elections in response to the mounting discontent of a citizenry living in an age of heightened political awareness and rising expectations. This trend culminated in May 1991 with the first truly free elections in over thirty years, ushering in a new political era. The Nepali Congress Party obtained a workable majority within the framework of a constitutional monarchy and affirmed the rise of a nascent democratic force.

One of the ramifications of the prodemocracy movement was the beginning of a process of integration in national politics and decision making. With an elected Parliament and demands for an equitable allocation of resources to different regions, it was likely that all regions would compete for equality in national politics and that the monopoly of power by select families would erode, as would the excessive influence of the Kathmandu Valley Brahman, Chhetri, and Newar elites.

At the beginning of 1990, the *panchayat* system still dominated Nepal. Although the institution itself was the object of derision from opponents of the *panchayat* system, it appeared unthreatened. Within a few months, however, its position eroded and then crumbled with bewildering speed. The surge of the successful prodemocracy movement sweeping Eastern Europe, parts of the Soviet Union, and several Asian countries profoundly inspired the Nepalese people. Also contributing to the sudden transformation were the economic woes of Nepal, exacerbated by India's refusal to renew a trade and transit agreement; widespread bureaucratic inefficiency and corruption at all levels of government; the misgivings openly expressed by the international donors over the country's inefficient use of aid; and a deplorable record on human rights.

In January 1990, the Nepali Congress Party held its first national convention in thirty years in Kathmandu. It was well attended by party delegates from all districts and observers from all political parties. Also present was a multiparty delegation from India, headed by Janata Dal (People's Party) leader Chandra Shekhar, who subsequently became India's prime minister. The Nepali Congress Party cooperated with the United Left Front parties, a coalition of seven communist factions, in a joint program to replace the *panchayat* system with a multiparty political system and launched the Movement for the Restoration of Democracy, or prodemocracy movement.

Beginning on February 18, 1990—the thirty-ninth anniversary of King Tribhuvan's declaration of a multiparty democracy and the thirtieth anniversary of the antidemocratic usurpation of power by the palace—a series of spontaneous and sometimes turbulent mass demonstrations rocked major cities. People took to the streets to demand the restoration of a multiparty democracy, human rights, and fundamental freedoms. The success of the Kathmandu *bandh* (general strike) by prodemocracy forces on March 2 was repeated in other parts of the country over the course of seven weeks. By the time the movement succeeded in totally uprooting the *panchayat* system, at least fifty people were dead, and thousands were injured as a result of the force used by the authorities in suppressing the agitation. The government also had incarcerated national and district-level leaders of both the Nepali Congress Party and the United Left Front.

Unable to contain the widespread public agitation against the *panchayat* system and the mounting casualties, and fearing for the survival of his own monarchical status, King Birendra lifted the ban on political parties on April 8. The unrest persisted. In the midst of continued violence, a royal proclamation on April 16 dissolved the Rashtriya Panchayat and invalidated provisions of the 1962 constitution inconsistent with multiparty democracy. The next day, the king named Nepali Congress Party President K.P. Bhattarai, a moderate who had spent fourteen years as a political prisoner, as prime minister and head of the interim government. The government also freed all political prisoners, lifted control of all domestic and foreign publications, and established a commission, known as the Mullick Commission, to investigate the recent loss of life and property.

The eleven-member Bhattarai cabinet, composed of four members of the Nepali Congress Party, three members of the United Left Front, two human rights activists, and two royal nominees, was immediately entrusted with the task of preparing a new constitution and holding a general election. Pending the adoption of a new constitution, the interim government agreed that Nepal should remain under the 1962 constitution. In the interest of continuity and orderly management of public business, the interim government resisted demands from the left for a mass purge of the bureaucracy and die-hard *panchayat* elements. Bhattarai's goal was national reconciliation in a multiparty democracy.

After nine months of politicking, the constitution was proclaimed on November 9, 1990. Elections to the House of Representatives were held on May 12, 1991. The new government faced the immediate problems of restoring law and order, providing economic relief to the populace, and establishing its claim to sound administration, a somewhat difficult task because the parties of the interim government had been in the opposition for a long period of time. Furthermore, pro-*panchayat* thugs who had tried to foment chaos and law and order problems to discredit the new government had to be brought under control. The situation improved as many former *panchayat* leaders who had previously supported moves for a multiparty democracy openly supported the political changes and offered to cooperate with the new government—taking advantage of political opportunism.

Political Parties

The Nepali Congress Party

The Nepali Congress Party, a reform-oriented centrist party, has been in continuous operation since it was founded under a slightly different name in 1947. Elected to office in 1959 in a landslide victory, the Nepali Congress Party government sought to liberalize society through a democratic process. The palace coup of 1960 led to the imprisonment of the powerful Nepali Congress Party leader, B.P. Koirala, and other party stalwarts; many other members sought sanctuary in exile in India.

Although political parties were prohibited from 1960 to 1963 and continued to be outlawed during the *panchayat* system under the aegis of the Associations and Organizations (Control) Act of 1963, the Nepali Congress Party persisted. The party placed great emphasis on eliminating the feudal economy and building a basis for socioeconomic development. It proposed nationalizing basic industries and instituting progressive taxes on land, urban housing, salaries, profits, and foreign investments. While in exile, the Nepali Congress Party served as the nucleus around which other opposition groups clustered and even instigated popular uprisings in the Hill and Tarai regions. During this time, the Nepali Congress Party refused the overtures of a radical faction of the Communist Party of Nepal for a tactical alliance.

Although the Nepali Congress Party demonstrated its ability to

Basantapur Square, close to Kathmandu's Durbar Square, site of the former royal palace, now a bustling venue for souvenir sellers and other vendors
Courtesy Harvey Follender

endure, it was weakened over time by defection, factionalism, and external pressures. Nevertheless, it continued to be the only organized party to press for democratization. In the 1980 referendum, it supported the multiparty option in opposition to the *panchayat* system. In 1981 the party boycotted the Rashtriya Panchayat elections and rejected the new government. The death in 1982 of B.P. Koirala, who had consistently advocated constitutional reforms and a broad-based policy of national reconciliation, further weakened the party.

In the 1980s, the Nepali Congress Party abandoned its socialistic economic program in favor of a mixed economy, privatization, and a market economy in certain sectors. Its foreign policy orientation was to nonalignment and good relations with India. Although the party also boycotted the 1986 elections to the Rashtriya Panchayat, its members were allowed to run in the 1987 local elections. In defiance of the ban on demonstrations, the Nepali Congress Party organized mass rallies in January 1990 that ultimately triggered the prodemocracy movement.

Following the humiliating defeat of party leader K.P. Bhattarai by the communist factions in the 1991 parliamentary elections, Girija Prasad (G.P.) Koirala was chosen by the Nepali Congress Party as leader of its Parliamentary Board. As prime minister, he formed the first elected democratic government in Nepal in thirty-two years. G.P. Koirala was the third of the Koirala brothers to become prime minister. Along with his elder brother, B.P. Koirala, he was arrested in 1960 and was not released until 1967. After a period of exile that began in 1971, he returned to Nepal in 1979 under a general amnesty. He was elected general secretary of the party in 1976 in a convention at Patna and played a key role in the prodemocracy movement. G.P. Koirala was known for favoring reconciliation with the left, but he also wanted to pursue national unity and Western-style democracy.

The Communist Parties

Like the Nepali Congress Party, the fractured communist movement was deeply indebted to its Indian counterpart, whose initiative had helped to found the Communist Party of Nepal (Marxist) in 1949 in Calcutta. Nepalese communists looked askance at the Nepali Congress Party leadership as willing collaborators of Indian expansionism and called for broad-based alliances of all progressive forces for the establishment of a people's democracy.

As many as seventeen factions, ranging from the quasi-establishment royal communists to extremely radical fringe groups, vied for leadership and control, preventing the movement from making significant gains. The proscription of political parties in 1960 affected the communists less severely than other parties because communist factions proved better at organizing and operating underground and at making the transition to covert activity. Little effort was exerted to detain communist leaders, and in the months following the palace coup d'état in 1960, the Communist Party of Nepal (Marxist) was allowed to operate with a perceptibly greater amount of freedom than any other party. The Communist Party of Nepal (Marxist-Leninist) was established in 1978, one of many splinter groups under the name Communist Party of Nepal. In spite of many vicissitudes encountered since the movement's inception, the communists maintained national attention because of continued support from the peasant and worker organizations and the fact that the country's poverty and deprivation offered a fertile ground for Marxist ideals. Support was maintained through the All Peasants Union and the Nepal Trade Union Congress.

Communist groups wielded significant influence in the universities and professional groups. The movement had a dedicated cadre of motivated youth who followed party discipline strictly. Whereas the Nepali Congress Party seemed to accommodate the old guard at the expense of the younger generation, communists more ardently

*Flags of the Communist
Party of Nepal and the
Nepali Congress Party fly
over a small urban shrine
near the center
of Kathmandu.
Courtesy
John N. Gunning*

sought younger members. Most of the mainstream communist groups in the 1980s believed in democracy and a multiparty system, recognized no international communist headquarters or leaders, and abjured the Maoism many had embraced earlier.

The United Left Front coalition, organized in late 1989, supported multiparty democracy. During the prodemocracy movement, it played a crucial role by joining the interim government led by the Nepali Congress Party and by submerging serious differences of opinion. Although differences in the communist camp were endemic when the movement was underground, the internal conflicts lessened as communists operated openly and began to look toward future electoral gains.

The success of the communist parties in the May 12, 1991, election came as a shock to the Nepali Congress Party, which had failed to repeat its 1959 landslide victory. Although there was some unity among the communist factions of the United Left Front, there was no agreement to share seats with the other factions or groups. The Communist Party of Nepal (United Marxist-Leninist) faction—formed as a result of a merger between the Communist Party of Nepal (Marxist) and the Communist Party of Nepal (Marxist-Leninist)—came in second to the Nepali Congress Party. The head of the communist leadership echelon was Madan Bhandari, son of a Brahman priest, who was working to turn his Communist Party of Nepal (United Marxist-Leninist) into a formidable

169

political power. He stunned the Nepali Congress Party in the 1991 elections by narrowly defeating its leader, K.P. Bhattarai, for a parliamentary seat in Kathmandu.

As a partner in the interim coalition government, the Communist Party of Nepal (United Marxist-Leninist) had endorsed, although reluctantly, the new constitution, which retained the monarchy. The communists received popular support for their allegations that the Nepali Congress Party was too close to India and was a threat to Nepal's sovereignty. Other mainstream communist leaders were Man Mohan Adhikari and Sahana Pradhan, both originally of the Communist Party of Nepal (Marxist); and Bishnu Bahadur Manandhar of the Communist Party of Nepal (Manandhar), another communist faction.

Other Political Parties

There was a phenomenal rise in the number of political parties—particularly between May and September 1990—as strategic maneuvers to participate in parliamentary elections and find a niche in postelection Nepal occurred. The Nepal Sadbhavana Party (Good Will Party), one of several regional and ethnic parties, was founded in April 1990. It aimed at promoting the interests of the Tarai Region, including the expulsion of the Hill people from Tarai and the establishment of a special relationship with India in the framework of nonalignment. A forum for people of Indian descent, the party also favored the introduction of Hindi as the second national language. Its ideology supported a democratic socialist society. Other Tarai Region parties included the Nepal Tarai Unity Forum, the Nepal Tarai Association, and the Nepal Tarai Muslim Congress Party.

Among the several ethnic parties were the National People's Liberation Front (Nepal Rashtriya Jana Mukti Morcha), the National Mongol Organization (Rashtriya Mongol Sanghatan), SETAMAGURALI (an acronym of names of different ethnic groups of eastern Nepal including the Tamang, Magar, and Gurung), the Front of the Kirat Aborigines (Nepal Kirat Adhibasi Janajiti Morch), the Freedom Front of the Limbu People (Limbuwan Mukli Morcha), and the Nepal Nationalist Gorkha Parishad, or Parishad (Nepal Rashtrabadi Gorkha Parishad). The Parishad, revived in September 1990, was founded in 1951 as part of Rana revivalist politics and had placed second in the 1959 general elections. Some of its senior leaders later joined the Nepali Congress or *pancha* camps.

Of those groups favoring the monarchy, two conservative parties received considerable attention. Hastily founded by two former prime ministers, both parties were called the National Democratic Party—suffixed with the names Thapa or Chand enclosed within brackets. Other parties of this political bent included the National Democratic Unity Panchayat Party (Rashtriya Prajatantrik Ekata Panchayat Party), Nepal Welfare Party (Nepal Janahit Party), United Democratic Party (Samyukti Prajatantra Party), and Nepal Panchayat Council (Nepal Panchayat Parishad).

Besides the Nepali Congress Party, fifteen centrist parties also had emerged. Most of these parties were founded by former members of the Nepali Congress Party and defecting *pancha* who had shifted allegiance to the multiparty system. The Women's Democratic Party aimed at promoting the rights, interests, and freedoms of Nepalese women.

Elections

The 1981 Elections

Growing political unrest, accompanied by massive demonstrations, forced King Birendra, as a palliative tactic, to call for a nationwide referendum to choose the form of government. Following the May 2, 1980, referendum—the subject of charges of rigging—the *panchayat* system was reaffirmed. However, members of the Rashtriya Panchayat would henceforth be elected directly by the people on the basis of universal adult suffrage.

In May 1981, the king promulgated the third amendment to the 1962 constitution incorporating the results of the referendum. There was no change in the fundamental principle of partylessness; all candidates for the Rashtriya Panchayat competed as individuals.

The first direct election to the Rashtriya Panchayat was held in May 1981. In the midst of an election boycott by the Nepali Congress Party and other banned political parties, the exercise only legitimized the administration of Prime Minister Thapa as a democratically elected popular government. Indirectly, however, the election was counterproductive because it intensified further the increasingly sharp divisions within the various *panchayat* and the continued opposition of the Nepali Congress Party, various communist factions, and peasants' and workers' organizations.

There were 1,096 candidates contesting 112 seats in the 1981 elections. Campaign appeals were made on regional, ethnic, and caste lines rather than on broad national issues. Among the contestants were forty-five candidates from pro-Moscow communist factions, thirty-six candidates from the Nepali Congress Party, and several multiparty *pancha*. Voter turnout was 63 percent. Despite

171

Thapa's reelection, more than 70 percent of the official candidates were defeated. Candidates who supported the multiparty system also fared poorly. The election of fifty-nine new members in the Rashtriya Panchayat indicated the voters' rejection of the old guard. The indirect participation of the political parties was a symbolic gesture toward national consensus and reconciliation; the chief protagonist was the moderate Nepali Congress Party leader, B.P. Koirala.

In the tradition of *panchayat* political patterns of instability, the quick fix of a referendum and new elections failed to restore political equilibrium to the system. Corruption and general administrative inertia further vitiated the political climate. Even senior *panchayat* leaders, who were openly critical of the system, became willing participants in intrigues, which only precipitated counterplots by paranoid palace advisers. Clashes between students, which were at times supported by faculty members, created disturbances throughout the country.

The 1986 Elections

Between the 1981 and 1986 elections, there was a growing rift among the *pancha*. Without a viable economic and political program, disillusionment with the *panchayat* system increased. In the face of a deteriorating economy, faltering development plans, and the failure of the *panchayati raj* to inspire motivation and confidence in an already demoralized bureaucracy, the credibility of the government waned. The banned political parties, especially the Nepali Congress Party, after initial efforts at reconciliation, concentrated on organizational work and the demand for political pluralism. Most political activities, however, were noticeable only within the *panchayat* system itself. Appointed in 1983, the new prime minister, Lokendra Bahadur Chand, had a no-confidence motion filed against him immediately after taking office. The motion was declared inadmissible on the grounds of errors in drafting, but this power struggle among different groups of *pancha* further undermined the *panchayat* system.

The uneasy political stalemate was upset when in late May 1985, the Nepali Congress Party, in preparation for the 1986 election, decided to launch a *satyagraha* (civil disobedience) campaign—in which many communists also participated—to demand reforms in the political system. A large number of Nepali Congress Party activists were quickly arrested. Although the campaign generally lacked popular support, it received considerable attention and interest among intellectuals and students, caused tension within the government, and further divided the already fractured *panchayat*. Kathmandu also was subjected to violence, including explosions that rocked the royal palace and other key buildings. There was further discontent when, at the *panchayat* workers' annual congress, the moot issue of government accountability to the legislature was disallowed from discussion.

In a politically charged atmosphere, the second quinquennial nationwide election to the Rashtriya Panchayat was held in May 1986. Slightly more than 9 million voters cast their ballots for 1,584 candidates for 112 seats. According to official sources, 60 percent of all eligible voters participated in the election.

The election was marked by a lack of enthusiasm, which partly reflected the Nepali Congress Party's boycott. A few communist factions contested the election. About 20 percent of the candidates were elected either on the basis of their roles as champions of the opposition or for their stand against the elite. Allegations of electoral malpractice also were widely voiced. The electoral success of forty-five Chettris and Thakuris, sixteen Hill Brahmans, and seven Newars indicated that the traditional power structure remained largely unaffected. Marich Man Singh Shrestha, a Newar, was appointed prime minister. Three women were elected to the Rashtriya Panchayat from the Tarai Region, but no Muslims were elected.

Local Elections in 1987

In contrast to the procedure followed in the 1986 elections, the Nepali Congress Party and a number of communist factions allowed their members to participate as individuals in the 1987 local elections. The Nepali Congress Party also made it clear that its local election strategy did not mean an end to its opposition or resistance to the *panchayat* system. In urban areas, especially in the Tarai Region, certain party members, as well as some communists, did very well and were returned to office in substantial numbers.

The 1991 Elections

For many Nepalese, participation in the democratic process meant either walking for hours along mountain paths or riding a yak to cast a ballot. Since most voters were illiterate, they had to choose a candidate according to the party's symbol as authorized by the election commission; for example, a tree signified the Nepali Congress Party and a sun represented the Communist Party of Nepal (United Marxist-Leninist).

Although forty-four parties were recognized by the Election Commission, only twenty parties actually contested the elections. The twenty parties ranged across the political spectrum from radical right to loyalist leftist and all except a leftwing radical faction, Masal (Torch), eagerly participated in the elections. Twelve parties did

173

not win a single seat and obtained a total of only about 82,500 votes, slightly more than 1 percent of the total valid votes. Many voters seemed to have fallen back on their age-old identification with caste or ethnic community. Younger voters favored the progressive leftist parties, as did voters in the urban areas.

The Nepali Congress Party won the first multiparty election in thirty-two years, taking 110 seats in the 205-member House of Representatives. The results of the elections, however, demonstrated that a coalition of various communist parties was a major political force in Nepalese politics, defying the international trend of dismantling communist parties and regimes. The Communist Party of Nepal (United Marxist-Leninist), a constituent of the United Left Front, won sixty-nine seats. The three other communist parties of the United Left Front coalition won a total of thirteen seats. Besides the Nepali Congress Party and the Communist Party of Nepal (United Marxist-Leninist) alliance, four other parties qualified for national party status, which meant they polled more than 3 percent of the total votes cast.

The election was marked by heavy voter turnout. Of a total of more than 11 million voters, about 7 million, or 65 percent, cast ballots, of which slightly more than 4 percent were declared invalid on technical grounds. The election results made it very clear that the promonarchists and those in favor of the panchayat system lacked national support. Communist parties won in the Kathmandu Valley and some parts of the eastern Tarai Region. The Nepali Congress Party won in other parts of the Tarai Region and in western Nepal. The National Democratic Party (Chand) won three seats, and the National Democratic Party (Thapa) won only one seat. The four members of those parties, six Nepal Sadbhavana Party members, and independents were expected to join the moderate Nepali Congress Party. All leftist elements under the Communist Party of Nepal (United Marxist-Leninist) umbrella were likely to form a solid opposition in Parliament to the Nepali Congress Party government.

The new House of Representatives included thirteen members of the dissolved Rashtriya Panchayat, five Muslims, seven women, and six members of the Parliament that had been dissolved in 1960. Although the number of women representatives was much lower than was hoped for, Muslim representation was comparable to their proportion of the population. Also notable was the performance of the ethnic or regional parties, in particular the Tarai-based Nepal Sadbhavana Party, which polled 4 percent of the valid votes, allowing it to claim the status of a national party. Out of the five seats in Kathmandu, the Nepali Congress Party

Election Commission building in Kathmandu, formerly a Russian hotel
Courtesy Janet MacDonald

won one seat; the rest were swept by the Communist Party of Nepal (United Marxist-Leninist). The average age of the newly elected members of the House of Representatives was forty-three.

Kathmandu citizens made it clear that they had enough of political dynasties. The son and wife of Nepali Congress Party figurehead Ganesh Man Singh ran for two of the high-profile seats; both were defeated by communist candidates. In the prestigious contest for a seat in Kathmandu, the Communist Party of Nepal (United Marxist-Leninist) general secretary, Madan Bhandari, defeated interim Prime Minister K.P. Bhattarai. The poor showing of the Nepali Congress Party in the urban areas may also be attributed to the fact that, given that the communists had been banned for thirty years, the party did not see them as potential opposition and was overconfident.

The continuing transition from a partyless *panchayat* system to a multiparty democracy was relatively peaceful, although there were some incidents of sporadic violence. Six deaths in preelection violence were reported, but no election-related deaths were confirmed on polling day. Police enforced a curfew during the long wait for election results. Because of election irregularities and violence, the Election Commission—which enjoyed the confidence of all the

175

parties—ordered repolling at 44 of 8,225 polling centers, affecting 31 constituencies.

In response to the interim government's invitation to international observers, a host of Asians, Europeans, and North Americans journeyed to Kathmandu. Among the observers was a sixty-four member international observation delegation, representing twenty-two countries, which was organized by Nepal's National Election Observation Committee. The committee was an offshoot of Nepal's Forum for the Protection of Human Rights. The international delegation concluded that the elections generally were conducted in a fair, free, and open manner and that the parties were able to campaign unimpaired. Complaints were received that equal and adequate access to radio and television was denied, however, and that the code of conduct and campaign spending limitations were violated. The delegation also recognized that, as confirmed by the Election Commission, from 5 to 10 percent of eligible voters were not registered and that there were some inaccuracies in voter lists.

On May 29, 1991, a Nepali Congress Party government was installed with G.P. Koirala as prime minister. The first session of Parliament was held on June 20. The new government faced two enormous tasks, both of which concerned India: the negotiation of a new trade and transit treaty, and the exploitation of Nepal's only major natural resource, water, for hydroelectric power for purchase by India. Further, although the Communist Party of Nepal (United Marxist-Leninist) faction wanted to end recruitment of the Gurkhas into the British and Indian armies, the Nepali Congress Party wanted neither to outrage the Gurkhas nor to deprive the country of the foreign remittances sent by the soldiers (see Gurkhas Serving Abroad, ch. 5).

The Media

Previous constitutions guaranteed freedom of expression as a basic right, but in practice this right was severely curtailed. Prepublication censorship, cancellation of registration for publication, and other similar restrictive regulations severely handicapped the freedom of the press, and journalists operated under constant threats of harassment and imprisonment. In 1960 the king decreed that all newspapers were required to obtain official clearance for reports of political activities. In 1962 a government-controlled news agency, Rashtriya Sambad Samity, was established to collect and distribute news about and within the country. The Samity monopoly continued until the success of the prodemocracy movement. In addition, provisions of the Freedom of Speech Publications Act of

1980 limited the publication of materials that might undermine the interests of sovereignty of the nation; contravene principles that underlie the constitution; or encourage, abet, or propagate party politics. This act was repealed in July 1990.

The constitution guarantees the freedom of the press as a fundamental right. It also prohibits the censoring of news items, articles, or any other reading materials and states that a press cannot be closed or seized for printing any news item, article, or any other reading materials. In addition, the registration of a newspaper or periodical cannot be cancelled for publishing offensive news articles or reading material. The operation of a free press is circumscribed, however, by vague restrictions against undermining the sovereignty and integrity of Nepal; disturbing the harmonious relations among the people of different castes, classes, or communities; violating decent public behavior morality; instigating crimes; or committing sedition or contempt of court. During the 1980s, several journalists were incarcerated and held without trial under the Public Security Act and the Treason Act.

The Nepalese press was supportive of the prodemocracy movement. When the government repressed the movement, the Central Committee of the Nepal Journalists Association, headed by Govinda Binyogi, issued a statement that declared all censorship, banning of newspapers, and arrests of journalists as illegal, unconstitutional, and undemocratic. The Nepal Journalists Association reported that between January and April 1990, forty journalists were arrested for comments criticizing the government. During the same period, several newspapers halted publication to protest the government's attempts at precensorship. More than ten papers had entire issues seized by government authorities when they ran articles considered overtly critical. Several newspapers were severely pressed financially after successive government seizures.

Since the momentous political changes of April 1990, freedom of the press has come into question only once, in November 1990, when authorities charged two reporters with slandering the royal family in print. Charges were dismissed in December following protests by the Nepal Journalist Association to the prime minister. An editor also was detained overnight in November 1990 for publishing insulting remarks against the queen, but charges were not pressed. As of mid-1991, there were no reports of the seizing or banning of foreign publications deemed to have carried articles unfavorable to the government or the monarchy.

In 1991 there were approximately 400 Nepalese newspapers and periodicals, including a dozen national dailies with a combined circulation of more than 125,000. The circulation of other newspapers, journals, and magazines was limited to only a few hundred copies each.

Except for two English dailies, *Rising Nepal* and *Commoner,* both published in Kathmandu, other widely circulating newspapers were published in Nepali. These included *Gorkhapatra, Samichhya, Matribhumi, Rastra Pukar, Daily News, Samaya,* and *Janadoot.* The number of publications in Hindi and Newari, however, was increasing in the late 1980s.

The daily *Gorkhapatra* and *Rising Nepal* were government organs. Before the success of the prodemocracy movement, both government dailies primarily provided coverage of official views, carried virtually no information on opposition activities, and muted criticism of the government. *Nepal Raj Patra,* the principal government publication since 1951, contained texts of laws, decrees, proclamations, and royal orders and was available in both English and Nepali.

Because of the government's near monopoly on domestic news, many newspaper readers relied on foreign publications. They relied on as *Statesman, Times of India,* and *Hindustan Times*—all from India—and the Pacific editions of *Time, Newsweek,* and *China Today,* published in India in Hindi, English, and Nepali.

Much of the fast proliferating printed matter was read only by a small elite and by government functionaries in the Kathmandu Valley. Staggeringly widespread illiteracy (about 33 percent of the population were literate in 1990), lack of a transport infrastructure, the general apathy of the rural people toward the affairs of Kathmandu—to which the press devoted a major share of coverage—and a general reliance on oral transmission of information rather than on the written word were among the factors that impeded the dissemination of publications. By April 1990, however, news coverage had broadened to reflect a wide range of views. Although in most circumstances editorial views reflected government policy, editors did at times exercise the right to publish critical views and alternative policies.

Electronic media consisted of radio and television programming controlled by the government. Radio Nepal broadcast on shortwave and medium-wave both in Nepali and English from transmitters in Jawalakhel and Khumaltar (see Communications, ch. 3). Nepal Television Corporation broadcast twenty-three hours of programs per week from its station at Singha Durbar, Kathmandu. Transmitters also were located at Pokhara, Biratnagar, and Hetauda. Prior to the unrest of 1990, programming closely reflected the views of the government. Although coverage of government criticism remained inadequate, programming in 1991 reflected a broader range of interests and political views. The Voice of America, the British Broadcasting Corporation, and several other European and Asian networks were monitored in Nepal.

Foreign Policy

A landlocked country, Nepal is sandwiched between two giant neighbors—China and India (see fig. 1; The Land, ch. 2). To the north, the Himalayas constitute a natural and mostly impassible frontier, and beyond that is the border with China. To the south, east, and west, Nepal is hemmed in by India. Without an outlet to the sea, Nepal has been dependent on India for international trade and transit facilities.

During the British Raj (1858-1947), Nepal sought geostrategic isolation. This traditional isolationism partially was the product of the relative freedom the country enjoyed from external intervention and domination. From the mid-nineteenth century, when Britain emerged as the unchallenged power in India and the Qing Dynasty (1644-1911) in China was in decline, Nepal made accommodations with Britain on the best possible terms. Without surrendering autonomy on internal matters, Nepal received guarantees of protection from Britain against external aggression and interference (see Rana Rule, ch. 1). London also considered a steady flow of Gurkha recruits from Nepal as vital to support Britain's security in India and its other colonial territories.

In the 1950s, Nepal began a gradual opening up and a commitment to a policy of neutrality and nonalignment. At the 1973 summit of the Nonaligned Movement in Algiers, King Birendra proposed that "Nepal, situated between two of the most populous countries of the world, wishes her frontiers to be declared a zone of peace." In Birendra's 1975 coronation address, he formally asked other countries to endorse his proposal. Since then, the concept of Nepal as a zone of peace has become a main theme of Kathmandu's foreign policy.

As of mid-1991, Nepal had been endorsed as a zone of peace by more than 110 nations. Many of these countries also recommended a regional approach to peace as the goal. Without the endorsement of India and the former Soviet Union, however, the prospect of broader international acceptance was dim.

At the beginning of the 1990s, Nepal had established diplomatic relations with approximately 100 countries. Nepal was an active member of the United Nations (UN) and participated in a number of its specialized agencies. Nepal also was a founding member of the South Asian Association for Regional Cooperation (SAARC) and had successfully negotiated several bilateral and multilateral economic, cultural, and technical assistance programs. Because of its geographical proximity to and historical links with China and India, Nepal's foreign policy was focused mainly on maintaining close and friendly relations with these two countries and on safeguarding its national security and independence. Nepal's relations with the United States, Europe, and the Soviet Union showed new signs of vitality in 1991.

Relations with India

Even after India had achieved independence from Britain in 1947, Nepalese-Indian relations continued to be based on the second Treaty of Sagauli, which had been signed with the government of British India in 1925. Beginning in 1950, however, relations were based on two treaties. Under the Treaty of Peace and Friendship, ratified in July 1950, each government agreed to acknowledge and respect the other's sovereignty, territorial integrity, and independence; to continue diplomatic relations; and, on matters pertaining to industrial and economic development, to grant rights equal to those of its own citizens to the nationals of the other residing in its territory. Agreements on all subjects in this treaty superseded those on similar matters dealt with in the previous treaties between Nepal and Britain. In the Treaty of Trade and Commerce, ratified in October 1950, India recognized Nepal's right to import and export commodities through Indian territory and ports. Customs could not be levied on commodities in transit through India.

India's influence over Nepal increased throughout the 1950s. The Citizenship Act of 1952 allowed Indians to immigrate to Nepal and acquire Nepalese citizenship with ease—a source of some resentment in Nepal. And, Nepalese were allowed to migrate freely to India—a source of resentment there. (This policy was not changed until 1962 when several restrictive clauses were added to the Nepalese constitution.) Also in 1952, an Indian military mission was established in Nepal. In 1954 a memorandum provided for the joint coordination of foreign policy, and Indian security posts were established in Nepal's northern frontier (see India, ch. 5). At the same time, Nepal's dissatisfaction with India's growing influence began to emerge, and overtures to China were initiated as a counterweight to India.

King Mahendra continued to pursue a nonaligned policy begun during the reign of Prithvi Narayan Shah in the mid-eighteenth century (see The Expansion of Gorkha, ch. 1). In the late 1950s and 1960s, Nepal voted differently from India in the UN unless India's basic interests were involved. The two countries consistently remained at odds over the rights of landlocked states to transit facilities and access to the sea.

Following the 1962 Sino-Indian border war, the relationship between Kathmandu and New Delhi thawed significantly. India suspended its support to India-based Nepalese opposition forces. Nepal extracted several concessions, including transit rights with other countries through India and access to Indian markets (see Foreign Trade, ch. 3). In exchange, through a secret accord concluded in 1965, similar to an arrangement that had been suspended in 1963, India won a monopoly on arms sales to Nepal.

In 1969 relations again became stressful as Nepal challenged the existing mutual security arrangement and asked that the Indian security checkposts and liaison group be withdrawn. Resentment also was expressed against the Treaty of Peace and Friendship of 1950. India grudgingly withdrew its military checkposts and liaison group, although the treaty was not abrogated.

Further changes in Nepalese-Indian relations occurred in the 1970s. India's credibility as a regional power was increased—and Nepal's vulnerability was reinforced—by the 1971 Indo-Soviet Treaty of Peace, Friendship, and Cooperation; the 1971 Indo-Pakistani War, which led to the emergence of an independent Bangladesh; the absorption of Sikkim into India in 1974; increased unofficial support of the Nepali Congress Party leadership in India; rebellions fomented by pro-Beijing Naxalite elements in 1973-74 in West Bengal State bordering Nepal; and India's nuclear explosion in 1974. Nepal adopted a cautious policy of appeasement of India, and in his 1975 coronation address King Birendra called for the recognition of Nepal as a zone of peace where military competition would be off-limits. India showed some flexibility in placating Nepal by distancing, if not disassociating, itself from the Nepalese opposition forces based in India, agreeing to a favorable trade and transit arrangement in 1978, and entering into another agreement on joint industrial ventures between Indian and Nepalese firms. The latter agreement, by opening the possibilities of India's investment, indirectly furthered India's domination of Nepal's economy. India also continued to maintain a high level of economic assistance to Nepal.

In the mid-1970s, Nepal pressed for substantial amendments to the 1971 trade and transit treaty, which was due to expire in 1976. India ultimately backed down from its initial position to terminate the 1971 treaty even before a new treaty could be negotiated. The 1978 agreements incorporated Nepal's demand for separate treaties for trade and transit. The relationship between the two nations improved over the next decade, but not steadily.

India continued to support the Nepalese opposition and refused to endorse Nepal as a zone of peace. In 1987 India urged expulsion of Nepalese settlers from neighboring Indian states, and Nepal retaliated by introducing a work permit system for Indians working in Nepal. That same year, the two countries signed an agreement setting up a joint commission to increase economic cooperation in trade and transit, industry, and water resources.

Relations between the two countries sank to a low point in 1988 when Kathmandu signed an agreement with Beijing to purchase weapons soon after a report that China had won a contract for constructing a road in the western sector to connect China with Nepal (see China, ch. 5). India perceived these developments as deliberately jeopardizing its security. India also was annoyed with the high volume of unauthorized trade across the Nepalese border, the issuance of work permits to the estimated 150,000 Indians residing in Nepal, and the imposition of a 55 percent tariff on Indian goods entering Nepal.

In retaliation for these developments, India put Nepal under a virtual trade siege. In March 1989, upon the expiration of the 1978 treaties on trade and transit rights, India insisted on negotiating a single unified treaty in addition to an agreement on unauthorized trade, which Nepal saw as a flagrant attempt to strangle its economy. On March 23, 1989, India declared that both treaties had expired and closed all but two border entry points.

The economic consequences of the trade and transit deadlock were enormous. Shortages of Indian imports such as fuel, salt, cooking oil, food, and other essential commodities soon occurred. The lucrative tourist industry went into recession. Nepal also claimed that the blockade caused ecological havoc since people were compelled to use already dwindling forest resources for energy in lieu of gasoline and kerosene, which came mostly via India (see Energy, ch. 3). To withstand the renewed Indian pressure, Nepal undertook a major diplomatic initiative to present its case on trade and transit matters to the world community.

The relationship with India was further strained in 1989 when Nepal decoupled its rupee (see Glossary) from the Indian rupee, which previously had circulated freely in Nepal. India retaliated by denying port facilities in Calcutta to Nepal, thereby preventing delivery of oil supplies from Singapore and other sources.

A swift turn in relations followed the success of the Movement for the Restoration of Democracy in early 1990. In June 1990, a joint Kathmandu-New Delhi communiqué was issued pending the finalization of a comprehensive arrangement covering all aspects of bilateral relations, restoring trade relations, reopening transit routes for Nepal's imports, and formalizing respect of each other's security concerns. Essentially, the communiqué announced the restoration of the status quo ante and the reopening of all border points, and Nepal agreed to various concessions regarding India's commercial privileges. Kathmandu also announced that lower cost was the decisive factor in its purchasing arms and personnel carriers from China and that Nepal was advising China to withhold delivery of the last shipment. The communiqué declared that Kathmandu and New Delhi would cooperate in industrial development, in harnessing the waters of their common rivers for mutual benefit, and in protecting and managing the environment.

Relations with Other South Asian Nations

Pakistan and Bangladesh

Nepal's relations with other South Asian nations were dominated by the search for alternate transit facilities and a reduction of India's influence. Nepal tried to stay clear of Indo-Pakistani rivalry, inasmuch as Nepal had a only minor role in the Kashmir dispute and had no involvement in several United States-sponsored security arrangements in the region in the early 1950s.

Nepal and Pakistan signed the protocol for establishing full diplomatic relations in 1962 and exchanged ambassadors in 1963. Two agreements between Kathmandu and Karachi (then Pakistan's capital) were signed in October 1962, calling for reciprocal most-favored-nation treatment. A January 1963 agreement provided Nepal with free trade and transit facilities through the port of Chittagong, East Pakistan (present-day Bangladesh). This arrangement somewhat reduced Nepal's dependence on India for import privileges, particularly after the establishment of an air link with East Pakistan later in the year. This endeavor to secure another transit route through East Pakistan had at best only limited potential because of the intervening Indian territory.

Nepal initially adopted a neutral posture during the Indo-Pakistan war of 1971 but immediately recognized the newly independent nation of Bangladesh on January 16, 1972. Two days after diplomatic relations were established with Dhaka, Islamabad broke off diplomatic relations with Kathmandu.

Nepal's focus shifted to Bangladesh as a permanent and much desired gateway to the sea. Bangladesh, friendly to India and close to Nepal's southern border, opened new potential for both trade and transit facilities.

Nepal's relations with Bangladesh improved when an anti-Indian faction seized power in Dhaka in August 1975. The turning point in Nepal-Bangladesh relations, however, occurred in April 1976 when the two countries signed four agreements relating to trade, transit, civil aviation, and technical cooperation. They also jointly issued a communiqué on maintaining close cooperation in the fields of power generation and the development of water resources. The transit agreement exempted all traffic-in-transit from transit duties or other charges. Six points of entry and exit for the movement of Nepalese traffic-in-transit through Bangladesh's ports and territory were designated. This transit agreement came at a crucial time—during Nepal's conclusion of a trade and transit agreement with a reluctant India. In 1986 Nepal was also gratified when Bangladesh wanted to involve Nepal in the issue of distribution and utilization of water from the Ganges River.

Bhutan

Nepal has shown interest in developing a mutually advantageous relationship with Bhutan, but substantial problems have persisted. Through its own treaty with India, signed in 1949, Bhutan had generally followed New Delhi's guidance in foreign policy matters. Bhutan had serious reservations over joining in regional and international organizational politics bearing Nepal's initiatives and had ignored the concept of a Himalayan federation. Another potential source of dissension in Nepalese-Bhutanese relations was the presence of a large Nepalese community in southern Bhutan. In the early 1990s, the large Nepalese population emerged as a potentially divisive issue between the two countries. In spite of these difficulties, Kathmandu maintained nonresident diplomatic relations with Thimpu (see Foreign Relations, ch. 6).

Sri Lanka and Maldives

As of mid-1991, Nepal had not cultivated bilateral relations with Sri Lanka or Maldives. Nevertheless, following a visit to Nepal by the Maldives president in May 1981, a cultural exchange and economic cooperation agreement was signed. The agreement, however, has remained dormant.

Nepal was interested in Sri Lanka's Tamil separatist movement because of its own potential problems with ethnic diversity. In line with its policy of deploring the violation of the territorial integrity of sovereign states, Nepal also expressed concern at India's military involvement in Sri Lanka during the 1980s. Nepal welcomed the conclusion of the Indo-Sri Lankan Accord of July 29, 1987.

Relations with China

The keystone of Nepal's China policy was maintaining equal

friendships with China and India while simultaneously seeking to decrease India's influence in Nepal and Nepal's dependence on India. Further, Kathmandu felt that the competition between its two giant neighbors—China and India—would benefit its own economic development.

The first recorded official relations with China and Tibet occurred near the middle of the seventh century. By the eighteenth century, Nepalese adventurism in Tibet led to Chinese intervention in favor of Tibet. The resultant Sino-Nepalese Treaty of 1792 provided for tribute-bearing missions from Nepal to China every five years as a symbol of Chinese political and cultural supremacy in the region (see The Making of Modern Nepal, ch. 1).

In the Anglo-Nepalese War of 1814–16, China refused Nepal's requests for military assistance and, by default, surrendered its dominant position in Nepal to the growing British influence. However, it appeared to be expedient for Nepal to retain the fiction of a tributary relationship with China in order to balance China against Britain.

Nepal invaded Tibet in 1854. Hostilities were quickly terminated when China intervened, and the Treaty of Thapathali was concluded in March 1856. The treaty recognized the special status of China, and Nepal agreed to assist Tibet in the event of foreign aggression.

Relations between Nepal and China and Tibet continued without critical incident until 1904, when British India sent an armed expedition to Tibet and Nepal rejected Tibet's request for aid to avoid risking its good relations with Britain. Beginning in 1908, Nepal stopped paying tribute to China.

By 1910, apprehensive of British activity in Tibet, China had reasserted its claim to sovereign rights in Tibet and feudatory missions from Nepal. In 1912 Nepal warned the Chinese representative at Lhasa that Nepal would help Tibet attain independent status as long as it was consistent with British interests. Nepal broke relations with China when the Tibetans, taking advantage of the Chinese revolution of 1911, drove the Chinese out.

When the Chinese communists invaded Tibet in 1950, Nepal's relations with China began to undergo drastic changes. Although annual Tibetan tribute missions appeared regularly in Nepal as late as 1953, Beijing had started to ignore the provisions of the 1856 treaty by curtailing the privileges and rights it accorded to Nepalese traders, by imposing restrictions on Nepalese pilgrims, and by stopping the Tibetan tributary missions.

The break between Kathmandu and Beijing continued until 1955 when relations were reestablished with China. The two countries established resident ambassadors in their respective capitals in July 1960.

In 1956 the Treaty of Thapathali was replaced by a new treaty under which Nepal recognized China's sovereignty over Tibet and agreed to surrender all privileges and rights granted by the old treaty. In 1962 Nepal withdrew its ambassador from Tibet and substituted a consul general. An agreement on locating and demarcating the Nepal-Tibet boundary was signed in March 1960. Within a month, another Treaty of Peace and Friendship was signed in Kathmandu.

The Sino-Nepal Boundary Treaty was signed in Beijing in October 1961. The treaty provided for a Sino-Nepal Joint Commission to agree on questions regarding alignment, location, and maintenance of the seventy-nine demarcation markers. The commission's findings were attached to the original treaty in a protocol signed in January 1963.

During the Sino-Indian conflict of 1962, Nepal reasserted its neutrality and warned that it would not submit to aggression from any state. Although the warning was directed at China, Nepal continued to support China's application for membership in the United Nations. A potential source of irritation in Sino-Nepalese relations was relieved in January 1964 when China agreed to release the frozen funds of Nepalese traders from Tibetan banks.

An agreement to construct an all-weather highway linking Kathmandu with Tibet was signed in October 1961—a time when neither Kathmandu nor Beijing had cordial relations with New Delhi. The Kathmandu-Kodari road opened in May 1967 but did not yield any commercial or trade benefits for Nepal. Because of the severe restrictions imposed by Beijing even before the road was opened, Kathmandu had closed its trade agencies in Tibet by January 1966. Although the highway had no economic or commercial value and was not viable as an alternate transit route, it was of strategic military importance to China. The highway established direct links between two major Chinese army bases within 100 kilometers of Kathmandu to forward bases at Gyirong in Tibet.

Throughout the latter half of the 1960s, Nepal's relations with China remained fairly steady. One exception was the belligerent activities of the Chinese officials in Nepal who eulogized and extolled the successes of the Cultural Revolution (1966-76) during the summer of 1967.

The emergence of a strident and confident India in the early 1970s introduced some new dimensions in Nepal's China policy. King Birendra did not abandon the policy of equal friendship between China and India but wanted to woo China to counter India's

United States Agency for International Development mission, located in the Rabi Bhavan complex, an old Rana palace in Kalimati Durbar, Kathmandu
Courtesy John N. Gunning

growing influence in the region. China had implicitly recognized India's predominance in the region, however, and was willing to oblige Nepal only to the extent of pledging support in safeguarding its national independence and preventing foreign interference.

In an open challenge to India's primacy in Nepal, Nepal negotiated a deal for the purchase of Chinese weapons in mid-1988. According to India, this deal contravened an earlier agreement that obliged Nepal to secure all defense supplies from India.

Nepal's overtures to China also had economic implications. Ever since an economic aid agreement between China and Nepal had been concluded in 1956, China's steadily increasing economic and technical assistance was being used to build up Nepal's industrial infrastructure and implement economic planning. According to a 1990 report, an estimated 750 Chinese workers were in Nepal, most of them working on road-building crews and small-scale development projects. The foreign trade balance also was in Nepal's favor. China reportedly has ceded some territory to Nepal to facilitate boundary demarcation and has endorsed Nepal as a zone of peace.

Relations with the United States

Nepal's relations with the United States were cordial. Diplomatic

relations at the legation level were established in 1947. Commercial relations were conducted according to the most- favored-nation
status. In August 1951, the two governments agreed to raise the
status of their respective diplomatic representations to the rank of
ambassador. It was not until August 1959, however, that each country established a resident embassy in each other's capital. The first
agreement for United States economic assistance was signed in
January 1951. By 1990 the United States commitment totaled approximately US$475 million.

In the late 1980s, United States economic assistance channeled
through the Agency for International Development averaged US$15
million annually. The United States also contributed to Nepal's
development through various multilateral institutions, businesses, and private voluntary organizations such as CARE, Save the
Children Federation, United Mission to Nepal, Seventh Day Ad-
ventists, the Coca-Cola Corporation, and Morrison Knudsen Corporation. Much of Washington's economic assistance has been in
the fields of health and family planning, environmental protection,
and rural development. Projects have included geological surveys,
road construction, agricultural development, and educational programs. The Peace Corps began operating in 1962 in Nepal, and
in 1991 it was the only such program still operational in South Asia.
The Peace Corps concentrated on agricultural, health, education,
and rural development programs.

United States policy toward Nepal supported three objectives—
peace and stability in South Asia, Nepal's independence and territorial integrity, and selected programs of economic and technical assistance to assist development. At the beginning of the Cold
War, the United States also had a significant strategic interest in
the country because Nepal was an outpost and a portal into China.

Although Kathmandu's primary interest in relations with
Washington was for economic and technical assistance, Nepal also
sought global support for its sovereignty and territorial integrity.
While on a state visit to the United States in December 1983, King
Birendra received President Ronald Reagan's endorsement of Nepal
as a zone of peace.

During Nepal's prodemocracy movement, the United States
Department of State voiced concern at the violent turn of events
in February 1990 and urged the government to start a dialogue
with the democratic forces in order to stop violence and repression. Congressman Stephen Solarz, Chairman of the House of
Representatives Foreign Affairs Subcommittee on Asia and the Pacific, and his colleagues twice visited Nepal and met with the king
and a wide range of political leaders undoubtedly to discuss events

relating to the prodemocracy movement. The United States-based Asia Watch human rights monitoring group published a detailed account of torture, repression, and inhumane treatment meted out to the detainees.

Relations with Britain

Nepalese-British relations spanned more than two centuries and generally were friendly and mutually rewarding (see From the Anglo-Nepalese War to World War II, ch. 5). Since the Treaty of Sagauli of 1816, when Britain began recruiting Gurkha troops, the British have had continuous official representation in Kathmandu. In 1855 a convention required the Rana prime ministers to seek unofficial British confirmation before assuming the powers of their office. The Ranas offered military assistance to the British during the Second Sikh War (1848–49), the Sepoy Rebellion of 1857, World War I (1914–18), and World War II (1939–45). During the Rana period, Nepal recognized Britain's leadership in foreign relations through numerous treaties and agreements. The Treaty of Sagauli was superseded in 1923 by the Treaty of Perpetual Peace and Friendship, which reconfirmed Nepal's independent status and remained virtually unchanged until Britain's paramountcy over India ended in 1947 and India inherited Britain's historic interest in Nepal. Britain endorsed Nepal as a zone of peace in 1980.

A minor irritant in the steady relationship between Kathmandu and London was Britain's policy, begun in the late 1980s, of gradually phasing out its employment of Gurkha soldiers. Remittances from the Gurkhas based in Britain and Hong Kong served as a stable source of foreign exchange earnings for Nepal. The dismissal in 1988 of more than 100 Gurkha soldiers based in Hong Kong caused such a furor in Nepal that the British minister of state for army supply visited Kathmandu. The minister stated that the incident was atypical and that the 5,000 Gurkhas stationed in Hong Kong would be maintained and assigned to Britain, Brunei, and elsewhere after 1997 when Hong Kong reverted to China. Britain announced in 1989, however, that the strength of the British Brigade of Gurkhas would be cut by 50 percent.

Relations with the Soviet Union

Relations between Nepal and the Soviet Union were cordial and cooperative. Diplomatic relations were established in 1956. In 1959 embassies were opened in Kathmandu and Moscow. A Soviet economic assistance program that concentrated on the industrial, health, and transportation sectors began shortly thereafter. The gross impact of Soviet aid, however, was inconsequential, and by 1990 it had trickled down only to limited training and technical assistance.

In support of India, the Soviet Union has resisted Nepal's repeated overtures to endorse it as a zone of peace. During a 1987 visit to Kathmandu, however, the Soviet deputy minister of foreign affairs stated that Moscow respected Nepal's constitution, in which the zone of peace concept was entrenched as a foreign policy goal.

Relations with Other Countries

Nepal has continually sought to establish good relations and an identity with the world community. However, because most countries recognized the primacy of India's leadership in the region, Nepal's continued efforts to expand its international activities, were of little use in solving its problems with India.

Nepal's contacts with the oil-rich Arab countries had increased in the late 1980s. A number of Nepalese citizens worked in several Middle Eastern countries, particularly the United Arab Emirates and Kuwait, and remittances from Nepalese nationals were a source of hard currency. Nepal was one of the first South Asian countries to condemn Iraq's aggression and takeover of Kuwait in August 1990. Kuwait also was an important source of development aid to Nepal.

Of the West European countries, the Federal Republic of Germany (West Germany) was Nepal's largest donor and, through 1986, provided more than Rs5.6 billion in economic and technical assistance for more than forty different projects ranging from health programs to hydroelectricity. France also had a role in assisting economic development. During the 1990 prodemocracy movement, France expressed its readiness to write off all its loans to Nepal, amounting to US$25 million, as a gesture of goodwill. The Swiss government also indicated its support of the movement and that it would probably increase its aid.

Nepal also sought to improve its international status by emphasizing its religious connections. In 1983 Nepal enlisted its support for the International Lumbini Development Project to present Lumbini, the birth place of Siddhartha Gautama, the Buddha, as a symbol of peace. Nepal continued to highlight its role as the only Hindu kingdom in the world (as stipulated in the constitution) by periodically convening the World Hindu Meet. Nepal also hosted meetings of The World Fellowship of Buddhists in Kathmandu.

International and Regional Organizations

Since the early 1950s, Nepal has pursued a calculated nonaligned policy and has become an active participant in international organizations. Nepal was admitted to the UN in 1955. Prior to its admission, Nepal already was a member of several specialized UN agencies, such as the Food and Agriculture Organization (1951); the United Nations Educational, Scientific, and Cultural Organization (1952); the World Health Organization (1953); and the Economic Council for Asia and the Far East (1954). Kathmandu often voted with the nonaligned group at the UN. In 1961 Nepal became a member of the World Bank and the International Monetary Fund (IMF—see Glossary). Nepal also was a member of the Universal Postal Union, the International Civil Aviation Organization, the International Committee of the Red Cross, and a host of other international organizations.

As a member of the Group of 77, Nepal was a vociferous champion for a new international economic order for the equitable distribution of resources and services between the developed countries and the developing world. In 1977 Nepal motivated its major foreign aid donors to form an aid-Nepal consortium to improve Nepal's ability to coordinate aid projects (see Foreign Aid, ch. 3).

Kathmandu tended to use its membership in international organizations as a forum to articulate its difficulties with New Delhi. For example, Nepal's position on the trade and transit disputes was aired at IMF and World Bank meetings. Nevertheless, most of the time Nepal voted with India in the UN. In 1987 Nepal enhanced its image in the UN when the General Assembly decided to establish a Regional Center for Peace and Disarmament in South Asia headquartered at Kathmandu. In June 1988, for the second time in twenty years, Nepal was elected to a two-year term as a nonpermanent member of the UN Security Council. At the request of the UN secretary general, Nepal sent observers and troops to supervise the Soviet troop withdrawal from Afghanistan.

Nepal also participated in various other forums for less-developed nations. In February 1985, Nepal hosted the twenty-fourth session of the Asian-African Legal Consultative Committee. Nepal participated in the thirtieth anniversary commemoration of the Asian-African Conference in Bandung, Indonesia, in 1985 and the extraordinary meeting of the Coordinating Bureau of the Nonaligned Countries on Namibia in New Delhi, at which it reiterated its support for the Namibian people.

In all the nonaligned summits held since 1961, the Nepalese delegation has been led by the king. In these summits, Nepal relentlessly has pleaded for the acceptance of peaceful coexistence and the right to remain free from military involvement.

Nepal scored a diplomatic victory in 1986 when, by unanimous decision, Kathmandu was chosen as the venue for the permanent secretariat of SAARC. In 1987 Nepal organized the first regional summit of SAARC in Kathmandu in which King Birendra reaffirmed a commitment to peace, stability, and regional cooperation. The success of this meeting and the conclusion of agreements to establish a SAARC food security reserve and to suppress terrorism enhanced Nepal's prestige. Although bilateral issues were not allowed to be raised in SAARC meetings, Nepal used the forum to parley with the smaller states of the region on the basis of a commonality of fear of Indian preeminence.

* * *

Scholarship on contemporary political developments in Nepal is limited. Although outdated, Leo E. Rose and John T. Scholz's *Nepal: Profile of a Himalayan Kingdom;* Leo E. Rose and Margaret W. Fisher's *The Politics of Nepal;* Frederick H. Gaige's *Regionalism and National Unity in Nepal;* and Rishikesh Shaha's *Nepali Politics* remain outstanding contributions on the subject. On recent political developments in Nepal, Rishikesh Shaha's *Politics in Nepal, 1980–1990* is an eminently readable account. The chapter on Nepal in Craig Baxter et al.'s *Government and Politics in South Asia* is useful in providing a regional perspective. Roop Singh Baraith's *Transit Politics in South Asia* and Parmanand's *The Nepali Congress since Its Inception* are useful collateral works. The Hoover Institution's *Yearbook on International Communist Affairs* covers activities of the Nepalese communists.

The complete text with amendments of the Nepali constitutions can be found in Albert P. Blaustein and Gisbert H. Flanz's *Constitutions of the Countries of the World.* Although Nepal's administrative structure is in transition, Hem Narayan Agrawal's *The Administrative System of Nepal* and Rishikesh Shaha's *Essays in the Practice of Government in Nepal* are basic resources. On human rights issues, Amnesty International's *Annual Report* and special reports as well as Asia Watch's special reports on Nepal are extremely useful.

There is no comprehensive up-to-date work on Nepal's international relations and foreign policy. Leo E. Rose's *Nepal: Strategy for Survival* and S.D. Muni's *Foreign Policy of Nepal* are notable works. Of the several works on bilateral relations, the following are useful: Ramakant's *Nepal-China and India;* Shankar Kumar Jha's *Indo-Nepal Relations;* T.R. Ghoble's *China-Nepal Relations and India;* and Rabindra K. Das's *Nepal and Its Neighbors.* For reportage on Nepalese politics and international affairs, weekly reports in the *Far Eastern*

Economic Review and its *Asia Yearbook,* annual essays on Nepal in *Asian Survey,* and *Europa World Year Book* are good sources. More detailed daily chronicles can be found in the Joint Publications Research Service's *JPRS Report: Near East and South Asia;* and the *Asian Recorder.* (For further information and complete citations, see Bibliography.)

Chapter 5. Nepal: National Security

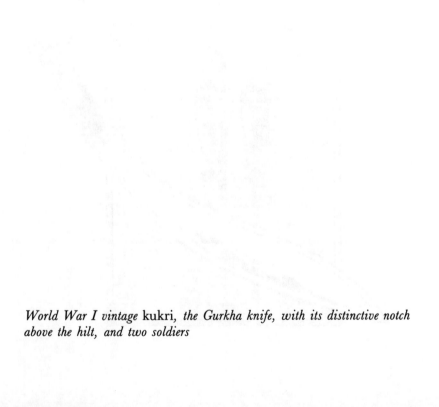

World War I vintage kukri, *the Gurkha knife, with its distinctive notch above the hilt, and two soldiers*

NEPAL IS RENOWNED for its fighting men, the fabled Gurkhas. The worldwide reputation of Nepalese soldiers as a superior fighting force can be attributed mainly to the qualities of the troops of Nepalese origin who have fought as contingents in the British Army since the early nineteenth century and for the Indian Army since its formation in 1947. With their long record of martial prowess and battlefield heroics, the Gurkhas provide one of the more colorful chapters of modern military history.

The history of the Royal Nepal Army is intertwined with that of the Rana Dynasty and its Shah predecessors (see Rana Rule, ch. 1). In the post-World War II era, the army served as a bastion of support for King Mahendra Bir Bikram Shah Dev and his heir, King Birendra Bir Bikram Shah Dev, Nepal's reigning monarch in late 1991. Many Nepalese opponents of the monarchy complained that the military was a reactionary institution bent on defending a quasifeudal system of government in the face of mounting popular calls for democratization. More conservative Nepalese, however, regarded a strong king and a traditional military beholden to royal patronage as essential elements of political stability and national independence. During the 1990 Movement for the Restoration of Democracy, or prodemocracy movement, which transformed Nepal's political system into a broad-based constitutional monarchy with elected civilian leaders, the army was used as a stabilizing force.

Nepal's military establishment in 1991 consisted of an army of 35,000 personnel. Organized largely along British lines, the force included fourteen infantry brigades, an airborne battalion, an air defense regiment, a small air services wing, and a variety of independent infantry companies and supporting units. Service in the army, an all-volunteer force, generally was held in high esteem by the general public; benefits and terms of service were attractive by local standards. Although its soldiers generally were well trained and highly motivated, Nepal lacked the resources to equip its army with anything beyond obsolete imported weapons. The officer corps had no political ambitions and invariably carried out the orders of the king and civilian authorities.

Although the military's stated mission was the classic one of defending the nation against hostile external attack, internal security—assisting the police, patrolling remote areas, and protecting the monarchy—constituted the military's primary mission. The

197

country's precarious geopolitical position between two giant neighbors, India and China, made anything more than a token conventional defense impractical. In order to ensure the country's survival,
Nepalese leaders have traditionally sought to maintain good relations with both neighbors and to obtain international recognition
of Nepal's de jure status as an independent buffer state. The protracted trade and transit dispute that poisoned Indo-Nepalese relations in 1989, although eventually resolved amicably in 1990,
reinforced the common Nepalese perception of an overbearing Indian government willing to use its economic and military advantages to intimidate its small Himalayan neighbor. Most Nepalese
regarded China as a more distant but benign power that served
as a strategic counterweight to India's supposed hegemonistic ambitions in the region.

Under the 1990 constitution, control over the nation's military
is vested in the king, although the elected civilian government acquired new authority over military affairs and national defense.
The 28,000-strong Nepalese Police Force, regarded by many observers as corrupt and inefficient, became a focus of the Nepali
Congress Party government that came to power in 1991. The new
government promised to reform the police system, overhaul the
judiciary, and improve the country's deteriorating law-and-order
situation. The constitution instituted significant reforms in human
rights and judicial practices, both of which were the objects of considerable domestic and foreign criticism.

Armed Forces and Society

Origins of the Legendary Gurkha

The term *Gurkha* (or, in Nepali, *Gorkha*) usually referred to soldiers of Nepalese origin who, over many generations, served in
the legendary British Brigade of Gurkhas. Other regiments designated as Gurkha still served in the Indian Army as of 1991. As
it has for more than 175 years, Nepal in the early 1990s served
as a source of recruits for Indian and British Gurkha regiments.
Retired British Gurkhas also served in specially raised security units
in Singapore and Brunei.

Soldiers who served in the Royal Nepal Army usually were not
called Gurkhas, although they also claimed to be the rightful heirs
of many of the same martial traditions as their countrymen who
were recruited to serve in foreign armies. The designation had no
distinct ethnic connotation but derived from the name of the old
kingdom of Gorkha (Gurkha), the territory that roughly encompassed

the present-day district of Gorkha, in the mountains some fifty-six kilometers west of Kathmandu. Soldiers from the kingdom of Gorkha established an international reputation for their martial qualities during the eighteenth century by their successful invasions of Tibet. As the Gorkha kingdom expanded eastward across the Himalayas to Sikkim, the king's warriors, taken from all groups in the area, came to be known as Gurkha soldiers. Legend had it that Gurkhas never drew their service-issued *kukri* (curved Nepalese knives) without drawing blood, even if it were their own. Although probably a tradition of a bygone era, the legend added immeasurably to the Gurkhas' reputation for toughness.

The exploits and legends surrounding the Gurkhas are among the more memorable of modern military history. The old Gorkha kingdom was established in the mid-sixteenth century by Dravya Shah, the founder of the dynasty of Shah Thakuri kings that have reigned in Nepal ever since (see The Expansion of Gorkha, ch. 1). Two centuries later, the Gorkha kingdom began a major expansion under the energetic, young King Prithvi Narayan Shah (reigned 1743–75), who conquered the Kathmandu Valley and unified numerous petty kingdoms while consolidating his control over an area substantially the same as that of modern Nepal. The first two regular Gurkha regiments, designated Sri Nath and Purano Gorakh, were raised in 1763. As Gorkha rule expanded, control over the conquered territories was left mainly to district governors (*bada hakim*), who were responsible for establishing military strong points and for maintaining a local militia.

The military prowess of the Nepalese soldier first became known in the eighteenth century, when forces from what was then known as Gorkha invaded Tibet. Within Nepal itself, certain ethnic groups, such as the Magar, Gurung, Limbu, Rai, Chhetri, and Thakuri, had much earlier won reputations as "warrior tribes." The Magar, Gurung, and Limbu furnished the bulk of the kingdom's soldiers up to the rank of captain. Higher ranks tended to be filled from the Thakuri, Chhetri, and Rai groups. These officers came almost exclusively from families of the ruling elite (see Caste and Ethnicity, ch. 2).

Until the middle of the nineteenth century, armies were raised when needed and disbanded when the need expired. This practice created a sizable reserve of trained veterans but resulted in a recurring unemployment problem. In general, only members of the higher castes were retained in military service between wars. The first steps toward the creation of a sizable permanent military establishment were taken by Prime Minister Bhimsen Thapa, who governed from 1804–37 and who raised the army's strength from

10,000 to 15,000 persons. He also built arsenals, ordnance workshops, and cantonments. The large parade ground constructed at Tundhikhel in Kathmandu during that period still was in use as of 1991.

From the Anglo-Nepalese War to World War II

Before the end of the eighteenth century, Gorkha rulers had sent successful military missions into Tibet and China. Pressure to the south and west, however, met resistance from the military forces of the British East India Company, which were expanding north of the Gangetic Plain into the Tarai and the foothills of the Himalayas. Increasingly frequent clashes of the opposing forces culminated in the Anglo-Nepalese War of 1814–16, in which the victorious British forces were impressed by the fighting qualities of their Gorkha opponents. When Nepal's General Amar Singh Thapa was forced to capitulate west of the Kali River in 1815, the remnants of his troops were accepted into the service of the British East India Company. By the 1816 Treaty of Sagauli, the British recognized the sovereignty of Nepal and received permission to recruit Nepalese soldiers (see The Making of Modern Nepal, ch. 1; Relations with Britain, ch. 4).

British recruiting efforts, which actually began in 1815, were carried on semiclandestinely even after the treaty came into force because all foreign military representatives were forbidden by Nepalese law to enter the country. The three battalions formed from General Thapa's conquered forces were expanded into regiments, and each regiment sent its own Gurkha recruiters into the interior. Applicants for service came almost entirely from the mountain areas. The ethnic groups represented included the Limbu and Rai from the Kiranti area in the east, the Magar, Gurung, and Tamang from the center, and the Chhetri and Thakuri castes from the west. These groups, eventually lumped together under the term *Gurkha*, became the backbone of British Indian forces along with other supposed "martial races" such as Sikhs, Dogras, Punjabis, and Pathans. Throughout the colonial era, the British raised the bulk of their military recruits from Nepal, Punjab, and the North-West Frontier.

The Gurkha reputation for martial prowess and obedience to authority was firmly established during the 1857–58 Sepoy Rebellion, which seriously threatened British ascendancy in South Asia. Some 9,000 Nepalese troops under Prime Minister Jang Bahadur Rana, in power from 1846–77, rendered valuable service to the British (see The Dictatorship of Jang Bahadur, ch. 1). Nepalese exploits in relieving the British resident in Lucknow made a lasting impression on British officials and strategists. Nepalese troops were awarded battle honors, and two additional regiments were raised.

Recruiting continued, and the adaptability of the Gurkha troops to various types and conditions of combat was demonstrated by their performance in the Second Afghan War (1878–80) and in the Boxer Uprising (1900). By 1908 the fabled Gurkha brigade had been formed. A flexible unit, the brigade numbered about 12,000 troops in peacetime and was organized in ten regiments, each consisting of two rifle battalions. Other Gurkha units included the Assam Rifles, Burma Rifles, Indian Armed Police, and Burma Military Police. Regiments and battalions were designated numerically. For example, the Second Battalion of the Seventh Gurkha Rifles was commonly referred to with pride by its members as the 2/7/GR.

Within Nepal itself, Prime Minister Ranoddip Singh, who governed from 1877 to 1885, introduced a militia system in the early 1880s by which the army could be rapidly expanded on short notice—an expedient which proved of great value to future British war efforts. Prime Minister Chandra Shamsher Rana, in power from 1901 to 1929, introduced many military reforms under a program to modernize government service. Among measures affecting the army were the adoption of translated British military manuals for the use of troop units, promotion examinations, improved standards of efficiency, reorganization of administrative processes, and payment of all ranks in cash, rather than in land tenure (*jagir*—see Glossary) or grain, as was formerly the practice. Despite these reforms, the officer corps above the grade of captain continued to be limited to members of the Rana family and to the Thakuri, Chhetri, and Rai ethnic groups. Barracks remained inadequate for accommodating all the men in the twenty-six battalions stationed in the Kathmandu Valley. Many soldiers had to seek their own food and lodging in towns and villages outside their garrisons.

Until 1914 the British recruited about 1,500 men per year to keep the twenty Gurkha battalions up to strength. As a rule, men from the same ethnic group were assigned to the same units. About seven regiments were composed of Magar, Tamang, and Gurung; two regiments were recruited from the Rai and Limbu; and one from the Chhetri and Thakuri. In many instances, several generations of one family served in the same regiment—a practice that continued in the early 1990s. The Magar, Gurung, and Rai, who over the years have supplied most of the recruits, are most closely associated with the fabled Gurkhas, but the Limbu, Chhetri, Tamang, Sunwar, and Thakuri also were included in the category.

On a percentage basis, the Gurung group provided a higher proportion of its total population for military service than any other group.

Under the British system, Gurkha regimental representatives examined and enlisted recruits within Nepal. From there recruits were sent to collection centers in northern India, primarily at Gorakhpur and at Ghum near Darjeeling, for final processing and assignment to units. The Nepalese government encouraged recruitment through assurances that service with British forces would be regarded as service in the Nepalese army and that special efforts would be made to provide employment for returning veterans. This policy was based on the view that returning veterans would add to the military strength of Nepal during emergencies (see Gurkhas Serving Abroad, this ch.). Relatively high pay and pensions as well as the opportunities for advancement in noncommissioned ranks also helped recruitment efforts.

During World War I (1914–18), the army was expanded and six new regiments, totaling more than 20,000 troops—all volunteers— were sent to India, most of them to the North-West Frontier Province, to release British and Indian troops for service overseas. Simultaneously, the Nepalese government agreed to maintain recruitment at a level that both would sustain the existing British Gurkha units and allow the establishment of additional ones. The battalions were increased to thirty-three with the addition of 55,000 new recruits, and Gurkha units were placed at the disposal of the British high command for service on all fronts. Many volunteers were assigned to noncombat units, such as the Army Bearer Corps and the labor battalions, but they also were in combat in France, Turkey, Palestine, and Mesopotamia. The Rana prime ministers urged Nepalese males to fight in the war. Of the more than 200,000 Nepalese who served in the British Army, there were some 20,000 Gurkha casualties.

Following the war, the Nepalese government requested that Britain cede portions of the Tarai in recognition of Kathmandu's contribution to the Allied war effort. London refused, but the Treaty of Perpetual Peace and Friendship, signed in December 1923, granted "unequivocal" recognition of Nepal's independence. This treaty formed the basis for Nepal's continued independence following the British withdrawal from India in 1947 (see The Rana Oligarchy, ch. 1).

In 1919 at the height of a civil disobedience campaign called by the Indian National Congress, Gurkha troops serving under British brigadier R.E.H. Dyer brutally suppressed a pro-independence political gathering in a walled courtyard outside the Sikh holy temple in Amritsar. Acting under Dyer's orders, the Gurkhas killed some

300 persons and wounded approximately 1,200 others. The episode generally was considered a watershed in the Indian independence movement. The Indian public, however, held Dyer and the British government responsible for the massacre and did not blame the soldiers who carried out the order to fire on unarmed civilians.

The British call to arms during World War II (1939–45) met with an enthusiastic response from the Rana prime ministers who again coerced Nepalese citizens into joining the British Army. At the outset of the war, ten Nepalese battalions arrived in India, where they served until the hostilities ended. By the close of 1946, various specialized units, such as paratroops, signal corps, engineers, and military police, had been established. Other elements served in Southeast Asia, particularly in Burma. The total number of Gurkha battalions in the British service increased to forty-five. In all, over 200,000 men passed through ten Gurkha training centers to serve in line units that fought on almost every front, although primarily in the Burmese, Middle Eastern, and North African theaters. Casualties in all theaters amounted to over 25,000 persons. Gurkha unit histories are replete with accounts of courageous stands in the face of heavy odds. In the two world wars, twelve Victoria Crosses (comparable to the United States Medal of Honor) were awarded to Gurkha soldiers.

Arrangements after World War II

The British ended their two-century rule over the subcontinent after World War II and agreed to an independent India, shorn of its Muslim-majority areas that had formed the new nation of Pakistan. Unlike most territories belonging to native princes, which were soon absorbed into the British successor states of India and Pakistan, Nepal and its feudal dynasty survived the British withdrawal intact. Still an independent entity, Nepal thus became a small South Asian state wedged between Asia's greatest land powers, India and China. Nepal nevertheless continued to provide a fertile recruiting ground for the British and Indian armies.

Under a tripartite agreement signed in 1947 by Nepal, India, and Britain, the Gurkha brigade was divided between British and Indian forces. Four regiments remained in the British service, and six passed to the new Indian Army, which recruited an additional regiment for a total of seven. Gurkha units in both military establishments played an important role throughout the postcolonial period. Gurkhas formed the backbone of the British counterinsurgency effort in Malaya that, by 1960, had crushed the communist offensive on the peninsula. Other Gurkha units fought in the defense of North Borneo against Indonesian-sponsored guerrillas in the early

1960s and also in the 1982 British campaign against Argentine forces in the Falkland Islands (called Islas Malvinas by Argentina). Throughout this period, Gurkha units were the mainstay of the British garrison in Hong Kong, which was scheduled to revert to China in 1997.

Gurkhas in the service of India have also played an important and colorful role in national defense, despite the early complaints of Indian nationalists that Nepalese soldiers were acting as British mercenaries or tools of the Ranas. According to Leo E. Rose, a noted historian of the period, "However critical the [Indian] Congress party may have been about the use of the Gurkhas by the British, their value was quickly recognized." The Rana regime sought to counter Indian criticism by specifying that Gurkhas in the Indian Army could not be used against Nepal, other Gurkha units, Hindus, or "unarmed mobs." No restrictions were imposed, however, on their use against Muslim mobs or against external enemies, including Pakistan and China.

Gurkhas, some of whom came from Nepalese families resident in the Indian Tarai, served with distinction in India's three wars with Pakistan (1947–48, 1965, and 1971). Many Indian Gurkhas also were stationed in the former North-East Frontier Agency (Arunachal Pradesh) when Chinese forces overran beleaguered Indian outposts along the disputed Sino-Indian frontier in 1962. A battalion served with distinction in the Congo (now Zaire) in the 1960s as part of the Indian Army contingent in the United Nations Operations in the Congo. Several battalions served with the Indian Peacekeeping Force in Sri Lanka from 1987 to 1990.

After World War II, the end of the British Raj (1858–1947), and the anti-Rana revolt of 1950–51, Nepal struggled to find its identity in a vastly changed Indian subcontinent. By 1950 all important army posts were held by members of the Rana ruling family. Many of the battalions had just returned from war duties in India and Burma; the battalions included some soldiers who had defected from British units and fought with the Japanese as part of the Indian National Army. The returning soldiers found that pay, rations, equipment, housing, and general conditions of service in Nepal contrasted unfavorably with what they had known under the British. Many of the general officers had never served in the lower ranks. The bulk of the army was stationed in the Kathmandu Valley, where the Rana government, aware of growing opposition, could keep potentially disloyal officers under surveillance. As remained true in 1991, British recruiters attracted the best candidates for military service because of improved prospects for advancement and higher pay. Those unable to land positions in the

Brigade of Gurkhas usually opted to serve in the Indian Army, leaving the Royal Nepal Army with the remaining large pool of recruits from which to choose.

Many World War II veterans were discharged at the end of their enlistments. Many of the officers who remained in service were unqualified to give proper training to the young replacements, and poor pay added to mounting discontent. By the time the revolt began in 1950, many soldiers were predisposed to defect to the anti-Rana forces (see The Return of the King, ch. 1). Most soldiers, however, remained loyal or, at a minimum, did not lend active support to political forces attempting to overthrow the Ranas. The officer corps, however, remained staunchly loyal to the king throughout the crisis. The organization leading the revolt, the Nepali Congress Party, developed a distrust of the army leadership that reportedly still persisted in some quarters in 1991. At the same time, memories of India's moral and limited matériel support for the 1950 uprising led some sections of the military to question the national loyalties of the Nepali Congress Party.

Legal Basis under the 1990 Constitution

The promulgation of the constitution in November 1990 opened a new era in Nepalese civil-military relations. Under the Ranas and the two monarchs of modern times, King Mahendra Bir Bikram Shah Dev (reigned 1955–72) and Birendra Bir Bikram Shah Dev (reigned 1972–   ), military and national defense decisions were the sole prerogative of the palace, acting on the advice of a small coterie of retainers and senior military commanders. Decisions were not ordinarily subject to the approval of elected bodies other than the narrowly based Rashtriya Panchayat, or National Panchayat, which served as a rubber stamp for the palace (see The Panchayat System under King Mahendra, ch. 1; The Panchayat Constitution, 1962, ch. 4).

Under the new constitutional order, the king retains his traditional authority as the supreme commander of the armed forces. The king, however, is not the sole source of authority in Nepal but rather a symbol of national unity. In a major break from past constitutional experiments, sovereignty is vested in the people, not in the person of the king. The distinction is important in that the military no longer acts solely as an instrument of the king but also is in principle subordinate to the authority of the popularly elected Parliament (see The Constitution of 1990, ch. 4).

During the protracted discussions that occurred in 1990 over the outlines of the new constitution, King Birendra, fearing that a future civilian government might radically undercut the military's prestige and with it the monarch's power or very existence, reportedly insisted on retaining ultimate authority over the military. Having to contend with independent centers of power that were beyond his direct control, Birendra realized that the military was his only reliable institutional base of support. Military commanders, for their part, feared that civilian politicians might attempt to politicize the army and undermine discipline. Consequently, the 1990 constitution represents a compromise between the king, who still retains many avenues to power should he choose, and a newly empowered civilian government.

Several provisions circumscribe the palace's previously unfettered right to employ the army as it sees fit. Unlike the legislature under the 1962 Panchayat Constitution, Parliament has real authority to determine and approve the annual defense budget. Although the role is not specified in the constitution, the civilian minister of defense oversees the day-to-day operations of the military. Conceivably, an assertive Parliament could hobble the king's authority over the army by denying funds. Day-to-day decisions affecting national security and military affairs are implemented by the king only with the advice and consent of the elected civilian government.

The power to appoint a chief of army staff, another traditional royal prerogative that afforded the palace direct control over the military, also is subject to the recommendation of an elected prime minister. This provision has the potential to precipitate a constitutional crisis should the king refuse the recommendation of the prime minister. The constitution offers no guidance should such a disagreement arise. In the first test of this clause, however, the newly elected Nepali Congress government of Girija Prasad (G.P.) Koirala assented to the appointment of General Gadul Shumsher Jang Bahadur Rana to head the Royal Nepal Army within days after assuming office in May 1991. The prime minister, the king, and the army were anxious to demonstrate that the new constitutional order was working.

Article 118 of the constitution mandates the formation of a three-person National Defence Council consisting of the prime minister, who chairs the body; the defense minister; and the chief of army staff, the nation's senior uniformed officer. According to this provision, the king "shall carry out the administration and deployment of the Royal Nepal Army on the recommendation of the National Defence Council." Although as of late 1991 there was no clear indication of the role this hybrid body performed, its formation underscored the insistence of King Birendra and the army that Parliament must not be solely responsible for national defense.

Soldiers at Sagarmatha National Park Headquarters
Courtesy Janet MacDonald

Accordingly, the National Defence Council will probably act as
an intermediary body between the Parliament and the king where
decisions affecting the military will be debated and negotiated. Under this arrangement, the army, still a critical component of political stability, also retains a formal say in national security affairs.

Despite Nepal's transition from an absolute monarchy to a
democracy, the king retains formidable emergency powers that,
if activated, would decisively tip the political balance of power in
his favor. Article 115, "Powers to Remove Difficulties," grants
the king the unilateral right to proclaim a state of emergency in
the event of a "grave crisis created by war, external attack, armed
revolt or extreme economic disorder." Under a state of emergency the king assumes direct rule and "may issue necessary orders
as are designed to meet the exigencies." Authority to implement
this provision is not clearly spelled out, but the king is specifically
authorized to suspend fundamental rights, except for habeas corpus and the right to organize political parties and unions. The
proclamation of an emergency must be submitted to the lower house
of Parliament within three months for approval by a two-thirds
majority, after which it may remain in effect for six months, with
one six-month renewal period. Although this provision was untested
as of September 1991, the king clearly has the authority to dissolve

the government and muster the nation's security forces to enforce royal decrees, if the situation warrants.

Provisions relating to the conduct of foreign affairs also have national security implications. Under Article 126, treaties with foreign governments must be ratified by a two-thirds majority of both houses of Parliament as opposed to the simple majority required for other bills. Specifically, the constitution mandates a two-thirds majority parliamentary assent to treaties bearing on "peace and friendship," defense and strategic alliances, the demarcation of national boundaries, and "national resources and distribution in the utilization thereof." One provision forbids passage of any treaty or agreement that "compromises the territorial integrity of Nepal." The rationale for these restrictions, although not spelled out in the constitution itself, clearly reflects widespread suspicions on the part of political parties and, in particular, the Nepalese public that an overbearing India might press for, or even dictate, treaty terms unfavorable to Nepal (see The Security Environment, this ch.).

Organization of the Armed Forces

The organizational structure of the Nepalese defense establishment reflected the country's indigenous military traditions, its long association with the British military, and reforms introduced by Indian military advisers in the 1950s and 1960s. There was strong reason to suspect that the basic changes introduced by the constitution as a result of the success of the prodemocracy movement would, in time, lead to new organizational arrangements and changes in command and control in line with the political realities that emerged in the early 1990s.

Following the British pattern, there was a Ministry of Defence, which, in conjunction with the king and the Parliament, was responsible for overseeing the military establishment. As with other government ministers, the minister of defense (a portfolio assumed by Prime Minister G.P. Koirala upon his government's assumption of office on May 29, 1991) was a cabinet official appointed by the prime minister. Under previous constitutions, the king ordinarily assumed the role of minister of defense, although routine oversight of the ministry was performed by a civilian bureaucrat or army officer who served at the pleasure of the king. The Ministry of Defence, located in Kathmandu, was responsible for overseeing routine matters such as pay, budget, and procurement, although the army high command retained broad discretion in matters relating to promotions and recruitment. Real command authority over military operations was generally reserved for the king, who acted in accordance with the wishes of the National

Defence Council and the elected civilian government. As of mid-1991, the degree of influence these newly chartered organizations had over military affairs could not be determined.

The nation's sole regular armed force was the Royal Nepal Army, also headquartered in Kathmandu. There was no separate air force. The army, however, operated a small air wing, primarily to transport troops within the country and to aid the civilian population during natural disasters. Because Nepal is landlocked, the country had no naval capabilities beyond a few small launches used by the army to patrol lakes and ford rivers (see Geography, ch. 2).

The Royal Nepal Army headquarters was patterned after the British and Indian systems. The highest post in army headquarters was that of chief of army staff, the only four-star billet in 1991. Directly below the chief were five staff sections: inspector general, quartermaster general, adjutant general, major general of ordnance, and the general staff general (see fig. 11). All sections were headed by major generals, a two-star billet. Of the five sections, the most important was the general staff general, as all army field echelons reported to army headquarters through him. This office also controlled functional directorates dealing with military operations, training, military intelligence, infantry brigades, and support units.

Defense Spending

Nepal was one of the poorest nations in the world. With a per capita income ranging from US$158 to US$180 per year, about 40 percent of the population living in conditions of absolute poverty, and virtually no marketable national resources, the country's fiscal resources for maintaining a standing army were woefully inadequate (see The Five-Year Plans, ch. 3). To compound matters, the country had virtually no capacity to provision its military beyond the most basic items such as food, clothing, and small-arms ammunition. Almost all of the army's equipment needs, such as air-defense guns and aircraft of all kinds, and its requirements for overhauling major equipment items were purchased abroad through scarce foreign exchange reserves or concessional terms. By any standard, the Royal Nepal Army faced severe resource constraints, even in comparison with other less-developed countries.

Nevertheless, resources earmarked for the military represented a modest defense burden. According to 1989 estimates, approximately US$33 million, or 1.2 percent of the gross national product (GNP—see Glossary), was budgeted for defense. The defense outlay represented approximately 6.2 percent of the central government expenditures budget. Health, education, and economic development clearly took priority over defense (see Regular and Development

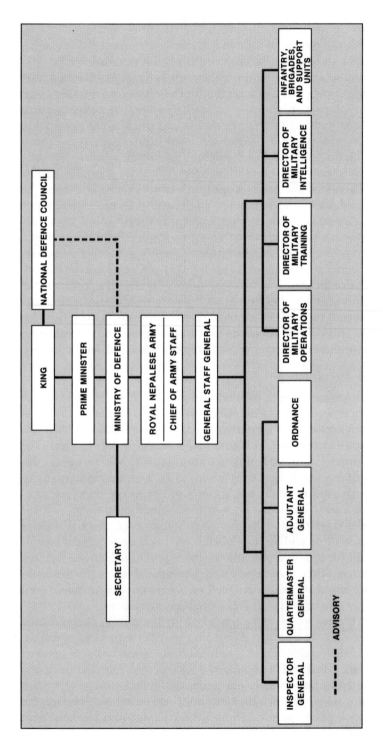

Figure 11. Nepal: Organization of the Armed Forces, 1991

Budget, ch. 3). Defense budget figures must be used with caution, however. Most observers suspected that actual outlays for the military were buried in other budget categories or else handled discreetly under accounts controlled by the royal family. Much of the defense budget, however, paid for routine recurring costs, particularly salaries and pensions. The defense budget traditionally was not subjected to close public scrutiny, and all but the most generalized statistics were a closely guarded secret. As of mid-1991, it was unclear whether this pattern would hold true. The Parliament, now genuinely representative, was constitutionally responsible for passing the annual budget and overseeing national defense requirements, but had not yet had a chance to prove itself in practice.

Missions

National Defense

The primary mission of the armed forces was defense of territorial integrity against external attack. Wedged between India and China, however, Nepal was clearly unable to mount anything more than a token conventional defense in the face of overwhelming odds. By necessity, governments in Kathmandu have always had to rely on diplomacy and the restraint of neighbors, rather than Nepal's military strength, to ensure national survival. During peacetime, the army's routine border defense duties included assisting the police in antismuggling operations and providing security in remote regions where there was no police presence.

In the event of conventional attack by either China or India, Nepalese military forces would mount a token defense to stall the enemy advance until international pressures could be mobilized to bring about a cease-fire and a return to the status quo. If international mediation failed, the military and police units that remained intact would withdraw from populated areas to lead a guerrilla war against occupation forces. Substantial numbers of Gurkha and Royal Nepal Army veterans also would be pressed into service, thereby multiplying the available military forces two or threefold. Nepal's position as a buffer state between two historically antagonistic powers also dictated that a beleaguered government in Kathmandu probably would appeal for assistance from the nonbelligerent neighbor.

Most of Nepal's population outside the Kathmandu Valley lived in hamlets that were either cut off from the rest of the country or else connected only to a local economy and communications infrastructure. Hence, the loss of some rural districts during a conventional conflict would not necessarily bring about the capitulation of the entire country. Semiautonomous guerrilla bands acting under the direction of retired or serving military officers could operate almost indefinitely and substantially raise the costs of an occupying force. However, loss of the valley, the political and cultural nerve center of the nation, could well mean the end of organized resistance. Partly for this reason, Nepal's national defenses were deployed primarily to defend the capital area in general and the national leadership in particular.

Geography also limited Nepal's capacity to mount a conventional defense of the nation. Although the Himalayas provided a nearly impenetrable shield against large-scale, rapid movement of troops from China, the harsh terrain also prevented Nepalese forces from erecting significant defenses along the 1,236-kilometer border. A paucity of roads, bridges, and airfields in the region would confine the Nepalese military response to provisioning scattered border outposts and positions near the mountainous tracks leading to some fifteen passes along the northern border (see Roads, ch. 3). The only land corridor of any significance in a conflict with China would be the main road, built with Chinese assistance, that connected Kathmandu with Tibet. New Delhi has repeatedly expressed its fears that the road could serve as a Chinese invasion route, not a Nepalese resupply route.

Mounting a conventional defense against India posed an equally daunting challenge. India boasted significant ground force assets along its 1,690-kilometer border with Nepal; moreover, these formations were connected by extensive lines of communication to the Indian heartland, where reinforcements could be introduced into Nepal in short order. Nepal had virtually no combat air capability and its rudimentary air defense assets were no match for the Indian Air Force, second in size and capabilities only to China's among Asia's air forces. Within Nepal, defense against a concerted Indian advance in the jungles and foothills of the Tarai was clearly impractical. Although the East-West Highway, or Mahendra Highway, connecting the extreme ends of the country was nearing completion in 1991, most of Nepal's approximately 4,500 kilometers of all-weather, motorable roads ran north-south, thereby complicating cross-country military movements. Avenues of approach leading north from India were considerably better developed than the generally primitive east-west lines of communication available to Nepalese forces. The country's rail network was limited to a forty-eight-kilometer spur line running from the border town of Raxaul to Amlekhganj and a fifty-three-kilometer narrow-gauge track from the Indian border town of Jaynagar to Janakpur and Bijalpura in Nepal.

Internal Security

Owing to its historical position as an instrument of royal authority, the army had always assumed the role of protecting the king against threats to his political as well as physical survival. In the modern era, the 28,000-strong Nepalese Police Force ordinarily was the first line of defense in combating incidents of political and criminal violence (see The Police System; The Judicial System, this ch.). A primary mission of the army, however, was to back up the police whenever additional coverage or firepower was required. This mission, known as "aid-to-the-civil-power" in British parlance, posed risks for the regular army. Detailing soldiers to arrest demonstrators, root out subversives, and fire on crowds risked tarnishing the army's reputation for impartiality. Moreover, overuse of the army in domestic peacekeeping tasks undermined military morale and discipline, upset routine training cycles, and diverted soldiers from conventional defense chores, such as border security. Ordinarily, the army preferred to leave routine internal security chores to the police.

The army has performed aid-to-the-civil-power duties, including riot control and disaster relief. In the 1960s and 1970s, for example, the army conducted sporadic counterinsurgency operations against Tibetan Khampa guerrillas operating in the remote mountains of northwestern Nepal. The campaign, which was finally suppressed in 1974, employed small army units trained in counterguerrilla tactics.

The army faced its most severe test during the strikes and demonstrations called by the Movement for the Restoration of Democracy, or prodemocracy movement, in the spring of 1990. The prodemocracy movement, composed of a broad spectrum of political parties led by the Nepali Congress Party and the United Left Front (a group of seven communist parties), staged a civil disobedience campaign in support of its demands for sweeping constitutional reforms. The police responded to the crescendo of protests by arresting movement leaders, closing the university and colleges, and censoring news reports of the disturbances. When these measures failed to check the demonstrations, security forces made mass arrests and resorted to firing on unruly, although usually unarmed, crowds. By March 1990, army units were heavily involved in putting down the protests and often staged "flag marches," or shows of force, to prevent crowds from gathering or to signal the government's determination to enforce emergency regulations. On April 6, the day after King Birendra reorganized his government and agreed to institute constitutional reforms, a crowd of as many as

200,000 strong gathered in downtown Kathmandu. By all accounts, the army panicked and fired on the crowd as it approached the palace, killing at least twenty-five protesters. All told, security forces reportedly killed at least fifty persons during the height of the protests between February and April.

The national elections held in May 1991 witnessed an unprecedented peacetime mobilization of military force in Nepal. Many observers of the Nepalese political scene predicted widespread violence. To head off any trouble, the entire army was put on alert and deployed throughout the country to ensure a free and fair election. Its missions included protecting polling booths, monitoring campaign rallies, and patrolling streets and highways. In addition, 42,000 retired police and soldiers were pressed into temporary service. By all accounts, the army performed well. A minimum of violence and few electoral irregularities were reported (see Elections, ch. 4). Once the voting was completed, the army returned to the barracks, police auxiliaries were relieved of their duties, and the regular police force resumed normal duties.

Force Dispositions and Capabilities

In 1991 the Royal Nepal Army, numbering approximately 35,000, was the country's sole military force. Army organization followed the British pattern. Field formations included fourteen infantry brigades. The brigades were numbered consecutively from one through sixteen (minus numbers eight and twelve, which were considered inauspicious according to Hindu astrology). The fourteen brigades, in turn, controlled a variety of units, including infantry battalions, an airborne unit, an air defense regiment, a signal battalion, a transportation regiment, an armored car company, and an unknown number of independent infantry companies and special forces units.

One of the army infantry battalions served as part of the United Nations Interim Force in Lebanon (UNIFIL) and performed peacekeeping duties in the Arab-Israeli dispute. Personnel in this battalion served six-month tours of duty, after which they returned home and were replaced by personnel drawn from other units on a rotating basis. Selection for service in UNIFIL was highly coveted by soldiers of all rank because those who served abroad received United Nations-scale pay and perquisites, as well as the opportunity to purchase consumer items that were unavailable or prohibitively expensive at home.

The peacetime disposition of forces underscored the fact that the army's primary mission was to back up local police in maintaining security in the Kathmandu Valley, the seat of government and the linchpin of political stability in the country. Fully half of the army brigades were garrisoned in or around the capitol, including the elite Royal Guards Brigade (the ninth) that served as the monarchy's praetorian guard. Additionally, many of the independent and specialized army units were attached to brigades stationed in Kathmandu. These units included an airborne battalion (known as the "para battalion") and various signal, engineer, artillery, transport, and medical units. Brigade headquarters outside the capital were located at Pokhara, Dipayal, and other towns across the country. Each of the brigades bore a distinctive unit nomenclature after the British fashion and wore distinctive arm patches. Lower echelon designations within each brigade included squadrons and troops (equivalent to United States Army companies and platoons, respectively).

Throughout its modern existence, the army has had to cope with shortages of virtually every category of weapon and equipment. Inventory consisted mostly of obsolete weapons purchased from, or donated by, India and Britain. This equipment included Ferret scout cars, various calibers of towed artillery pieces and mortars, and a diverse array of small arms. During wartime and declared national emergencies, the military had the authority to commandeer private and state-owned transport assets, such as trucks and buses for ferrying troops and supplies. Some miscellaneous equipment items, such as communications gear, small arms, and air defense guns, were purchased from France, Germany, the United States, and China. Nepal lacked both the financial resources to purchase major equipment items and a foreign benefactor willing to supply armaments on a grant or concessional basis. Consequently, it was unlikely that Nepal could sustain high-intensity combat operations without massive foreign assistance provided on a timely basis.

The army also supported a modest air wing known as the Royal Nepal Army Air Service. Based in Kathmandu and subordinate to a brigade, the organization was established in 1979. Its missions were to transport troops to far-flung outposts that were inaccessible by road, to fly paratroopers to drop zones, and to assist in civilian relief operations in the aftermath of natural disasters such as floods or avalanches. In 1991 the army air service inventory included fixed-wing aircraft, such as Indian-made HS–748 turboprops, Skyvans, and a DeHaviland Twin Otter. Its helicopter inventory included Pumas, a Bell 2061, Allouettes, and Chetaks (Indian-made Allouettes). In all, the air order of battle totalled about fourteen aircraft of all descriptions, none of which was believed to be armed with guns or missiles. Consequently, the army air service was considered a logistics support element as opposed to an offensive strike asset.

Pilots were trained abroad, primarily in India and Britain. The force reportedly suffered critical shortages of maintenance personnel, owing to the scarcity of technically competent recruits and the attraction of lucrative job offers in the Persian Gulf and elsewhere. There were thirty-six airfields in Nepal that could be used for military airlift operations. Many of the airfields were configured for short takeoff and landing (STOL) aircraft operated by Royal Nepal Airlines, the government-owned commercial airline. Commercial aircraft could be pressed into military service during emergencies (see Civil Aviation, ch. 3). In 1991 the inventory of Royal Nepal Airlines totalled eighteen aircraft.

Recruitment, Training, and Morale

In 1991 recruitment into the all-volunteer Royal Nepal Army theoretically was open to all citizens regardless of caste, religion, or ethnic background. In practice, however, recruits tended to be drawn from the ethnic and caste groups that have traditionally supplied the bulk of the Nepalese and Gurkha regiments; the military apparently preferred to recruit from ethnic groups drawn from the mountain areas and the Kathmandu Valley (see Armed Forces and Society, this ch.). Not only were these groups the traditional source of military recruitment, but they generally were presumed to be untainted by any real or imagined loyalties to India. As with similar complaints leveled against Kathmandu's preferential recruitment policies for government service, residents of the Tarai Region voiced complaints of official discrimination in military recruitment. According to press reports, residents of the Tarai Region, known as *madhesis* (''midlanders''), constituted some 40 percent of Nepal's population but were severely underrepresented in the army and police. More than 89 percent of the country was Hindu; accordingly, the religious composition of the army was thought to be almost exclusively Hindu, with a smattering of Buddhists.

Even though Nepalese, British, and Indian recruiters competed annually for the best candidates for military service, none of the forces had ever encountered a dearth of recruits. In a population of over 19 million persons, there were about 4.5 million physically fit males between the ages of fifteen and forty-nine available for military service; about 225,000 males annually reached military age, which was eighteen years (see Population, ch. 2). In the early 1990s, the army revealed no personnel mobilization plan in the event of war or a declared national emergency, nor was there any known contingency plan to institute conscription during or in

*Parading on New Road, Kathmandu, in celebration of the
royal* kumari, *the virgin goddess*
Courtesy Harvey Follender

anticipation of an emergency. Retired soldiers, however, customarily
were regarded as a valuable resource that the government could
rely upon during wartime. Over 100,000 military pensioners of the
Nepalese, Indian, and British armies resided in Nepal. This group
could provide a pool of military personnel in an emergency. All
Nepalese service personnel were liable for call-up after retirement.

The different languages that characterized the social mosaic of
Nepalese society posed no formidable obstacle because virtually
all soldiers spoke Nepali (referred to in British and Indian regiments as "Gurkhali"). Most officers, because of the higher educational requirements demanded of them, possessed at least a limited
knowledge of English. Personnel who aspired to be general officers
or to attend military training courses abroad invariably were fluent
in English.

Caste and ethnic differences were minimized by the longstanding policy of assigning recruits from the same area and ethnic groups
to the same unit, a policy also practiced in British and Indian Gurkha regiments. Low-caste enlistees often were assigned to service
units, whereas officer ranks were staffed largely by upper-caste
recruits (primarily Chhetris) and those applicants with long family
histories of army service.

217

Women played a marginal role in the armed forces in the early 1990s. Professional opportunities for women in Nepal were restricted. A woman's station in life generally was confined to raising children, maintaining the home, and performing agricultural and handicraft labor (see Women's Status and Role in Society, ch. 2). A limited number of women served in the armed forces as physicians, nurses, nursing assistants, and parachute packers attached to the para battalion. Pay scales were the same as those of males, although prospects for promotion within the few job categories open to women were limited.

Recruitment regulations prescribed that qualified candidates for enlistment appear before a selection and recruiting board composed of an officer from the Department of the Adjutant General and four other officers. Candidates were required to be between eighteen and twenty-three years of age, physically fit, and at least 161 centimeters tall. Exceptions were made for honorably discharged former Gurkha soldiers who were under the age of thirty-six, physically fit, and had not been convicted of a criminal offense. Appointment was confirmed only after the candidate's statements regarding residence, age, caste, and address were attested to by the army or civil service. A recruit could be dismissed at any time during the first year of training.

Upon entering the service, the recruit signed a contract to participate in drills and training prescribed by army regulations and to obey orders wherever he or she might be sent. Enlistment lasted for an initial period of ten years, except for former Gurkhas, who enlisted for three years. All recruits were required to take an oath to protect the life and throne of the king and to arrest or report any person threatening the king. As of 1991, the army had not revised this oath so that recruits also swore to uphold the constitution, as was the practice in many democracies. Military indoctrination at all levels still was closely associated with the defense of the king, who many Nepalese regarded as the reincarnation of the Hindu god Vishnu. Devotion to duty thus carried with it a marked element of religious devotion to the person of the king (see Religion and Society, ch. 2).

Military pay scales generally were the same as Nepalese government civilian pay scales. Although they were abysmally low by Western standards, military pay and benefits were quite attractive by Nepalese standards, and military service was highly sought after. Moreover, job security, promotion prospects, and economic attractions offered by military service were virtually unmatched in the small private sector, particularly for applicants with limited education and job skills. Pay scales also included allocations for rations and travel allowances while on duty and en route home during leave periods. Officers received housing, medical, and educational benefits, and family allowances that also were attractive by Nepalese standards. Soldiers earned pensions after seventeen years of service; maximum pension benefits could reach 60 percent of a soldier's final pay rate.

The army maintained a liberal leave policy that contributed to good morale. Leave was of three types: ordinary, home, and sick. The maximum twenty days' annual ordinary leave was not cumulative from year to year. Home leave accrued to soldiers after one year of service at the rate of forty-five days each year. Sick leave of up to fifteen days annually was authorized. Ration and travel allowances were included as part of the leave policy.

Beyond pay and leave, other factors that contributed to good morale within the ranks included opportunities to acquire an education and job skills—attributes that were transferable to civilian life. Moreover, military service carried with it the prestige of serving in a profession that was highly regarded by most of the Nepalese public.

The quality of military personnel, particularly within the enlisted ranks, was regarded by most observers as excellent. Nepalese troops are renowned for their toughness, stamina, adaptability to harsh climates and terrain, and willingness to obey orders.

Because the incidence of infectious diseases was high in the general population, malaria, tuberculosis, syphilis, and dysentery probably were present in any pool of recruits in spite of efforts to screen out the physically unfit before enlistment. In the service, however, medical care, adequate diet, and hygienic measures greatly reduced the incidence of disease, and experience in the varied environments of Asia, Europe, North Africa, and the Middle East has shown that illness in Nepalese units was not a serious problem. As of 1991, there was no indication that the army screened recruits or serving personnel for acquired immune deficiency syndrome (AIDS), and there were no publicly revealed statistics citing the incidence of AIDS within the military.

Before assignment to units, enlistees received almost a year of training under officers and noncommissioned officers specially chosen for this task. The long training period was necessitated by the high illiteracy rate—almost 70 percent nationally—making the recruitment of soldiers with anything beyond a rudimentary education difficult. Many recruits had to be taught elementary skills, such as using a telephone and driving. On the whole, soldiers probably were sufficiently trained for effective guerrilla operations or for combat in small units—the types of warfare most likely to occur.

The army supported a number of schools scattered around the country that instructed individual personnel and whole units in specialized skills, such as jungle operations, communications, medicine, and mountain warfare. A limited number of enlisted personnel and noncommissioned officers were sent to India each year for specialized training not offered in Nepal.

Training for aid-to-civil-power duties, such as riot control, was not covered extensively during the training cycle. The military generally preferred to let the police perform such functions, which most senior officers trained under the British model did not regard as "proper soldiering." That army personnel were, of necessity, becoming better acquainted with police tactics was suggested by the increased use of the army in aid-to-civil-power duties during the riots and protests that rocked the country during the 1990 prodemocracy movement, the massive army deployment to prevent violence during the national elections staged in May 1991, and the peacekeeping experience acquired during service in Lebanon.

Officer training was modeled on that of the Indian Army. This training, in turn, was strongly influenced by its long association with the British military establishment. An Indian Military Mission arrived in Kathmandu in 1952 soon after an attempted coup to assist in correcting discipline problems and organizational defects. With a staff of 100 personnel commanded by a major general, the mission implemented significant reforms in training, recruitment, promotion, and virtually every aspect of military life. In 1958 the Indian Military Mission was replaced by the Indian Military Training and Advisory Group consisting of twenty officers. This group functioned in Kathmandu until 1963, when it was renamed the Military Liaison Group and its responsibilities were reduced to liaison work on common defense problems. Nepalese nationalists complained, however, that the army's dependence on India for military training and direction was repugnant. Following significant rifts in Indo-Nepalese relations in the late 1960s, the Indian advisory group closed its offices for good (see Relations with India, ch. 4). The only Indian military presence in Nepal in 1991 consisted of a defense attaché at the high commission in Kathmandu and Gurkha recruitment centers located at Pokhara and Dharan. The only other countries with defense attachés posted to Kathmandu in 1991 were the United States, Britain, China, the Soviet Union, and Pakistan.

Although Nepalese officers still were sent to India for a variety of advanced or specialized courses as of 1991, basic officer training for "gentleman" recruits was conducted at the Royal Nepal

Military Academy at Kharipati near Kathmandu. Modeled after the Indian Military Academy and Sandhurst, the academy conducted a fifteen-month training course. Classes, usually numbering between 50 and 100 students, were divided into four cadet companies named after famous Nepalese military victories. At the conclusion of training, newly commissioned second lieutenants were assigned to units according to their specialties and the needs of the army.

Those officers who showed promise for promotion to higher commands competed throughout their careers for highly prized training assignments in the United States, Britain, Germany, India, Pakistan, and Bangladesh. Nepalese officers were not known ever to have received military training in the Soviet Union or in East European countries. A handful of army personnel may have gone to China in 1988, however, to train on the air defense guns purchased by Nepal at that time. Chinese military advisers have never been posted to Nepal, owing, in part, to Kathmandu's awareness of India's extreme sensitivity over Chinese activities in the country (see Relations with China, ch. 4).

Over the years, Nepalese officers have attended the United States Army Command and Staff College at Fort Leavenworth, Kansas; the Army War College at Carlisle Barracks, Pennsylvania; and a number of other military schools and institutions. Most expenses for this training were covered by funds appropriated under the International Military Education Training (IMET) program. The program has been open to Nepalese officers since 1947, when Nepal and the United States exchanged diplomatic recognition.

Rank Structure and Insignia

Royal Nepal Army rank structure was, like most other aspects of military life, a blending of British, Indian, and Nepalese practices. Except for honorary military titles, most commissioned officer ranks were the same as their United States and British equivalents. Exceptions included the titles field marshal (equivalent to the United States general of the armies) and colonel in chief of the army. As of 1991, Nir Shamsher Jang Bahadur Rana was the only field marshal; Crown Prince Dipendra Bir Bikram Shah Dev was the colonel in chief. Nepal's senior officer corps in 1991 numbered one general, five major generals, and about twenty-one brigadier generals. Officers' insignia displayed a variety of symbols; all, however, bore the emblem of the crossed *kukri* that identified Gurkha soldiers the world over.

Between the commissioned officers and the enlisted ranks was a separate category of junior commissioned officers (JCOs), who

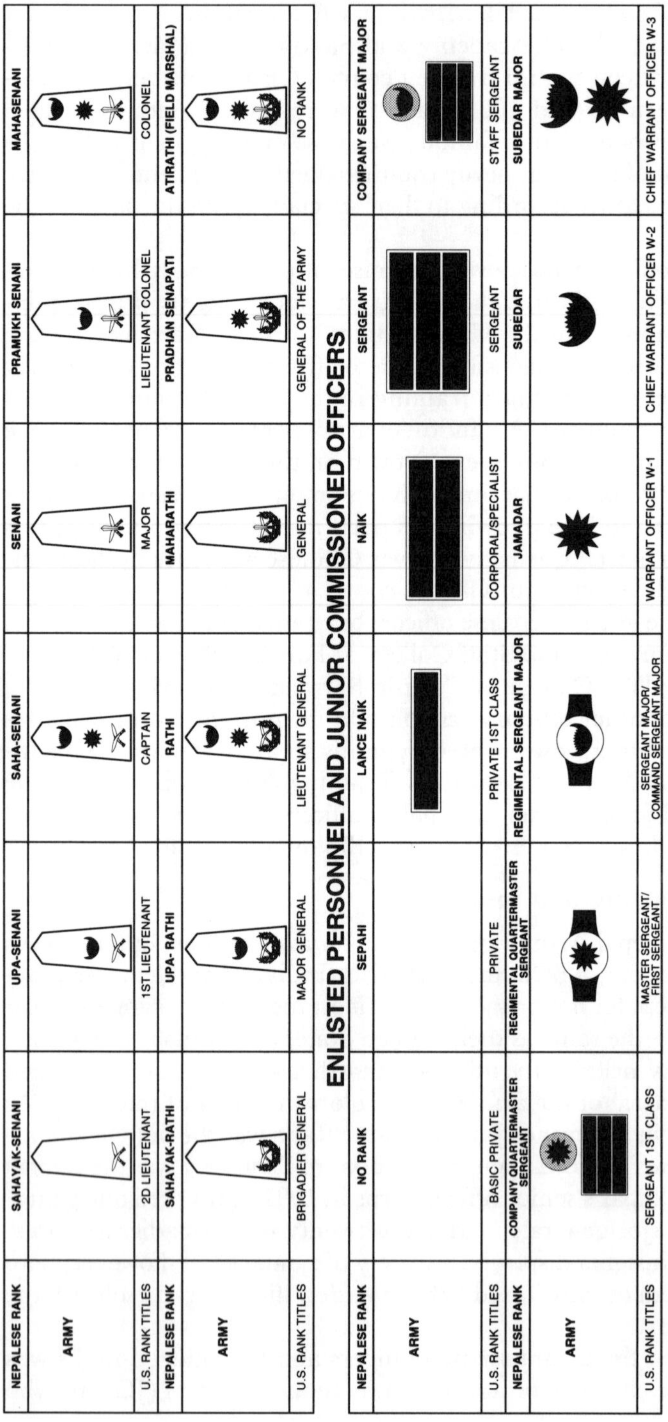

OFFICERS

NEPALESE RANK	SAHAYAK-SENANI	UPA-SENANI	SAHA-SENANI	SENANI	PRAMUKH SENANI	MAHASENANI
ARMY						
U.S. RANK TITLES	2D LIEUTENANT	1ST LIEUTENANT	CAPTAIN	MAJOR	LIEUTENANT COLONEL	COLONEL
NEPALESE RANK	SAHAYAK-RATHI	UPA- RATHI	RATHI	MAHARATHI	PRADHAN SENAPATI	ATIRATHI (FIELD MARSHAL)
ARMY						
U.S. RANK TITLES	BRIGADIER GENERAL	MAJOR GENERAL	LIEUTENANT GENERAL	GENERAL	GENERAL OF THE ARMY	NO RANK

ENLISTED PERSONNEL AND JUNIOR COMMISSIONED OFFICERS

NEPALESE RANK	NO RANK	SEPAHI	LANCE NAIK	NAIK	SERGEANT	COMPANY SERGEANT MAJOR
ARMY						
U.S. RANK TITLES	BASIC PRIVATE	PRIVATE	PRIVATE 1ST CLASS	CORPORAL/SPECIALIST	SERGEANT	STAFF SERGEANT
NEPALESE RANK	COMPANY QUARTERMASTER SERGEANT	REGIMENTAL QUARTERMASTER SERGEANT	REGIMENTAL SERGEANT MAJOR	JAMADAR	SUBEDAR	SUBEDAR MAJOR
ARMY						
U.S. RANK TITLES	SERGEANT 1ST CLASS	MASTER SERGEANT/ FIRST SERGEANT	SERGEANT MAJOR/ COMMAND SERGEANT MAJOR	WARRANT OFFICER W-1	CHIEF WARRANT OFFICER W-2	CHIEF WARRANT OFFICER W-3

Figure 12. Nepal: Military Ranks and Insignia, 1991

acted as a bridge between the officers and their troops. Adapted from the colonial commissioned officer system of the old British Indian Army, JCOs were roughly equivalent to United States Army warrant officers (although few JCOs were skilled technicians). JCOs were selected from noncommissioned officer ranks and advanced through a three-tier ranking system (*jamadar, subedar,* and *subedar major*). At the bottom of the military hierarchy were the "other ranks" (commonly referred to as ORs). These included several ranks of noncommissioned officers, *sepahis* (or, the Anglo-Indian corruption, "sepoys") and *jawans,* who together made up the bulk of the army (see fig. 12). Although the lowest army ranks had their equivalents in the Brigade of Gurkhas and the colonial successor armies of India, Pakistan, and Bangladesh, the Royal Nepalese Army maintained a distinct nomenclature not found anywhere else.

Gurkhas Serving Abroad

Despite Nepalese sensitivities over domestic and foreign criticism of allowing foreign armies to recruit "mercenaries" in Nepal, various Gurkha units continued to serve outside Nepal in the early 1990s. The only Nepalese-controlled unit abroad, however, was the Nepalese army battalion posted to the United Nations Interim Force in Lebanon. Small Nepalese contingents also have served in United Nations peacekeeping forces in Korea and the Congo (now Zaire). Unlike neighboring states, such as Bangladesh and Pakistan, Nepal did not contribute military personnel to the international coalition that defeated Iraqi forces and liberated Kuwait in the 1991 Operation Desert Storm campaign.

From Kathmandu's perspective, the military and economic advantages accruing from foreign recruitment of Gurkhas far outweighed occasional criticism. Militarily, the presence of over 100,000 trained and disciplined Gurkha veterans was a valuable human resource. Service abroad widened their horizons, and military training and discipline taught them not only how to obey, but also how to give orders. Many Gurkhas gained specialized skills in communications and engineering units, and most have had some training in such practical subjects as sanitation, hygiene, agriculture, and the building trades. The Gurkhas also played an important role in the country's economy. The cash flow derived from annual pensions, remittances to families, or monies taken home in a lump sum by discharged veterans or by service personnel on leave represented a major source of the country's foreign exchange. Remittances and pensions contributed by British Gurkhas were estimated in 1991 to total over US$60 million annually, or over twice the value of Britain's annual foreign aid commitment to Nepal.

Pensions from Indian Gurkhas also represented a major revenue source. Gurkhas returning from duty in Hong Kong also were able legally to import a few kilograms of gold bullion duty free.

In some Gurung villages, about half of the families had one or more pensioners. For many families, hope of financial solvency rested on their sons returning home with a substantial sum saved during a three-year enlistment. Such income also directly benefited the economy, as money circulated in the purchase of consumer goods, the payment of debts, the purchase of land, or investment in small commercial ventures.

The British Brigade of Gurkhas was the most famous unit. By 1991 the brigade comprised about 8,000 soldiers—five infantry battalions and supporting units—most of whom were posted to Hong Kong. There was considerable uncertainty over the brigade's future, however. Cutbacks in British military commitments in Europe, coupled with plans to cede control of Hong Kong to China in 1997, left the brigade's future in doubt. Under a proposed scheme, the brigade would be based in Britain and would induct fewer than 150 Nepalese recruits annually. An informal lobby of former Gurkha regimental commanders exerted tremendous political pressure whenever the British Parliament considered changes in Gurkha force structure. Although some Britons considered the existence of foreign-recruited units anachronistic in a modern sophisticated army, much of the British public and defense establishment harbored strong sentimental attachments to the Brigade of Gurkhas.

As of 1991, there were more than 100,000 Gurkhas serving in over forty Indian infantry battalions and elsewhere in the Indian Army. Their pay and pensions, though not as generous as British benefits, also represented a significant contribution to the Nepalese economy. Almost all of the Indian Gurkhas served in ethnically distinct regiments commanded by non-Gurkha officers. In addition, about twenty-five battalions of Assam Rifles, a specialized paramilitary force descended from the old British unit of the same name, were staffed almost exclusively by Gurkha recruits. Gurkhas played no appreciable role in Indian services other than the army and paramilitary forces. As during the British Raj, successive Indian governments called upon Gurkha regiments on numerous occasions to put down domestic disturbances that were beyond the control of local police. Ethnically homogeneous Gurkha units often were considered more reliable than mixed units that might be tempted to side with ethnic kin embroiled in a dispute.

Singapore has maintained a small Gurkha contingent attached to the Singapore Police since the early 1950s. Composed entirely of British Gurkha veterans and commanded by British officers, the contingent performed guard duties and assisted the local police in routine security chores. The sultan of Brunei also maintained a 900-person Gurkha Reserve Unit equipped with light infantry weapons. As with the Singapore unit, the Brunei Gurkhas all were British Army veterans. The unit functioned primarily as a praetorian guard that protected the sultan—reputedly the richest man in the world—against any internal or external threat that might arise.

Military Justice

The military court system consisted basically of courts-martial, similar in composition and jurisdiction to those of the Indian Army. Courts-martial were of four kinds: general, district, summary general, and summary. A general court-martial was convened by the king or an officer deputized by him. It consisted of five or more officers, each with three or more years of commissioned service. Attending the court, but not a member, was an officer of the Department of the Judge Advocate General or an officer designated by the judge advocate general. The court was authorized to impose any sentence prescribed by army regulations. A district court-martial consisted of three or more officers, each with a minimum of three years of commissioned service, and could impose any sentence other than the death penalty. A summary general court-martial consisted of three or more officers, with no requirement as to the length of their commissioned service. A summary court-martial was convened by an officer of the rank of battalion commander or above, who acted as the court.

The death sentence, banned in civilian cases under the 1990 constitution, was imposed for treason, mutiny, desertion, inciting panic, and surrender of troops, arms, or garrisons to the enemy with a finding of cowardice. Authorized punishment for dereliction of military duties or regulations in time of war generally was twice as severe as that prescribed for the same offense committed in peacetime. Contact with foreign diplomats and attachés, however innocuous, was strictly forbidden. A few high-ranking officers in army headquarters were allowed to interact with foreigners but only on official matters. Failure to observe this rule could damage a soldier's promotion prospects or lead to disciplinary action.

The disciplinary powers of officers and noncommissioned officers were more extensive than in the United States military service. Unit commanders could impose up to thirty days' confinement in prison or restriction to barracks. The most common forms of company punishment included extra guard duty, suspension from duty or from supervisory assignments, fines of up to fourteen days' pay, detention of pay until a financial or property loss was compensated, reprimand, and warning. Junior commanders could demote officers with the rank of *hudda* (sergeant) or lower.

The Police System

Until the middle of the nineteenth century, police and judicial functions in many areas were in the hands of local princes (rajas), who were virtually autonomous rulers of their people. The central government ruled outside the capital and delegated authority to the local governors, later known as *bada hakim,* who in turn depended on village heads and village councils to maintain order in their respective communities. The scope and intensity of police and judicial activities varied largely with local leaders and customs. Caste status and standing with the authorities also greatly influenced court judgments and police attitudes. Efforts by the central government to enlarge its authority over local affairs generally were regarded by the isolated tribal groups as encroachments on their traditional independence. Thus, old practices tended to persist in the hinterland despite changes in the government and government policy in Kathmandu.

The Ranas did not establish a nationwide police system, although Prime Minister Chandra Shamsher Rana, who served from 1901 to 1929, somewhat modernized the police forces in Kathmandu, other large towns, and some parts of the Tarai. Police functions in outlying areas, because of the relative isolation of most communities, generally were limited to the maintenance of order by small detachments of the centrally controlled police personnel supplemented by a few locally recruited police.

Following the anti-Rana revolt that began in 1950, the government began to modernize the police system and improve its effectiveness. Assistance was requested from India, and an Indian police official was sent to Kathmandu to help reorganize the police force. Some Nepalese police were sent to police training academies in India.

Nepal's police system in the early 1990s owed its modern origins to the Nepal Police Act, enacted by King Mahendra in 1955. Besides defining police duties and functions, the act effected a general reduction in the size of the police force and a complete reorganization of its administrative structure along Indian lines.

In accordance with the Nepal Police Act, Nepal was divided into three geographical zones (sometimes called "ranges" in Indian parlance). Each of the zonal headquarters, under a deputy inspector general of police, was responsible for several subsections composed of four or five police districts operating under a superintendent of police. A district superintendent was in charge of the police stations in his area. Each station normally was supervised by a head constable who was in charge of several constables performing basic police functions, such as crime investigations and arrests. Each constable was customarily responsible for three or four villages.

Under the constitution, law and order at the district level continues to be the responsibility of the chief district officer, who is selected from among senior cadre civil servants under the Ministry of Home Affairs. Other district administrative officers work in coordination with the chief district officer. Despite the abolition of the *panchayat* (see Glossary) system, no significantly different alternative system had emerged as of mid-1991. During the interim, village and municipal development committees, consisting of persons nominated by chief district officers, replaced village and town *panchayat,* which had exercised administrative and some quasi-judicial functions at the local level. At the local level, maintenance of law and order is the responsibility of the *chowki hawaldar* (local police officer), who reports to the *thana* (station inspector). All local police officers work under the supervision of the chief district officer.

At the apex of the system was the Nepalese Police Force, centrally administered by the Ministry of Home Affairs. The Central Police Headquarters, commanded by the inspector general of the Nepalese Police Force, had a criminal investigation division; intelligence, counter-intelligence, motor transport and radio sections; a traffic policy branch; and a central training center.

The police system formerly had been overseen by the king and his advisers, with little or no public accountability. Under the partyless *panchayat* system, the public generally regarded the police as instruments of the king and his local political supporters. Nepalese police were poorly paid and poorly trained, even by Nepalese standards.

The administration of justice was often arbitrary and, according to international human rights organization, brutal. A 1989 United States congressional report on human rights in Nepal noted ''continuing reports of beatings and other brutal treatment of prisoners by police officials, particularly in rural areas.'' The report also noted that arbitrary arrest and detention were ''common. . . . Because communication links in Nepal are limited, local officials have a great deal of autonomy and exercise wide discretion in handling law and order issues.''

Although the Nepalese police system in the early 1990s still was generally regarded as inefficient and corrupt, most observers believed that Nepal's transition from a feudal monarchy to a parliamentary democracy had greatly improved the chances for police reform and the curtailing of human rights abuses by the police. As in the case of the army, police loyalties were severely tested during the 1990 nationwide prodemocracy movement. Although acting under the guidance of the palace, the police generally did not take sides in the political standoff. Even though police excesses occurred, force discipline did not break down.

Shortly after his election to office, Prime Minister G.P. Koirala pledged that improving law and order and protecting human rights would be his administration's top priorities. Koirala's critics noted, however, that his tough law-and-order stance was intended less to promote human rights reforms and more as a political signal to communist elements threatening to mount street protests against the new democratic government. In April 1991, Nepal acceded to the International Covenant on Civil and Political Rights and the Convention Against Torture and Other Cruel, Inhuman, or Degrading Treatment.

State-supported penal institutions, including the central prison in Kathmandu and jails in most district capitals, had long been targets of considerable criticism on the part of human rights activists. According to various reports on human rights, prison conditions were unsanitary and degrading. Prisoners were segregated into three categories. Class C prisons, the lowest and most numerous type of prison, were populated with common criminals who often were subjected to beatings and abuse at the hands of police jailers. The higher prison categories were reserved for persons with political connections or higher social status. Conditions in these facilities generally were better than in Class C prisons. Women were incarcerated separately from men although in equally poor conditions. Mentally ill persons often were placed in jails because most communities lacked other, more appropriate, long-term care facilities. In an effort to address some of these problems, the Koirala government shifted prison administration and management from the police to the Ministry of Home Affairs shortly after assuming office in 1990.

The Judicial System
The Legal Code

The judicial system initiated under the Ranas, despite some limited reforms, remained traditional in character in the early 1990s. The Muluki Ain of 1854, the legal code introduced by the first Rana prime minister, Jang Bahadur Rana, combined ancient Hindu sanctions and customary law and common laws modeled on the

British and Indian codes with the rules of behavior that had evolved over the centuries among the Newars in the Kathmandu Valley (see The Kot Massacre, ch. 1).

The Muluki Ain was amended several times and was completely revised in 1963. Over the years, the Muluki Ain blended royal edicts, proclamations, and piecemeal legislation. The entire corpus of law was consolidated in a compilation called the Ain Sangraha. Customs were applied in the absence of legislative provisions or judicial procedures.

The revised code sought to promote social harmony and declared all persons theoretically equal in the eyes of the law, thus ending legal discrimination based on caste, creed, and sex. The code granted the right to divorce, permitted intercaste marriages, and abolished the laws sanctioning untouchability. These provisions were drafted at the behest of the king. A uniform family law was applicable to all religious communities and was contained in the Muluki Ain. When the code was silent, however, the custom of the particular community applied. The code remained the existing substantive law in 1991.

The Court System

The official text of the Muluki Ain was published in Nepali; few statutes were available in English. Statutes were cited by the years of enactment. The *Nepal Raj Patra,* the government gazette, issued at irregular intervals, published all new legislation. Official texts of Supreme Court decisions were published monthly in the *Nepal Kanoon Patriki,* the Nepalese law journal, which also contained the official texts of new legislation and articles on legal topics. The Nepal Act Series, published by the Law Book Management Board in Kathmandu, by arrangement with government ministries, was a compilation of all Nepalese laws and statutes.

Under the vague instrument of the Muluki Ain prior to its 1963 revision, magistrates and justices had wide latitude in deciding cases according to their own interpretations. There was a motive for caution, however, in the provision that if a higher court reversed the decision of a lower court, the magistrate of the lower court was liable to a fine, corporal punishment, or even execution. Court procedures varied greatly. The accuser was placed in jail along with the accused. Writs of habeas corpus were not issued. Prisoners often waited many months before trial. The onus of proof of innocence rested on the accused, who was tried without a jury.

Under the rules, no one could be convicted of a criminal charge without a confession, but confessions were commonly extracted by torture. The Rana courts had both executive and judicial powers, and the prime minister was the supreme judicial authority whose decision on a given case was final.

Reforms enacted under the constitution of 1948 and in the first years following the 1951 overthrow of Rana rule modernized many features of the feudal-based legal system. The prime minister was divested of judicial powers and no longer functioned as the highest court of appeal. The Supreme Court Act of 1952 established the Supreme Court as the highest judicial body, with powers and structure corresponding generally to those of the Supreme Court of India. Special traveling courts were organized and were sent into the districts to provide citizens easier access to the legal system. These courts were empowered to audit public accounts, hear complaints of all kinds, make arrests, hold trials, and impose sentences. An important step toward a unified judicial system came in 1956 with the establishment, mostly in the Tarai, of a series of district courts that heard civil and criminal cases. Appeals courts were set up in Kathmandu. The 1962 Panchayat Constitution stipulated that the king was solely responsible for appointing judges and providing judicial overview.

Under the Panchayat Constitution, the court system was headed by the Supreme Court, composed of a chief justice, nine judges, and a small secretarial staff. Below the Supreme Court were fourteen zonal courts, which, in turn, oversaw seventy-five district courts throughout the country. All the lower courts had both civil and criminal jurisdiction. Although the judiciary technically was independent, in practice the courts never were assertive in challenging the king or his ministers.

The constitution promulgated in 1990 reorganized the judiciary, reduced the king's judicial prerogatives, and made the system more responsive to elected officials. Under the new system, the king appointed the chief justice of the Supreme Court and the other judges (no more than fourteen) of that court on the recommendation of the Judicial Council. Below the Supreme Court, the constitution established fifty-four appellate courts and numerous district courts. The judges of the appellate and district courts also were appointed by the king on the recommendation of the Judicial Council. The Judicial Council, established in the wake of the prodemocracy movement and incorporated into the constitution, monitored the court system's performance and advised the king and his elected government on judicial matters and appointments. Council membership consisted of the chief justice of the Supreme Court, the minister of justice, the two most senior judges of the Supreme Court, and a distinguished judicial scholar. All lower court decisions, including acquittals, were subject to appeal. The Supreme Court was the court of last resort, but the king retained the right to grant pardons and suspend, commute, or remit any sentence levied by any court.

The new judicial system still was in its infancy as of 1991. Some observers noted that judicial appointments had remained a source of patronage by which the elected government rewarded its supporters. Others feared that Nepal lacked the legal resources to staff an expanding and modern judicial system. The growing backlog of legal cases, many of them initiated during the 1990 prodemocracy upheaval, also threatened to overwhelm the system. Despite these drawbacks, however, most observers of the legal system felt the changes were forward-looking and progressive.

The Security Environment

Throughout its modern existence, Nepalese foreign policy architects and defense planners have had to perform a precarious balancing act to ensure the nation's survival. As a protective measure, foreign troops were not allowed to be based in Nepal. This restriction remained in force as of 1991. Neither China nor India harbored territorial ambitions in Nepal; indeed, unlike many other land boundaries in South Asia, Nepal's frontiers were regarded by India and China as valid international boundaries. Nor did Nepal possess any natural resources or other economic assets that were coveted by either neighbor. Nevertheless, the country's geostrategic position between China's restive Tibetan population and the Indian heartland placed it in a vulnerable position.

Terrain, weather, and logistic considerations presented special problems for defense planners and for any foreign forces that might have to operate in the country. Ground units had to be equipped to cope with climatic extremes of monsoonal rains and drought as well as jungle heat and high-altitude cold. Nepal's terrain ranged from the world's highest and most deeply gorged mountains to the swamps and dense jungles of the Tarai (see The Land, ch. 2). Troops operating in Nepal had ample cover, but cross-country movement was extremely difficult. The use of motor transport—often in short supply in the Nepalese army—was impractical except for the short stretches where roads existed. Further, many roads and bridges were unsuitable for heavy military vehicles. In the higher elevations, supplies were moved by pack animals or human porters. Throughout the country, the terrain lent itself to the ambush and hit-and-run tactics that Nepalese units would employ during a partisan struggle. Thus, local inhabitants familiar with the countryside and accustomed to its severe climatic conditions would have a decided tactical advantage over invading forces.

In the lowlands, ground movement was virtually impossible during the wet season because of extensive flooding, washed-out bridges, and deep mud. In the mountains, troops had to march single file over precarious trails subject to washouts, landslides, avalanches of boulders, ice, and snow. Stream crossing points often were limited to fords and unstable suspension bridges. Supply drops by helicopters and airplanes—both critically short in the Nepalese army—could be made only in favorable weather and in the restricted areas accessible to troops. Tribhuvan International Airport outside Kathmandu was the country's only airfield with sufficient capacity for large-scale military airlift and resupply operations. The airport's refueling capacity and aircraft maintenance facilities were marginal, however. Only five of Nepal's thirty-eight airfields had permanent-surface runways.

Tropical diseases, such as malaria, and the danger of suffering pulmonary edema and frostbite during high-altitude operations further inhibited force sustainability. Medical equipment and supplies, most of which were imported from India, also were in short supply. Water supplies, although usually available in all but the most mountainous regions, often were contaminated and unfit for human consumption unless treated. Although army medical services were adequate for routine peacetime health care of soldiers and their families, sustained combat operations probably would overwhelm the country's underdeveloped health services. The army's premier medical facility, Birendra Hospital, was located in Kathmandu. As food production in most areas was barely sufficient to support the local population, wartime destruction of the agricultural infrastructure, particularly in the fertile Kathmandu Valley, would be likely to result in shortages and famine unless India or other foreign donors provided immediate emergency relief.

India

Although landlocked Nepal was surrounded by both India and China, the kingdom's geographic, economic, and cultural orientation was more closely linked to India. Whereas many Nepalese stressed the differences that defined Nepal's national existence, India's policy makers tended to stress the similarities that bound the two countries together. According to New Delhi's perception, South Asia constituted an integral security unit in which India played the lead role. Many Nepalese resented this interpretation and accused India of being insensitive to Nepal's status as an independent nation.

Despite New Delhi's insistence that stable, independent neighbors were vital to India's security, many Nepalese regarded India as a regional bully. Because of these differing attitudes, Nepal's relations with India oscillated considerably over the years, particularly in matters relating to security.

In a speech before Parliament in 1950, the Indian prime minister, Jawaharlal Nehru, summed up India's security concerns vis-à-vis Nepal. He stated: "From time immemorial, the Himalayas have provided us with magnificent frontiers. . . . We cannot allow that barrier to be penetrated, because it is also the principal barrier to India. Therefore, as much as we appreciate the independence of Nepal, we cannot allow anything to go wrong in Nepal or permit that barrier to be crossed or weakened, because that would be a risk to our own security." Nehru and his successors subsequently stated that any Chinese attack on Nepal would be regarded as aggression against India.

In 1950 China forcibly annexed Tibet, which New Delhi regarded as a buffer zone shielding the subcontinent from real or potential Chinese incursions. Nepal thus came to play a much larger role in India's security calculations. Fearing that China might eventually subvert or invade Nepal, India signed a Treaty of Peace and Friendship with the Rana regime in 1950. Although not a formal military alliance, the treaty required both parties to consult and "devise effective countermeasures" in the event of a security threat to either country. Nepal's inclusion in the Indian defense perimeter was made explicit by an exchange of secret letters—later made public—that accompanied the treaty, stating inter alia that "neither government shall tolerate any threat to the security of the other by a foreign aggressor." To assuage Nepalese fears of Indian domination, the treaty also stipulated that Indian forces could be introduced into the country only at the invitation of the Nepalese government. The two sides simultaneously signed a trade and transit agreement that extended reciprocal rights with regard to bilateral trade and residential arrangements as well as transshipment of Nepalese goods through India.

In 1952 the Indian Military Mission arrived in Kathmandu to reorganize Nepal's armed forces and bring the kingdom's defenses more in line with India's security requirements. In implementing changes, Nepal drastically reduced the size of its postwar army and revamped its training and organization along Indian lines. Indian advisers also played key roles in training the civil service and police force. Many Nepalese—military officers and civil servants, in particular—were outraged by India's actions, which they saw as an insult to national self-respect. Indian influence was further strengthened, however, by the cooperation of both countries' militaries on several occasions in the 1950s, when at Nepal's request

Indian troops helped quell disturbances near their common boundary. As Sino-Indian tensions mounted in the late 1950s, Indian soldiers and technicians assisted in staffing some of the checkposts on the frontier with Tibet. Despite close military ties, Nepal, however, has never allowed garrisoning of Indian troops or joint military exercises in the country.

In 1962 Indian and Chinese forces fought a brief but decisive war over desolate stretches of their disputed frontier. India's unprepared forces suffered a humiliating defeat, despite the fact that China unilaterally withdrew its forces after several weeks of heavy fighting. Although Nepal did not become embroiled in the fighting and both belligerents respected the kingdom's territorial integrity, the war reinforced Nepalese perceptions of their country's perilous role as a Sino-Indian security buffer.

Because of India's growing influence and Nepal's corresponding dependence on India, international diplomacy has always been a vital element of Nepal's survival strategy. Nepal was an active participant and a voice of moderation in the United Nations (UN) and the Nonaligned Movement, although the viability of the latter organization was in doubt after the end of the Cold War (see International and Regional Organizations, ch. 4). In addition, Nepal firmly supported the South Asian Association for Regional Cooperation (SAARC—see Glossary) headquartered in Kathmandu. SAARC eschewed any role in regional security because the threats perceived by Nepal and the other small states of the region were often at variance with those perceived by India.

In 1975 King Birendra proposed that the UN declare Nepal a zone of peace, where military competition would be off-limits. In Birendra's view, the proposal symbolized Nepal's desire to maintain cordial relations with both its neighbors by placing internationally sanctioned restrictions on the use of military force (see Foreign Policy, ch. 4).

Nepalese-Indian relations underwent major jolts over a protracted period starting in 1988. In June of that year, Birendra concluded a secret arms purchase with China, whereby Beijing would supply obsolescent air defense artillery at bargain prices. India probably learned of the deal within days or weeks of the agreement and protested vigorously that Birendra's action had violated the spirit, if not the letter, of the 1950 treaty. Although the appearance of a limited number of vintage air defense weapons hardly represented a threat to Indian Air Force contingency plans, India interpreted the sale as a dangerous precedent that could not go unchallenged. As bilateral tensions mounted, India added other complaints regarding Nepal's supposed insensitivity to India's vital interests. Birendra, capitalizing on nationalistic fervor, was intransigent and insisted that Nepal had the sovereign right to determine its own defense requirements. He also pointed out that Nepal's use of air defense assets against India would never arise as long as Indian fighters respected Nepalese air space; New Delhi countered that the only plausible use for the weapons was against India.

In March 1989, the Nepal-India trade and transit agreement came up for renewal. India's prime minister, Rajiv Gandhi, refused to extend the agreement unless Nepal agreed to meet India's commercial and defense concerns. After both sides refused to back down, India allowed the agreement to lapse and closed thirteen of the fifteen border checkposts that regulated most of Nepal's trade with the outside world. The blockade was a severe blow to Nepal. The Chinese rail line in Tibet ended 800 kilometers short of the Nepalese border, and the road linking Kathmandu and Tibet was closed much of the year by avalanches and monsoon landslides. The Nepalese army was pressed into action to keep Nepal's section of the road open to the extent possible. Pakistan and Bangladesh were hardly in a position to supply major assistance because their only land routes to Nepal traversed India. The Soviet Union, the United States, and other Western powers quietly declined to take sides and urged India and Nepal to return to the bargaining table.

In the final analysis, the dispute underscored a central geopolitical reality: landlocked Nepal did not have the military, diplomatic, or economic clout to withstand an Indian blockade as long as the government in New Delhi was willing to risk international opprobrium and press its case against the kingdom. Many Nepalese saw New Delhi's actions as ''punishment'' for Birendra's show of independence and as a manifestation of India's supposed policy of isolating and subjugating its smaller neighbors. Some Nepalese observers, however, criticized Birendra's handling of the dispute, arguing that the king harnessed popular fervor against India to rally patriotic support behind the palace.

Some fifteen months of economic dislocations and diplomatic recriminations placed heavy pressure on both sides to halt the slide in relations. Finally, both sides reaffirmed the 1950 treaty, and Kathmandu agreed not to purchase defense items abroad without consulting New Delhi. Birendra requested that China stop delivery of a final shipment of air defense equipment. Relations gradually returned to normal and improved significantly after Nepal's democratically elected government assumed office in May 1991. The dispute convinced many Nepalese, however, that India had the capacity and will to pressure small neighbors in pursuit of its foreign policy objectives—a message that New Delhi clearly intended to convey to Beijing.

China

Nepal's security relations with China dated at least as far back as the eighteenth century. In the nineteenth century, Nepal gained the upper hand over Tibet, then a semiautonomous vassal state of China. In the latter part of the twentieth century, however, Nepal's dealings with China generally had been kept on an even keel, except when India expressed strong disapproval, as in the aftermath of China's 1988 sale of air defense weapons to Nepal.

The earliest defense pact with China was the Sino-Nepalese Treaty of 1792, signed after the Chinese had defeated the forces of the Gorkha kingdom at Nawakot, some seven kilometers northwest of modern Kathmandu. Under this treaty, the signatories agreed that they would regard China as a "father" to them and affirmed their understanding that China would come to the aid of Nepal should it ever be invaded by a foreign power—although no such assistance occurred during the Anglo-Nepalese War of 1814–16 (see The Enclosing of Nepal, ch. 1). In the mid-nineteenth century, however, forces from the kingdom of Gorkha were on the move northward. The Nepalese-Tibetan Treaty of Thapathali, signed in 1856 at the conclusion of a successful two-year campaign in Tibet, stipulated that Tibet pay annual tribute to Nepal and grant certain extraterritorial rights to Nepalese traders. It also pledged a mutual policy of nonaggression, and China agreed to come to Nepal's assistance should Nepal be invaded by the forces of "any other prince." A century later, in September 1956, the agreement was replaced by a treaty of amity and commerce with China's new communist regime, ending Nepal's tributary income and extraterritorial privileges.

Although China offered to sign nonaggression or mutual defense pacts with Nepal, the kingdom always turned down the offers in deference to Indian sensitivities. In the 1950s, Nepal's anticommunist rulers, spurred on by Indian advisers, regarded China as a potential threat and enacted various military reforms and laws to combat Chinese propaganda and subversion. In 1961 King Mahendra visited Beijing and signed an agreement to construct a highway, named the Arniko Highway, from Kathmandu to Kodari on the Tibetan border. As of 1991, this highway remained the only major artery linking the two countries. Nepal generally preferred to keep relations with China low-key to avoid offending India. The 1988 decision to purchase Chinese air defense weapons was a glaring exception to this rule.

Royal Nepal Army
soldier at the gate
of the old
royal palace,
Kathmandu
Courtesy
Harvey Follender

Internal Security Considerations

Nepalese police, backed from time to time by the army, combat routine crimes in addition to monitoring numerous political strikes and demonstrations. The incidence of organized political violence was low, however. Nepal was not a fertile breeding ground for international terrorism because most political violence was committed by Nepalese dissidents to further their own domestic political agendas.

In the mid-1980s, small antimonarchist and communist groups conducted a series of bombings in the Kathmandu Valley to dramatize their opposition to Birendra's rule. In June 1984, clandestine Maoist bands such as the Samyuktha Mukti Bahini (Socialist Liberation Army), the Democratic Front, and the United Liberation Torch Bearers mounted a campaign of bombings and assassinations intended to spark a revolution. Their actions had the opposite effect, however, as moderate opposition politicians condemned the violence and rallied around the king. The opposition civil disobedience campaign was called off, and the Rashtriya Panchayat passed a stringent antiterrorist ordinance to put down the threat. By August 1984, over 1,000 suspected terrorists and sympathizers were imprisoned under provisions of antiterrorist legislation promulgated by the king.

The following year, another bombing in downtown Kathmandu killed eight persons and wounded twenty-two others. The sensational crime was perpetrated by the Jan Morcha (People's Front), a Tarai-based antimonarchist group with ties to political thugs in the Indian border states of Uttar Pradesh and Bihar. Several Jan Morcha leaders who fled to India were convicted of the bombing in absentia. In June 1991, following the installation of the Nepali Congress Party government, King Birendra pardoned the exiled terrorists as a gesture of political goodwill.

The ethnic tensions that spilled across Nepal's international boundaries also posed security and foreign policy problems. In 1987 the Nepalese minority residing in the mountainous northern districts of the Indian state of West Bengal mounted a violent agitation demanding statehood within the Indian union for Indian citizens of Nepalese origins. The standard bearer of the campaign was the Gorkha National Liberation Front led by Subhas Ghising, a former noncommissioned officer in an Indian Gurkha regiment. The communist state government of West Bengal complained of Nepalese collusion with the agitators after Ghising openly solicited Kathmandu's support and called on Gurkhas in the Indian Army to back the demand for a separate "Gorkhaland." The situation worsened when Indian police crossed the Nepalese border while pursuing Gurkha militants. Although Kathmandu probably was sympathetic to the plight of the Nepalese minority, any appearance of support for the statehood agitation was scrupulously avoided for fear of angering New Delhi. Official Nepalese support for the movement never was proven. By 1991 the Gorkhaland agitation had subsided after New Delhi, West Bengal, and Gurkha militants negotiated a political settlement that fell short of statehood.

In the 1980s, some of the young, militant Nepalese population residing in the southern part of Bhutan began to complain of systematic discrimination at the hands of the Bhutanese government. As many as 6,000 ethnic Nepalese refugees fled to Nepal. Because there were another 16,000 Nepalese refugees who had fled from Bhutan to India, the ethnic dispute in Bhutan threatened to become a transregional security problem involving all three states (see Political Developments, ch. 6).

The strong communist showing in the 1991 election was a disturbing development from the perspective of Birendra and the army. The Nepali Congress Party, a longtime political and ideological foe of the communists, also harbored deep misgivings over communist political intentions. Many observers feared that the relatively open political environment would allow disciplined communist cadres to mount street protests, paralyze the government, and force a showdown with the king and the army. Army officers, most of whom rejected the antimonarchist platform of the communists, invariably regarded the communists as a potential security menace and a threat to the throne. There was no evidence in late 1991 that the some twenty Nepalese communist factions then in existence commanded any appreciable support within the army rank-and-file.

The Military in the Early 1990s

In the early 1990s, the military retained its generally privileged position in society. Constitutional arrangements mandating an unprecedented degree of civilian control over national defense and military affairs still were being ironed out, however, and the country's experiment in participatory democracy still was in an embryonic stage. The Royal Nepal Army's position during the 1990 prodemocracy campaign prompted many observers to predict that the military would willingly accept its role in the new constitutional order. Other observers, noting possibilities of heightened political competition and strife in the kingdom, were not so sanguine. Nepal, however, has never experienced a military coup d'état—although the 1960 palace coup by King Birendra was backed by the military. In sum, the military's position in society and its subservience to civilian authority was a continuing process, not a settled fact.

There were calls from some political quarters, particularly radical communists and a section of the intelligentsia, to abolish the monarchy, overhaul the military chain of command, slash the defense budget, and ban Indian and British military recruiting of Nepalese citizens. These objectives were not shared by the ruling Nepali Congress Party government, King Birendra, large sections of the Nepalese public, and the military itself—all of which voiced unequivocal opposition to any political attempts to radically alter traditional patterns of civil-military relations. By 1991 the Royal Nepal Army, long a bulwark of the monarchy, appeared to be adjusting to the new requirements laid down by the constitution and the new democratically elected government. Most civilian politicians also recognized the value of maintaining a disciplined, reliable military that could enforce public order, symbolize the nation's independence, and allow the government to proceed with the monumental task of improving the economic well-being of its citizens.

* * *

There are numerous popular works detailing the history, traditions, and martial prowess of the Gurkhas. Among the more interesting are such vintage publications as Francis Ivan Simms Tuker's *Gorkha: The Story of the Gurkhas of Nepal,* Byron Farwell's *The Gurkhas,* and Robin Adshead's *Gurkha: The Legendary Soldier.* John Masters's classic novel *Bugles and a Tiger* provides colorful insight into the Gurkha tradition. For insights into the British Indian Army from which the Royal Nepalese Army traces its origin, see Stephen P. Cohen's monograph, *The Indian Army.*

Unfortunately, there is no comprehensive work on Nepal's army, as most publications deal with Gurkha regiments. Basic information on Nepal's order of battle can be obtained from the annual, *The Military Balance;* periodic articles in *Far Eastern Economic Review, Asian Defence Journal,* and *India Today* shed some light on Nepalese military and defense topics. Nepal's English-language press is generally unenlightening on issues relating to defense; the government-controlled *Rising Nepal* is probably the best source for photos, commentaries, and a flavor of local opinion. Leo E. Rose's *Nepal: Strategy for Survival* ranks as the best source on Nepal's defense and foreign policy concerns, although it is somewhat dated. Historical documents relating to Nepal's defense can be found in *Documents on Nepal's Relations with India and China, 1949-1966,* edited by A.S. Bhasin. Niranjan Koirala's "Nepal in 1990: End of an Era" in the February 1991 issue of *Asian Survey* provides a succinct summary of the Indo-Nepalese trade and transit dispute.

Annual updates on Nepal in *Asian Survey* and the Far Eastern Economic Review's *Asia Yearbook* are useful sources on Nepalese defense affairs; the Hoover Institution's annual *Yearbook on International Communist Affairs* details the activities of Nepalese communists; and the Department of State's annual *Country Reports on Human Rights Practices for 1990* highlights Nepal's record and accomplishments in human rights. A much darker view of the problem can be found in Amnesty International's *Nepal: A Pattern of Human Rights Violations.* (For further information and complete citations, see Bibliography.)

Table B. Bhutan: Chronology of Important Events

Period	Description
ca. 500 B.C.	State of Monyul established; continues to A.D. 600.
ca. A.D. 630–640	Early Buddhist temples built.
747	Guru Rimpoche visits Bhutan; founds Nyingmapa sect several years later.
ca. 810	Independent monarchies develop.
830s–840s	Tibetan Buddhist religion and culture firmly established.
eleventh century	Bhutan occupied by Tibetan-Mongol military forces.
1360s	Gelugpa sect monks flee to Bhutan from Tibet.
1616	Drukpa monk Ngawang Namgyal arrives from Tibet, seeking freedom from Dalai Lama.
1629	First Westerners—Portuguese Jesuits—visit Bhutan.
1629–47	Successive Tibetan invasions of Bhutan end in withdrawal or defeat.
1651	Ngawang Namgyal dies; theocratic Buddhist state rules unified Bhutan (called Drukyul) and joint civil-religious administration established; summer capital established at Thimphu, winter capital at Punakha. Drukpa subsect emerges as dominant religious force.
1680s–1700	Bhutanese forces invade Sikkim.
1714	Tibetan-Mongolian invasion thwarted.
1728	Civil war accompanies struggle for succession struggle to throne.
1730	Bhutan aids raja of Cooch Behar against Indian Mughals.
1760s	Cooch Behar becomes de facto Bhutanese dependency; Assam Duars come under Bhutanese control.
1770	Bhutan-Cooch Behar forces invade Sikkim.
1772	Cooch Behar seeks protection from British East India Company.
1772–73	British forces invade Bhutan.
1774	Bhutan signs peace treaty with British East India Company.

Table B.—Continued

Period	Description
1787	Boundary disputes plague Bhutanese-British Indian relations.
1826–28	Border tensions between Bhutan and British increase after British seize Lower Assam, threaten Assam Duars.
1834–35	British invade Bhutan.
1841	British take control of Bhutanese portion of Assam Duars and begin annual compensation payments to Bhutan.
1862	Bhutan raids Sikkim and Cooch Behar.
1864	Civil war in Bhutan; British seek peace relationship with both sides.
1864–65	Duar War waged between Britain and Bhutan.
1865	Treaty of Sinchula signed; Bhutan Duars territories ceded to Britain in return for annual subsidy.
1883–85	Period of civil war and rebellion leads to a united Bhutan under Ugyen Wangchuck.
1904	Ugyen Wangchuck helps secure Anglo—Tibetan Convention on behalf of Britain.
1907	Theocracy ends; hereditary monarchy, with Ugyen Wangchuck as Druk Gyalpo (Dragon King), established.
1910	China invades Tibet, laying claim to Bhutan, Nepal, and Sikkim; Treaty of Punakha signed with Britain, stipulating annual increase of stipend to Bhutan and Bhutan's control of own internal affairs.
1926	Ugyen Wangchuck dies and is succeeded by Jigme Wangchuck.
1947	British rule of India and British association with Bhutan end.
1949	Treaty of Friendship signed with India, essentially continuing 1910 agreement with Britain.
1952	Third Druk Gyalpo, Jigme Dorji Wangchuck, enthroned.
1953	National Assembly established as part of government reform.
1961	First five-year plan introduced.
1962	Indian troops retreat through Bhutan during Sino-Indian border war.
1964	Jigme Palden Dorji assassinated; factional politics emerge.
1965	Assassination attempt on Jigme Dorji Wangchuck.

Table B. —Continued

Period	Description
1966	Thimphu made year-round capital.
1968	Druk Gyalpo decrees that sovereign power is to reside in National Assembly.
1971	Bhutan admitted to United Nations.
1972	Fourth Druk Gyalpo, Jigme Singye Wangchuck, succeeds upon father's death.
1974	New monetary system established separate from India's.
1986	One thousand illegal foreign laborers—mostly Nepalese—expelled.
1989	Unrest among Nepalese minority brings government efforts to ameliorate differences between ethnic communities as well as additional government restrictions.
1990	Antigovernment terrorist activities initiated; ethnic Nepalese protesters in southern Bhutan clash with Royal Bhutan Army; violence and crime increase; citizen militias formed in progovernment communities.
1991	Jigme Singye Wangchuck threatens to abdicate in face of hard-line opposition in National Assembly to his efforts to resolve ethnic unrest; cancels participation in annual three-day South Asian Association for Regional Cooperation (SAARC) conference because of unrest at home; attends abbreviated one-day SAARC session in Colombo, Sri Lanka.

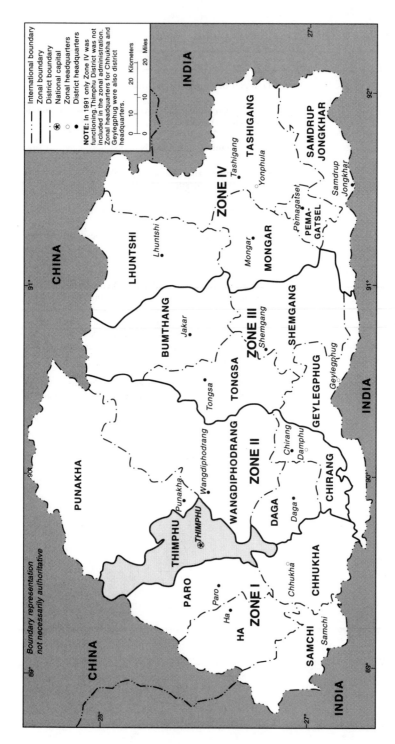

Figure 13. Bhutan: Administrative Divisions, 1991

Bhutan: Country Profile

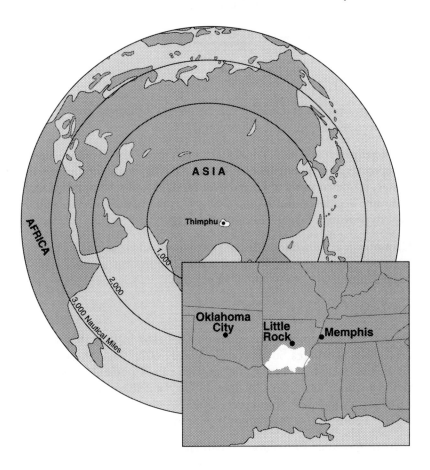

Country

Formal Name: Kingdom of Bhutan (Drukyul, literally, Land of the Thunder Dragon).

Short Form: Bhutan.

Term for Citizens: Bhutanese.

Capital: Thimphu.

Note: The Country Profile contains updated information as available.

Date of Unification: 1651, when theocratic Buddhist state of Drukyul was unified by Ngawang Namgyal.

National Holiday: December 17, National Day, when Ugyen Wangchuck became first hereditary king.

Geography

Location and Size: Landlocked between China and India; total land area 44,500 square kilometers.

Topography: Rugged, mountainous, snowcapped or glacier-covered terrain in north, part of Himalayas; high mountains in center, southern spurs of Himalayas; foothills and subtropical plains in south. Highest point Kulha Gangri (7,554 meters). Numerous, rapidly flowing, largely unnavigable rivers.

Climate: Varies with altitude. Year-round snow in north, heavy monsoon rains in west, drier but temperate in central and eastern areas, humid and subtropical in south.

Society

Population: Estimates vary widely: 1,660,167 in July 1992 based on foreign estimates but more likely only 600,000, size given by Bhutanese government; annual growth rate 2 percent. About 45 percent under age fifteen in late 1980s. In 1985, only 5 percent in urban areas; low population density—thirty-one persons per square kilometer for total area, higher average for habitable land.

Ethnic Groups: Officially 72 percent of Bhutanese of Tibetan (Ngalop), Indo-Mongoloid (Sharchop), and aboriginal (Drokpa, Lepcha, and Doya) origin; 28 percent, Nepalese origin. Nepalese may constitute as much as 40 percent.

Language: Dzongkha official national language using *chhokey* (Tibetan script) for written expression; Ngalopkha (on which Dzongkha is based) spoken in west; Sharchopkha in east; Nepali in south; English widely understood throughout school system.

Religion: 70 percent Mahayana Buddhists (predominantly Drupka subsect), approximately 25 percent Hindus, 5 percent Muslims. Indeterminate but small number of Bon adherents.

Education: Noncompulsory, free eleven-year education (primary—grades one through five; junior high—grades six through eight;

upper-secondary schools—grades nine through eleven). Primary level attended by about 25 percent of school-age population; junior high and high schools attended by around 8 percent and 3 percent, respectively. In 1991 one junior college and two technical schools. Entire system supervised by Department of Education. Literacy rate 30 percent for males, 10 percent for females in early 1990s.

Health: In early 1980s, life expectancy 45.9 for women and men. Infant mortality rate 137 per 1,000 in 1990. Health-care system in late 1980s included twenty-nine general hospitals, forty-six dispensaries, and sixty-seven basic health units, four indigenous-medicine dispensaries, and fifteen malaria education centers with total capacity 932 beds. Severe shortage of health-care personnel: 142 physicians and 678 paramedics in 1988. Gastrointestinal infections most common illness.

Economy

Salient Features: Underdeveloped economy with ties to India because of geographic position and historical relationship. Predominantly agricultural; limited industrial activity; services—particularly related to tourism—growing part of economy. Development of hydroelectric capabilities for domestic use and export also increasingly important. Increasing domestic concern and international cooperation with respect to environmental protection and resource conservation. Development funding—major component in economic development. Once 100 percent from India, but increasingly from domestic sources, European countries, and international organizations. Less than 1 percent of population involved in industrial work.

Gross National Product (GNP): Nu3.9 billion (1988; Nu—ngultrum). Per capita GNP US$440.

Gross Domestic Product (GDP): Nu3.4 billion (1988).

Agriculture: Including fishing and forestry, 46.2 percent of GDP projected for 1991. Traditionally self-sufficient in food production; rice imports increased in late 1980s. About 87 percent of population involved in agriculture. Less than 6 percent of land cultivable; most farms terraced or use illegal *tsheri* (shifting cultivation). Major crops corn and rice. Cash crops oranges, apples, and cardamon. Livestock raised throughout country. Fish an important dietary supplement. Modest use of irrigation and fertilizers. Up to 70 percent of country covered with forests; lumber industry about 15 percent of GDP.

Industry: 26.4 percent of GDP projected for 1991. Only 1 percent of population involved in industry and construction in late 1980s. Basic industries: handicrafts, cement, food processing, wood milling, and distilling; 400 small-scale cottage and industrial units. Limestone for cement production major mining and quarrying product. Hydroelectric power major energy producer.

Services: 29 percent of GDP projected for 1991. Most commercial services tourist-oriented plus domestic-oriented wholesale and retail trade. Tourism largest foreign-exchange earner (US$2 million in 1987).

Resources: High-grade limestone and slate; marble, dolomite, and graphite; deposits of copper, gypsum, lead, tin, tungsten, zinc, coal, beryl, mica, pyrites, tufa, and talc. Abundant water for hydroelectric power sources.

Foreign Trade: Principally with India. Total exports Nu1.2 billion in 1990, primarily electricity and processed raw materials. Total imports Nu1.8 billion in 1990, primarily rice and manufactured goods.

Balance of Payments: Early 1980s trade imbalance—imports 80 percent of total trade—decreased as decade progressed. Exports represented 40 percent, imports 60 percent of total annual trade in 1990.

Foreign Aid: Once 100 percent dependent on India for development funds and government revenue; since 1960s major inputs from Colombo Plan, World Bank, United Nations, and private sources, plus domestic contributions, decreased Indian aid to 27.5 percent (Nu2.6 billion) of total input in Sixth Development Plan (1987–92).

Currency/Exchange Rate: Ngultrum (Nu). US$1 = Nu18.3 (January 1991). Ngultrum on par with Indian rupee.

Fiscal Year: July 1 to June 30.

Transportation and Communications

Roads: In 1989, 2,280 kilometers of roads, 77 percent paved. Most principal towns linked by surfaced road network in south; mountainous terrain in north makes transportation difficult. Nearly 7,000 vehicles registered in 1988. Bus service major public transportation.

Airports: International facility at Paro, small airport at Yonphula; helipads throughout country. Druk-Air service from Paro; five flights weekly to Bangkok, Calcutta, New Delhi, Dhaka, and Kathmandu.

Telecommunications: Modern telecommunications link major towns; international microwave telephone service through satellite ground stations in Thimphu, Calcutta, and New Delhi.

Government and Politics

Government: World's only Buddhist kingdom. De facto constitutional monarchy with Druk Gyalpo (Dragon King) head of state and head of government. Royal family members serve as close advisers and heads of some ministries. Main executive organs Royal Advisory Council and Council of Ministers. Since August 1991 eight ministries, with establishment of new Ministry of Planning. Unicameral National Assembly (Tshogdu); two-thirds of its 150 members—representatives of general public—indirectly elected every three years; balance made up of monastic representatives appointed by Buddhist hierarchy and government officials appointed by Druk Gyalpo.

Politics: No legal political parties; political activities carried out by elite factions. Starting in late 1980s, unrest among Nepalese minority in south led to government's parallel efforts to accommodate ethnic communities and restrict separatist activities amid increasing discontent and violence.

Judiciary: Civil law system heavily influenced by Buddhist law based on seventeenth-century code. Druk Gyalpo final level of appeal. High Court and district courts; minor civil disputes adjudicated by village heads.

Administrative Divisions: Four administrative zones (*dzongdey*) planned to provide central government services at local levels; in 1991 eighteen districts (*dzongkhag*), ten of which were divided into subdistricts (*dungkhag*); and 191 village groups (*gewog*). Thimphu District not included in zonal administration. Municipal corporations at Thimphu and Phuntsholing; 4,500 other villages and settlements. Nineteenth district—Gasa (part of Punakha District)—to be established under Seventh Development Plan (1992–97).

Foreign Relations: Major aid recipient from India, international organizations, and developed countries. Traditionally relied first on Britain and then on India to direct foreign affairs; increasingly

249

asserted independence since joining United Nations in 1971. In 1991 maintained diplomatic relations with only sixteen nations. Member of Asian Development Bank, Colombo Plan for Cooperative, Economic and Social Development in Asia and the Pacific, Coordination Bureau of Nonaligned Movement, International Civil Aviation Organization, International Development Association, International Monetary Fund, International Telecommunications Union, South Asian Association for Regional Cooperation, United Nations and its affiliated agencies, and Universal Postal Union.

Media: *Kuensel,* government-owned weekly newspaper. Bhutan Broadcasting Service offers shortwave radio programming; daily FM broadcasts in Thimphu; no television reception.

National Security

Armed Forces: Royal Bhutan Army numbered about 6,000 in 1990.

Military Units and Equipment: Four operational wings headquartered in Changju, Damthang, Goinchawa, and Yonphula; each organized into companies, platoons, and sections. Airport security unit at Paro. Royal Body Guards—elite VIP protection unit; some members with counterinsurgency training. Modern small arms; obsolescent Indian-supplied equipment.

Military Budget: Unknown.

Foreign Military Relations: India de facto protector, weapons supplier, and provider of advanced training.

Paramilitary: Village security long-standing tradition. Modern militia controlled by central government. Universal militia training by Royal Bhutan Army instituted 1989. Uniformed Forest Guards trained by Royal Bhutan Army to protect forests and support border security.

Police Forces: Royal Bhutan Police, subordinate to Royal Bhutan Army; headquarters in each district and subdistrict; provide border security.

Chapter 6. Bhutan

Bhutan's national symbol. The traditional sacred wheel of Buddhism is used to symbolize the king (center) surrounded by his ministers (the spokes). The two dragons surrounding the wheel stand for religious and secular administration. The jeweled umbrella, a Buddhist symbol of luck, suggests spiritual protection for the people of Bhutan; the lotus blossom at the bottom represents peace and gentleness.

"In THE THUNDER DRAGON KINGDOM, adorned with sandalwood, the protector who guards the teachings of the dual system; he, the precious and glorious ruler, causes dominion to spread while his unchanging person abides in constancy, as the doctrine of the Buddha flourishes, may the sun of peace and happiness shine on the people." These few words—the text of the national anthem of Bhutan—sum up much about the spirit and culture of a society that sprang from an aboriginal people and was enriched by Tibetan, Mongol, and Indo-Burman migrants. Buddhism has been a pervasive influence in Bhutan throughout most of its history and has long been the state religion and source of civil law. Unified Bhutan has had two forms of monarchy: from the sixteenth century to the early twentieth century, a dual system of shared civil and spiritual rule; and since 1907 the hereditary monarchy of the Wangchuck family.

Once one of the many independent Himalayan kingdoms and principalities, Bhutan, like Nepal, is situated between two Asian powers, India and China, which, at best, have had an uneasy standoff politically and militarily for nearly half a century (see fig. 2). Bhutan's independence has long been at issue in the geopolitical maneuverings between Tibet (and later China) and India. In the late twentieth century, Bhutan has fended off this external threat with conscientiously planned economic development. A serious internal threat to Bhutan's traditional identity started peacefully in the 1950s and 1960s among the growing Nepalese minority, which represented 28 percent or more of the population in the early 1990s and emerged as a sometimes violent "prodemocracy" movement in the late 1980s. The 1990s promised to be a crucial period for the monarchy as it continued to foster economic and administrative reform amid efforts to retain traditional culture and to assuage minority unrest.

Historical Setting

Origins and Early Settlement, A.D. 600–1600

Although knowledge of prehistoric Bhutan has yet to emerge through archaeological study, stone tools and weapons, remnants of large stone structures, and megaliths that may have been used for boundary markers or rituals provide evidence of civilization as early as 2000 B.C. The absence of neolithic mythological legends argues against earlier inhabitation. With a little more certainty, historians theorize about the existence of the state of Lhomon (literally, southern darkness) or Monyul (dark land, a reference to the Monpa aboriginal peoples of Bhutan), possibly a part of Tibet that was then beyond the pale of Buddhist teachings (see Religious Tradition, this ch.). Monyul is thought to have existed between 500 B.C. and A.D. 600. The names Lhomon Tsendenjong (southern Mon sandalwood country) and Lhomon Khashi (southern Mon country of four approaches), found in ancient Bhutanese and Tibetan chronicles, may also have credence and have been used by some Bhutanese scholars when referring to their homeland. Variations of the Sanskrit words Bhota-ant (end of Bhot, an Indian name for Tibet) or Bhu-uttan (meaning highlands) have been suggested by historians as origins of the name Bhutan, which came into common foreign use in the late nineteenth century and is used in Bhutan only in English-language official correspondence. The traditional name of the country since the seventeenth century has been Drukyul—country of the Drukpa, the Dragon People, or the Land of the Thunder Dragon—a reference to the country's dominant Buddhist sect.

Some scholars believe that during the early historical period the inhabitants were fierce mountain aborigines, the Monpa, who were of neither the Tibetan or Mongol stock that later overran northern Bhutan. The people of Monyul practiced the shamanistic Bon religion, which emphasized worship of nature and the existence of good and evil spirits. During the latter part of this period, historical legends relate that the mighty king of Monyul invaded a southern region known as the Duars, subduing the regions of modern Assam, West Bengal, and Bihar in India.

Arrival of Buddhism

The introduction of Buddhism occurred in the seventh century A.D., when Tibetan king Srongtsen Gampo (reigned A.D. 627–49), a convert to Buddhism, ordered the construction of two Buddhist temples, at Bumthang in central Bhutan and at Kyichu in the Paro Valley (see fig. 13). Buddhism replaced but did not eliminate the Bon religious practices that had also been prevalent in Tibet until the late sixth century. Instead, Buddhism absorbed Bon and its believers. As the country developed in its many fertile valleys, Buddhism matured and became a unifying element. It was Buddhist literature and chronicles that began the recorded history of Bhutan.

In A.D. 747, a Buddhist saint, Padmasambhava (known in Bhutan as Guru Rimpoche and sometimes referred to as the Second

Buddha), came to Bhutan from India at the invitation of one of the numerous local kings. After reportedly subduing eight classes of demons and converting the king, Guru Rimpoche moved on to Tibet. Upon his return from Tibet, he oversaw the construction of new monasteries in the Paro Valley and set up his headquarters in Bumthang. According to tradition, he founded the Nyingmapa sect—also known as the "old sect" or Red Hat sect—of Mahayana Buddhism, which became for a time the dominant religion of Bhutan. Guru Rimpoche plays a great historical and religious role as the national patron saint who revealed the tantras—manuals describing forms of devotion to natural energy—to Bhutan. Following the guru's sojourn, Indian influence played a temporary role until increasing Tibetan migrations brought new cultural and religious contributions.

There was no central government during this period. Instead, small independent monarchies began to develop by the early ninth century. Each was ruled by a *deb* (king), some of whom claimed divine origins. The kingdom of Bumthang was the most prominent among these small entities. At the same time, Tibetan Buddhist monks (*lam* in Dzongkha, Bhutan's official national language) had firmly rooted their religion and culture in Bhutan, and members of joint Tibetan-Mongol military expeditions settled in fertile valleys. By the eleventh century, all of Bhutan was occupied by Tibetan-Mongol military forces.

Rivalry among the Sects

By the tenth century, Bhutan's political development was heavily influenced by its religious history. Following a period in which Buddhism was in decline in Tibet in the eleventh century, contention among a number of subsects emerged. The Mongol overlords of Tibet and Bhutan patronized a sequence of subsects until their own political decline in the fourteenth century. By that time, the Gelugpa or Yellow Hat school had, after a period of anarchy in Tibet, become a powerful force resulting in the flight to Bhutan of numerous monks of various minor opposing sects. Among these monks was the founder of the Lhapa subsect of the Kargyupa school, to whom is attributed the introduction of strategically built *dzong* (fortified monasteries—see Glossary). Although the Lhapa subsect had been successfully challenged in the twelfth century by another Kargyupa subsect—the Drukpa—led by Tibetan monk Phajo Drugom Shigpo, it continued to proselytize until the seventeenth century. The Drukpa subsect, an unreformed Nyingmapa group in Tibet, spread throughout Bhutan and eventually became a dominant form of religious practice. Between the twelfth century and the seventeenth century, the two Kargyupa subsects vied with one another from their respective *dzong* as the older form of Nyingmapa Buddhism was eclipsed.

Theocratic Government, 1616–1907

Consolidation and Defeat of Tibetan Invasions, 1616–51

In the seventeenth century, a theocratic government independent of Tibetan political influence was established, and premodern Bhutan emerged. The theocratic government was founded by an expatriate Drukpa monk, Ngawang Namgyal, who arrived in Bhutan in 1616 seeking freedom from the domination of the Gelugpa subsect led by the Dalai Lama (Ocean Lama) in Lhasa. After a series of victories over rival subsect leaders and Tibetan invaders, Ngawang Namgyal took the title *shabdrung* (At Whose Feet One Submits, or, in many Western sources, *dharma raja*), becoming the temporal and spiritual leader of Bhutan. Considered the first great historical figure of Bhutan, he united the leaders of powerful Bhutanese families in a land called Drukyul. He promulgated a code of law and built a network of impregnable *dzong,* a system that helped bring local lords under centralized control and strengthened the country against Tibetan invasions. Many *dzong* were extant in the late twentieth century.

Tibetan armies invaded Bhutan around 1629, in 1631, and again in 1639, hoping to throttle Ngawang Namgyal's popularity before it spread too far. The invasions were thwarted, and the Drukpa subsect developed a strong presence in western and central Bhutan, leaving Ngawang Namgyal supreme. In recognition of the power he accrued, goodwill missions were sent to Bhutan from Cooch Behar in the Duars (present-day northeastern West Bengal), Nepal to the west, and Ladakh in western Tibet. The ruler of Ladakh even gave a number of villages in his kingdom to Ngawang Namgyal. During the first war with Tibet, two Portuguese Jesuits—the first recorded Europeans to visit—passed through Bhutan on their way to Tibet. They met with Ngawang Namgyal, presented him with firearms, gunpowder, and a telescope, and offered him their services in the war against Tibet, but the *shabdrung* declined the offer.

Bhutan's troubles were not over, however. In 1643 a joint Mongol-Tibetan force sought to destroy Nyingmapa refugees who had fled to Bhutan, Sikkim, and Nepal. The Mongols had seized control of religious and civil power in Tibet in the 1630s and established Gelugpa as the state religion. Bhutanese rivals of Ngawang Namgyal encouraged the Mongol intrusion, but the Mongol force was easily defeated in the humid lowlands of southern Bhutan. Another Tibetan invasion in 1647 also failed.

During Ngawang Namgyal's rule, administration comprised a state monastic body with an elected head, the Je Khenpo (lord abbot), and a theocratic civil government headed by the *druk desi* (regent of Bhutan, also known as *deb raja* in Western sources). The *druk desi* was either a monk or a member of the laity—by the nineteenth century, usually the latter; he was elected for a three-year term, initially by a monastic council and later by the State Council (Lhengye Tshokdu). The State Council was a central administrative organ that included regional rulers, the *shabdrung's* chamberlains, and the *druk desi*. In time, the *druk desi* came under the political control of the State Council's most powerful faction of regional administrators. The *shabdrung* was the head of state and the ultimate authority in religious and civil matters. The seat of government was at Thimphu, the site of a thirteenth-century *dzong,* in the spring, summer, and fall. The winter capital was at Punakha, a *dzong* established northeast of Thimphu in 1527. The kingdom was divided into three regions (east, central, and west), each with an appointed *ponlop,* or governor, holding a seat in a major *dzong.* Districts were headed by *dzongpon,* or district officers, who had their headquarters in lesser *dzong.* The *ponlop* were combination tax collectors, judges, military commanders, and procurement agents for the central government. Their major revenues came from the trade between Tibet and India and from land taxes.

Ngawang Namgyal's regime was bound by a legal code called the Tsa Yig, which described the spiritual and civil regime and provided laws for government administration and for social and moral conduct. The duties and virtues inherent in the Buddhist dharma (religious law) played a large role in the new legal code, which remained in force until the 1960s.

Administrative Integration and Conflict with Tibet, 1651–1728

To keep Bhutan from disintegrating, Ngawang Namgyal's death in 1651 apparently was kept a carefully guarded secret for fifty-four years. Initially, Ngawang Namgyal was said to have entered into a religious retreat, a situation not unprecedented in Bhutan, Sikkim, or Tibet during that time. During the period of Ngawang Namgyal's supposed retreat, appointments of officials were issued in his name, and food was left in front of his locked door.

Ngawang Namgyal's son and stepbrother, in 1651 and 1680, respectively, succeeded him. They started their reigns as minors under the control of religious and civil regents and rarely exercised authority in their own names. For further continuity, the concept of multiple reincarnation of the first *shabdrung*—in the form of either his body, his speech, or his mind—was invoked by the Je Khenpo and the *druk desi,* both of whom wanted to retain the power they had accrued through the dual system of government. The last person recognized as the bodily reincarnation of Ngawang Namgyal died in the mid-eighteenth century, but speech and mind reincarnations, embodied by individuals who acceded to the position of *shabdrung,* were recognized into the early twentieth century. The power of the state religion also increased with a new monastic code that remained in effect in the early 1990s. The compulsory admission to monastic life of at least one son from any family having three or more sons was instituted in the late seventeenth century. In time, however, the State Council became increasingly secular as did the successive *druk desi, ponlop,* and *dzongpon,* and intense rivalries developed among the *ponlop* of Tongsa and Paro and the *dzongpon* of Punakha, Thimphu, and Wangdiphodrang.

During the first period of succession and further internal consolidation under the *druk desi* government, there was conflict with Tibet and Sikkim. Internal opposition to the central government resulted in overtures by the opponents of the *druk desi* to Tibet and Sikkim. In the 1680s, Bhutan invaded Sikkim in pursuit of a rebellious local lord. In 1700 Bhutan again invaded Sikkim, and in 1714 Tibetan forces, aided by Mongolia, invaded Bhutan but were unable to gain control.

Civil Conflict, 1728-72

Civil war ensued when the "first reincarnation" of Ngawang Namgyal, Jigme Dakpa, was recognized as the *shabdrung* in 1728. A rival claimant, however, was promoted by opposition forces supported by Tibet. The Tibetan-backed forces were defeated by Jigme Dakpa's supporters, but the political system remained unstable. Regional rivalries contributed to the gradual disintegration of Bhutan at the time the first British agents arrived.

In the early eighteenth century, Bhutan had successfully developed control over the principality of Cooch Behar. The raja of Cooch Behar had sought assistance from Bhutan against the Indian Mughals in 1730, and Bhutanese political influence was not long in following. By the mid-1760s, Thimphu considered Cooch Behar its dependency, stationing a garrison force there and directing its civil administration. When the *druk desi* invaded Sikkim in 1770, Cooch Behari forces joined their Bhutanese counterparts in the offensive. In a succession dispute in Cooch Behar two years later, however, the *druk desi*'s nominee for the throne was opposed by a rival who invited British troops, and, in effect, Cooch Behar became a dependency of the British East India Company.

British Intrusion, 1772–1907

Under the Cooch Behari agreement with the British, a British expeditionary force drove the Bhutanese garrison out of Cooch Behar and invaded Bhutan in 1772–73. The *druk desi* petitioned Lhasa for assistance from the Panchen Lama, who was serving as regent for the youthful Dalai Lama. In correspondence with the British governor general of India, however, the Panchen Lama instead castigated the *druk desi* and invoked Tibet's claim of suzerainty over Bhutan.

Failing to receive help from Tibet, the *druk desi* signed a Treaty of Peace with the British East India Company on April 25, 1774. Bhutan agreed to return to its pre-1730 boundaries, paid a symbolic tribute of five horses to Britain, and, among other concessions, allowed the British to harvest timber in Bhutan. Subsequent missions to Bhutan were made by the British in 1776, 1777, and 1783, and commerce was opened between British India and Bhutan and, for a short time, Tibet. In 1784 the British turned over to Bhutanese control the Bengal Duars territory, where boundaries were poorly defined. As in its other foreign territories, Bhutan left administration of the Bengal Duars territory to local officials and collected its revenues. Although major trade and political relations failed to develop between Bhutan and Britain, the British had replaced the Tibetans as the major external threat.

Boundary disputes plagued Bhutanese-British relations. To reconcile their differences, Bhutan sent an emissary to Calcutta in 1787, and the British sent missions to Thimphu in 1815 and 1838. The 1815 mission was inconclusive. The 1838 mission offered a treaty providing for extradition of Bhutanese officials responsible for incursions into Assam, free and unrestricted commerce between India and Bhutan, and settlement of Bhutan's debt to the British. In an attempt to protect its independence, Bhutan rejected the British offer. Despite increasing internal disorder, Bhutan had maintained its control over a portion of the Assam Duars more or less since its reduction of Cooch Behar to a dependency in the 1760s. After the British gained control of Lower Assam in 1826, tension between the countries began to rise as Britain exerted its strength. Bhutanese payments of annual tribute to the British for the Assam Duars gradually fell into arrears, however. The resulting British demands for payment and military incursions into Bhutan in 1834 and 1835 brought about defeat for Bhutan's forces and a temporary loss of territory.

The British proceeded in 1841 to annex the formerly Bhutanese-controlled Assam Duars, paying a compensation of 10,000 rupees a year to Bhutan. In 1842 Bhutan gave up control to the British of some of the troublesome Bengal Duars territory it had administered since 1784.

Charges and countercharges of border incursions and protection of fugitives led to an unsuccessful Bhutanese mission to Calcutta in 1852. Among other demands, the mission sought increased compensation for its former Duars territories, but instead the British deducted nearly 3,000 rupees from the annual compensation and demanded an apology for alleged plundering of British-protected lands by members of the mission. Following more incidents and the prospect of an anti-Bhutan rebellion in the Bengal Duars, British troops deployed to the frontier in the mid-1850s. The Sepoy Rebellion in India in 1857–58 and the demise of the British East India Company's rule prevented immediate British action. Bhutanese armed forces raided Sikkim and Cooch Behar in 1862, seizing people, property, and money. The British responded by withholding all compensation payments and demanding release of all captives and return of stolen property. Demands to the *druk desi* went unheeded, as he was alleged to be unaware of his frontier officials' actions against Sikkim and Cooch Behar.

Britain sent a peace mission to Bhutan in early 1864, in the wake of the recent conclusion of a civil war there. The *dzongpon* of Punakha—who had emerged victorious—had broken with the central government and set up a rival *druk desi* while the legitimate *druk desi* sought the protection of the *ponlop* of Paro and was later deposed. The British mission dealt alternately with the rival *ponlop* of Paro and the *ponlop* of Tongsa (the latter acted on behalf of the *druk desi*), but Bhutan rejected the peace and friendship treaty it offered. Britain declared war in November 1864. Bhutan had no regular army, and what forces existed were composed of *dzong* guards armed with matchlocks, bows and arrows, swords, knives, and catapults. Some of these *dzong* guards, carrying shields and wearing chainmail armor, engaged the well-equipped British forces.

The Duar War (1864–65) lasted only five months and, despite some battlefield victories by Bhutanese forces, resulted in Bhutan's defeat, loss of part of its sovereign territory, and forced cession of formerly occupied territories. Under the terms of the Treaty of Sinchula, signed on November 11, 1865, Bhutan ceded territories in the Assam Duars and Bengal Duars, as well as the eighty-three-square-kilometer territory of Dewangiri in southeastern Bhutan, in return for an annual subsidy of 50,000 rupees.

Druk Gyalpo Jigme Singye Wangchuck, Bhutan's fourth hereditary monarch
Courtesy Permanent Mission of the Kingdom of Bhutan, United Nations

In the 1870s and 1880s, renewed competition among regional rivals—primarily the pro-British *ponlop* of Tongsa and the anti-British, pro-Tibetan *ponlop* of Paro—resulted in the ascendancy of Ugyen Wangchuck, the *ponlop* of Tongsa. From his power base in central Bhutan, Ugyen Wangchuck had defeated his political enemies and united the country following several civil wars and rebellions in 1882–85. His victory came at a time of crisis for the central government, however. British power was becoming more extensive to the south, and in the west Tibet had violated its border with Sikkim, incurring British disfavor. After 1,000 years of close ties with Tibet, Bhutan faced the threat of British military power and was forced to make serious geopolitical decisions. The British, seeking to offset potential Russian advances in Lhasa, wanted to open trade relations with Tibet. Ugyen Wangchuck saw the opportunity to assist the British and in 1903–4 volunteered to accompany a British mission to Lhasa as a mediator. For his services in securing the Anglo-Tibetan Convention of 1904, Ugyen Wangchuck was knighted and thereafter continued to accrue greater power in Bhutan.

Establishment of the Hereditary Monarchy, 1907

Ugyen Wangchuck's emergence as the national leader coincided with the realization that the dual political system was obsolete and ineffective. He had removed his chief rival, the *ponlop* of Paro, and installed a supporter and relative, a member of the pro-British

Dorji family, in his place. When the last *shabdrung* died in 1903 and a reincarnation had not appeared by 1906, civil administration came under the control of Ugyen Wangchuck. Finally, in 1907, the fifty-fourth and last *druk desi* was forced to retire, and despite recognitions of subsequent reincarnations of Ngawang Namgyal, the *shabdrung* system came to an end.

In November 1907, an assembly of leading Buddhist monks, government officials, and heads of important families was held to end the moribund 300-year-old dual system of government and to establish a new absolute monarchy. Ugyen Wangchuck was elected its first hereditary Druk Gyalpo (Dragon King, reigned 1907–26; see The Monarchy, this ch.). The Dorji family became hereditary holders of the position of *gongzim* (chief chamberlain), the top government post. The British, wanting political stability on their northern frontier, approved of the entire development.

Britain's earlier entreaties in Lhasa had unexpected repercussions at this time. China, concerned that Britain would seize Tibet, invaded Tibet in 1910 and asserted political authority. In the face of the Chinese military occupation, the Dalai Lama fled to India. China laid claim not only to Tibet but also to Bhutan, Nepal, and Sikkim. With these events, Bhutanese-British interests coalesced.

A new Bhutanese-British agreement, the Treaty of Punakha, was signed on January 8, 1910. It amended two articles of the 1865 treaty: the British agreed to double their annual stipend to 100,000 rupees and "to exercise no interference in the internal administration of Bhutan." In turn, Bhutan agreed "to be guided by the advice of the British Government in regard to its external relations." The Treaty of Punakha guaranteed Bhutan's defense against China; China, in no position to contest British power, conceded the end of the millennium-long Tibetan-Chinese influence.

Much of Bhutan's modern development has been attributed by Bhutanese historians to the first Druk Gyalpo. Internal reforms included introducing Western-style schools, improving internal communications, encouraging trade and commerce with India, and revitalizing the Buddhist monastic system. Toward the end of his life, Ugyen Wangchuck was concerned about the continuity of the family dynasty, and in 1924 he sought British assurance that the Wangchuck family would retain its preeminent position in Bhutan. His request led to an investigation of the legal status of Bhutan vis-à-vis the suzerainty held over Bhutan by Britain and the ambiguity of Bhutan's relationship to India. Both the suzerainty and the ambiguity were maintained.

Development of Centralized Government, 1926-52

Ugyen Wangchuck died in 1926 and was succeeded by his son, Jigme Wangchuck (reigned 1926–52). The second Druk Gyalpo continued his father's centralization and modernization efforts and built more schools, dispensaries, and roads. During Jigme Wangchuck's reign, monasteries and district governments were increasingly brought under royal control. However, Bhutan generally remained isolated from international affairs.

The issue of Bhutan's status vis-à-vis the government of India (was Bhutan a state of India or did it enjoy internal sovereignty?) was reexamined by London in 1932 as part of the issue of the status of India itself. It was decided to leave the decision to join an Indian federation up to Bhutan when the time came. When British rule over India ended in 1947, so too did Britain's association with Bhutan. India succeeded Britain as the de facto protector of the Himalayan kingdom, and Bhutan retained control over its internal government. It was two years, however, before a formal agreement recognized Bhutan's independence.

Following the precedent set by the Treaty of Punakha, on August 8, 1949, Thimphu signed the Treaty of Friendship Between the Government of India and the Government of Bhutan, according to which external affairs, formerly guided by Britain, were to be guided by India (see Foreign Relations, this ch.). Like Britain, India agreed not to interfere in Bhutan's internal affairs. India also agreed to increase the annual subsidy to 500,000 rupees per year. Important to Bhutan's national pride was the return of Dewangiri. Some historians believe that if India had been at odds with China at this time, as it was to be a decade later, it might not have acceded so easily to Bhutan's request for independent status.

Modernization under Jigme Dorji, 1952-72

The third Druk Gyalpo, Jigme Dorji Wangchuck, was enthroned in 1952. Earlier he had married the European-educated cousin of the *chogyal* (king) of Sikkim and with her support made continual efforts to modernize his nation throughout his twenty-year reign. Among his first reforms was the establishment of the National Assembly—the Tshogdu—in 1953. Although the Druk Gyalpo could issue royal decrees and exercise veto power over resolutions passed by the National Assembly, its establishment was a major move toward a constitutional monarchy (see Structure of the Government, this ch.).

When the Chinese communists took over Tibet in 1951, Bhutan closed its frontier with Tibet and sided with its powerful neighbor to the south. To offset the chance of Chinese encroachment, Bhutan began a modernization program. Land reform was accompanied by the abolition of slavery and serfdom and the separation of the judiciary from the executive branch of government. Mostly funded by India after China's invasion of Tibet in 1959, the modernization program also included the construction of roads linking the Indian plains with central Bhutan. An all-weather road was completed in 1962 between Thimphu and Phuntsholing, the overland gateway town on the southwest border with India. Dzongkha was made the national language during Jigme Dorji's reign (see Social System, this ch.). Additionally, development projects included establishing such institutions as a national museum in Paro and a national library, national archives, and national stadium, as well as buildings to house the National Assembly, the High Court (Thrimkhang Gongma), and other government entities in Thimphu. The position of *gongzim*, held since 1907 by the Dorji family, was upgraded in 1958 to *lonchen* (prime minister) and was still in the hands of the Dorji. Jigme Dorji Wangchuck's reforms, however, although lessening the authority of the absolute monarchy, also curbed the traditional decentralization of political authority among regional leaders and strengthened the role of the central government in economic and social programs.

Modernization efforts moved forward in the 1960s under the direction of the *lonchen,* Jigme Palden Dorji, the Druk Gyalpo's brother-in-law. In 1962, however, Dorji incurred disfavor with the Royal Bhutan Army over the use of military vehicles and the forced retirement of some fifty officers. Religious elements also were antagonized by Dorji's efforts to reduce the power of the state-supported religious institutions. In April 1964, while the Druk Gyalpo was in Switzerland for medical care, Dorji was assassinated in Phuntsholing by an army corporal. The majority of those arrested and accused of the crime were military personnel and included the army chief of operations, Namgyal Bahadur, the Druk Gyalpo's uncle, who was executed for his part in the plot.

The unstable situation continued under Dorji's successor as acting *lonchen,* his brother Lhendup Dorji, and for a time under the Druk Gyalpo's brother, Namgyal Wangchuck, as head of the army. According to some sources, a power struggle ensued between pro-Wangchuck loyalists and ''modernist'' Dorji supporters. The main issue was not an end to or lessening of the power of the monarchy but ''full freedom from Indian interference.'' Other observers believe the 1964 crisis was not so much a policy struggle as competition for influence on the palace between the Dorji family and the Druk Gyalpo's Tibetan mistress, Yangki, and her father. Nevertheless, with the concurrence of the National Assembly, Lhendup Dorji and other family members were exiled in 1965. The tense political situation continued, however, with an assassination attempt on the Druk Gyalpo himself in July 1965. The Dorjis were not implicated in the attempt, and the would-be assassins were pardoned by the Druk Gyalpo.

In 1966, to increase the efficiency of government administration, Jigme Dorji Wangchuck made Thimphu the year-round capital. In May 1968, the comprehensive Rules and Regulations of the National Assembly revised the legal basis of the power granted to the National Assembly. The Druk Gyalpo decreed that henceforth sovereign power, including the power to remove government ministers and the Druk Gyalpo himself, would reside with the National Assembly. The following November, the Druk Gyalpo renounced his veto power over National Assembly bills and said he would step down if two-thirds of the legislature passed a no-confidence vote. Although he did nothing to undermine the retention of the Wangchuck dynasty, the Druk Gyalpo in 1969 called for a triennial vote of confidence by the National Assembly (later abolished by his successor) to renew the Druk Gyalpo's mandate to rule.

Diplomatic overtures also were made during Jigme Dorji Wangchuck's reign. Although always seeking to be formally neutral and nonaligned in relations with China and India, Bhutan also sought more direct links internationally than had occurred previously under the foreign-policy guidance of India. Consequently, in 1962 Bhutan joined the Colombo Plan for Cooperative, Economic, and Social Development in Asia and the Pacific (Colombo Plan; see Glossary) and in 1966 notified India of its desire to become a member of the United Nations (UN). In 1971 after holding observer status for three years, Bhutan was admitted to the UN. In an effort to maintain Bhutan as a stable buffer state, India continued to provide substantial amounts of development aid.

Jigme Dorji Wangchuck ruled until his death in July 1972 and was succeeded by his seventeen-year-old son, Jigme Singye Wangchuck. The close ties of the Wangchuck and Dorji families were reemphasized in the person of the new king, whose mother, Ashi Kesang Dorji (*ashi* means princess), was the sister of the *lonchen,* Jigme Palden Dorji. Jigme Singye Wangchuck, who had been educated in India and Britain, had been appointed *ponlop* of Tongsa in May 1972 and by July that year had become the Druk Gyalpo. With his mother and two elder sisters as advisers, the new Druk Gyalpo was thrust into the affairs of state. He was often seen among the people, in the countryside, at festivals, and, as his reign progressed, meeting with foreign dignitaries in Bhutan and abroad. His formal coronation took place in June 1974, and soon thereafter the strains between the Wangchucks and Dorjis were relieved with the return that year of the exiled members of the latter family. The reconciliation, however, was preceded by reports of a plot to assassinate the new Druk Gyalpo before his coronation could take place and to set fire to the Tashichhodzong (Fortress of the Glorious Religion, the seat of government in Thimphu). Yangki was the alleged force behind the plot, which was uncovered three months before the coronation; thirty persons were arrested, including high government and police officials.

Entering the Outside World, 1972–86

When civil war broke out in Pakistan in 1971, Bhutan was among the first nations to recognize the new government of Bangladesh, and formal diplomatic relations were established in 1973. An event in 1975 may have served as a major impetus to Bhutan to speed up reform and modernization. In that year, neighboring Sikkim's monarchy, which had endured for more than 300 years, was ousted following a plebiscite in which the Nepalese majority outvoted the Sikkimese minority. Sikkim, long a protectorate of India, became India's twenty-second state.

To further ensure its independence and international position, Bhutan gradually established diplomatic relations with other nations and joined greater numbers of regional and international organizations. Many of the countries with which Bhutan established relations provided development aid (see Foreign Economic Relations, this ch.). Moderization brought new problems to Bhutan in the late 1980s (see Political Developments, this ch.).

The Society and Its Environment
Geography
The Land

Landlocked Bhutan is situated in the eastern Himalayas and is mostly mountainous and heavily forested. It is bordered for 470 kilometers by Tibet (China's Xizang Autonomous Region) to the north and northwest and for 605 kilometers by India's states of Sikkim to the west, West Bengal to the southwest, Assam to the south and southeast, and Arunachal Pradesh (formerly the North-East Frontier Agency) to the east. Sikkim, an eighty-eight-kilometer-wide territory, divides Bhutan from Nepal, while West Bengal separates Bhutan from Bangladesh by only sixty kilometers. At its longest east-west dimension, Bhutan stretches around 300 kilometers;

it measures 170 kilometers at its maximum north-south dimension, forming a total of 46,500 square kilometers, an area one-third the size of Nepal. In the mid-1980s, about 70 percent of Bhutan was covered with forests; 10 percent was covered with year-round snow and glaciers; nearly 6 percent was permanently cultivated or used for human habitation; another 3 percent was used for shifting cultivation (*tsheri*), a practice banned by the government; and 5 percent was used as meadows and pastures. The rest of the land was either barren rocky areas or scrubland.

Early British visitors to Bhutan reported ''dark and steep glens, and the high tops of mountains lost in the clouds, constitut[ing] altogether a scene of extraordinary magnificence and sublimity.'' One of the most rugged mountain terrains in the world, it has elevations ranging from 160 meters to more than 7,000 meters above sea level, in some cases within distances of less than 100 kilometers of each other. Bhutan's highest peak, at 7,554 meters above sea level, is north-central Kulha Gangri, close to the border with China; the second highest peak, Chomo Lhari, overlooking the Chumbi Valley in the west, is 7,314 meters above sea level; nineteen other peaks exceed 7,000 meters (see fig. 14).

In the north, the snowcapped Great Himalayan Range reaches heights of over 7,500 meters above sea level and extends along the Bhutan-China border. The northern region consists of an arc of glaciated mountain peaks with an arctic climate at the highest elevations. Watered by snow-fed rivers, alpine valleys in this region provide pasturage for livestock tended by a sparse population of migratory shepherds.

The Inner Himalayas are southward spurs of the Great Himalayan Range. The Black Mountains, in central Bhutan, form a watershed between two major river systems, the Mo Chhu and the Drangme Chhu (*chhu* means river). Peaks in the Black Mountains range between 1,500 meters and 2,700 meters above sea level, and the fast-flowing rivers have carved out spectacular gorges in the lower mountain areas. The woodlands of the central region provide most of Bhutan's valuable forest production. Eastern Bhutan is divided by another southward spur, the Donga Range. Western Bhutan has fertile, cultivated valleys and terraced river basins.

In the south, the Southern Hills, or Siwalik Hills, the foothills of the Himalayas, are covered with dense deciduous forest, alluvial lowland river valleys, and mountains that reach to around 1,500 meters above sea level. The foothills descend into the subtropical Duars Plain. Most of the Duars Plain proper is located in India, and ten to fifteen kilometers penetrate inside Bhutan. The Bhutan Duars has two parts. The northern Duars, which abuts the

Himalayan foothills, has rugged, slopping terrain and dry porous soil with dense vegetation and abundant wildlife. The southern Duars has moderately fertile soil, heavy savanna grass, dense mixed jungle, and freshwater springs. Taken as a whole, the Duars provides the greatest amount of fertile flatlands in Bhutan. Rice and other crops are grown on the plains and mountainsides up to 1,200 meters. Bhutan's most important commercial centers—Phuntsholing, Geylegphug, and Samdrup Jongkhar—are located in the Duars, reflecting the meaning of the name, which is derived from the Hindi *dwar* and means gateway. Rhinoceros, tigers, leopards, elephants, and other wildlife inhabit the region.

Climate

Bhutan's climate is as varied as its altitudes and, like most of Asia, is affected by monsoons. Western Bhutan is particularly affected by monsoons that bring between 60 and 90 percent of the region's rainfall. The climate is humid and subtropical in the southern plains and foothills, temperate in the inner Himalayan valleys of the southern and central regions, and cold in the north, with year-round snow on the main Himalayan summits.

Temperatures vary according to elevation. Temperatures in Thimphu, located at 2,200 meters above sea level in west-central Bhutan, range from approximately 15°C to 26°C during the monsoon season of June through September but drop to between about – 4°C and 16°C in January (see table 22, Appendix). Most of the central portion of the country experiences a cool, temperate climate year-round. In the south, a hot, humid climate helps maintain a fairly even temperature range of between 15°C and 30°C year-round, although temperatures sometimes reach 40°C in the valleys during the summer.

Annual precipitation ranges widely in various parts of the country. In the severe climate of the north, there is only about forty millimeters of annual precipitation—primarily snow. In the temperate central regions, a yearly average of around 1,000 millimeters is more common, and 7,800 millimeters per year has been registered at some locations in the humid, subtropical south, ensuring the thick tropical forest, or savanna. Thimphu experiences dry winter months (December through February) and almost no precipitation until March, when rainfall averages 20 millimeters a month and increases steadily thereafter to a high of 220 millimeters in August for a total annual rainfall of nearly 650 millimeters.

Bhutan's generally dry spring starts in early March and lasts until mid-April. Summer weather commences in mid-April with occasional showers and continues through the premonsoon rains of late June. The summer monsoon lasts from late June through late September with heavy rains from the southwest. The monsoon weather, blocked from its northward progress by the Himalayas, brings heavy rains, high humidity, flash floods and landslides, and numerous misty, overcast days. Autumn, from late September or early October to late November, follows the rainy season. It is characterized by bright, sunny days and some early snowfalls at higher elevations. From late November until March, winter sets in, with frost throughout much of the country and snowfall common above elevations of 3,000 meters. The winter northeast monsoon brings gale-force winds down through high mountain passes, giving Bhutan its name—Drukyul, which in the Dzongkha language means Land of the Thunder Dragon.

River Systems

Bhutan has four major river systems: the Drangme Chhu; the Puna Tsang Chhu, also called the Sankosh; the Wang Chhu; and the Torsa Chhu. Each flows swiftly out of the Himalayas, southerly through the Duars to join the Brahmaputra River in India, and thence through Bangladesh where the Brahmaputra (or Jamuna in Bangladesh) joins the mighty Ganges (or Padma in Bangladesh) to flow into the Bay of Bengal. The largest river system, the Drangme Chhu, flows southwesterly from India's state of Arunachal Pradesh and has three major branches: the Drangme Chhu, Mangde Chhu, and Bumthang Chhu. These branches form the Drangme Chhu basin, which spreads over most of eastern Bhutan and drains the Tongsa and Bumthang valleys. In the Duars, where eight tributaries join it, the Drangme Chhu is called the Manas Chhu. The 320-kilometer-long Puna Tsang Chhu rises in northwestern Bhutan as the Mo Chhu and Pho Chhu, which are fed by the snows from the Great Himalayan Range. They flow southerly to Punakha, where they join to form the Puna Tsang Chhu, which flows southerly into India's state of West Bengal. The tributaries of the 370-kilometer-long Wang Chhu rise in Tibet. The Wang Chhu itself flows southeasterly through west-central Bhutan, drains the Ha, Paro, and Thimphu valleys, and continues into the Duars, where it enters West Bengal as the Raigye Chhu. The smallest river system, the Torsa Chhu, known as the Amo Chhu in its northern reaches, also flows out of Tibet into the Chumbi Valley and swiftly through western Bhutan before broadening near Phuntsholing and then flowing into India.

Glaciers

Glaciers in northern Bhutan, which cover about 10 percent of the total surface area, are an important renewable source of water for Bhutan's rivers. Fed by fresh snow each winter and slow melting in the summer, the glaciers bring millions of liters of fresh water to Bhutan and downriver areas each year. Glacial melt added to monsoon-swollen rivers, however, also contributes to flooding and potential disaster.

Population

Size, Structure, and Settlement Patterns

When Bhutan's first national census was conducted in 1969, the population officially stood at 930,614 persons. Before 1969 population estimates had ranged between 300,000 and 800,000 people. The 1969 census has been criticized as inaccurate. By the time the 1980 census was held, the population reportedly had increased to approximately 1,165,000 persons (see table 23, Appendix). The results of the 1988 census had not been released as of 1991, but preliminary government projections in 1988 set the total population at 1,375,400 persons, whereas UN estimates stood at 1,451,000 people in 1988. Other foreign projections put the population at 1,598,216 persons in July 1991. It is likely, however, that Bhutan's real population was less than 1 million and probably as little as 600,000 in 1990. Moreover, the government itself began to use the figure of "about 600,000 citizens" in late 1990.

The annual growth rate in 1990 was 2 percent. Although the wide variation in population size makes all projections flawed, experts believe that the population growth rate is valid. The birth rate was 37 per 1,000, and the death rate was 17 per 1,000. In 1988 UN experts had estimated Bhutan would have a population of 1.9 million by 2000 and 3 million by 2025. The average annual population growth rate was estimated at 1.9 percent during the period from 1965 to 1970 and 1.8 percent during the period 1980 to 1985. Rates of change were projected to increase to 2.1 percent by 1990 and 2.3 percent by 2000 and to decrease to 1.41 percent by 2025. Total fertility rates (the average number of children born during a woman's reproductive years) have declined since the 1950s, however. The rate stood at 6.0 in 1955 and 5.5 in 1985 and was expected to decline to 3.7 by 2005 and 2.5 by 2025. The infant mortality rate was the highest in South Asia in 1990: 137 deaths per 1,000 live births. Despite the declining population growth most of Bhutan's people were young. By the late 1980s, 45 percent of the population was under fifteen years of age. However, the greater number of female infant deaths resulted in one of the world's lowest male-female ratios (97.2 females to 100 males; see fig. 15).

Life expectancy at birth had increased significantly since the 1950s, when it stood at only 36.3 years. By the early 1980s, life expectancy had reached 45.9 years. In 1989 the UN projected that life expectancy at birth in Bhutan would reach 55.5 years by 2005 and 61.8 years by 2025, still low compared with other South Asian countries and with the other least developed nations of the world.

Overall population density was thirty-one persons per square kilometer in the late 1980s, but because of the rugged terrain distribution was more dense in settled areas. The regions in the southern Duars valleys and eastern Bhutan around the fertile Tashigang Valley were the most populous areas. As was common among the least developed nations, there was a trend, albeit small, toward urbanization. Whereas in 1970 only 3 percent of the population lived in urban settings, the percentage had increased to 5 percent in 1985. UN specialists projected the urban population would reach 8 percent by 2000. With the exception of Tuvalu, Bhutan had the lowest urban population of any country among the forty-one least developed nations of the world.

Thimphu, the capital, the largest urban area, had a population of 27,000 persons in 1990. Most employed residents of Thimphu, some 2,860 in 1990, were government employees. Another 2,200 persons worked in private businesses and cottage industries. The city advanced toward modernization in 1987 with the installation of meters to regulate water consumption, the naming of its streets, and the erection of street signs. The only other urban area with a population of more than 10,000 residents was Phuntsholing in Chhukha District.

Ethnic Groups

Bhutan's society is made up of four broad but not necessarily exclusive groups: the Ngalop, the Sharchop, several aboriginal peoples, and Nepalese. The Ngalop (a term thought to mean the earliest risen or first converted) are people of Tibetan origin who migrated to Bhutan as early as the ninth century. For this reason, they are often referred to in foreign literature as Bhote (people of Bhotia or Tibet). The Ngalop are concentrated in western and northern districts. They introduced Tibetan culture and Buddhism to Bhutan and comprised the dominant political and cultural element in modern Bhutan.

The Sharchop (the word means easterner), an Indo-Mongoloid people who are thought to have migrated from Assam or possibly Burma during the past millennium, comprise most of the population of eastern Bhutan. Although long the biggest ethnic group in Bhutan, the Sharchop have been largely assimilated into the Tibetan-Ngalop culture. Because of their proximity to India, some

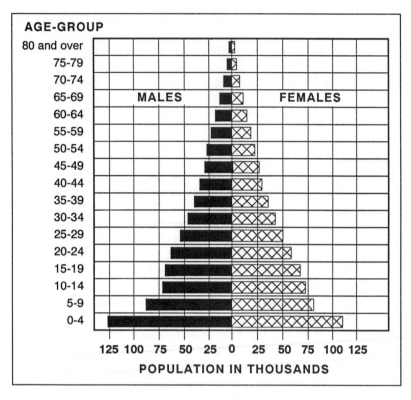

Source: Based on information from Bhutan, Planning Commission, Central Statistical Office, *Statistical Yearbook of Bhutan, 1989*, Thimphu, May 1990, 2.

Figure 15. Bhutan: Population Distribution by Age and Sex, 1988

speak Assamese or Hindi. They practice slash-and-burn and *tsheri* agriculture, planting dry-rice crops for three or four years until the soil is exhausted and then moving on.

The third group consists of small aboriginal or indigenous tribal peoples living in scattered villages throughout Bhutan. Culturally and linguistically part of the populations of West Bengal or Assam, they embrace the Hindu system of endogamous groups ranked by hierarchy and practice wet-rice and dry-rice agriculture. They include the Drokpa, Lepcha, and Doya tribes as well as the descendants of slaves who were brought to Bhutan from similar tribal areas in India. The ex-slave communities tended to be near traditional population centers because it was there that they had been pressed into service to the state. Together, the Ngalop, Sharchop, and tribal groups were thought to constitute up to 72 percent of the population in the late 1980s.

The remaining 28 percent of the population were of Nepalese origin. Officially, the government stated that 28 percent of the national population was Nepalese in the late 1980s, but unofficial estimates ran as high as 30 to 40 percent, and Nepalese were estimated to constitute a majority in southern Bhutan. The number of legal permanent Nepalese residents in the late 1980s may have been as few as 15 percent of the total population, however. The first small groups of Nepalese, the most recent of the major groups to arrive in Bhutan, emigrated primarily from eastern Nepal under Indian auspices in the late nineteenth and early twentieth centuries. Mostly Hindus, the Nepalese settled in the southern foothills and are sometimes referred to as southern Bhutanese. Traditionally, they have been involved mostly in sedentary agriculture, although some have cleared forest cover and conducted *tsheri* agriculture. The most divisive issue in Bhutan in the 1980s and early 1990s was the accommodation of the Nepalese Hindu minority. The government traditionally attempted to limit immigration and restrict residence and employment of Nepalese to the southern region. Liberalization measures in the 1970s and 1980s encouraged intermarriage and provided increasing opportunities for public service. More in-country migration by Nepalese seeking better education and business opportunities was allowed.

Bhutan also had a sizable modern Tibetan refugee population, which stood at 10,000 persons in 1987. The major influx of 6,000 persons came in 1959 in the wake of the Chinese army's invasion and occupation of Tibet. The Tibetan expatriates became only partially integrated into Bhutanese society, however, and many were unwilling to accept citizenship. Perceiving a lack of allegiance to the state on the part of Tibetans, the government decided in 1979 to expel to India those who refused citizenship. India, after some reluctance, acceded to the move and accepted more than 3,100 Tibetans between 1980 and 1985. Another 4,200 Tibetans requested and received Bhutanese citizenship. Although Bhutan traditionally welcomed refugees—and still accepted a few new ones fleeing the 1989 imposition of martial law in Tibet—government policy in the late 1980s was to refuse more Tibetan refugees.

Languages

Bhutanese speak one or more of four major, mutually unintelligible languages. Traditionally, public and private communications, religious materials, and official documents were written in *chhokey,* the classical Tibetan script, and a Bhutanese adaptive cursive script was developed for correspondence. In modern times, as in the past, *chhokey,* which exists only in written form, was understood only by the well educated. The official national language, Dzongkha (language of the *dzong*), has developed since the seventeenth century. A sophisticated form of the Tibetan dialect spoken by Ngalop villagers in western Bhutan, it is based primarily on the vernacular speech of the Punakha Valley. In its written form, Dzongkha uses an adaptive cursive script based on *chhokey* to express the Ngalop spoken language. Ngalopkha is spoken in six regional dialects with variations from valley to valley and village to village; Dzongkha, however, through vigorous government education programs had become widely understood throughout Bhutan by the 1970s.

The other languages include Sharchopkha, or Tsangla, a Mon language spoken in eastern districts; Bumthangkha, an aboriginal Khen language spoken in central Bhutan; and Nepali, or Lhotsam, predominantly spoken in the south. Seven other Khen and Mon languages also are spoken in Bhutan. Hindi is understood among Bhutanese educated in India and was the language of instruction in the schools at Ha and Bumthang in the early 1930s as well as in the first schools in the ''formal'' education system from the beginning of the 1960s.

Along with Dzongkha and English, Nepali was once one of the three official languages used in Bhutan. Dzongkha was taught in grades one through twelve in the 1980s. English was widely understood and was the medium of instruction in secondary and higher-level schools. Starting in the 1980s, college-level textbooks in Dzongkha were published, and in 1988 a proposal was made to standardize Dzongkha script. Sharchopkha, Bumthangkha, and Nepali also were used in primary schools in areas where speakers of those languages predominated. In 1989, however, Nepali was dropped from school curricula.

Part of the government's effort to preserve traditional culture and to strengthen the contemporary sense of national identity (*driglam namzha*—national customs and etiquette) has been its emphasis on Dzongkha-language study. The Department of Education declared in 1979 that because Dzongkha was the national language, it was ''the responsibility of each and every Bhutanese to learn Dzongkha.'' To aid in language study, the department also published a Dzongkha dictionary in 1986.

Social System

Society

Bhutan's traditional society has been defined as both patriarchal and matriarchal, and the member held in highest esteem served as the family's head. Bhutan also has been described as feudalistic and characterized by the absence of strong social stratification. In premodern times, there were three broad classes: the monastic community, the leadership of which was the nobility; lay civil servants who ran the government apparatus; and farmers, the largest class, living in self-sufficient villages. In the more militaristic premodern era, Bhutan also had an underclass of prisoners of war and their descendants, who were generally treated as serfs or even as slaves. In modern times, society was organized around joint family units, and a class division existed based on occupation and, in time, social status. With the introduction of foreign practices in recent centuries and increasing job mobility outside the village, however, emphasis has been placed on nuclear family units.

Social status is based on a family's economic station. Except among the Hindu Nepalese in southern Bhutan, there was no caste system. Although Bhutanese were endogamous by tradition, modern practices and even royal decrees encouraged ethnic integration in the late twentieth century. Primogeniture dictated the right of inheritance traditionally, although in some central areas the eldest daughter was the lawful successor. In contemporary Bhutan, however, inheritance came to be more equally distributed among all children of a family.

Except for the royal family and a few other noble families, Bhutanese do not have surnames. Individuals normally have two names, but neither is considered a family name or a surname. Some people adopt their village name, occasionally in abbreviated form, as part of their name, using it before their given name. Wives keep their own names, and children frequently have names unconnected to either parent. Some individuals educated abroad have taken their last name as a surname, however. A system of titles, depending on age, degree of familiarity, and social or official status, denotes ranks and relationships among members of society. The title *dasho,* for example, is an honorific used by a prince of the royal house, a commoner who marries a princess, a nephew of the Druk Gyalpo, a deputy minister, other senior government officials, and others in positions of authority.

Although adherents of Buddhism, Bhutanese are not vegetarians and occasionally eat beef, especially in western Bhutan. Pork, poultry, goat and yak meat, and fish are consumed on a limited scale. Rice and increasingly corn are staples. Despite a scarcity of milk, dairy products, such as yak cheese and yak cheese byproducts, are part of the diet of upland people. Meat soups, rice or corn, and curries spiced with chilies comprise daily menus; beverages include buttered tea and beer distilled from cereals. Wild vegetation, such as young ferns, also is harvested for table food.

Traditional clothing still was commonly worn in the early 1990s, and, indeed, its use was fostered by government decree. Women wore the *kira,* an ankle-length dress made of a rectangular piece of cloth held at the shoulders with a clip and closed with a woven belt at the waist, over a long-sleeved blouse. Social status was indicated by the amount of decorative details and colors of the *kira* and the quality of the cloth used. Men wore the *gho,* a wraparound, coatlike, knee-length garment, with a narrow belt. Both men and women sometimes wore elaborate earrings, and both sexes also wore scarves or shawls, white for commoners and carefully specified colors, designs, and manners of folding for higher ranking individuals. Only the Druk Gyalpo and the Je Khenpo were allowed to wear the honorific saffron scarf. Other officials were distinguished by the color of the scarves they wore: orange for ministers and deputy ministers, blue for National Assembly and Royal Advisory Council members, and red or maroon for high religious and civil officials, district officers, and judges (anyone holding the title of *dasho*). Stripes on scarves of the same base color denoted greater or lesser ranks.

Marriage and Family Life

The traditional practice, arranged marriages based on family and ethnic ties, has been replaced in the late twentieth century with marriages based on mutual affection. Marriages were usually arranged by the partners in contemporary Bhutan, and the minimum age was sixteen for women and twenty-one for men. The institution of child marriage, once relatively widespread, had largely declined as Bhutan modernized, and there were only remnants of the practice in the late twentieth century. Interethnic marriages, once forbidden, were encouraged in the late 1980s by an incentive of a Nu10,000 (for value of the ngultrum—see Glossary) government stipend to willing couples. The stipend was discontinued in 1991, however. Marriages of Bhutanese citizens to foreigners, however, have been discouraged. Bhutanese with foreign spouses were not allowed to obtain civil service positions and could have their government scholarships cancelled and be required to repay portions already received. Foreign spouses were not entitled to citizenship by right but had to apply for naturalization.

Polyandry was abolished and polygamy was restricted in the midtwentieth century, but the law in the 1990s still allowed a man as many as three wives, providing he had the first wife's permission. The first wife also had the power to sue for divorce and alimony

Bhutanese girl, wearing traditional kira *and jewelry*
Courtesy Bhutan Travel, Inc., New York (Marie Brown)

if she did not agree. In the 1980s, divorce was common, and new laws provided better benefits to women seeking alimony.

Family life, both traditionally and in the contemporary period, was likely to provide for a fair amount of self-sufficiency. Families, for example, often made their own clothing, bedding, floor and seat covers, tablecloths, and decorative items for daily and religious use. Wool was the primary material, but domestic silk and imported cotton were also used in weaving colorful cloth, often featuring elaborate geometric, floral, and animal designs. Although weaving was normally done by women of all ages using family-owned looms, monks sometimes did embroidery and appliqué work. In the twentieth century, weaving was possibly as predominant a feature of daily life as it was at the time of Bhutan's unification in the seventeenth century.

Landholdings varied depending on the wealth and size of individual families, but most families had as much land as they could farm using traditional techniques. A key element of family life was the availability of labor. Thus, the choice of the home of newlyweds was determined by which parental unit had the greatest need of supplemental labor. If both families had a sufficient supply of labor, then a bride and groom might elect to set up their own home.

Role of Women

Although officially the government has encouraged greater participation of women in political and administrative life, male members of the traditional aristocracy dominate the social system.
Economic development has increased opportunities for women to
participate in fields such as medicine, both as physicians and nurses;
teaching; and administration. By 1989 nearly 10 percent of government employees were women, and the top civil service examination graduate in 1989 was a woman. During their government
careers, women civil servants were allowed three months materni-
ty leave with full pay for three deliveries and leave without pay
for any additional deliveries. Reflecting the dominance of males
in society, girls were outnumbered three to two in primary and
secondary-level schools.

Women in the 1980s played a significant role in the agricultural
work force, where they outnumbered men, who were leaving for
the service sector and other urban industrial and commercial activities. In the mid-1980s, 95 percent of all Bhutanese women from
the ages of fifteen to sixty-four years were involved in agricultural
work, compared with only 78 percent of men in the same age range.
Foreign observers have noted that women shared equally with men
in farm labor. Overall, women were providing more labor than
men in all sectors of the economy. Less than 4 percent of the total
female work force was unemployed, compared with nearly 10 percent of men who had no occupation.

The government founded the National Women's Association of
Bhutan in 1981 primarily to improve the socioeconomic status of
women, particularly those in rural areas. The association, at its
inaugural session, declared that it would not push for equal rights
for women because the women of Bhutan had already come to "enjoy equal status with men politically, economically, and socially."
To give prominence to the association, the Druk Gyalpo's sister,
Ashi Sonam Chhoden Wangchuck, was appointed its president.
Starting in 1985, the association became a line item in the government budget and was funded at Nu2.4 million in fiscal year (FY—
see Glossary) 1992. The association has organized annual beauty
contests featuring traditional arts and culture, fostered training in
health and hygiene, distributed yarn and vegetable seeds, and introduced smokeless stoves in villages.

Housing

Bhutanese housing has a distinct character from that of other
Himalayan countries. Relatively spacious compared with those of

neighboring societies, houses took advantage of natural light and, because of the steep terrain, were usually built in clusters rather than in rows. Timber, stone, clay, and brick were typical construction materials in upland Ngalop areas. Family residences frequently had three stories, with room for livestock on the first or ground story, living quarters on the second story, additional living quarters and storage on the third story, and an open space between the third story and the roof for open-air storage. Large stones were used to weigh down wooden roofs against fierce Himalayan storms. Among Buddhism's contributions to Bhutan were its rich architectural embellishments. The walls of residences and public buildings, inside and outside, were subject to colorful decoration, as were furniture, cupboards, stairs, window frames, doors, and fences. Wooden shutters rather than scarce glass were used throughout the 1980s. Buddhist motifs and symbolic colors also were extensively used. Sharchop houses of stone and timber were sometimes built on hillsides. In the southern areas inhabited by Nepalese, Assamese, and Bengalis, housing was more likely to consist of bamboo and thatched roof houses and mud and thatch dwellings. The construction of housing often was a cooperative task of the community.

Festivals

Bhutan has numerous public holidays, most of which center around traditional seasonal, secular, and religious festivals. They include winter solstice (around January 1, depending on the lunar calendar), lunar new year (January or February), the Druk Gyalpo's birthday and the anniversary of his coronation, the official start of monsoon season (September 22), National Day (December 17), and various Buddhist and Hindu celebrations. Even the secular holidays have religious overtones, including religious dances and prayers used to bless the day.

Masked dances and dance dramas are common traditional features at festivals. Energetic dancers wearing colorful wooden or composition face masks employ special costumes and music to depict a panoply of heroes, demons, death heads, animals, gods, and caricatures of common people. The dances enjoy royal patronage and preserve not only ancient folk and religious customs but also perpetuate the art of mask making.

Religious Tradition

Buddhism

Mahayana Buddhism was the state religion, and Buddhists comprised about 70 percent of the population in the early 1990s.

Although originating from Tibetan Buddhism, Bhutanese Buddhism differs significantly in its rituals, liturgy, and monastic organization. The state religion has long been supported financially by the government through annual subsidies to monasteries, shrines, monks, and nuns. In the modern era, support of the state religion during the reign of Jigme Dorji Wangchuck included the manufacture of 10,000 gilded bronze images of the Buddha, publication of elegant calligraphied editions of the 108-volume *Kanjur* (Collection of the Words of the Buddha) and the 225-volume *Tenjur* (Collection of Commentaries), and the construction of numerous *chorten* (stupas) throughout the country. Guaranteed representation in the National Assembly and the Royal Advisory Council, Buddhists constituted the majority of society and were assured an influential voice in public policy.

In 1989 some 1,000 monks (*lam,* or *gelong,* novices) belonged to the Central Monastic Body in Thimphu and Punakha, and some 4,000 monks belonged to district monastic bodies. The hierarchy was headed by the Je Khenpo, who was assisted by four *lonpon* or masters, each in charge of religious tradition, liturgy, lexicography, or logic. The *lonpon,* one of whom, the Dorji Lonpon, normally succeeded the current Je Khenpo, had under them religious administrators and junior monastic officials in charge of art, music, and other areas. Gelugpa monks were celibate, but Nyingmapa monks were not so restricted and could marry, raise families, and work in secular occupations while performing liturgical functions in temples and homes. In all, there were some 12,000 monks in Bhutan in the late 1980s. There were also active congregations of nuns, but no figures were readily available.

The majority of Bhutan's Buddhists are adherents of the Drukpa subsect of the Kargyupa (literally, oral transmission) school, one of the four major schools of Tibetan Buddhism, which is itself a combination of the Theravada (monastic), Mahayana (messianic), and Tantrayana (apocalyptic) forms of Buddhism. Tibetan Buddhism holds that salvation can be achieved through the intercession of compassionate bodhisattvas (enlightened ones) who have delayed their own entry into a state of *nibbana* (see Glossary), or nirvana, enlightenment and selfless bliss, to save others. Emphasis is put on the doctrine of the cosmic Buddha, of whom the historical Buddha—Siddhartha Gautama (ca. 563-ca. 483 B.C.)—was only one of many manifestations. Bodhisattvas are in practice treated more as deities than as enlightened human beings and occupy the center of a richly polytheistic universe of subordinate deities; opposing, converted, and reformed demons; wandering ghosts; and saintly humans that reflects the shamanistic folk religion of the

regions into which Buddhism expanded. Tantrism contributed eso-
teric techniques of meditation and a repertoire of sacred icons,
phrases, gestures, and rituals that easily lent themselves to practical (rather than transcendental) and magical interpretation.

The Kargyupa school was introduced into Tibet from India and
into Bhutan from Tibet in the eleventh century. The central teaching of the Kargyupa school is meditation on *mahamudra* (Sanskrit
for great seal), a concept tying the realization of emptiness to freedom from reincarnation. Also central to the Kargyupa school are
the dharma (laws of nature, all that exists, real or imaginary), which
consist of six Tantric meditative practices teaching bodily self-control
so as to achieve nirvana. One of the key aspects of the Kargyupa
school is the direct transmission of the tenets of the faith from teacher
to disciple. The Drukpa subsect, which grew out of one of the four
Kargyupa sects, was the preeminent religious belief in Bhutan by
the end of the twelfth century (see Origins and Early Settlement,
A.D. 600–1600, this ch.).

Monasteries and convents were common throughout Bhutan in
the late twentieth century. Both monks and nuns kept their heads
shaved and wore distinguishing maroon robes. Their days were
spent in study and meditation but also in the performance of rituals
honoring various bodhisattvas, praying for the dead, and seeking
divine intercession on behalf of the ill. Some of their prayers involved chants and singing accompanied by conch shell trumpets,
thighbone trumpets (made from human thighbones), metal horns
up to three meters long, large standing drums and cymbals, hand
bells, temple bells, gongs, and wooden sticks. Such monastic music
and singing, not normally heard by the general public, has been
reported to have "great virility" and to be more melodious than
its Tibetan monotone counterparts.

To bring Buddhism to the people, numerous symbols and structures are employed. Religious monuments, prayer walls, prayer
flags, and sacred mantras carved in stone hillsides were prevalent
in the early 1990s. Among the religious monuments are *chorten,*
the Bhutanese version of the Indian stupa. They range from simple rectangular "house" *chorten* to complex edifices with ornate steps,
doors, domes, and spires. Some are decorated with the Buddha's
eyes that see in all directions simultaneously. These earth, brick,
or stone structures commemorate deceased kings, Buddhist saints,
venerable monks, and other notables, and sometimes they serve
as reliquaries. Prayer walls are made of laid or piled stone and in-
scribed with Tantric prayers. Prayers printed with woodblocks on
cloth are made into tall, narrow, colorful prayer flags, which are
then mounted on long poles and placed both at holy sites and at

dangerous locations to ward off demons and to benefit the spirits of the dead. To help propagate the faith, itinerant monks travel from village to village carrying portable shrines with many small doors, which open to reveal statues and images of the Buddha, bodhisattavas, and notable lamas.

Bon

Before the introduction of Buddhism, animistic worship, generally categorized as Bon in the Himalayas, was prevalent in Bhutan. The sun, moon, sky, and other natural elements were worshiped, and doctrine was transmitted orally from generation to generation. Bon, from a Tibetan word meaning invocation or recitation, has priests—*bonpo*—who perform exorcisms, burial rites, and divinations to tame threatening demons and to understand the wishes of the gods. Imported from Tibet and India, perhaps in the eighth century, Bon doctrine became so strongly reinvigorated by Buddhism that by the eleventh century it reasserted itself as an independent school apart from Buddhism. Conversely, Bon influenced popular Buddhism, infusing it with an appreciation for omens and demons felt to influence daily life profoundly. Bon established a canon of teachings and continued to be practiced in modern Bhutan.

Hinduism and Islam

The minority religion of Bhutan is Hinduism, whose adherents—those of Nepalese origin—officially constitute 28 percent of the population (see Hinduism, ch. 2). Despite Buddhism's status as the state religion, Hindus had de facto freedom of religion. The Druk Gyalpo decreed major Hindu festivals as national holidays, and the royal family participated in them. An even smaller religious minority—about 5 percent of the population in 1989—practiced Islam. Although foreign religious personnel were permitted to work in Bhutan, primarily as educators, they were not allowed to proselytize.

Education

Western-style education was introduced to Bhutan during the reign of Ugyen Wangchuck (1907–26). Until the 1950s, the only formal education available to Bhutanese students, except for private schools in Ha and Bumthang, was through Buddhist monasteries. In the 1950s, several private secular schools were established without government support, and several others were established in major district towns with government backing. By the late 1950s, there were twenty-nine government and thirty private primary schools, but only about 2,500 children were enrolled. Secondary

The twelfth-century Chendibji chorten, *a religious monument dominated by the Buddha's all-seeing eyes*
Courtesy Bhutan Travel, Inc., New York (Marie Brown)

education was available only in India. Eventually, the private schools were taken under government supervision to raise the quality of education provided. Although some primary schools in remote areas had to be closed because of low attendance, the most significant modern developments in education came during the period of the First Development Plan (1961-66), when some 108 schools were operating and 15,000 students were enrolled (see Role of the Government, this ch.).

The First Development Plan provided for a central education authority—in the form of a director of education appointed in 1961—and an organized, modern school system with free and universal primary education. Since that time, following one year of preschool begun at age four, children attended school in the primary grades—one through five. Education continued with the equivalent of grades six through eight at the junior high level and grades nine through eleven at the high school level. The Department of Education administered the All-Bhutan Examinations nationwide to determine promotion from one level of schooling to the next. Examinations at the tenth-grade level were conducted by the Indian School Certificate Council. The Department of Education also was responsible for producing textbooks; preparing course syllabi and in-service training for teachers; arranging training and study abroad; organizing interschool tournaments; procuring foreign assistance for education programs; and recruiting, testing, and promoting teachers, among other duties.

The core curriculum set by the National Board of Secondary Education included English, mathematics, and Dzongkha. Although English was used as the language of instruction throughout the junior high and high school system, Dzongkha and, in southern Bhutan until 1989, Nepali, were compulsory subjects. Students also studied English literature, social studies, history, geography, general science, biology, chemistry, physics, and religion. Curriculum development often has come from external forces, as was the case with historical studies. Most Bhutanese history is based on oral traditions rather than on written histories or administrative records. A project sponsored by the United Nations Education, Scientific, and Cultural Organization (UNESCO) and the University of London developed a ten-module curriculum, which included four courses on Bhutanese history and culture and six courses on Indian and world history and political ideas. Subjects with an immediate practical application, such as elementary agriculture, animal husbandry, and forestry, also were taught.

Bhutan's coeducational school system in 1988 encompassed a reported 42,446 students and 1,513 teachers in 150 primary schools, 11,835 students and 447 teachers in 21 junior high schools, and 4,515 students and 248 teachers in 9 high schools. Males accounted for 63 percent of all primary and secondary students. Most teachers at these levels—70 percent—also were males. There also were 1,761 students and 150 teachers in technical, vocational, and special schools in 1988.

Despite increasing student enrollments, which went from 36,705 students in 1981 to 58,796 students in 1988, education was not compulsory. In 1988 only about 25 percent of primary-school-age children attended school, an extremely low percentage by all standards. Although the government set enrollment quotas for high schools, in no instance did they come close to being met in the 1980s. Only about 8 percent of junior high-school-age and less than 3 percent of high-school-age children were enrolled in 1988.

Bhutan's literacy rate in the early 1990s, estimated at 30 percent for males and 10 percent for females by the United Nations Development Programme (UNDP), ranked lowest among all least developed countries. Other sources ranked the literacy rate as low as 12 to 18 percent.

Some primary schools and all junior high and high schools were boarding schools. The school year in the 1980s ran from March through December. Tuition, books, stationery, athletic equipment, and food were free for all boarding schools in the 1980s, and some high schools also provided clothing. With the assistance of the World Food Programme of the Food and Agriculture Organization of the United Nations (FAO), free midday meals were provided in some primary schools.

Higher education was provided by Royal Bhutan Polytechnic just outside the village of Deothang, Samdrup Jongkhar District, and by Kharbandi Technical School in Kharbandi, Chhukha District. Founded in 1973, Royal Bhutan Polytechnic offered courses in civil, mechanical, and electrical engineering; surveying; and drafting. Kharbandi Technical School was established in the 1970s with UNDP and International Labour Organisation assistance. Bhutan's only junior college—Sherubtse College in Kanglung, Tashigang District—was established in 1983 as a three-year degree-granting college affiliated with the University of Delhi. In the year it was established with UNDP assistance, the college enrolled 278 students, and seventeen faculty members taught courses in arts, sciences, and commerce leading to a bachelor's degree. Starting in 1990, junior college classes also were taught at the Yanchenphug High School in Thimphu and were to be extended to other high schools thereafter.

Education programs were given a boost in 1990 when the Asian Development Bank (see Glossary) granted a US$7.13 million loan for staff training and development, specialist services, equipment and furniture purchases, salaries and other recurrent costs, and facility rehabilitation and construction at Royal Bhutan Polytechnic. The Department of Education and its Technical and Vocational Education Division were given a US$750,000 Asian Development Bank grant for improving the technical, vocational, and training sectors. The New Approach to Primary Education, started in 1985, was extended to all primary and junior high schools in 1990 and stressed self-reliance and awareness of Bhutan's unique national culture and environment.

Most Bhutanese students being educated abroad received technical training in India, Singapore, Japan, Australia, New Zealand, Britain, Germany, and the United States. English-speaking countries attracted the majority of Bhutanese students. The vast majority returned to their homeland.

Health

Bhutan's health-care development accelerated in the early 1960s with the establishment of the Department of Public Health and the opening of new hospitals and dispensaries throughout the country.

By the early 1990s, health care was provided through some twenty-nine general hospitals (including five leprosy hospitals, three army hospitals, and one mobile hospital), forty-six dispensaries, sixty-seven basic health units, four indigenous-medicine dispensaries, and fifteen malaria eradication centers. The major hospitals were in Thimphu, Geylegphug, and Tashigang. Hospital beds in 1988 totaled 932. There was a severe shortage of health-care personnel with official statistics reporting only 142 physicians and 678 paramedics, about one health-care professional for every 2,000 people, or only one physician for almost 10,000 people. Training for health-care assistants, nurses' aides, midwives, and primary health-care workers was provided at Thimphu General Hospital's Health School, which was established in 1974. Graduates of the school were the core of the national public health system and helped staff the primary care basic health units throughout the country. Additional health-care workers were recruited from among volunteers in villages to supplement primary health care.

The most common diseases in the 1980s were gastrointestinal infections caused by waterborne parasites, mostly attributable to the lack of clean drinking water. The most frequently treated diseases were respiratory tract infections, diarrhea and dysentery, worms, skin infections, malaria, nutritional deficiencies, and conjunctivitis. In 1977 the World Health Organization (WHO) declared Bhutan a smallpox-free zone. In 1979 a nationwide immunization program was established. In 1987, with WHO support, the government envisioned plans to immunize all children against diphtheria, pertussis, tetanus, polio, tuberculosis, and measles by 1990. The government's major medical objective by 2000 was to eliminate waterborne parasites, diarrhea and dysentery, malaria, tuberculosis, pneumonia, and goiter. Progress in leprosy eradication was made in the 1970s and 1980s, during which time the number of patients had decreased by more than half, and by 1988 the government was optimistic that the disease could be eliminated by 2000.

It was estimated in 1988 that only 8 persons per 1,000 had access to potable water. Despite improved amenities provided to the people through government economic development programs, Bhutan still faced basic health problems. Factors in the country's high morbidity and death rates included the severe climate, less than hygienic living conditions, for example long-closed-up living quarters during the winter, a situation that contributes to the high incidence of leprosy, and smoke inhalation from inadequately ventilated cooking equipment. Nevertheless, in 1980 it was estimated that 90 percent of Bhutanese received an adequate daily caloric intake.

Although there were no reported cases of acquired immune deficiency syndrome (AIDS), the Department of Public Health set up a public awareness program in 1987. With the encouragement of the WHO, a "reference laboratory" was established at the Thimphu General Hospital to test for AIDS and human immunodeficiency virus (HIV) as a precautionary measure. To further enhance awareness, representatives of the National Institute of Family Health were sent to Bangladesh in 1990 for training in AIDS awareness and treatment measures.

The Economy

The Economic Context

Bhutan, recognized by international aid agencies as one of the poorest of the least developed countries of the world, had a primarily subsistence agricultural economy in the early 1990s. In the late 1980s, around 95 percent of the work force was involved in the agricultural sector (agriculture, livestock, forestry and logging, and fishing). The government projected that the agriculture sector would produce 46.2 percent of the nation's gross domestic product (GDP—see Glossary) for 1991, representing a decade-long slight decline as government services and electric power generation increased. Manufacturing and construction, although important, were expected to contribute only 14.2 percent of the projected total GDP (nearly Nu4.1 billion) for 1991 (see table 24, Appendix). The gross national product (GNP—see Glossary) was nearly Nu3.9 billion in 1988, and in the same year, the GDP had risen to Nu3.4 billion (see table 25, Appendix). The World Bank (see Glossary) calculated Bhutan's 1989 per capita GNP, based on revised population estimates (600,000 persons), at US$440.

Despite these seemingly bleak economic indicators, the actual quality of life was comparatively better than that of countries to the north and south. World Bank analysts believed the numbers were low because of inaccurate population estimates and differences in measuring subsistence output and barter transactions, as well as the difficulties in reconciling the differences between fiscal-year and calendar-year accounts. Nutritional intakes, and the availability of housing, land, livestock, and fuel, all pointed to higher per capita income. And, when measured in 1980 constant prices, according to Bhutanese government statistics, the economy experienced a highly respectable 8.8 percent annual growth rate during the 1980s.

Although Bhutan has a minuscule private sector, it was growing in the late twentieth century in conjunction with government development plans. It was controlled, however, by a small sector of society, members of the royal family, and individuals or families with government ties. The Companies Act of 1989 provided for the separation of all public and joint sector corporations from the civil service by mid-1990, and, as a result, certain key enterprises became independent of the government.

Role of the Government

Planning and Reform

Government played a pervasive role in Bhutan's economy. Since 1961 the economy has been guided through development plans, which the Development Secretariat and later the Planning Commission directed, subject to the National Assembly's approval. In the World Bank's 1989 appraisal, "Coming late to the development scene, Bhutan was eager to avoid mistakes committed elsewhere. Although strongly dependent on foreign aid, it was determined to follow its own set of priorities, keep public finance on an even keel, build up a well trained but lean bureaucracy, and prevent environmental damage from overexploitation of the forests or uncontrolled growth of tourism." To help avoid further mistakes, the government used traditional social institutions and involved people at the local level in planning and implementation for their own district, subdistrict, or village. "As a result of these factors," said the World Bank, "development in Bhutan has been remarkably free from seeing economic, social, or cultural disruption."

India fully funded the First Development Plan (1961–66). The first plan, for which Nu107.2 million was allocated, and the Second Development Plan (1966–71), for which Nu202.2 million was allocated, focused primarily on developing modern budgeting techniques (see table 26, Appendix). According to some foreign observers, the first two plans failed to set priorities and achieve economic-sector integration as might be expected of genuine development planning. The major economic-planning emphasis was on public works, primarily roads; forestry; health care; and education (see table 27, Appendix).

To make planning more effective, the Planning Commission was established to formulate the Third Development Plan (1971–76), and the Druk Gyalpo served as its chairman until 1991. Under the third plan, public works, still primarily roads, continued to take a significant share of the Nu475.2 million development budget (17.8 percent) but had decreased from its 58.7 percent share in the first plan and its 34.9 percent share in the second plan. Education gradually increased (from 8.8 to 18.9 percent) in the first three plans. The second and third plans were paid for primarily by India, although about 3 percent of total funding became available through the UN, starting with the third plan. Despite amounts budgeted for planned development, there were additional capital expenditures outside the formal development plan, including public works (mostly road construction) and hydroelectric plants.

One of the major achievements of the Fourth Development Plan (1976–81) was the establishment of district (or *dzongkhag*) planning committees to stimulate greater local involvement, awareness of government development policies, and local development proposals. The committees, however, had no decision-making powers. Nevertheless, agricultural and animal husbandry came to the fore, taking 29 percent of the Nu1.106 billion allocated for the fourth plan. It was during the fourth plan that Bhutan made its first effort to establish the value of the GDP, which in 1977 amounted to Nu1.0 billion. In that year, GDP was distributed among agricultural and related activities, 63.2 percent; services, 13.1 percent; government administration, 10.4 percent; rental income, 8.1 percent; and manufacturing and mining, 5.2 percent. Per capita GDP was estimated at US$105.

The Fifth Development Plan (1981–87) sought the expansion of farmland to increase the production of staple crops, such as rice, corn, wheat, barley, buckwheat, and millet. The plan also emphasized improvements in livestock, soil fertility, plant protection, and farm mechanization. Its total planned allocation was Nu4.3 billion, but the actual outlay came to Nu4.7 billion. Financing the planning process grew increasingly complex, as indicated by the fifth plan's multilateral funding sources. However, domestic revenue sources for development planning had increased significantly, and the fifth plan included development projects that would further decrease dependence on external assistance. Such concepts as self-reliance in each district, decentralization of the development administration, greater public input in decision making, better control of maintenance expenditures, and more efficient and effective use of internal resources became increasingly important.

The Sixth Development Plan (1987–92) focused on industry, mining, trade, and commerce (13.3 percent) and power generation projects (13.1 percent), with education's allocation decreasing slightly to 8.1 percent from 11.2 percent during the fifth plan. At Nu9.5 billion, the sixth plan was considerably more expensive than its predecessor. It included programs that, if successfully implemented, would mean far-reaching reforms. The goals included strengthening government administration, promoting the national identity, mobilizing internal resources, enhancing rural incomes, improving rural housing and resettlement, consolidating and improving services, developing human resources, promoting public involvement in development plans and strategies, and promoting national self-reliance. Perhaps the key ingredient, self-reliance, promised to provide for more popular participation in the development process and to result in improved rural conditions and services as well as better government administration and human-resource development. With greater self-reliance, it was hoped that Bhutan would begin exploiting markets in neighboring countries with manufacturing, mining, and hydroelectric projects in the 1990s. Faced with rising costs, Bhutan postponed some projects requiring large inputs of capital until the Seventh Development Plan (1992–96).

No major changes were expected in overall sectoral development in the seventh plan. Preliminary planning indicated emphasis on "consolidation and rehabilitation" of developments achieved under previous plans, more attention to environmental concerns, and enhancement of women's role in economic and social development.

From their inception, the development plans have been aimed at energizing the rest of the economy and promoting economic self-reliance. Windfall revenues from export receipts normally were used to reduce foreign debt and dependence on foreign aid. Planners also sought to involve the immediate beneficiaries of economic development. Representatives in the National Assembly and district officials were encouraged to become involved in projects, such as roads and bridges, schools, health-care facilities, and irrigation works, in their district. Some costs for the projects were borne through self-help, such as households providing labor. Government planners also have endeavored to increase rural income through initiatives in the farming sector, such as stock-breeding programs, promotion of cash crops, and advanced agro-technology. Central government efforts also were aimed at increasing the quality of life by providing electrification, modern water and sanitation systems, better cooking equipment, and insulation for houses.

Budgets

Key to the budgetary process since 1949 has been the annual subsidy given to Bhutan by the Indian government. In the late 1980s, the subsidy stood at 40 percent of total revenue, but this proportion was significantly less than the nearly 100 percent New Delhi once provided. The rest was funded by international aid organizations and a few domestic sources.

Weaving on a backstrap loom, an important home industry
Courtesy Bhutan Travel, Inc., New York (Marie Brown)

During most of the 1980s, the budget ran a deficit. Only in 1984, out of the four years between 1983 and 1986, did government revenues exceed expenditures, and revenues depended heavily on foreign aid. In other years, revenue shortfalls reached as much as Nu207 million (in 1985). In FY 1989, Bhutan's revenues of nearly Nu1.7 billion (US$99 million) were exceeded by expenditures of nearly Nu2.2 billion (US$128 million, of which US$65 million were for capital expenditures).

Monetary System

The monetary system in the early 1990s was based on the decimal-system ngultrum, which was established as the nation's currency and first used to keep financial accounts in 1974. Prior to 1957, a nondecimal system using both Indian and Bhutanese rupees was employed, and the decimal-based rupee was the standard currency between 1957 and 1974. Since at least the eighteenth century, Bhutan had had its own coinage system, and the Indian rupee also freely circulated as a medium of exchange. Until the 1960s, however, most financial transactions were carried out using barter arrangements. Although Indian rupee notes were used extensively, in 1971 the government had to withdraw some 350,000 *tikchung* (a Bhutanese coin worth half a rupee) from circulation

293

because of the inconvenience of using them in large financial transactions. In 1991 the Indian rupee continued to be legal tender in Bhutan, and the ngultrum was at par with it. The Reserve Bank of India determined the exchange rate between the ngultrum and other foreign currencies. External transactions were handled by Bhutan's Ministry of Finance, which provided foreign exchange for most currency and capital transactions. The ministry also had approval authority over all capital transactions. Starting in 1985, the ministry delegated most foreign-exchange transactions to the Royal Monetary Authority.

Banking and Credit

The Royal Monetary Authority, since its establishment in 1982, has served as the central bank of Bhutan and maintained its headquarters in Thimphu. The authority was responsible for issuing currency, implementing monetary policy, coordinating financial institution activities, and holding the government's foreign-exchange earnings. Among its initial duties was the administration of financial assistance to rural development, a duty later delegated to the Bhutan Development Finance Corporation when it was founded in 1988.

The Bank of Bhutan, the nation's commercial bank, was established in 1968 as a joint venture with the Chartered Bank of India, which owned 25 percent of the bank. In 1970 the State Bank of India took over the Bhutanese assets controlled by the Chartered Bank of India. Since its establishment, the Bank of Bhutan's board of directors, has been composed of key officials from the economic ministries and departments and two officials from the Indian banks. The bank was restructured in 1971. To ensure that it would have sufficient funds at its disposal, government departments were required to deposit all of their accounts with the government-run bank until 1982, when the Royal Monetary Authority was established. Since 1982 the Bank of Bhutan has served as the retail banking agent for the Royal Monetary Authority. The bank's principal office was in Phuntsholing; in 1991 there were twenty-six branch offices throughout the country. The Bank of Bhutan was able to give relatively large loans for capital programs, such as irrigation projects in the south-central region. Among its retail banking activities was the issuance of rupee-denomination travelers' cheques; this activity was started in 1974.

The Bhutan Development Finance Corporation, upon its establishment in 1988, took over the administration of rural financial assistance from the Royal Monetary Authority. Loans were granted for improving farmlands, acquiring livestock, and meeting short-term, seasonal requirements. At least some of the funding for the corporation came from the Asian Development Bank, including an initial US$2.5 million loan in 1988 for the expansion of small- and medium-sized, private-sector industrial development. By 1991 the corporation had been privatized.

Nonbank financial institutions also were set up as part of the economic modernization process. Insurance was offered by the Royal Insurance Corporation of Bhutan, which was established in 1975 with its headquarters in Phuntsholing. Starting in 1980, individuals could invest their savings in the newly established Unit Trust of Bhutan. The trust, with its main office in Phuntsholing, channeled invested funds, for which it issued shares called units, into industrial and commercial development. The Government Employees' Provident Fund, established in 1986; the Bhutan Development Finance Corporation; and other nonbank institutions were small and constrained by the rudimentary use of money in the economy.

Government-Owned Corporations

The government owned several trading corporations. The Food Corporation of Bhutan in Phuntsholing was involved in retailing, marketing, storage, importing and exporting agricultural products, regulating agricultural commerce and processing, and managing rural finance through loans from the Bank of Bhutan and the Royal Insurance Corporation. The National Commission for Trade and Industry in Thimphu provided quality control for proposed industrial projects, and the State Trading Corporation of Bhutan in Phuntsholing was the government's import and export management agency.

Foreign Economic Relations

Aid

Whereas Bhutan was once nearly totally dependent on India not only for its development assistance but also for its entire government revenue, it increasingly turned to various international organizations, such as the United Nations, the Colombo Plan, the World Bank, and the Asian Development Bank, for loans. Since the 1960s, Bhutan, through the Colombo Plan, has received aid from several countries in the form of farm machinery, motor vehicles, school books and laboratory equipment, livestock, seeds, dairy equipment, medicine, and refrigeration and irrigation systems. Participating countries included Japan, Australia, New

Zealand, Britain, Austria, Switzerland, West Germany, and Canada. The World Bank granted a US$9 million interest-free loan to help with the development of a calcium carbide plant near Phuntsholing. As of 1990, total Asian Development Bank loans to Bhutan since the latter joined in 1982 amounted to US$30 million. In 1987 and 1988 alone, the bank approved loans totalling more than US$6.9 million to cover the modernization of industrial estates and to provide foreign currency for the Bhutan Development Finance Corporation, which in turn provided credit for agricultural projects and private-sector businesses. Asian Development Bank loans to Bhutan for 1990–93 were projected at US$35 million, plus a grant of more than US$4.85 million; the aid was for technical assistance.

The Sixth Development Plan saw increased involvement of aid both through UN auspices and the non-profit Swiss organization Helvetas (Swiss Association for Technical Assistance). Helvetas began providing funding to Bhutan in 1975 through contributions from association members and the Swiss government. In 1990, for example, Helvetas contributed Nu32.8 million (69 percent of total foreign aid) to establish the Natural Resources Training Institute, a two-year technical training school. The Japanese government gave Nu74 million in grants for agricultural development and audio training equipment in 1990–91.

In 1989 the World Food Programme approved a two-year US$700,000 project to establish food reserves that would help Bhutan handle local emergencies and interruptions of food supplies. The FAO sponsored a program to assist Bhutan in achieving food self-sufficiency by 1992.

Another form of aid received by Bhutan was through international and foreign volunteer programs. A UN volunteer program initiated in 1980 brought foreign specialists in to assist and advise in the areas of education, health, engineering, animal husbandry, agriculture, and urban planning. By 1990 Japan, New Zealand, Britain, and Canada also were operating volunteer programs in Bhutan.

In addition to the substantial aid it received, Bhutan was itself an aid giver. For example, in 1987 Bhutan provided disaster relief aid to Maldives (Nu1 million), Bangladesh (Nu0.5 million), and India (Nu5 million).

Foreign Debt

At the start of the 1980s, Bhutan's external debt was small, but as the decade progressed it increased significantly. Whereas it stood at US$2.7 million in 1984, the debt jumped to US$21 million in 1985 and reached US$70.1 million in 1989. Although efforts have been made to reduce dependence on foreign aid inputs, an increasing amount of aid, other than that received from India, has been in the form of loans rather than outright grants. Whereas Bhutan had no foreign debt outside of India in the early 1980s, by the mid-to-late 1980s, loans—primarily from the World Bank and the Asian Development Bank—comprised 30 percent of foreign assistance and represented about 17 percent of its GDP.

Trade

Traditionally, most foreign trade was with Tibet. By 1960, however, following the closing of the Bhutan-China border and the development of closer ties with India, formal trade with India replaced that with Tibet. Although banned by the Bhutan government by 1961, barter trade with Tibet has persisted. Since 1960 nearly all of Bhutan's exports (93 percent in 1989) and the majority of its imports (67 percent in 1989) have been with India (see table 28, Appendix). Payments for imports in the 1980s were usually made with Indian rupees. There were no import duties on Indian imports, and, in accordance with the 1949 friendship treaty between Bhutan and India, there was duty-free transit of imports from other countries (see Foreign Relations, this ch.).

Both imports and exports increased steadily during the 1980s, from a total of Nu805.9 million in 1983 to more than Nu2.9 billion in 1990 (see table 29, Appendix). The balance of trade also improved as the decade progressed. In 1983, for example, only 20 percent of trade was in exported goods, whereas 80 percent was imports; this negative trade balance improved markedly by 1990, however, when exports accounted for 40.2 percent and imports for 59.8 percent of foreign trade (see table 30, Appendix). Although there was little trade with the United States, in recognition of its economic status Bhutan was granted an exemption in 1985 from the competitive trade requirements provided by the United States' Generalized System of Preferences.

Exports, which reached almost Nu1.2 billion in 1990, consisted primarily of cement, talc, fruit (mostly oranges) and fruit products, alcoholic beverages, resin, cardamom, lumber products, potatoes, and handicrafts. Although most trade was with India, such specialties as timber, cardamom, and liquor were exported to Bangladesh, Singapore, and countries in the Middle East and Western Europe. The opening of thirteen border crossings with customs facilities for Bhutan's exports and imports also eased trade with Nepal and Bangladesh. An increasingly important export to India was surplus power from Bhutan's Chhukha Hydel Project, which earned Bhutan

Nu22.3 million in FY 1988; that figure increased to nearly Nu399 million only two years later.

Imports amounted to nearly Nu1.8 billion in 1990. They consisted of raw materials; textiles; cereals; fuel; investment goods, including motor vehicles; and other consumer goods, primarily from India.

Agriculture

Bhutan was traditionally self-sufficient in food production. Most of Bhutan's citizens and a significant amount of its GDP were devoted to the agricultural sector in the late 1980s. About 87 percent of the population was involved in agriculture, and a projected 30.5 percent of GDP was expected to be produced through farming, animal husbandry, and fishing in 1991. Most agriculture was carried out with traditional methods and at the subsistence level. Faced with constraints of a shortage of cultivable and pasture land, lack of technical knowledge, logistical difficulties, and a shortage of skilled labor and managerial expertise, agricultural development was difficult. Grain production had not met demand, and imports were rising in the late 1980s. Shortages of feed contributed to low livestock productivity. Cash crops, such as oranges, apples, and cardamom, were significant, but they produced too little income to influence the overall economy. Government interest in agriculture was ensured during the First Development Plan (1961–66), with the establishment of agriculture and animal husbandry departments to oversee model farms, research, and crop and herd improvement, a trend which continued through subsequent development plans.

Farming

Crop farming was projected to produce 20.3 percent of GDP in 1991. Only about 15 percent of Bhutan's extremely mountainous land was arable, and less than 6 percent was under permanent cultivation. Because rainfall and temperatures changed radically from one valley to the next, there were significant variations in the kinds of crops that were raised in neighboring communities. Most farms were small, with 90 percent of nearly 65,000 landholders having less than five hectares. Nearly 50 percent of those farms used terraced cultivation; another 18 percent were in valleys. Although banned by the government, *tsheri* cultivation accounted for 32 percent of the agricultural land use and about 3 percent of the total land in the early to mid-1980s.

The major cereal crops in the 1980s were corn, rice, wheat and barley, buckwheat, and millet. Other major annual crops were

Threshing rice
Courtesy Bhutan Travel, Inc., New York (Marie Brown)

potatoes, chilies, vegetables, soya beans, pulses, and mustard. Horticultural crops included oranges, apples, and cardamom. Corn and rice were by far the most prevalent crops, producing 81,000 tons and 80,000 tons, respectively, in 1988. In the same year, a total of 51,000 tons of oranges, 50,000 tons of potatoes, 16,000 tons of wheat, 7,000 tons of millet, 4,000 tons of barley, and 4,000 tons of apples were produced. Total cereal production, however, only increased from 154,000 tons in 1979 to 205,000 tons in 1987.

Despite increases in paddy production, with 26,000 hectares under cultivation in 1989, rice was imported. Bhutan had once been an exporter of rice to Tibet, but its growing urban population plus the nonfarm immigrant and migrant population put a severe constraint on previous self-sufficiency in rice production. With a total cereal demand of 200,000 tons by 1987, some 20,000 tons of rice and 12,000 tons of wheat were being imported from India annually. Nonfood crops, such as jute, which was produced by fewer than 2 percent of Bhutan's farmers, also were grown. A small amount of tobacco was produced, with a reported crop of 100 tons in 1987, the same amount produced annually for nearly a decade.

Animal Husbandry

The most common livestock types traditionally and in the late

299

1980s, in order of numbers of head, were cattle, poultry, pigs, goats, sheep, yaks, and horses. Buffaloes, donkeys, and mules also were raised. Although all types of livestock were raised throughout the country, cattle tended to predominate in the east and south, horses in the east, yaks and pigs in the west, and goats and poultry in the south. Milk production stood at 31,000 tons in 1987. Development priorities under the Sixth Development Plan included livestock crossbreeding, improved animal health care, increased individual land ownership, and a better balance between herd size and feed availability. As a result of these efforts, livestock production increased modestly from 5,000 tons of beef, veal, pork, mutton, and lamb in 1980 to 7,000 tons annually by 1987.

Fisheries

A less productive but still significant food source resulted from fishing, both from cold-water streams and lakes (primarily trout) and warm-water fisheries (primarily carp). A growing demand for fish as a dietary supplement was reported in the mid-1970s following a 1974 FAO aquaculture study and a 1976 FAO survey of rivers and lakes to determine the level of fish stock. Fisheries were developed, and carp were imported from Assam. In 1977 the Department of Animal Husbandry established a Fishery Development Programme, initially for stocking rivers with game fish and for developing commercial capability as a long-term goal. Between 1979 and 1987, an average of 1,000 tons of fish were caught or produced annually. Another FAO survey was conducted in 1981, and the government included fishery development for the first time in the Fifth Development Plan. The Integrated Fisheries Development Project was started at Geylegphug in 1985. The National Warm Water Fish Culture Centre supplied fish to farmers, and some twenty-one tons of carp were produced at fisheries for local and national consumption. To control cold-water fishing, the Department of Forestry issued fishing licenses and enforced seasonal and fish-size prohibitions.

Irrigation and Fertilization

Through the Bank of Bhutan, the government helped finance irrigation projects in south-central Bhutan. By 1986 some 350 kilometers of new irrigation channels had been constructed, and another 395 kilometers of old channels had been repaired. Irrigation, however, was of only limited applicability because of the terrain. More attention was needed for rainfed crops, such as potatoes, wheat, and corn, than for rice and cash crops in irrigated areas.

Fertilizer use was limited. Although nitrogenous fertilizers were used at a rate of 100 tons a year and phosphate and potash fertilizers were used in indeterminant amounts throughout the 1980s, they were not a major agricultural factor.

Forestry

One of Bhutan's significant natural resources in the late twentieth century was its rich forests and natural vegetation. Bhutan's location in the eastern Himalayas, with its subtropical plains and alpine terrain, gives it more rainfall than its neighbors to the west, a factor greatly facilitating forest growth. The forests contain numerous deciduous and evergreen species, ranging from tropical hardwoods to predominantly oak and pine forests.

The small population and the general absence of overdevelopment in Bhutan contributed to forest preservation. Because of the terrain, the more accessible forests had been overcut whereas remote forests remained largely in their natural state. A progressive government-sponsored forestry conservation policy strove to balance revenue needs with ecological considerations, water management, and soil preservation. Success in managing its forest resources had long been critical to the local environment and economy and also affected downstream floodplains in India and Bangladesh.

The Department of Forestry was established in 1952 to oversee conservation and exploitation of the country's significant forestry resources. After an initial decade of development, forestry-resource exploitation increased with the start of the First Development Plan in 1961. Uncontrolled felling of trees in the 1970s by private companies in logging areas and by rural populations along roads and in main valleys stripped hillsides and caused serious erosion. *Tsheri* cultivation, forest fires, and overgrazing also contributed to the degradation of the forestry resource.

In 1971 the Forestry School was established at Kalikhola in southern Bhutan. It was moved to Taba in the northern Thimphu Valley in 1977. The school provided basic instruction in forestry and forest management and trained foresters and Forest Guards (see Paramilitary, this ch.).

In 1981 some 3.3 million hectares, or between 70 and 74 percent of the land, were forested, but in 1991 foreign estimates indicated a shrinking forest of only 60 to 64 percent of the land. Even more conservative estimates indicated that closer to 50 percent of Bhutan's territory still was forested in the late 1980s, and about 15 percent of GDP was produced through the nation's important forest industry.

According to UN statistics, in the decade between 1978 and 1987 Bhutan harvested an average of nearly 3.2 million cubic meters of roundwood and produced 5,000 cubic meters of sawn wood per year. Of this total, nearly 80 percent was for commercial use (paper pulp, veneers, plywood, particle board, and firewood), and the remainder was for housing construction and public works.

Before hydroelectric power and other modern energy sources were available, wood was the almost exclusive source of fuel for heating, cooking, and lighting. The provision of electricity, as well as better regulation of fuelwood collectors and more aggressive reforestation projects, was seen in the 1980s as a key factor in forest conservation. Because affordable electricity was not available throughout the country, the government established fuelwood plantations near villages to accommodate daily needs and to promote forest conservation.

Recognizing the potential value of its forestry resource, Bhutan became increasingly conscientious about forestry management in the 1970s. Starting in 1977, the World Wildlife Fund began supporting Bhutan's forest management through organizing forest ranger training programs, supplying funds for forest boundary demarcation, building guard posts, and constructing a patrol road for what was later to be designated the Royal Manas National Park. Bhutan rejected World Bank aid to build a major dam on the Manas Chhu in 1986 that would have flooded this major conservation area on the southern Bhutan-India border. By 1989 Bhutan had developed nine other forest and wildlife preserves, also mostly along the southern border with India.

In the face of increasing denuded hillsides, private logging was banned, and strict standards for public-sector logging operations were established in 1979. Farmers were warned against burning off forests to clear land for *tsheri* cultivation, and Forest Guards were trained in increasing numbers to help preserve the valuable resources. Surveying, demarcation, conservation, and management plans for harvesting forest products were part of the Fifth Development Plan's focus on forestry preservation. Wildlife sanctuaries also were developed. One of the immediate results of forestry sector regulation, however, was a sharp decrease in revenues since the late 1970s. In 1991 the government, with assistance from UNDP and the World Wildlife Fund, established a trust fund for environmental conservation. Initially in the amount of US$20 million, the UNDP-administered fund was aimed at producing up to US$1 million per year for training in forestry and ecology, surveying forests, reviewing and implementing management plans for protected areas, and supporting government environmental offices, public awareness programs, and integrated conservation and development programs.

Industry, Mining, Energy, and Commerce

Industry

Only 1 percent or less of the work force was involved in industry and construction in the late 1980s, and industrial production and construction represented only 14.2 percent of GDP projected for 1991. Handicrafts, cement, food processing, wood milling, and distilling were the major industries. In the late 1980s, there about 400 small-scale cottage and industrial units. There also were two cement plants under the Penden Cement Authority; a joint venture (the government-sponsored Tashi Commercial Corporation in conjunction with the World Bank, Norway, and Kuwait), a Bhutan Carbide and Chemicals calcium carbide plant (near Phuntsholing), and factories for processing fruit, for manufacturing paper pulp, wood veneers, and particle board (Gedu Wood Manufacturing Corporation and Bhutan Board Products), and for producing resin and turpentine. Additionally, there were three distilleries and a salt iodization plant. Other small industrial enterprises manufactured such consumer goods as soap, confectionaries, and furniture. Most of the larger industries, established since Bhutan's economic modernization began in the 1960s, were themselves modern and used a considerable amount of labor-saving technology. The largest industries employed no more than sixty or seventy workers. Many of the newly developing industries began making public stock offerings in the late 1980s.

Mining

The mining and quarrying industry was projected to produce 1.5 percent of GDP in 1991. Limestone—used in cement production—and clay were the major minerals being extracted in the mid-1980s. Mineral production also has included marble, dolomite, graphite, and slate. In addition, deposits of copper, gypsum, lead, tin, tungsten, zinc, coal, beryl, mica, pyrites, tufa, and talc have been found, primarily through an exploration program operated initially by the Geological Survey of India and, starting in 1982, in cooperation with the Geological Survey of Bhutan. Although not being exploited as much as other minerals, Bhutan's slate deposits have been described by experts as some of the best in the world. Bhutan's high-quality limestone deposits and energy resources were expected to take on increasing importance in the 1990s because of the contributions they could make to the ferrosilicon industry, which the government hoped to invest in through Bhutan Carbide and Chemicals.

Energy

Electricity and gas production was expected by the government to account for 10.7 percent of GDP in 1991. Hydroelectric power has long been a very important aspect of Bhutan's economic development as a low-cost energy source supporting more capital-intensive industries, such as forestry, mining, and cement and calcium carbide production. Bhutan's steep mountains, deep gorges, and fast-flowing rivers create abundant hydroelectric potential, which the government began to develop in the early 1960s with India's assistance. In 1981 Bhutan generated 22 million kilowatt-hours of energy from hydroelectric sources. A major plant in southwest Bhutan—the 18,000-kilowatt Jaldhaka hydroelectric plant—furnished electricity locally and exported the balance to India's West Bengal. The major expansion of hydroelectric facilities started in 1975 on the Wang Chhu between Thimphu and Phuntsholing. Known as the Chhukha Hydel Project, it helped boost the nation's fledgling industrial development. The 336-megawatt Chhukha plant came on line in 1986 and was synchronized with the Indian grid that same year, and additional capacity became available in 1988. The Nu2.44 billion Chhukha project was 60 percent paid for by India and budgeted outside the normal development plan process. It was planned that Bhutan would sell at low cost all power to West Bengal that it did not consume itself. At the same cost, Bhutan also hoped to re-import some of that power through the Indian power grid into southern districts. The Chhukha project was important not only because it supplied electric power to western and southern districts but also because it provided a major source of income for the government. The project's gross annual income was projected at Nu380 million in 1989. In 1989 nearly 95 percent of Bhutan's government-installed power generation—a total of 355 megawatts—was supplied by Chhukha, and a total of some 20 principal towns and 170 villages had been electrified. By 1990 Thimphu's commercial district had an underground cable system for its power supply.

Besides the Chhukha project, government installations included seven minihydroelectric plants, each averaging 7,350 kilowatts capacity; twelve microhydroelectric plants, each averaging 340 kilowatts capacity; and eight diesel-powered generation stations, each averaging 6,000 kilowatts capacity. Because domestic consumption was low (just over 16 megawatts, more than 80 percent of which was consumed by industry), ample power could be exported to India. The project not only cut domestic electricity costs in half, but also revenues from electricity sold to India were nearly equal to the total government revenue from all domestic sources. Smaller enterprises, such as the 1.5-megawatt Gyetsha Mini-Hydel, which was inaugurated in 1989, brought badly needed power to Bumthang and was expected to provide additional power to neighboring districts by 1993. Another major plant, a proposed 60-megawatt plant at Kurichu in eastern Bhutan, was included in the Sixth Development Plan (1987–92).

Other sources of energy included biogas, which was used in some districts for lighting and cooking and was primarily generated from cow dung. Solar energy was used for a variety of purposes, including heating dwellings and greenhouses and lighting hospitals. Despite the potential solar energy that might be produced, Bhutan's mountainous terrain prevents maximum use. The same mountains are funnels for powerful winds, however, providing another viable renewable energy source. High-technology windmills were installed in Wangdiphodrang in 1987 to produce electricity to run irrigation pumps.

Still another source of fuel in the 1980s was wood. Although Bhutanese had greater access to electric power than they had had previously, traditional methods of cooking and heating required readily available fuel. In the mid-1980s, Bhutan produced a coal equivalent of 982,000 tons of fuelwood per year to meet domestic needs. Coal itself was available in reserve in some 1.3 million tons, but recovery was difficult and the quality was poor.

Commerce

Commercial services were projected to generate 7.4 percent of GDP in 1991. Much of Bhutan's commerce revolved around tourist-oriented hotels and restaurants, and wholesale and retail trade made up the balance. The Bhutan Chamber of Commerce and Industry served as a formal conduit between government and private-sector businesses. The chamber was established with government sanction and leadership in 1980, but it made a slow start. In 1984 the first meeting was held between chamber members and heads of government departments, and the Trade Information Centre was established as a unit of the Department of Trade and Commerce to provide trade and commercial information to both the public and private sectors. Despite these initiatives, the Bhutan Chamber of Commerce and Industry had to be reorganized in 1987; the intent was that the chamber would play a "vital role" in coordinating activities in the government and private sectors and promoting socioeconomic development. The Druk Gyalpo himself criticized the chamber in 1988 for its "extremely poor and disappointing performance" and urged it to take on a greater role in national development and to help build a strong and dynamic economy. Despite these initiatives, the Bhutan Chamber of Commerce and Industry had only forty members in 1989.

Labor Force

"The economy of Bhutan is characterized by the predominance of people engaged in self-employment," reported the government's Planning Commission in 1989, "particularly those working their own land." Statistics available for the mid-1980s revealed that 87 percent of the working-age population was involved in agricultural work, another 3.4 percent in government services, 0.9 percent in business, 2 percent in "other" occupations, and 6.5 percent— mostly teenagers and young adults—that had no stated occupation. In the late 1980s, there was a serious shortage of indigenous nonagricultural labor and, in the government's view, an overabundance of foreign laborers. To carry out the construction of roads, hydropower plants, and other infrastructure development so important to modernization, the government, however, has had to depend upon foreign laborers. Low wages for laborers, ties to agricultural work, and a dispersed population led to the influx of migrant labor, primarily Nepalese, estimated to have reached 100,000 in 1988.

The increase in the number of foreign laborers in Bhutan during the 1980s resulted in a government campaign to identify and expel the growing number of those without work permits. In a crackdown starting in 1986, some 1,000 illegal foreigners were expelled. Most were Nepalese; Bangladeshis and Indians made up the balance. By 1988 the crackdown had reduced the number of foreign workers and provided opportunities for some 4,000 unemployed Bhutanese to join the work force.

Trade union activity was not legalized until 1991. There was no collective bargaining, and labor-related issues were nil in a society in which less than 1 percent of the population was involved in industrial work. Bhutan was not a member of the International Labour Organisation.

Transportation and Communications

Roads

Until 1961, because of the lack of paved roads, travel in Bhutan was by foot or on muleback or horseback. The 205-kilometer trek from the Indian border to Thimphu took six days. Modern road construction began in earnest during the First Development Plan (1961–66). The first paved road, 175-kilometers-long, was completed in 1962 (a branch road later linked Paro with the Phuntsholing-Thimphu road). Described as a jeep track, it linked Thimphu and Phuntsholing with Jaigaon, West Bengal. The travel time by motor vehicle from the border to Thimphu had shrunk to six hours. Some 30,000 Indian and Nepalese laborers were imported to build the road with Indian aid at a time when India was bolstering its strategic defense against a possible Chinese invasion. Bhutanese also were obliged to donate labor for the construction work. Another road connecting Tashigang with Tawang, Arunachal Pradesh, also was built.

By the mid-1970s, about 1,500 kilometers of roads had been built, largely by manual labor. There was a linked network of 2,280 kilometers of roads in 1989; at least 1,761 kilometers of these were paved with asphalt, and 1,393 kilometers were classified as national highways (see fig. 16). Despite the construction of surfaced roads linking the principal towns in the south, the mountainous terrain elsewhere makes travel even from one valley to the next quite difficult. Most roads run in river valleys. As part of the Sixth Development Plan, the Department of Public Works, in cooperation with the Indian Border Roads Organization, made plans to construct and upgrade 1,000 kilometers of roads and to extend the road network through the five major river valleys by 1992. Motorable roads were not the only important development. It was estimated as part of the Fifth Development Plan that Bhutan also needed some 2,500 kilometers of mule tracks to connect the nation's 4,500 settlements.

A mountainous country with numerous watersheds, Bhutan also had numerous bridges. Built as part of the road modernization program, most were of reinforced or prestressed concrete for motorable roads and of modular, prefabricated timber on secondary roads. Suspended footbridges joined paths across precipices and waterways.

Nationwide, some 6,910 vehicles were registered in 1988, including 1,235 private automobiles, 250 taxis, 118 buses, 1,105 four-wheel-drive vehicles, and 1,249 trucks. The most prevalent form of transportation was motorcycles and scooters, with some 2,882 registered in 1988. Diplomatic offices registered the balance of transportation vehicles. Most vehicles were of Indian, Japanese, and European manufacture. The Bhutan Government Transport Service operated a fleet of buses nationwide and provided minibus service twice a day between Thimphu and Phuntsholing. A subsidiary of the Royal Insurance Corporation, the Transport Corporation of Bhutan also ran bus service between Phuntsholing and Calcutta. In FY 1989, the government bus service carried 1.2 million passengers. Starting in 1985, private companies operated some bus routes. The greater availability of transportation increased opportunities for Bhutanese citizens to travel within their country and abroad. There was no railroad system, but a small monorail trail was inaugurated in Paro in 1990. It was used to haul produce to market.

Civil Aviation

The national air carrier of Bhutan was established in 1981 as Royal Bhutan Airlines, known as Druk-Air. Thrice-weekly, ninety-minute service between Paro and Calcutta was inaugurated in 1983 using a Dornier 228–200 twenty-seat airplane purchased from West Germany. A second Dornier was later added, increasing round-trips between Paro and Calcutta to five weekly during the busy spring and fall tourist seasons. By 1991 Druk-Air operated international flights to Bangkok, Calcutta, New Delhi, Dhaka, and Kathmandu. In November 1988, Druk-Air began using a four-engine, eighty-seat British Aerospace BAe 146–100 airplane for its five flights weekly: two from Bangkok and Dhaka, two from New Delhi and Kathmandu, and one from Calcutta. The cabin crew was trained by Thai Airways. By 1989 the two Dornier aircraft had been taken out of service. As Druk-Air flights increased, so did the number of passengers. In 1983 some 2,800 passengers were carried, and by 1987, the latest year for which statistics were reported by the government, 8,700 passengers were carried.

Travelers arriving at the one-story international terminal in Paro—the only airport with a permanent-surface runway—were transported by minibus to Thimphu. The Paro airport had its runway extended from 1,500 meters to 2,000 meters in 1988 and was further improved with a new hangar and an extended runway in 1990. There was a small, paved-runway airport at Yonphula, Tashigang District but it was seldom used. Thimphu was served by air only by helicopter, but helipads were available throughout the country.

Aviation in Bhutan in the 1980s and early 1990s was regulated by the Department of Civil Aviation and Transport. Under the Ministry of Communications, the department provided weather data and air traffic controllers. Druk-Air, although government owned, was a separate entity from the regulatory department.

Posts and Telecommunications

Mail and telecommunications services in 1991 were under the jurisdiction of the Ministry of Communications's Department of Posts and the Department of Telecommunications, respectively.

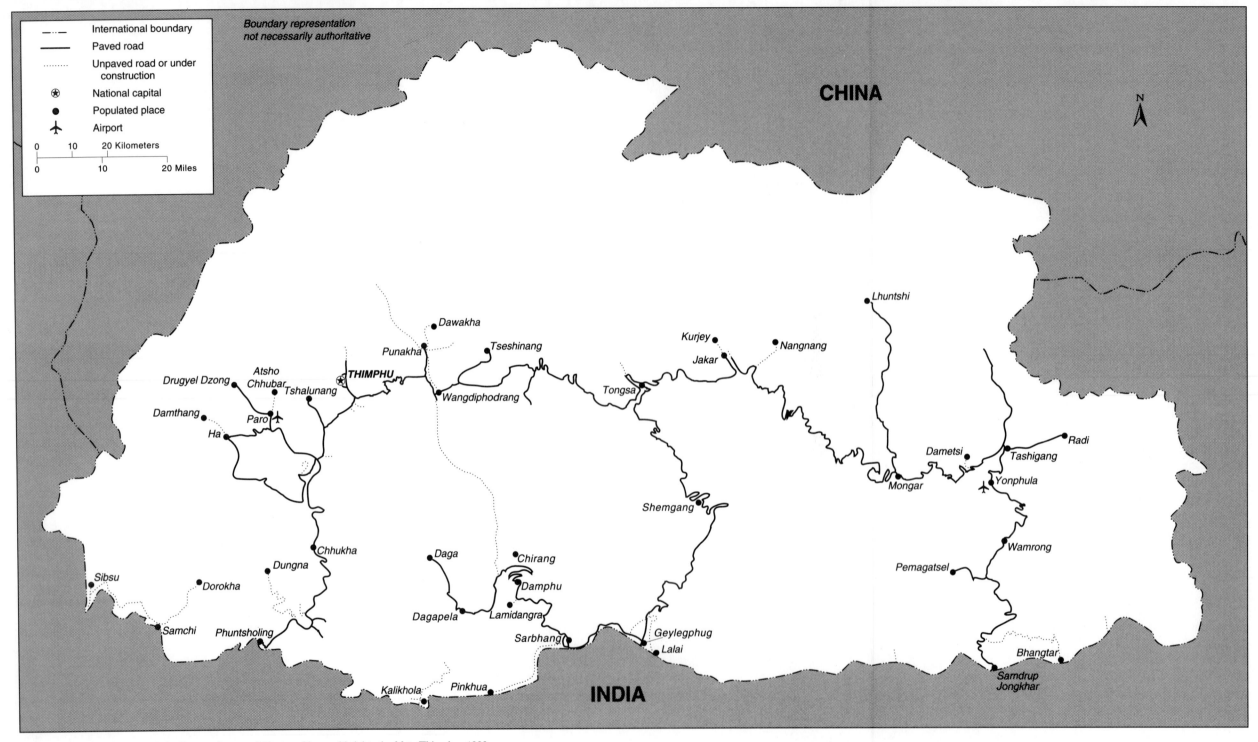

Source: Based on information from Bhutan, Survey of Bhutan, *Bhutan: Administrative Map,* Thimphu, 1988.

Figure 16. Bhutan: Transportation System, 1988

With a labor force of nearly 900 employees, the departments worked hard to modernize Bhutan's telecommunications and to provide links with other nations.

Although a courier system for internal official mail had been in existence for centuries, the modern postal system was introduced only in 1962. Prior to then, external mail was sent through Tibet or India. Bhutan's first postage stamps were issued in 1955 for internal use only. After the construction of modern roads, post offices were built throughout the kingdom. Bhutan joined the Universal Postal Union, a specialized agency of the UN, in 1969. Thereafter, improvements were made in handling international mail and foreign parcels. By 1988 there were two general post offices, fifty-five main post offices, and twenty-eight branch post offices.

The sale of commemorative postage stamps has been a foreign-exchange earner for Bhutan since 1962, when the first internal- and external-use stamps were issued, with the help of a London printer, in rupee demoninations. Until tourism passed the sale of colorful stamps to foreign collectors as the major foreign-exchange earner in 1974, the sale of postal stamps was the nation's principal source of foreign revenue. Sales averaged around US$44,000 a year in the 1970s, peaking at US$100,000 in 1979. In a related activity, Bhutan also issued commemorative gold and silver coins as a revenue generator.

As of 1991, Bhutan had more than 750 kilometers of telephone trunk lines, one digital telephone exchange in Thimphu, and twelve analog exchanges in other areas. The Department of Telecommunications planned to modernize all telephone exchanges and to connect all eighteen districts to the digital system by 1997. The telephone exchange in Thimphu by 1990 had a 10,000-line capability. As the 1990s began, there were nearly 2,000 telephones or one telephone for about every 700 people according to official information. Internationally, Thimphu was linked by a microwave system through Hashimara to satellite ground stations in Calcutta and New Delhi. The link, financed by India in 1984, provided sixty channels and had a potential for 300 channels when fully operational. Additionally, using a twenty-terminal French Sagem telex system, service between Thimphu and Phuntsholing was installed in 1986, and international service through New Delhi was connected in 1987; this facility was relocated to Calcutta in 1990. In 1989 the installation of a Japanese-equipped ground satellite station at Thimphu using International Telecommunications Satellite Organization (Intelsat) circuits substantially enhanced international telephone service.

There were thirty-nine point-to-point high-frequency radio stations, including two installed in Bhutan's embassies in New Delhi and Dhaka in 1988 for internal administrative communications. There also were eight telegraph offices. The government-run Bhutan Broadcasting Service in Thimphu started with three hours of broadcasts per week in 1973 and had expanded to thirty hours per week by 1988. An FM station in Thimphu and shortwave receivers throughout the rest of the country received its daily programming in Dzongkha, English, Sharchopkha, and Nepali. Whereas there were only 7,000 radio receivers in Bhutan in 1980, by 1988 between 15,000 and 22,000 sets were reported. In 1991 a new broadcasting complex was opened in Thimphu under the auspices of the Department of Telecommunications. Built with Indian aid, the complex included a high-power fifty-kilowatt shortwave transmitter capable of covering all of Bhutan and neighboring areas. There was no domestic television, but there was a big demand for videos, especially in the larger towns.

Tourism

Tourism has been an important industry and the country's largest foreign-exchange earner since its inception in 1974. Most tourists visit cultural sites—particularly *dzong* and temples—and observe seasonal festivals featuring masked dances and archery contests (archery is the national sport of Bhutan) or go on trekking expeditions on foot or mounted on horses or yaks. Limited to land travelers from India until Druk-Air's international service became operational in 1983, tourism was closely controlled by the state-run tourism agency, the Bhutan Tourism Corporation. Tourism reaped increasing foreign exchange in its first decade, ranging from US$300,000 from 390 visitors in 1976 to US$1.4 million from 1,325 visitors in 1982. By 1984 some 2,000 tourists visited Bhutan annually. By 1987 revenues had risen to more than US$2 million earned from the 2,524 tourists who visited the country that year. The government then decided to limit the number of tourists to around 2,000 a year and restricted access seasonally and to certain historical, cultural, and scenic sites. These restrictions resulted in decreases to 2,199 tourists and to revenues of US$1.9 million in 1988. In 1991, however, the Ministry of Trade, Industry, and Tourism announced plans to gradually double the number of entry visas granted and to reduce the charges levied on tour operators. The changes provided for the privatization of the Bhutan Tourism Corporation. In addition, whereas only group tours were allowed before 1991, after that date individual tourists were granted visas for prearranged tours. Visited from 1987 to 1990 by only a

Paro, the air gateway to Bhutan and a major district seat
Courtesy Ann Kinney

few travelers, many of Bhutan's religious sites were becoming more accessible to tourists in 1991. However, a substantial per person tariff, ranging from US$80 to US$200 per day depending on the time of year and type of package visit, was kept and helped boost revenues.

Opened to increasing tourism, Bhutan planned to turn over its government-run hotels to private management to improve its lodging accommodations. The largest number of tourists from a single nation, nearly 600 in 1988, came from the United States, and tourists from West Germany and Japan were close behind in numbers.

Government and Politics

The Monarchy

The hereditary monarchy of Bhutan was established in 1907 after 300 years of dual theocratic-civil government (see Establishment of the Hereditary Monarchy, 1907, this ch.). The Druk Gyalpo—the king—is both head of state and head of government. In the process of coming to power, the first Druk Gyalpo, Ugyen Wangchuck, who reigned from 1907 to 1926, unified the nation, established friendly relations with Britain, and set his dynasty's

313

political agenda. As of 1991, there had been three other hereditary monarchs: Jigme Wangchuck (1926–52), Jigme Dorji Wangchuck (1952–72), and Jigme Singye Wangchuck (since 1972). December 17, the anniversary of the day Ugyen Wangchuck became the first hereditary monarch in 1907, is Bhutan's National Day.

Established as an absolute monarchy in 1907, Bhutan first moved toward a constitutional monarchy in 1953 with the foundation of its National Assembly. In 1963 the monarch's title was changed from "His Highness" to "His Majesty the Druk Gyalpo" in a move to assert a distinct Bhutanese identity. The Druk Gyalpo retained veto power over actions of the National Assembly until 1969 when the National Assembly, following his 1968 decree, became the kingdom's sovereign institution. After 1969, the National Assembly could remove the Druk Gyalpo through a no-confidence vote, and he no longer had veto power. To secure the Wangchuck Dynasty, however, should the Druk Gyalpo be dethroned through a no-confidence vote, the Wangchuck family member next in line of succession would automatically take the throne. Also beginning in 1969, at the insistence of the Druk Gyalpo a "democratic monarchy" was to be determined through triennial votes of confidence in the Druk Gyalpo's rule—a system later abolished.

In 1972 Jigme Singye Wangchuck succeeded his father, Jigme Dorji Wangchuck, who had involved the young prince in the work of government and had appointed him crown prince and *ponlop* of Tongsa only a few months before dying. After his accession to the throne in 1972, the new Druk Gyalpo was assisted by his uncle, Dasho (Prince) Namgyal Wangchuck, and his elder sisters, Ashi Sonam Chhoden Wangchuck and Ashi Dechen Wangmo Wangchuck, who served in the ministries of finance and development as the Druk Gyalpo's representatives. (Ashi Sonam Chhoden Wangchuck later became minister of finance.) Jigme Singye Wangchuck was formally enthroned in June 1974.

In 1979 Jigme Singye Wangchuck privately married four sisters who were descendants of two of the *shabdrung,* the rulers of the old dual system of government. In 1988, in order to legitimize the eventual succession to the throne for his oldest son, Dasho Jigme Gesar Namgyal Wangchuck, the Druk Gyalpo and his four sister-queens were married again in a public ceremony in Punakha. At the time of the public wedding, it was reported that the Druk Gyalpo lived in a small, simply furnished house, across from the Tashichhodzong (Fortress of the Glorious Religion), the year-round central government complex in Thimphu. His four queens each maintained separate residences. The Druk Gyalpo's mother, the Dowager Queen Pemadechen (Ashi Kesang Dorji), continued to reside in the royal palace at Dechenchholing, living as a Buddhist nun. The Tashichhodzong, a stone-and-timber structure, has thick whitewashed walls, seven towers covered with red roofs, and a series of interior courtyards. The entire structure is richly ornamented. The current Tashichhodzong complex, which has more than 100 rooms, was completed in 1969 after seven years of construction on the site of an older *dzong* of the same name. Originally built in the twelfth century, the Tashichhodzong had been rebuilt in the eighteenth century and required the 1962–69 reconstruction because of damage over the centuries from fires and earthquakes. It also was the residence of the spiritual leader of Bhutan, the Je Khenpo, during the summer.

After coming to the throne in 1972, Jigme Singye Wangchuck became increasingly interested in economic development and traveled extensively throughout the country. He also has traveled a great deal outside of Bhutan, attending international meetings and personally representing his country in New Delhi on frequent occasions. A young, vigorous head of state unafraid to break from the bureaucracy and constraints of his office—including his trips to the countryside where the Druk Gyalpo could be seen ''serving the people''—Jigme Singye Wangchuck presented the monarchy as progressive and symbolic of national unity.

Structure of the Government

Legal Basis

Bhutan does not have a written constitution or organic laws. The 1907 document submitted by the monastic and government leaders was an agreement only to establish an absolute hereditary monarchy. Bhutan's only legal or constitutional basis is the 1953 royal decree for the Constitution of the National Assembly. The 1953 constitution set forth eighteen succinct ''rules'' for the procedures of the National Assembly and the conduct of its members. The May 1968 revision reiterated and elucidated some of the eighteen rules but revised others. Beginning in 1969, the powers of the speaker of the National Assembly were strengthened, and the Druk Gyalpo's veto power was eliminated.

Legislature

The unicameral National Assembly—the Tshogdu—comprises the legislative branch of government. The National Assembly has the power to enact civil, criminal, and property laws; to appoint and remove ministers; to debate policy issues as a means of providing input to government decision making; and to control the

315

Tashichhodzong complex, Bhutan's seat of government in Thimphu
Courtesy Elsa Martz

auditor general, who has approval authority over government expenditures (see fig. 17).

Since its establishment in 1953, the National Assembly has varied in size from 140 to 200 members. According to Rule 7 of the Constitution of the National Assembly, the legislature sets its size every five years. The National Assembly has three categories of members: representatives of the people elected by indirect vote every three years and comprising between half and two-thirds of the National Assembly membership; monastic representatives, also appointed for three-year terms and constituting about one-third of the membership; and government officials nominated by the Druk Gyalpo. The first woman member of the National Assembly was seated in 1979.

In 1989 there were 150 members in the National Assembly, 100 of whom were representatives of the general public. Under 1981 rules, qualified citizens over twenty-five years of age can be nominated at general public meetings by village heads and adult representatives of each household (*gung*) and "joint family." Once nominations are certified by village heads and local government officials, they are forwarded to the speaker of the National Assembly for "final declaration of the nominee as a member of the National Assembly." The other fifty members are made up of monastic representatives nominated by the Central Monastic Body in Thimphu (or Punakha in the winter) and eight district monastic bodies, members of the Council of Ministers (Lhengye Shungtsong), members of the Royal Advisory Council (Lodoi Tsokde), secretaries of various government departments, district heads, others nominated by the government, and a representative nominated by the Bhutan Chamber of Commerce and Industry. The National Assembly meets at least once and sometimes twice a year—in May and June and again in October and November; each session lasts about four weeks. Emergency sessions can also be called by the Druk Gyalpo.

The National Assembly elects a speaker from among its members and is authorized to enact laws, advise the government on constitutional and political matters, and hold debates on important issues. Executive-branch organizations are responsible to the National Assembly. Powers of the National Assembly include directly questioning government officials and forcing ministers to resign if there is a two-thirds no-confidence vote.

National Assembly votes are secret in principle, but in practice decisions are almost always made by reaching a public consensus. The National Assembly, housed in the Tashichhodzong, provides a forum for presenting grievances and redressing administrative problems. The Druk Gyalpo cannot formally veto bills that the National Assembly passes, but he can refer them back for reconsideration. Although criticism of the Druk Gyalpo was not permitted in the public media, it was allowed and took place in National Assembly debates in the 1980s.

Executive

At the apex of the executive branch is the Druk Gyalpo, who is both head of state and head of the government. Responsible to him are two advisory and executive organizations: the Royal Advisory Council and the Council of Ministers. There also is the Royal Secretariat, which serves as an intermediary between the Druk Gyalpo and the Council of Ministers.

The Royal Advisory Council was mentioned in the 1953 Constitution of the National Assembly (members of the council are concurrently members of the National Assembly), but it took on greater importance in 1965 when the Druk Gyalpo installed representatives elected by the monastic bodies and the National Assembly. In 1989 the council's membership included a representative of the government, two representatives of the monasteries, six regional representatives, and a chairperson, all serving for five-year terms. The chairperson and the government representative are appointed by the Druk Gyalpo; the two monks represent the central and district monastic bodies. Monk representatives, according to 1979 regulations for council membership, are required to be literate and "highly knowledgeable about the Drukpa Kargyupa religion." Monk nominees are subject to the approval of the speaker of the National Assembly. The regional representatives are elected by the National Assembly from a list endorsed by village assemblies. Representing the southeastern, southwestern, western, eastern, central, and the Thimphu-Paro-Ha regions, they are required to be literate, knowledgeable about Bhutanese traditional culture and customs with "some knowledge of modern customs and etiquette," "well-behaved and able to speak well," "able to shoulder responsibility, and far-sighted." As the principal consulting body to the Druk Gyalpo, the Royal Advisory Council is a key state organization and interacts most directly with the National Assembly.

Chaired by the Druk Gyalpo, the Council of Ministers was established in 1968 with the approval of the National Assembly. In 1991 it comprised seven ministers and the Druk Gyalpo's representative in each ministry (agriculture; communications; finance; foreign affairs; home affairs; social services; and trade, industry, and tourism). The largest ministry by far was the Ministry of Social Services, which ran the nation's education and health systems and

319

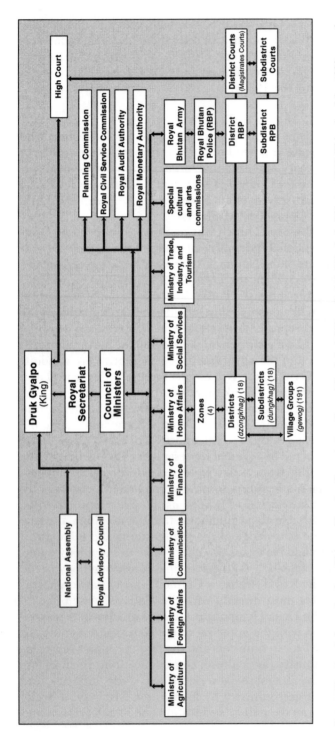

Source: Based on information from Bhutan, Planning Commission, Central Statistical Office, *Statistical Yearbook of Bhutan, 1989*, Thimphu, May 1990, x; and United States, Central Intelligence Agency, Directorate of Intelligence, *Reference Aid: Chiefs of State and Cabinet Members of Foreign Governments*, Washington, March–April 1991, 8–9.

Figure 17. Bhutan: Structure of the Government, 1991

included nearly 26 percent of all civil service employees. Two of the ministers in 1990—the minister of finance (Ashi Sonam Chhoden Wangchuck) and the minister of home affairs (Dasho Namgyal Wangchuck)—were members of the royal family.

Until the 1960s, the Royal Secretariat played a major role in government affairs. The key officials of the Royal Secretariat were the Druk Gyalpo's representative in the Royal Bhutan Army, the royal chief secretary, and the royal finance secretary. After the establishment of the Council of Ministers and subsequent shift of administrative and financial matters out of the palace, however, the Royal Secretariat's day-to-day role diminished in importance. Relations between the two bodies have been described as cordial, nevertheless, and ministers usually were selected from among Royal Secretariat personnel.

Judiciary

The highest-level court is the Supreme Court of Appeal—the Druk Gyalpo himself. The Supreme Court of Appeal hears appeals of decisions emanating from the High Court (Thrimkhang Gongma). In 1989 the High Court, which was established in 1968 to review lower-court appeals, had six justices (including a chief justice), two of whom were elected by the National Assembly and four of whom were appointed by the Druk Gyalpo, for five-year terms. Each district has a magistrate's court (Dzongkhag Thrimkhang), headed by a magistrate or *thrimpon,* from which appeals can be made to the High Court. Minor civil disputes are adjudicated by a village head. All citizens have been granted the right to make informal petitions to the Druk Gyalpo, some of which have been made reportedly by citizens who flagged down the Druk Gyalpo's automobile as he toured the nation.

Civil Service

Bhutan's government employees have been under the authority of the Royal Civil Service Commission since its establishment in 1982. Part of the commission's mandate was to reform government service. With assistance from the UNDP, the commission held a conference in 1986 and assessed the civil service. Plans were laid out for providing in-country and foreign training, improving training effectiveness, and organizing a system by which personnel and training management would be linked within departments. Civil service rules adopted in 1989 established procedures for government employment and prohibited civil servants from being assigned to their home districts. Starting in 1989, candidates for government service were given only one opportunity to pass the civil service selection examination. Once they were selected, promotions were available through seventeen grades, from the lowest clerk to just below the deputy minister level.

In an efficiency drive in the late 1980s, the civil service was reduced through reorganization (the government was scaled down from thirty-three entities at and above the department level in 1985 to nineteen in 1989), reassignment to local government, retirements, and "voluntary resignations." In 1987 there were 13,182 civil service workers, but by 1989 the number of regular civil service employees had dropped to 11,099. An additional 3,855 persons worked under government contract or as "wage" employees throughout all parts of the government. More than 1,650 of them, however, were employed by government-run industries, and another 848 worked for the Chhukha Hydel Project. The total number of persons working under the civil service in July 1989 was 15,802. Later in 1989, however, all public and joint sector corporation employees were removed from the civil service rolls. Because of the national shortage of skilled workers, 3,137 members of the civil service in 1989 were reportedly "nonnationals," mostly ethnic Nepalese.

Local Government

Local government in 1991 was organized into four zones, or *dzongdey,* and eighteen districts, or *dzongkhag* (see fig. 13). Before the zonal administration system was established beginning in 1988 and 1989, the central government interacted directly with district governments. The new level of administration was established, according to official sources, to "bring administration closer to the people" and to "expedite projects without having to refer constantly to the ministry." In other words, the zonal setup was to provide a more efficient distribution of personnel and administrative and technical skills. The zonal boundaries were said to be dictated by geophysical and agroclimatic considerations. Zonal administrators responsible for coordinating central policies and plans acted as liaisons between the central ministries and departments and district governments. Each zonal headquarters had nine divisions: administration, accounts, agriculture, animal husbandry, education, engineering, health, irrigation, and planning. The divisions were staffed with former civil service employees of the Ministry of Home Affairs and with technical personnel from the various sectors in the districts. Four zones were established in 1988 and 1989: Zone I, including four western districts, seated at Chhukha; Zone II, including four west-central districts, seated at Damphu; Zone III, including four east-central districts, seated at Geylegphug; and Zone IV, including five eastern districts, seated at Yonphula. Although

Thimphu District and Thimphu Municipality were within the boundaries of Zone I, they remained outside the zonal system. By 1991, however, only Zone IV was fully functioning.

Eighteen districts comprised local government at the next echelon. Each district was headed by an appointed district officer (*dzongda,* assisted by a deputy district officer, *dzongda wongmo* or *dzongrab*), who was responsible for development planning and civil administration. Formerly appointed by the Druk Gyalpo, district officers have been appointed by the Royal Civil Service Commission since 1982. Each district also had a district development committee comprising elected representatives and government officials.

Districts were further subdivided into subdistricts (*dungkhag*) and village blocks or groups (*gewog*). Ten of the eighteen districts had subdistricts, which were further subdivided into village groups. The subdistrict served as an intermediate level of administration between district government and some villages in larger districts. These same districts also had village groups that were immediately subordinate to the district government. In the remaining eight smaller districts, village groups were directly subordinate to the district government. In 1989 there were 191 village groups, 67 of which were organized into 18 subdistricts and 124 of which were immediately subordinate to the district government. Subdistrict officers (*dungpa*) led the subdistricts, and village heads (*gup* in the north, *mandal* in the south) were in charge of the village groups. Despite greater central government involvement with economic development programs since the 1960s, villages continued to have broad local autonomy. There were 4,500 villages and settlements in 1991.

Bhutan also has two municipal corporations—Thimphu and Phuntsholing—headed by mayors (*thrompon*). Thimphu's municipal corporation was set up in 1974 as an experiment in local self-government. Headed by a chairperson, the corporation concentrated on sanitation and beautification projects. A superintending engineer, an administrative officer, a plant protection officer, and a tax collector served under a chief executive officer. Ward councillors carried out local representation in the city's seven wards. In subsequent years, municipal boards were set up in the larger towns.

Political Developments

The political forces that shaped Bhutan after its seventeenth-century unification were primarily internal until the arrival of the British in the eighteenth century. Thereafter, British pressure and protection influenced Bhutan and continued to do so until Britain's withdrawal from the mainland of South Asia in 1947. The nationalist movements that had brought independence to India had significant effects on Sikkim and Nepal. Because of its relative isolation, however, they left Bhutan largely unaffected until the growing Nepalese minority became increasingly exposed to the radical politics of Nepalese migrants from India. These migrants brought political ideas inspired by Indian democratic principles and agitation to the minority community in southern Bhutan. By 1950 the presence of that community had resulted in government restrictions on the cultivation of forest lands and on further migration.

Expatriate Nepalese, who resettled in West Bengal and Assam after leaving Bhutan, formed the Bhutan State Congress in 1952 to represent the interests of other expatriates in India as well as the communities they had left behind. An effort to expand their operations into Bhutan with a *satyagraha* (nonviolent resistance) movement in 1954 failed in the face of the mobilization of Bhutan's militia and a lack of enthusiasm among those Nepalese in Bhutan who did not want to risk their already tenuous status. The government further diffused the Bhutan State Congress movement by granting concessions to the minority and allowing Nepalese representation in the National Assembly. The Bhutan State Congress continued to operate in exile until its decline and gradual disappearance in the early 1960s. The leaders in exile were pardoned in 1969 and permitted to return.

Despite the absence of political parties, political activities carried out by elite political factions have played a role since the 1960s. These factional politics have generally been devoid of ideology, focusing instead on specific issues or events. Only with the 1964 assassination of Lonchen Jigme Palden Dorji did factional politics cause a national crisis (see Modernization under Jigme Dorji, 1952–72, this ch.).

Government decrees promulgated in the 1980s sought to preserve Bhutan's cultural identity in a "one nation, one people" policy called *driglam namzha* (national customs and etiquette). The government hoped to achieve integration through requiring national dress—the *kira* for women and the *gho* for men—at formal gatherings (by a May 1989 decree that was quickly reversed) and insisting that individual conduct be based on Buddhist precepts. The government stressed standardization and popularization of Dzongkha, the primary national language, and even sponsored such programs as the preservation of folksongs used in new year and marriage celebrations, house blessings, and archery contests.

Other cultural preservation efforts, especially those aimed at traditional Bhutanese arts and crafts that had long been under royal family patronage, were embodied in the Sixth Development Plan. Bhutan participated in the Olympic Games and in other international games, and imported high-tech bows for use in national archery tournaments, although for a time only the simple traditional bow was permitted in contests within Bhutan. In 1989 Nepali ceased to be a language of instruction in schools, and Dzongkha was mandated to be taught in all schools. In 1989 the government also moved to implement the Citizenship Act of 1985, which provided that only those Nepalese immigrants who could show they had resided in Bhutan for fifteen or twenty years (depending on occupational status), and met other criteria, might be considered for grants of citizenship by naturalization. An earlier law, passed in 1958, had for the first time granted Bhutanese citizenship to Nepalese landed settlers who had been in Bhutan for at least ten years. To ameliorate some of the differences between the ethnic communities, interethnic marriages among citizens, once forbidden, were allowed as a means of integrating the Nepalese.

Bhutan's concern heightened in the late 1980s when Nepalese liberation movements emerged in India. In 1988 some ethnic Nepalese in Bhutan again began protesting the alleged discrimination against them. They demanded exemption from the government decrees aimed at enhancing Bhutanese national identity by strengthening aspects of traditional culture (under the rubric of *driglam namzha*). It was likely that they were inspired by prodemocracy activities in their homeland as well as by democratic, Marxist, and Indian social ideas picked up during their migration through or education in India (see Political Parties, ch. 4).

The reaction to the royal decrees in Nepalese majority communities surfaced as ethnic strife directed against non-Nepalese-origin people. Reactions also took form as protest movements in Nepal and India among Nepalese who had fled Bhutan. The Druk Gyalpo was accused of "cultural suppression," and his government was charged by antigovernment leaders with human rights violations, including the torture of prisoners; arbitrary arrest and detention; denial of due process; and restrictions of freedoms of speech and press, peaceful organization and assembly, and workers' rights.

Antigovernment protest marches involved more than 20,000 participants, including some from a movement that had succeeded in coercing India into accepting local autonomy for ethnic Nepalese in West Bengal, who crossed the border from West Bengal and Assam into six Bhutan districts. In February 1990, antigovernment activists detonated a remote-control bomb on a bridge hear Phuntsholing and set fire to a seven-vehicle convoy. In September 1990, clashes occurred with the Royal Bhutan Army, which was ordered not to fire on protesters. The men and women marchers were organized by S.K. Neupane and other members of the illegal Bhutan People's Party, which reportedly urged the marchers to demand democracy and human rights for all Bhutanese citizens. Some villagers willingly joined the protests; others did so under duress. The government branded the party, reportedly established by antimonarchists and backed by the Nepali Congress Party and the Marxist-Leninist faction of the Communist Party of Nepal, as a terrorist organization. The party allegedly led its members—said to be armed with rifles, muzzle-loading guns, knives, and homemade grenades—in raids on villages in southern Bhutan, disrobing people wearing traditional Bhutanese garb; extorting money; and robbing, kidnapping, and killing people. Reportedly, there were hundreds of casualties, although the government admitted to only two deaths among security forces. Other sources indicated that more than 300 persons were killed, 500 wounded, and 2,000 arrested in clashes with security forces. Along with the above-mentioned violence, vehicle hijackings, kidnappings, extortions, ambushes, and bombings took place, schools were closed (some were destroyed), and post offices, police, health, forest, customs, and agricultural posts were destroyed. For their part, security forces were charged by the Bhutan People's Party, in protests made to Amnesty International and the International Human Rights Commission, with murder and rape and carrying out a "reign of terror." In support of the expatriate Nepalese, the general secretary of the Nepali Congress Party, the ruling party in Nepal, called on the Druk Gyalpo to establish a multiparty democracy.

The Bhutanese government admitted only to the arrest of forty-two people involved in "anti-national" activities in late 1989, plus three additional individuals who had been extradited from Nepal. All but six were reportedly later released; those remaining in jail were charged with treason. By September 1990, more than 300 additional prisoners held in the south were released following the Druk Gyalpo's tour of southern districts.

In the face of government resistance to demands that would institutionalize separate identities within the nation, protesters in the south insisted that the Bhutan People's Party flag be flown in front of administrative headquarters and that party members be allowed to carry the *kukri*, a traditional Nepalese curved knife, at all times. They also called for the right not to wear the Bhutanese national dress and insisted that schools and government offices stay closed until their demands were met. The unmet demands were accompanied by additional violence and deaths in October 1990. At the same time, India pledged "all possible assistance that the royal government might seek in dealing with this problem'' and assured that it would protect the frontier against groups seeking illegal entry to Bhutan.

By early 1991, the press in Nepal was referring to insurgents in southern Bhutan as ''freedom fighters.'' The Bhutan People's Party claimed that more than 4,000 advocates of democracy had been arrested by the Royal Bhutan Army. Charges were made that some of those arrested had been murdered outside Bhutanese police stations and that some 4,200 persons had been deported.

Supporting the antigovernment activities were expatriate Nepalese political groups and supporters in Nepal and India. Between 2,000 and 12,000 Nepalese were reported to have fled Bhutan in the late 1980s, and according to a 1991 report, even high-level Bhutanese government officials of Nepalese origin had resigned their positions and moved to Nepal. Some 5 million Nepalese were living in settlements in India along the Bhutan border in 1990. Nepalese were not necessarily welcome in India, where ethnic strife conspired to push them back through the largely unguarded Bhutanese frontier. The Bhutan People's Party operated among the large Nepalese community in northern India. A second group, the Bhutan People's Forum for Human Rights (a counterpart of the Nepal People's Forum for Human Rights), was established in Nepal by a former member of Bhutan's National Assembly, Teknath Rizal. In November 1989, Rizal was allegedly abducted in eastern Nepal by Bhutanese police and returned to Thimphu, where he was imprisoned on charges of conspiracy and treason. The Bhutan Students Union and the Bhutan Aid Group-Nepal also were involved in political activism.

The government explained its cultural identity programs as a defense against the first political problems since the Wangchuck Dynasty was established in 1907 and the greatest threat to the nation's survival since the seventeenth century. Its major concern was to avoid a repeat of events that had occurred in 1975 when the monarchy in Sikkim was ousted by a Nepalese majority in a plebiscite and Sikkim was absorbed into India. In an effort to resolve the interethnic strife, the Druk Gyalpo made frequent visits to the troubled southern districts, and he ordered the release of hundreds of arrested ''antinationals.'' He also expressed the fear that the large influx of Nepalese might lead to their demand for a separate state in the next ten to twenty years, in much the same way as happened in the once-independent monarchy of Sikkim in the 1970s. To deter and regulate Nepalese migration into Bhutan from India, the Druk Gyalpo ordered more regular censuses, improved border checks, and better government administration in the southern districts. The more immediate action of forming citizens' militias took place in October 1990 as a backlash to the demonstrations. Internal travel regulations were made more strict with the issue of new multipurpose identification cards by the Ministry of Home Affairs in January 1990.

By the end of 1990, the government admitted the serious effects of the antigovernment violence. It was announced that foreign-exchange earnings had dropped and that the GDP had decreased significantly because of terrorist activities.

Ethnic problems were not Bhutan's only political concern in the early 1990s. Rumors persisted that the exiled family of Yangki, the late Druk Gyalpo's mistress, including an illegitimate pretender to the throne, were garnering support among conservative forces in Bhutan to return to a position of authority.

The Media

In 1986 a weekly government news bulletin, *Kuensel,* was reformatted under the same title and also published weekly as Bhutan's only newspaper. Published by the Ministry of Communications' Department of Information, *Kuensel* had a total circulation in 1988 of 12,500 and was published in Dzongkha, Nepali, and English. Indian and other foreign newspapers also were available. Bhutan's low literacy rate, however, means that the majority of the population is not affected by the print media. Oral tradition is very strong, however, and radio broadcasts are widely listened to.

Bhutan Broadcasting Service, established in 1973 and given its current name in 1986, operated under the auspices of the Department of Information; it offered thirty hours a week of shortwave radio programming in Dzongkha, Sharchopkha, Nepali, and English. There was daily FM programming in Thimphu and shortwave reception throughout the rest of the nation in the early 1990s. In 1991 there were thirty-nine public radio stations for internal communications. There were also two stations used exclusively for communications with Bhutan's embassies in New Delhi and Dhaka and thirteen stations used by hydrologists and meteorologists. There were no television stations in Bhutan in the early 1990s, and a 1989 royal decree ended the viewing of foreign television by mandating the dismantling of antennas. The government wanted to prevent Indian and Bangladeshi broadcasts from reaching Bhutan's citizens.

Foreign Relations

Historically, Bhutan's foreign policies were greatly influenced by Tibet. Bhutan acknowledged Tibet's influence over it until 1860 and continued to pay a nominal tribute to Tibet until the mid-1940s, although not necessarily on a friendly basis. Despite religious and cultural affinities, most of Bhutan's elite were refugees who had fled Tibet for religious reasons over the centuries. From 1865 to 1947, Britain guided Bhutan's foreign affairs. Thereafter Bhutan's foreign relations until the early 1970s were under the guidance of India, with which Bhutan had had official diplomatic relations from 1949. During the 1970s and 1980s, however, Bhutan became a member of the UN and its affiliated agencies; established formal diplomatic relations with fifteen other nations, primarily in South Asia and Scandinavia; actively participated in the South Asian Association for Regional Cooperation (SAARC—see Glossary) and the Nonaligned Movement; spoke out against, among other subjects, nuclear proliferation and terrorism; and had a peripatetic head of state who traveled abroad widely (see table 31, Appendix). By the early 1990s, Bhutan's foreign policies were effectively autonomous.

A shortage of diplomatic officials limited Thimphu's missions in New York and Geneva (established in 1985) and meant that the nation could only staff embassies in New Delhi, Dhaka, and Kuwait. Bhutan had only one employee, a computer programmer, at the SAARC headquarters in Kathmandu in late 1990. Only India and Bangladesh had representatives in Thimphu in 1991; other nations generally gave dual accreditation to their ambassadors in New Delhi to enable them to represent their countries' interests in Thimphu. Similarly, because of the shortage of diplomatic personnel, the head of the Bhutanese UN mission in Geneva, for example, also served as ambassador to Austria, Denmark, Finland, the Netherlands, Norway, Sweden, the European Economic Community (EEC), and several UN affiliates. The ambassador to Kuwait is accredited to Switzerland because of Swiss rules that disallow the UN representative in Geneva to also be accredited to Switzerland. Honorary consuls represented Bhutan in Singapore, Hong Kong, Macao, Ōsaka, and Seoul, and the Republic of Korea (South Korea) had an honorary consul in Thimphu.

Bhutan had no formal diplomatic relations with the United States as of 1991. It was one of only seven sovereign nations in the world with which the United States did not maintain formal representation. Informal contact was maintained, however, between the embassies of Bhutan and the United States in New Delhi, and Bhutan's permanent mission at the United Nations in New York had consular jurisdiction in the United States. It has been speculated that Bhutan, in light of India's close relations with the Soviet Union, had elected to keep equidistant from both superpowers. Nevertheless, during a visit with a United States senator in 1985, the Druk

Gyalpo personally expressed strong support for the United States as the principal bulwark against the Soviet Union in South Asia. The United States ambassador to New Delhi was among numerous emissaries of nations without diplomatic ties to pay courtesy calls in Thimphu in the 1980s. Contacts with the Soviet Union and other communist countries were nil.

India

Bhutan is bounded on three sides by India. From east to west, the Indian states of Sikkim, West Bengal, Assam, and Arunachal Pradesh (formerly the North-East Frontier Agency) border Bhutan. In view of the long-standing political disputes and border confrontations between India and China, Bhutan has long been part of India's strategic defense plan (see Strategic Location, this ch.). In the view of some Indian strategists, Bhutan was a weak link in India's defense against China.

The key document guiding relations with India is the Treaty of Friendship Between the Government of India and the Government of Bhutan of 1949. The ten-article treaty, in force in perpetuity, calls for peace between the two countries and assures Indian noninterference in Bhutan's internal affairs in return for Bhutan's agreeing ''to be guided by the advice of the Government of India in regard to its external relations'' (Article 2). The treaty provides for compensation by India at a higher rate than provided in the 1865 and 1910 British treaties, and it returned Bhutan's Dewangiri territory seized by Britain in the Duar War. It also guarantees free trade between the countries and duty-free transit across India of Bhutan's imports. Furthermore, the treaty assures the rights of citizens of each country and the extradition of criminals seeking refuge in either country.

Events in Tibet have had causal effects on Bhutan-Indian relations. When the Chinese communists took over Tibet in 1951, Bhutan braced itself against a renewed external threat with a modernization program and a new defense posture. In his first visit to Bhutan in 1958, Indian prime minister Jawaharlal Nehru reiterated India's wish that Bhutan remain an independent country, ''taking the path of progress according to your will.'' Following precedent, Bhutan sided with India when the Chinese army occupied Tibet in 1959 and a border dispute emerged between China and India. Nehru declared in the Indian parliament in November 1959 that ''any aggression against Bhutan . . . would be regarded as an aggression against India.'' A de facto alliance developed between Bhutan and India by 1960, and Indian aid increasingly bolstered Bhutan's strategic infrastructure development. In times of crisis between India and China or between Bhutan and China, India was quick to assure Bhutan of military assistance. Concerns were raised by Bhutan, however, during the 1971 Indo-Pakistani War when there were doubts about India's ability to protect Bhutan against China (which sided with Pakistan) while fighting a two-front war.

In 1960 the Druk Gyalpo had said that Bhutan was not 100 percent independent because of the 1949 treaty, and until Bhutan emerged into the world of international diplomacy by joining the UN in 1971, Article 2 of the treaty seemed intact. Admission to the UN, however, changed Bhutan's perspective on the world beyond India and Thimphu's traditional dependence on New Delhi. Two years later, Bhutan and Bangladesh exchanged diplomatic recognition, hinting further at Thimphu's independent attitude. A new interpretation of the relationship emerged in 1974 when Bhutan's minister of foreign affairs said that Bhutan's following India's advice and guidance on foreign policy matters was optional. Bhutan had raised its representation in India to the ambassadorial level in 1971 and in 1978 changed the name of its diplomatic office in New Delhi from the Royal Bhutan Mission to the Royal Bhutan Embassy to further reflect its sovereign status. A new trade agreement between Bhutan and India in 1972 exempted from export duties goods from Bhutan to third countries.

The Druk Gyalpo's statement in 1979 that the 1949 treaty needed to be "updated" was still another move asserting independence. Members of the National Assembly speaking just before the Druk Gyalpo's "update" announcement made the interpretation that Article 2 only required Bhutan to seek India's advice and guidance on matters of external affairs. Bhutan exerted its independent stance at the Nonaligned Movement summit conference in Havana, also in 1979, by voting with China and some Southeast Asian countries rather than with India on the issue of allowing Cambodia's Khmer Rouge to be seated at the conference. Bhutan's votes in the UN on such issues as the status of landlocked nations also did not follow India's leads.

Despite a history of good relations between Bhutan and India, bilateral border issues long went unresolved. Indo-Bhutanese borders had been delineated in the Treaty of Peace of 1865 between Bhutan and Britain, but it was not until the period between 1973 and 1984 that a detailed delineation and demarcation was made. Border demarcation talks with India generally resolved disagreements except for several small sectors, including the middle zone between Sarbhang and Geylegphug and the eastern frontier with Arunachal Pradesh.

China

The other nation that borders Bhutan is China, with which Bhutan had no diplomatic relations as of mid-1991. Bhutan and China have long had differences with respect to the delineation of their common border, which follows natural features—the watershed of the Chumbi Valley in the northwest and the crest of the Great Himalayan Range of mountains in the north. The part of China that borders Bhutan—Tibet, or the Xizang Autonomous Region— has important historical, cultural, and religious ties to Bhutan (see Origins and Early Settlement, A.D. 600-1600, this ch.). China had been heavily involved in Tibetan affairs since the 1720s, and it was through this involvement that Bhutan and China had their first direct relations. Bhutanese delegations to the Dalai Lama came into contact with the Chinese representatives in Lhasa, but there never was a tributary relationship with Beijing. Relations with Tibet itself, never particularly good, were strained considerably when Bhutan sided with Britain in the early 1900s. Trying to secure its southwestern flank against increasing foreign aggression, China claimed a vague suzerainty over Bhutan in the period just before the Chinese Revolution of 1911. The new Republic of China let the claim lapse, however, and it never again was raised publicly.

Tension in Bhutan-China relations increased with the Chinese occupation of Tibet in 1951 and again rose with the anti-Chinese revolts in eastern and central Tibet between 1954 and 1958. The massive Tibetan uprisings in 1959 and the flight to India of the Dalai Lama, as well as the heightened presence of Chinese forces on the ill-defined frontier, alerted Bhutan to the potential threat it faced, and its representative in Tibet was withdrawn. Included in the territory occupied by the Chinese People's Liberation Army were the eight western Tibetan enclaves administered by Bhutan since the seventeenth century. New Delhi intervened with Beijing on behalf of Thimphu regarding the enclaves, but the Chinese refused to discuss what they considered a matter between China and Bhutan. Another problem with China emerged at this time as the result of the flight to Bhutan of some 6,000 Tibetan refugees. The specter of renewed Chinese claims to Bhutan, Sikkim, and Nepal was raised after China published a map in 1961 that showed alterations of traditional Sino-Bhutanese and other Himalayan borders in Beijing's favor. Bhutan responded with an embargo on cross-border trade and closer links with India.

During this period, Thimphu continued to withstand Beijing's mixture of threats and offers of conciliation in the form of economic aid and assurance of independence. Tension was renewed during the 1962 Sino-Indian border war when the Chinese army outflanked Indian troops, who, with permission of Bhutanese authorities, retreated through southeastern Bhutan. More fearful of China than confident of India's ability to defend it, Bhutan formally maintained a policy of neutrality while quietly expanding its relations with India. Cross-border incursions by Chinese soldiers and Tibetan herders occurred in 1966, but tensions generally lessened thereafter and during the 1970s. In 1979 a larger than usual annual intrusion by Tibetan herders into Bhutan brought protests to Beijing from both Thimphu and New Delhi. China, again seeking a direct approach with Bhutan, ignored the Indian protest but responded to the one from Bhutan. As part of its policy of asserting its independence from India, Bhutan was open to direct talks, whereas India continued to see the Sino-Bhutan boundary issue as intimately related to the Sino-Indian border dispute. A series of border talks has been held annually since 1984 between the ministers of foreign of affairs of Bhutan and China, leading to relations that have been characterized by the two sides as ''very good.''

Other Countries

Bhutan, the second nation to do so, recognized the newly independent Bangladesh in 1971, and diplomatic relations were established in 1973. Bangladesh was the only country other than India with which Bhutan had diplomatic relations at the time and, in the view of some foreign observers, perhaps the only country with which India would have allowed Bhutan to develop bilateral relations. For Bhutan, however, the step was an important symbolic move that provided a new trade outlet as well as another access to the sea. Water and flood control, a major multilateral issue involving the great Himalayan watersheds that run through China, Bhutan, and India into flood-prone Bangladesh have been perennial concerns between Thimphu and Dhaka.

Bhutan, with its sizeable Nepalese minority, has been particularly cautious in its relations with Nepal in deference to Indian sensitivities. In 1969 the Nepal-Bhutan Friendship and Cultural Society was established in Kathmandu to facilitate good relations, but formal diplomatic ties were not established until 1983, the same year SAARC was founded. Given the ethnic unrest among Nepalese in Bhutan, at the request of the Nepal-Bhutan Friendship and Cultural Society, the Bhutan-Nepal Friendship Association was formed in 1989 to help defuse tensions.

Participation in International Organizations

Historically, Bhutan's foreign relations had been limited primarily to contacts with Tibet, India, and Britain. A major step was taken in the 1960s as Bhutan began to join international organizations. It first became a member of the Colombo Plan in 1962, which put the kingdom into contact with member states throughout South Asia and Southeast Asia for purposes of fostering cooperative economic development. Bhutan joined the Universal Postal Union in 1969, putting it into contact with some 137 countries. UN membership was achieved in 1971, followed by the gaining of seats in the UN's specialized and related agencies, including the International Monetary Fund (IMF—see Glossary) and the World Bank. A founding member of SAARC in 1983, Bhutan had also established relations with the Coordination Bureau of the Nonaligned Countries (the headquarters of the Nonaligned Movement), the Group of 77, the Asian Development Bank, and the European Community. By 1990, Bhutan belonged to 119 international, regional, and special interest organizations (see table 32, Appendix).

In 1975 Bhutan and four other landlocked Asian countries (Afghanistan, Laos, Mongolia, and Nepal) were granted special status as "least developed landlocked countries" by the UN Economic and Social Commission for Asia and the Pacific (ESCAP) in coordination with the United Nations Conference on Trade and Development (UNCTAD) and UNDP. Despite these organizations' intentions to assist Bhutan and the other countries in dealing with international transit problems, Bhutan declined to participate in their work.

Perhaps the most significant international participation Bhutan embarked on in the 1980s was membership in SAARC. SAARC's agenda excluded bilateral issues and political programs from the organization's debates and confined committee and summit discussions to areas where member nations must find common ground for achieving mutual economic benefit. Bhutan became involved in useful working group discussions on agriculture and livestock, rural development, meteorology, telecommunications, science and technology, health and population, transportation, postal cooperation, and trade and industrial cooperation.

Heads-of-state meetings of SAARC have taken Jigme Singye Wangchuck abroad on several occasions. The integration of Bhutan into SAARC activities also involved the country with a variety of issues of concern to poor undeveloped nations as well as increasing its participation in the Nonaligned Movement. In Bhutan's extensive multilateral diplomatic activities in the 1980s, officials saw their country emerging as an "Eastern Geneva" providing a "venue for peace-making efforts in South Asia."

National Security

Strategic Location

Bhutan is a strategic buffer state wedged between India and China. After centuries of close ties to Tibet and less definite connections to China, Bhutan developed a southerly political orientation, first with British India and then with independent India. British troops in or near Bhutan presented a considerable deterrent to China from the eighteenth century until the early twentieth century. Britain's withdrawal from India in 1947 and India's replacement of Britain as Bhutan's protector coincided with the communist military victory in China in 1949.

Because of its location in India's strategic defense system, Bhutan has long had foreign defense arrangements, first with Britain and then with independent India. Despite common international policy goals of Indian and Chinese leaders, territorial problems between the two powers continued to define Bhutan's buffer status. The 1962 border war between India and China had serious implications for Bhutan and could have embroiled it in the fighting. Thimphu permitted Indian troops to cross Bhutanese territory and Chinese airplanes allegedly violated Bhutanese air space. In addition, China reportedly had six divisions stationed near the borders of Bhutan, Sikkim, and Nepal. China had its own boundary disputes with Bhutan, and Chinese troops reportedly breached the Bhutanese frontier on several occasions in 1966, 1970, and 1979. In each case, New Delhi attempted to represent Thimphu's interests in protest notes to Beijing, all of which were rejected.

As the Chinese threat grew, India became increasingly involved in the buildup of Bhutan's indigenous defensive capability, specifically in the training and equipping of the Royal Bhutan Army (see Armed Forces, this ch.). The headquarters of the Indian Military Training Team (IMTRAT) in Bhutan was located in Ha District, which is adjacent to Tibet's Chumbi Valley, where China routinely kept large concentrations of troops, at the junction of the Bhutanese, Indian, and Chinese borders.

The 1949 Indo-Bhutanese treaty makes no reference to India's defense of Bhutan except what might be inferred from Article 2 of the treaty. Prime Minister Nehru, however, declared in 1958 that acts of aggression against Bhutan would be taken as acts of aggression against India itself. Also, by the terms of the 1949 treaty, Bhutan has the right to import arms, munitions, and other military matériel from or through India as long as the Indian government is satisfied that such imports do not threaten India. Bhutan, on the other hand, agreed not to export or allow private citizens to export any arms, ammunition, or military equipment. The Indian Ministry of Defence also made provisions for the rapid deployment of helicopter-borne troops to Bhutan in the event of a Chinese invasion and made related plans for air force operations. Suggestions from within the Bhutanese government to allow Indian troops to be stationed in Bhutan were rejected. An important defensive consideration has been the construction of extensive roads with major assistance from the Indian government's paramilitary Border Roads Organization.

Armed Forces

The Royal Bhutan Army was organized as a regular military force in the 1950s with the encouragement of India and in response to China's takeover of Tibet. Following the establishment of a national militia in 1958, the government announced a new conscription system the same year and plans for a standing army of 2,500 troops with modern equipment. Military training was given to all able-bodied men, and by 1963 the standing army was well established. A reorganization in 1968 led several years later to an increase in the army to 4,850 troops and a campaign aimed at recruiting 600 additional troops per year. In 1990 the Royal Bhutan Army was composed of 6,000 men and was backed by a growing militia. Two women were recruited for the army's airport security unit in 1989, but no other women soldiers have been noted.

The army's primary mission was border defense, but it also has assisted the Royal Bhutan Police in performing internal security duties (see Police Force, this ch.). The army also provided security at the Paro airport and regulated the sale, ownership, and licensing of civilian-owned firearms. For ceremonial occasions, the army had a band, some members of which were trained in India.

The army's supreme commander in 1991 was the Druk Gyalpo; day-to-day operations were under the charge of the chief operations officer. The chief operations officer held the rank of colonel until 1981, when the position was upgraded to major general (see table 33, Appendix). In 1991 the chief operations officer was Major General Lam Dorji. Organizationally, the army headquarters ranked at the ministry level and was immediately subordinate to the Council of Ministers.

As of 1978, the Royal Bhutan Army consisted of its headquarters in Thimphu, a training center at Tenchholing, four operational wings, and an airport security unit at Paro. Wing 1 had its headquarters in Changjukha (Geylegphug), Wing 2 at Damthang, Wing 3 at Goinichawa, and Wing 4 at Yonphula. Organized into companies, platoons, and sections, the troops were assigned to the

Royal Bhutan Army camp at Tashi Makhang, Punakha District
Courtesy Bhutan Travel, Inc., New York (Marie Brown)

wings deployed primarily in border areas. The army also operated hospitals in Lungtenphug, Wangdiphodrang, and Yonphula.

Most if not all of the army's weapons in the 1980s were manufactured in India. Rifles, bayonets, machine guns, and 81mm mortars have been noted in the army's weapons inventory, but some were believed to be obsolescent. Figures on defense expenditures were not publicly available and, in budgetary information published by the Planning Commission, were found only in general government costs.

The army has traditionally been a small, lightly armed conscript force. The majority of its officers and noncommissioned officers were trained by IMTRAT, which was commanded by an Indian Army brigadier at the Wangchuck Lo Dzong Military Training School, established in 1961 in Ha District. Recruits were trained at the Army Training Centre established in 1957 at Tenchholing in Wangdiphodrang District. IMTRAT also offered a one-to-two-month precourse for officers and enlisted personnel selected for advanced training in India. Royal Bhutan Army cadets were sent to the Indian National Defence Academy at Pune, followed by training at the Indian Military Academy at Dehra Dun, from which they were commissioned as second lieutenants. It was reported in 1990 that members of the Royal Body Guards (an elite VIP protection unit commanded by a lieutenant colonel) had completed counterinsurgency and jungle warfare training in the Mizo Hills in India, the Indian College of Combat, and the Indian Military Academy.

The army conducted an annual recruitment drive. Families with two or more sons were expected to have one son serve in the army. Individuals between sixteen and twenty-four years of age, having a minimum height of 150 centimeters and minimum weight of fifty-two kilograms, were eligible for recruitment. Selected from among volunteers and conscripts, recruits were given ten to twelve months of basic training that included weapons proficiency, "field craft," signals, map reading, tae kwon do, and physical fitness. Soldiers also were expected to achieve proficiency in Dzongkha, Nepali, and English. Annual salaries started at Nu300 plus food, clothing, and accommodations.

Since the 1970s, one of the army's goals has been self-sufficiency. The Army Welfare Committee was established in 1978 to oversee the Army Welfare Project, which provided housing, food, and income for the Royal Bhutan Army and the Royal Body Guards. It was charged with taking care of individual army personnel problems and providing pensions to retirees. Although some labor for the Army Welfare Project was provided by army personnel, the project was administered by civil service employees and contractors. By 1979 a pilot project, the Lapchekha Agriculture Farm in Wangdiphodrang District, had been established to provide food for army units in western Bhutan. The farm comprised 525 hectares with a potential for an additional 113 hectares of arable land. Army personnel constructed a twenty-one-kilometer-long canal to irrigate the farm and worked there for three months each year. Revenues from the farm and other welfare projects helped provide benefits to retired and disabled personnel in the form of pensions and loans and, in the case of landless retirees, agricultural land grants. Army careerists could retire, depending on their rank, between the ages of thirty-seven and forty-five years of age. Preretirement training in farming was provided to army personnel. All retirees received pensions, and those disabled during service received both a pension and free medical care. In 1985 the Army Welfare Project generated Nu40 million in sales of farm services and products, which ranged from such practical civil activities as fence electrification to protect sugarcane farms from wild elephants in Geylegphug District to entrepreneurial endeavors, such as the manufacture and sale of rum to the Indian Army and Indian Air Force.

Paramilitary

Militia

Historically, the government raised militia forces during times of crisis during the period of theocratic rule (1616–1907). They were commanded by a *dapon* (arrow chief in Dzongkha). In modern times, a 5,000-strong militia was raised in 1958 as part of the defensive strategy against China. Militia personnel were trained by army officers who had been trained at the Indian Military Academy. Their primary function was as a first line of defense along frontier areas with China. Following an Indian inspection tour in 1961, the government was advised to step up militia recruitment. In 1967 the militia was reorganized on a national basis, with compulsory military training being given for three months each year for three years to men twenty to twenty-five years of age. After the initial three-year training phase, militia personnel were placed on reserve status.

In a move said by the Druk Gyalpo to reinforce Bhutan's security, new militia training was initiated in 1989. In the early 1980s, weapons training for all male citizens between ages sixteen and sixty was considered, but, in view of national security and public works projects to which the army already was committed, it was postponed. In 1990 ninety-four students were enlisted in a program at the Tenchholing army camp. Candidates for militia training included individuals who had completed at least the tenth grade, new college graduates, and members of the civil service. Starting in 1989, new male civil service entrants were required to take a three-week militia training course.

In reaction to the "prodemocracy" demonstrations by ethnic Nepalese in southern Bhutan in September 1990, the government announced that more than 1,000 citizens had volunteered to join militia groups. The army was to provide training for around 500 militia members to assist the "badly under strength" police in dealing with mob attacks. Recruits were men and women from among civil servants and urban residents. Militia trainees pledged to give their "full support and loyalty" to *tsawa sum* (country, king, and people) and a total commitment to defend the nation.

Forest Guards

The Forest Guards, a uniformed government service with paramilitary capabilities, had been in existence since the early 1970s. Under the jurisdiction of the Department of Forestry, Forest Guards were trained in two six-month classes per year at the Forestry School. Recruits learned first aid, forest-fire fighting, marksmanship,

339

physical training, and traditional Bhutanese customs. Small arms training was imparted by the Royal Bhutan Army. Besides guarding Bhutan's important forest resources, the Forest Guards provided border-security support to the Royal Bhutan Police.

Police Force

The Royal Bhutan Police was established with personnel reassigned from the army on September 1, 1965, a day thereafter marked as Police Day throughout Bhutan. Starting with only a few hundred personnel in 1965, by the late 1970s the force had more than 1,000 constables and officers. Recruits—grade six graduates and above—were trained at the Police Training Centre in Zilnon Namgyeling, Thimphu District, and, after 1981, at a police training center in Jigmiling, Geylegphug District. The curriculum consisted of weapons training, tae kwon do, physical training with and without arms, law, simple investigation techniques, "turn-out drill," check-post duties, traffic control, public relations, and *driglam namzha*. Recruits were also trained for other unspecified duties and to escort important visitors.

Since the establishment of the police force in 1965, Indian police advisers and instructors have been used. Starting in 1975, Bhutanese instructors, trained in India for one year, began training recruits at the Zilnon Namgyeling Police Training Centre. Advanced training for selected police officers in fields such as criminology, traffic control, and canine corps has taken place in India and other countries. In 1988, following specialized training in India, a female second lieutenant established a fingerprint bureau in Thimphu. Besides having access to training at the Indian Police Academy in Hyderabad, some students were also sent to the Police Executive Development Course in Singapore.

Besides performing their standard police functions, members of the Royal Bhutan Police also served as border guards and firefighters and provided first aid. In 1975, in response to the increased number of traffic accidents resulting from the development of roads and the increased number of motor vehicles, the police established an experimental mobile traffic court staff with Royal Bhutan Police personnel and a judicial official to make on-the-spot legal decisions.

Organizationally subordinate to the Royal Bhutan Army, the Royal Bhutan Police in 1991 was under the command of Major General Lam Dorji, who was also chief of operations of the army, under the title inspector general or commandant. There were police headquarters in each district and subdistrict.

Traffic control on Norzin Lam, Thimphu's main street
Courtesy Bhutan Travel, Inc., New York (Marie Brown)

Legal System

Criminal Justice

Bhutan's civil and criminal codes are based on the Tsa Yig, a code established by the *shabdrung* in the seventeenth century. The Tsa Yig was revised in 1957 and ostensibly replaced with a new code in 1965. The 1965 code, however, retained most of the spirit and substance of the seventeenth-century code. Family problems, such as marriage, divorce, and adoption, usually were resolved through recourse to Buddhist or Hindu religious law. In modern Bhutan, village heads often judged minor cases and district officials adjudicated major crimes.

Trials in the 1980s were public, and it was the practice of the accuser and the accused personally to put their cases to judges. There were no lawyers in Bhutan's legal system until the 1980s, and decisions were made on the facts of each case as presented by the litigants. Judges appointed by the Druk Gyalpo were responsible for investigations, filing of charges, prosecution, and judgment of defendants. Serious crimes were extremely rare throughout the twentieth century, although there were reports of increased criminal activity in the 1980s and early 1990s with the influx of foreign laborers, widening economic disparities, and greater contact with foreign cultures.

Penal Code

Arrests can be made only under legal authority. Exile, stated as a punishment in the 1953 Constitution of the National Assembly, and its 1968 revision, is not used as a form of punishment, and mutilation was abolished in 1965. Fines, according to various reports, ranged from the equivalent of US$10 to US$55, and jail sentences from seven days to one month were levied against citizens who violated a compulsory but not widely enforced 1989 royal decree that they wear the national dress at formal gatherings to preserve and promote Bhutanese culture. With respect to international criminal law, in 1988 the National Assembly ratified a SAARC convention on terrorism, which Bhutan has consistently condemned in international forums. It provided for extradition of terrorists.

The last half of the twentieth century was a momentous period in Bhutan's long historical development. The nation moved from a traditional system of governance to a de facto constitutional monarchy while retaining its firm Buddhist religious basis. Physical isolation was overcome with major road construction and advances in telecommunications that linked the various parts of the country and gave greater access to the outside world. International air travel brought tourism and greater amounts of foreign exchange needed for economic development. Having observed the problems encountered by other developing nations, Bhutan sought a more controlled economic and infrastructure development with the assistance of major foreign and international organizations. Once exclusively reliant on India for trade and aid, the kingdom broadened its import/export base and diversified its sources of economic assistance markedly during this period.

Despite these positive achievements, Bhutan faced serious political problems in the early 1990s. The Nepalese minority in southern Bhutan had been a source of serious ethnic disturbances and even terrorist acts, and its demands for greater participation in the political process had been on the rise since the mid-1980s. The threat to the indigenous population of gradually being outnumbered by politically active immigrant Nepalese raised for Bhutan's leaders the specter of Sikkim's annexation by India in 1974, when that kingdom's indigenous Buddhist people became a minority in their own country and lost political power. The question of how to modernize the nation politically remained a crucial one, and

Bhutan's independence and sovereignty hung in the balance as the 1990s progressed.

*   *   *

The annual writings of Brian Shaw in the Far Eastern Economic Review's *Asia Yearbook, Statesman's Year-Book,* and Europa's *The Far East and Australasia* and *Europa World Year Book* provide an excellent and up-to-date overview of all facets of Bhutanese history, society, economy, politics, and other sectors. *Bhutan: The Early History of a Himalayan Kingdom* by Michael Aris provides a detailed view of Bhutan's historical origins as derived from Bhutanese primary sources. Bhutan's general history is well covered in *History of Bhutan* by Bikrama Jit Hasrat. The Bhutan Planning Commission's *Statistical Yearbook of Bhutan* provides copious information on many sectors of society and the economy. Social and economic developments are cogently presented in Pradyumna P. Karan's *Bhutan: Development Amid Environmental and Cultural Preservation,* and his earlier book, *Bhutan: A Physical and Cultural Geography,* provides key information on geography. The World Bank's *Bhutan: Development in a Himalayan Kingdom* and *Bhutan: Development Planning in a Unique Environment* are excellent analyses of economic development. Articles by Sukhdev Shah and S.W.R. de A. Samarasinghe in *Asian Survey* also provide useful analyses of the economy of Bhutan. Political developments from the seventeenth to the mid-twentieth century are well presented in Leo E. Rose's *The Politics of Bhutan.* The weekly official newspaper *Kuensel* [Thimphu] is a good source of current official information on government and popular activities. To keep abreast of subsequent publications on Bhutan, the Association for Asian Studies' annual *Bibliography of Asian Studies* should be consulted. (For further information and complete citations, see Bibliography.)

Appendix

Table 1. *Metric Conversion Coefficients and Factors*

When you know	Multiply by	To find
Millimeters	0.04	inches
Centimeters	0.39	inches
Meters	3.3	feet
Kilometers	0.62	miles
Hectares (10,000 m²)	2.47	acres
Square kilometers	0.39	square miles
Cubic meters	35.3	cubic feet
Liters	0.26	gallons
Kilograms	2.2	pounds
Metric tons	0.98	long tons
....	1.1	short tons
....	2,204	pounds
Degrees Celsius	1.8	degrees Fahrenheit
(Centigrade)	and add 32	

Table 2. *Nepal: Population Growth, Selected Years, 1911–2001*

Year	Population (in thousands)	Growth Rate (in percentages)
1911	5,639	n.a.
1921	5,574	−0.13
1931	5,533	−0.07
1941	6,284	1.16
1952/54	8,473	2.27
1961	9,413	1.64
1971	11,556	2.05
1981	15,023	2.62
2001 *	23,593	2.30

n.a.—not applicable.
* Projected as medium variant.

Source: Based on information from Nepal, National Planning Commission, Secretariat, Central Bureau of Statistics, *Statistical Pocket Book: Nepal, 1988,* Kathmandu, 1988, 21.

*Table 3. Nepal: Population Density and Agricultural Density by Region,
1961, 1971, and 1981*

Region	1961 [1]	1971	1981
Population density [2]			
Mountain Region	n.a.	22	25
Hill Region	n.a.	99	117
Tarai Region	101	128	193
NEPAL	64	79	102
Agricultural density [3]			
Mountain Region	n.a.	9.3	10.6
Hill Region	n.a.	6.5	7.6
Tarai Region	2.4	3.1	4.7
NEPAL	3.8	4.7	6.1

n.a.—not available.
[1] Mountain and Hill regions together had population density figure of 53 and agricultural density figure of 5.6.
[2] Persons per square kilometer of total land.
[3] Persons per hectare of cultivable land.

Source: Based on information from Nanda R. Shrestha, *Landlessness and Migration in Nepal*,
Boulder, Colorado, 1990, 121.

Table 4. Nepal: Lifetime Regional Migration, 1971 and 1981

		Place of Birth			
Place of Enumeration	Year	Mountain Region	Hill Region	Tarai Region	Total
Mountain Region	1971	n.a.	9,258	440	9,698
	1981	n.a.	33,423	2,196	35,619
Hill Region	1971	15,667	n.a.	9,699	25,366
	1981	134,254	n.a.	35,669	169,923
Tarai Region	1971	33,990	376,074	n.a.	410,064
	1981	162,832	561,211	n.a.	724,043
TOTAL	1971	49,657	385,332	10,139	445,128
	1981	297,086	594,634	37,865	929,585 *

n.a.—not applicable.
* Excludes migration flows within the same region; including these flows would bring the total to
1,272,300 persons.

Source: Based on information from Nanda R. Shrestha, *Landlessness and Migration in Nepal*,
Boulder, Colorado, 1990, 27.

Table 5. *Nepal: Reasons for Lifetime Regional Migration by Region and Sex, 1981*

Reason	Mountain to Mountain	Mountain to Hill	Mountain to Tarai	Hill to Mountain	Hill to Hill	Hill to Tarai	Tarai to Mountain	Tarai to Hill	Tarai to Tarai
Males									
Trade and commerce	48.3	48.5	21.6	7.6	14.9	5.4	43.8	22.4	8.5
Agriculture	5.7	6.1	35.9	2.5	23.2	50.2	5.2	5.9	38.1
Service	2.3	3.4	4.3	7.5	15.2	7.5	15.2	12.2	10.8
Study and training	0.2	1.1	4.8	0.4	3.9	4.6	1.8	4.4	4.1
Marriage	0.6	0.5	0.5	1.2	2.4	0.7	1.5	1.2	2.3
Not stated and other	42.9	40.4	32.8	80.8	40.2	31.5	32.5	53.8	36.2
Total males *	100.0	100.0	100.0	100.0	00.0	100.0	100.0	100.0	100.0
Females									
Trade and commerce	40.6	42.4	20.1	4.4	6.5	3.9	26.6	12.7	4.2
Agriculture	5.4	5.2	25.4	1.3	8.6	31.9	2.3	3.4	10.6
Service	0.3	0.6	0.7	0.1	1.3	1.1	2.0	1.8	0.9
Study and training	0.2	0.5	2.7	0.3	1.0	2.0	0.8	1.9	1.3
Marriage	16.2	15.2	14.6	33.1	49.1	24.0	31.7	26.8	52.0
Not stated and other	37.2	36.1	36.4	60.2	3.4	37.0	36.5	53.4	31.0
Total females *	100.0	100.0	100.0	100.0	100.0	100.0	100.0	100.0	100.0

* Figures may not add to total because of rounding.

Source: Based on information from Nanda R. Shrestha, *Landlessness and Migration in Nepal,* Boulder, Colorado, 1990, 30.

349

Table 6. Nepal: Reasons for External Absentee Migration by Region and Sex, 1981

Region and Sex	Trade and Commerce	Agriculture	Service	Study and Training	Marriage	Not Stated and Other	Total
Mountain Region							
Males							
Number	n.a.	n.a.	n.a.	n.a.	n.a.	n.a.	61,263
Percentage	1	8	67	2	0	22	100
Females							
Number	n.a.	n.a.	n.a.	n.a.	n.a.	n.a.	16,247
Percentage	1	7	11	3	1	77	100
Total Mountain Region							
Number	1,048	5,863	43,010	1,498	267	25,824	77,510
Percentage	1	8	56	2	0	33	100
Hill Region							
Males							
Number	n.a.	n.a.	n.a.	n.a.	n.a.	n.a.	237,747
Percentage	0	3	79	2	0	16	100
Females							
Number	n.a.	n.a.	n.a.	n.a.	n.a.	n.a.	49,668
Percentage	0	2	12	3	2	81	100
Total Hill Region							
Number	1,213	7,576	195,610	6,756	1,181	77,079	289,415
Percentage	0	3	68	2	0	27	100

Table 6. —Continued

Region and Sex	Trade and Commerce	Agriculture	Service	Study and Training	Marriage	Not Stated and Other	Total
Tarai Region							
Males							
Number	n.a.	n.a.	n.a.	n.a.	n.a.	n.a.	27,438
Percentage	1	2	67	7	1	22	100
Females							
Number	n.a.	n.a.	n.a.	n.a.	n.a.	n.a.	8,614
Percentage	0	2	8	5	23	62	100
Total Tarai Region							
Number	262	666	19,144	2,386	2,148	11,446	36,052
Percentage	0	2	53	7	6	32	100
NEPAL							
Males							
Number	n.a.	n.a.	n.a.	n.a.	n.a.	n.a.	326,448
Percentage	1	4	76	2	0	17	100
Females							
Number	n.a.	n.a.	n.a.	n.a.	n.a.	n.a.	74,529
Percentage	0	3	12	3	4	78	100
TOTAL NEPAL							
Number	2,523	14,105	257,764	10,640	3,596	114,349	400,977
Percentage	1	3	64	3	1	28	100

n.a.—not available.

Source: Based on information from Nanda R. Shrestha, *Landlessness and Migration in Nepal*, Boulder, Colorado, 1990, 36.

Table 7. *Nepal: Distribution of Population*
by Mother Tongue, 1981

Mother Tongue	Number	Percentage
Nepali	8,767,361	58.4
Maithili	1,668,309	11.1
Bhojpuri	1,142,805	7.6
Tharu	545,685	3.6
Tamang	522,416	3.5
Newari	448,746	3.0
Abadhi	234,343	1.5
Rai and Kirati	221,353	1.5
Magar	212,681	1.4
Gurung	174,464	1.2
Limbu	129,234	0.9
Bhote (or Bhotia) and Sherpa	73,589	0.5
Rajbansi	59,383	0.4
Satar	22,403	0.1
Danuwar	13,522	0.1
Sunwar	10,650	0.1
Santhal	5,804	—
Thakali	5,289	—
Other	764,802	5.1
TOTAL	15,022,839	100.0

—means negligible.

Source: Based on information from Nepal, National Planning Commission, Secretariat,
Central Bureau of Statistics, *Statistical Pocket Book: Nepal, 1988,* Kathmandu, 1988, 24.

Table 8. Nepal: Distribution of Land by Region and Size of Holding, 1981
(in hectares)

Region	Under 0.5	0.5 to 1.0	1.0 to 3.0	3.0 to 5.0	Over 5.0	Total
Mountain Region						
Households						
Number	131,703	37,767	23,423	2,534	2,151	197,578
Percentage	66.7	19.1	11.8	1.3	1.1	100.0
Holdings						
Number	24,563	27,787	31,403	9,842	28,992	122,587
Percentage	20.0	22.7	25.6	8.0	23.7	100.0
Average holding .	0.2	0.7	1.3	3.9	13.5	0.6
Hill Region						
Households						
Number	541,988	194,403	250,203	41,468	17,158	1,045,220
Percentage	51.9	18.6	23.9	4.0	1.6	100.0
Holdings						
Number	98,731	145,776	375,079	157,383	162,735	939,704
Percentage	10.5	15.5	39.9	16.7	17.4	100.0
Average holding .	0.2	0.7	1.5	3.8	9.5	0.9
Tarai Region						
Households						
Number	434,210	123,250	262,386	75,667	55,645	951,158
Percentage	45.6	13.0	27.6	8.0	5.8	100.0
Holdings						
Number	38,705	91,367	463,521	288,447	519,386	1,401,426
Percentage	2.7	6.5	33.1	20.6	37.1	100.0
Average holding .	0.1	0.7	1.8	3.8	9.3	1.5
TOTAL						
Households						
Number	1,107,901	355,420	536,012	119,669	74,954	2,193,956
Percentage	50.5	16.2	24.4	5.5	3.4	100.0
Holdings						
Number	161,999	264,930	870,003	455,672	711,113	2,463,717
Percentage	6.6	10.7	35.3	18.5	28.9	100.0
Average holding .	0.2	0.8	1.6	3.8	9.5	1.1

Source: Based on information from Nanda R. Shrestha, *Landlessness and Migration in Nepal*, Boulder, Colorado, 1990, 127.

Table 9. Nepal: Planned Expenditures in the Public Sector, 1970-90
(in percentages)

Sector	Fourth Plan (1970-75)	Fifth Plan (1975-80)	Sixth Plan (1980-85)	Seventh Plan (1985-90)
Agriculture	26.0	30.0	29.4	30.6
Transportation	41.2	25.4	20.6	17.7
Industry	18.4	21.2	21.9	26.0
Social services	14.4	23.5	28.1	25.7
TOTAL *	100.0	100.0	100.0	100.0

* Figures may not add to total because of rounding.

Source: Based on information from Badri Prasad Shreshtha, *Nepalese Economy in Retrospect and Prospect,* Kathmandu, 1990, 22.

Table 10. Nepal: Public Sector Development Expenditures
and Foreign Aid, 1956-90
(in millions of rupees) [1]

Period	Planned Development Expenditures	Foreign Aid Value	Foreign Aid Percentage of Development Expenditures
First Plan (1956-61)	382.9 [2]	382.9	100.0
Second Plan (1962-65)	614.7	478.3	77.8
Third Plan (1965-70)	1,639.1	919.2	56.1
Fourth Plan (1970-75)	3,356.9	1,509.1	45.0
Fifth Plan (1975-80)	8,832.5	4,240.8	48.0
Sixth Plan (1980-85)	22,090.1	10,585.2	47.9
Seventh Plan (1985-90)	29,000.0	20,480.0	70.6
1985-86	6,213.3	3,491.5	60.1 [3]
1986-87	7,377.9	3,990.9	68.8 [3]
1987-88	9,428.0	5,892.6	62.5 [3]

[1] For value of the rupee—see Glossary.
[2] Actual amount disbursed.
[3] As published.

Source: Based on information from Babu Ram Shrestha, *Managing External Assistance in Nepal,* Kathmandu, 1990, 45, 118-19.

Table 11. Nepal: Government Budget, Fiscal Years 1987-90
(in millions of rupees) [1]

	1987	1988	1989 [2]	1990 [3]
Expenditures				
Regular	4,135.2	4,676.9	5,765.1	6,651.2
Development	7,378.0	9,428.0	9,495.5	13,590.7
Total expenditures	11,513.2	14,104.9	15,260.6	20,241.9
Revenues				
Regular	5,975.1	7,350.4	7,540.7	8,500.6
Foreign grants	1,285.1	2,076.8	1,817.9	8,000.6
Total revenues	7,260.2	9,427.2	9,358.6	16,501.2
Deficit	4,253.0	4,677.7	5,902.0	3,740.7
Loans				
Foreign	2,705.8	3,815.8	4,169.4	7,767.4
Internal	1,644.7	1,130.0	1,130.0	1,750.0
Total loans	4,350.5	4,945.8	5,299.4	9,517.4
Cash balance (- means surplus) [4]	-97.5	-268.0	602.6	n.a.

n.a.—not available.
[1] For value of the rupee—see Glossary.
[2] Revised estimate.
[3] Estimate.
[4] Figures may not add to total because of rounding.

Source: Based on information from Nepal, National Planning Commission, Secretariat, Central Bureau of Statistics, *Statistical Pocket Book: Nepal, 1990,* Kathmandu, 1990, 199.

Table 12. Nepal: Direction of Foreign Trade, Fiscal Years 1989, 1990, and 1991
(in millions of rupees) [1]

	1989	1990 [2]	1991 [3]
Exports			
India	1,034.9	666.6	1,348.0
Other	3,160.4	4,568.9	4,182.1
Total exports	4,195.3	5,235.5	5,530.1
Imports			
India	4,238.7	4,646.3	5,574.5
Other	12,025.0	13,755.2	11,281.9
Total imports	16,263.7	18,401.5	16,856.4
Trade balance			
India	-3,203.8	-3,979.7	-4,226.5
Other	-8,864.6	-9,186.3	-7,099.8
Total trade balance	-12,068.4	-13,166.0	-11,326.3

[1] For value of the rupee—see Glossary.
[2] Provisional.
[3] Provisional; first nine months of fiscal year.

Source: Based on information from Nepal Rastra Bank, Research Department, *Main Economic Indicators,* Kathmandu, February-April 1991, Table 17.

Table 13. *Nepal: Exports to India by Commodity Group, Fiscal Years 1986-89* [1]
(in millions of rupees) [2]

Commodity Group	1986	1987	1988	1989 [3]
Food and live animals	573.0	560.0	773.2	463.1
Tobacco and beverages	0.1	2.7	1.8	1.1
Crude materials and inedibles, except				
fuels	364.5	460.0	390.0	212.4
Mineral fuels and lubricants	0.2	0.2	0.8	—
Animal and vegetable oils and fats	56.0	73.8	144.1	94.8
Chemicals and drugs	1.0	1.2	11.1	16.5
Manufactured goods classified chiefly by				
materials	201.7	193.1	228.5	180.2
Machinery and transportation equipment .	37.5	0.9	0.1	4.2
Miscellaneous manufactured goods	6.8	10.8	15.7	18.3
Other	0.3	0.2	2.5	—
TOTAL	1,241.1	1,302.9	1,567.8	990.6

—means negligible.
[1] Based on customs data.
[2] For value of the rupee—see Glossary.
[3] Provisional.

Source: Based on information from Nepal, National Planning Commission, Secretariat, Central Bureau of Statistics, *Statistical Pocket Book: Nepal, 1990,* Kathmandu, 1990, 252.

Table 14. *Nepal: Exports by Country, Fiscal Years 1985-88* *
(in percentages)

Country	1985	1986	1987	1988
Bangladesh	—	—	0.3	—
Britain	9.4	6.1	10.1	10.0
China	n.a.	n.a.	—	—
Hong Kong	1.5	2.8	0.7	0.3
Japan	1.2	0.6	1.6	0.8
Pakistan	—	0.1	0.1	—
Singapore	6.2	12.3	6.4	1.2
Soviet Union	8.6	3.8	2.6	1.6
United States	43.2	45.8	36.5	37.1
West Germany	13.1	13.7	18.2	26.7
Other	16.8	14.8	23.5	22.3
TOTAL	100.0	100.0	100.0	100.0

—means negligible.
n.a.—not available.
* Excluding India.

Source: Based on information from Nepal, National Planning Commission, Secretariat, Central Bureau of Statistics, *Statistical Pocket Book: Nepal, 1990,* Kathmandu, 1990, 243.

Table 15. Nepal: Exports by Commodity Group, Fiscal Years 1986–89 [1]
(in millions of rupees) [2]

Commodity Group	1986	1987	1988	1989 [3]
Food and live animals	835.6	703.7	804.4	540.5
Tobacco and beverages	0.2	3.5	10.1	5.0
Crude materials and inedibles, except fuels	412.9	491.1	513.7	245.2
Mineral fuels and lubricants	0.2	0.2	0.8	n.a.
Animal and vegetable oils and fats	61.3	117.1	171.5	98.1
Chemicals and drugs	2.5	2.0	12.6	24.3
Manufactured goods classified chiefly by materials	900.0	1,009.6	1,601.6	1,986.5
Machinery and transportation equipment	38.6	2.6	0.5	5.7
Miscellaneous manufactured goods	826.5	661.5	996.9	1,250.1
Other	0.3	0.2	2.5	n.a.
TOTAL	3,078.1	2,991.5	4,114.6	4,155.4

n.a.—not available.
[1] Based on customs data.
[2] For value of the rupee—see Glossary.
[3] Provisional.

Source: Based on information from Nepal, National Planning Commission, Secretariat, Central Bureau of Statistics, *Statistical Pocket Book: Nepal, 1990,* Kathmandu, 1990, 249.

Table 16. Nepal: Imports by Country, Fiscal Years 1985–88 *
(in percentages)

Country	1985	1986	1987	1988
Britain	6.4	1.9	3.0	3.0
China	6.4	5.8	4.4	5.6
Hong Kong	2.8	3.5	3.2	2.6
Japan	22.3	28.7	22.9	20.8
Singapore	5.1	6.4	12.4	13.1
South Korea	10.1	8.8	9.2	6.9
Soviet Union	11.3	3.4	0.1	4.6
Thailand	2.2	2.0	2.5	1.8
United States	3.1	3.3	1.4	2.1
West Germany	4.8	5.2	5.0	8.1
Other	25.5	31.0	35.9	31.4
TOTAL	100.0	100.0	100.0	100.0

* Excluding India.

Source: Based on information from Nepal, National Planning Commission, Secretariat, Central Bureau of Statistics, *Statistical Pocket Book: Nepal, 1990,* Kathmandu, 1990, 244.

Table 17. Nepal: Imports by Commodity Group, Fiscal Years 1986–89 [1]
(in millions of rupees) [2]

Commodity Group	1986	1987	1988	1989 [3]
Food and live animals	971.1	1,028.9	1,523.7	1,291.1
Tobacco and beverages	113.0	144.0	172.2	203.7
Crude materials and inedibles,				
except fuels	393.0	657.2	1,306.9	1,165.4
Mineral fuels and lubricants	1,054.0	929.5	1,049.9	1,128.4
Animal and vegetable oils and fats ..	102.0	175.9	352.6	345.6
Chemicals and drugs	1,170.2	1,287.6	1,495.3	1,541.4
Manufactured goods classified				
chiefly by materials	2,759.5	3,226.8	3,359.2	4,678.8
Machinery and transportation				
equipment	2,134.7	2,784.1	4,143.7	4,861.2
Miscellaneous manufactured goods ..	637.2	664.0	729.1	1,020.2
Other	6.7	7.3	7.0	4.7
TOTAL	9,341.4	10,905.3	14,139.6	16,240.5

[1] Based on customs data.
[2] For value of the rupee—see Glossary.
[3] Provisional.

Source: Based on information from Nepal, National Planning Commission, Secretariat, Central Bureau of Statistics, *Statistical Pocket Book: Nepal, 1990,* Kathmandu, 1990, 254.

Table 18. Nepal: Disbursement of Foreign Loans and Grants, Selected Fiscal Years, 1984–90
(in millions of rupees) *

Source	1984	1985	1989	1990
Bilateral				
Grants	765.5	756.9	1,363.8	1,674.0
Loans	217.7	399.4	507.8	1,000.6
Total bilateral	983.2	1,156.3	1,871.6	2,674.6
Multilateral				
Grants	111.1	166.5	316.8	301.3
Loans	1,453.2	1,353.6	5,158.6	4,959.0
Total multilateral	1,564.3	1,520.1	5,475.4	5,260.3
TOTAL	2,547.5	2,676.4	7,347.0	7,934.9

* For value of the rupee—see Glossary.

Table 19. Nepal: Disbursement of Foreign Aid, Fiscal Years 1976–86
(in millions of rupees) *

Fiscal Year	Committed	Disbursed	Difference
1976	1,415.7	505.6	910.1
1977	1,911.2	556.9	1,354.3
1978	1,956.2	848.4	1,107.8
1979	2,417.3	980.4	1,436.9
1980	1,911.6	1,340.5	571.1
1981	4,012.6	1,462.2	2,550.4
1982	2,886.1	1,723.2	1,162.9
1983	2,959.2	2,075.9	883.3
1984	3,099.6	2,547.5	552.1
1985	5,991.4	2,676.4	3,315.0
1986	9,504.2	3,491.5	6,012.7

* For value of the rupee—see Glossary.

Source: Based on information from Babu Ram Shrestha, *Managing External Assistance in Nepal,* Kathmandu, 1990, 94, 116.

Table 20. Nepal: Power and Irrigation Facilities, 1956–90
(in hectares)

Period	Area
First Plan (1956–61)	5,200
Second Plan (1962–65)	1,035
Third Plan (1965–70)	52,860
Fourth Plan (1970–75)	37,733
Fifth Plan (1975–80)	95,425
Sixth Plan (1980–85)	172,649
Seventh Plan (1985–90)	217,845
TOTAL	582,747

Source: Based on information from Nepal, National Planning Commission, Secretariat, Central Bureau of Statistics, *Statistical Pocket Book: Nepal, 1990,* Kathmandu, 1990, 117.

Table 21. Nepal: Production of Principal Crops, Fiscal Years 1986–89
(in thousands of tons)

Crop	1986	1987	1988	1989 *
Barley	23	25 *	24	27
Corn	874	868	901	1,072
Jute	61	23	15	18
Millet	138	137	150	183
Oilseeds	79	83	94	99
Potatoes	357	395	567	640
Rice (paddy)	2,804	2,372	2,981	3,283
Sugarcane	558	616 *	814	903
Tobacco	5	5	4	5
Wheat	598	701	744	830

* Estimate.

Source: Based on information from Nepal, National Planning Commission, Secretariat,
Central Bureau of Statistics, *Statistical Pocket Book: Nepal, 1990,* Kathmandu, 1990, 40.

Table 22. Bhutan: Climatic Statistics, Selected Stations, 1988

Station	Average Annual Precipitation [1]	Temperature [2]	
		Minimum	Maximum
Chhukha	1,566	8.7	27.6
Daga	1,282	7.5	25.3
Damphu	1,818	6.5	23.4
Gedu	3,498	4.2	23.7
Samchi	4,290	16.3	32.0
Shemgang	1,743	6.4	20.1
Thimphu	646	-3.8	25.6
Tongsa	1,259	-0.1	21.7
Wangdiphodrang	639	4.6	28.3

[1] In millimeters.
[2] In degrees Celsius.

Source: Based on information from Bhutan, Planning Commission, Central Statistical Office,
Statistical Yearbook of Bhutan, 1989, Thimphu, May 1990, 28–33.

Table 23. Bhutan: Population by District, 1969 and 1980

District	1969	1980
Bumthang	n.a.	n.a.
Chhukha	n.a.	97,200
Chirang	80,357	104,500
Chotse	46,316	n.a.
Daga	n.a.	27,700
Dar	16,908	n.a.
Gardzong	10,344	n.a.
Geylegphug	n.a.	112,800
Ha	21,356	17,100
Ja	37,816	n.a.
Lhuntshi	45,651	36,900
Mongar	121,252	71,300
Pangdzong	21,212	n.a.
Pemagatsel	n.a.	35,100
Punakha	n.a.	34,500
Rinpung (Paro)	63,032	39,800
Samchi	57,161	138,900
Samdrup Jongkhar	n.a.	72,200
Shemgang	53,136	43,300
Tashigang	234,708	170,000
Thimphu	60,027	64,600
Tongsa	n.a.	28,600
Wangdiphodrang	n.a.	47,700
Wangdzong	61,338	n.a.
TOTAL	930,614	1,142,200 *

n.a.—not available.
* A total of 1,165,000 was provided by Bhutan's Central Statistical Office.

Source: Based on information from Leo E. Rose, *The Politics of Bhutan*, Ithaca, 1977, 41; and Bhutan, Planning Commission, Central Statistical Office, *Statistical Yearbook of Bhutan, 1989*, Thimphu, May 1990, 2.

Table 24. Bhutan: Gross Domestic Product by Sector,
Selected Years, 1981–91 [1]
(in percentages)

Sector	1981	1983	1985	1987	1989 [2]	1991 [2]
Crop farming	25.9	26.3	24.7	20.3	20.5	20.3
Livestock	12.3	11.9	11.7	10.5	10.3	10.2
Forestry and logging	14.7	15.0	16.2	15.2	15.0	15.7
Fishing	—	—	—	—	—	—
Total agriculture, forestry, and fishing	59.2	53.2	52.6	46.0	45.8	46.2
Mining and quarrying	0.6	0.6	0.9	1.0	1.3	1.5
Manufacturing	4.9	5.5	5.5	5.8	4.8	5.2
Electricity and gas	0.2	0.4	0.3	10.7	12.0	10.7
Construction	11.2	13.6	12.4	9.9	8.9	9.0
Commercial services [3]	12.2	9.7	8.6	7.0	7.5	7.4
Transportation, storage, and communications	4.5	4.4	4.4	3.6	4.0	4.1
Finance, insurance, real estate, and business services	6.3	5.7	6.4	6.0	5.8	5.9
Community, social, and personal services [4]	9.5	8.8	11.1	11.8	11.5	11.6
(Less imputed bank service charges)	-2.3	-1.9	-2.2	-1.8	-1.6	-1.6
TOTAL	100.0	100.0	100.0	100.0	100.0	100.0

—means negligible.
[1] Based on current prices.
[2] Projected.
[3] Wholesale and retail trade, hotels, and restaurants.
[4] Includes government administration and defense.

Source: Based on information from Bhutan, Planning Commission, Central Statistical Office, *Statistical Yearbook of Bhutan, 1989,* Thimphu, May 1990, 82, 84.

Table 25. Bhutan: Value and Growth Rate of Gross Domestic Product, Selected Years, 1980–91 [1]

Year	Value [2]	Growth Rate [3]
1980	1,095	n.a.
1981	1,280	16.9
1982	1,498	17.0
1983	1,754	17.0
1984	2,060	17.5
1985	2,350	14.1
1986	2,759	17.4
1987	3,531	28.0
1988 [4]	3,441	7.6
1989 [4]	3,633	5.6
1990 [4]	3,835	5.6
1991 [4]	4,049	5.6

n.a.—not available.
[1] Based on current prices.
[2] In millions of ngultrum; for value of the ngultrum—see Glossary.
[3] In percentages.
[4] Projected for Sixth Development Plan (1987–92).

Source: Based on information from Bhutan, Planning Commission, Central Statistical Office, *Statistical Yearbook of Bhutan, 1989,* Thimphu, May 1990, 82, 84.

Table 26. Bhutan: Allocation and Sources of Funds under Development Plans, 1961–92

Development Plan	Funds Allocated [1]	Sources of Funds [2]		
		Domestic [3]	India	Other [4]
First (1961–66)	107	0.0	100.0	0.0
Second (1966–71)	202	1.1	98.9	0.0
Third (1971–76)	475	6.9	89.8	3.3
Fourth (1976–81)	1,106	5.4	77.1	17.5
Fifth (1981–87)	4,711	31.0	42.8	26.2
Sixth (1987–92)	9,500 [5]	34.7	27.5	37.8

n.a.—not available.
[1] In round millions of ngultrum; for value of the ngultrum—see Glossary.
[2] In percentages.
[3] Domestic revenues and internal loans.
[4] External grants and loans (includes financial gap).
[5] Proposed.

Source: Based on information from World Bank, *Bhutan: Development Planning in a Unique Environment,* Washington, 1989, 26, 28, 33.

Table 27. Bhutan: Allocation of Funds under Development Plans by Sector or Business, 1961–92
(in percentages)

Sector or Business	First (1962–66)	Second (1966–71)	Third (1971–76)	Fourth (1976–81)	Fifth (1981–87)	Sixth (1987–92)
Agriculture	1.8	10.7	12.3	23.4	9.0	9.2
Food Corporation of Bhutan	0.0	0.0	0.0	0.0	2.9	1.1
Animal husbandry	1.4	2.9	5.1	5.6	3.5	3.5
District administration .	n.a.	n.a.	n.a.	n.a.	n.a.	2.5
Druk-Air	0.0	0.0	0.0	0.0	0.0	4.1
Education	8.8	17.7	18.9	12.2	11.2	8.1
Forestry	3.0	3.4	6.0	10.0	4.9	4.4
General government ...	n.a.	n.a.	n.a.	n.a.	24.0	20.6
Geological survey	0.0	0.0	0.0	0.0	0.0	0.4
Health	2.9	8.3	8.0	4.9	5.1	4.2
Industry, mining, trade, and commerce	1.0	0.5	5.3	15.8	7.0	13.3
Information and broadcasting	0.1	0.7	0.8	1.0	0.8	1.0
Posts and telegraphs ...	0.5	2.9	2.4	1.5	1.4	0.7
Power generation [1]	1.4	4.5	6.3	4.6	7.3	13.1
Public works	58.7	34.9	17.8	11.6	16.9	9.3
Road transportation and aviation	7.0	5.9	2.0	0.0	0.6	0.5
Telecommunications ...	0.0	0.0	3.1	3.4	0.7	1.4
Tourism	0.0	0.0	3.0	1.1	0.6	0.0
Urban development ...	0.0	0.0	0.0	0.0	4.0	2.6
Other	13.4	7.7	8.9	4.9	0.0	0.0
TOTAL [2]	100.0	100.0	100.0	100.0	100.0	100.0

n.a.—not available.
[1] Excluding the Chhukha Hydel Project.
[2] Figures may not add to total because of rounding.

Source: Based on information from Bhutan, Planning Commission, Central Statistical Office, *Statistical Yearbook of Bhutan, 1989,* Thimphu, May 1990, 79.

Table 28. Bhutan: Major Trade with India, Selected Years, 1981–87
(in millions of ngultrum) *

Commodity	1981	1983	1985	1987
Exports				
Cement	35.7	35.2	55.0	103.2
Timber	16.0	8.2	46.8	121.2
Cardamom	10.8	8.0	38.0	21.9
Ginger	—	—	—	2.0
Fruit products	4.5	11.0	21.2	2.6
Potatoes	15.6	5.1	16.1	23.2
Oranges	17.2	3.6	13.3	19.7
Resin	7.2	8.1	10.7	6.0
Alcoholic beverages	1.0	4.4	7.8	17.5
Soft drinks	—	—	—	4.2
Veneers	0.3	3.0	6.9	0.9
Apples	0.1	0.5	6.1	8.9
Methyl	4.9	0.3	3.2	1.9
Blockboard	—	0.1	14.8	29.3
Electricity	—	—	—	275.9
Dolomite	—	—	—	13.2
Other	52.9	69.7	30.1	31.1
Total exports	166.2	157.2	270.0	702.4
Imports				
Diesel oil	28.0	40.4	53.4	45.1
Gasoline	11.7	13.4	16.2	20.3
Kerosene	n.a.	n.a.	n.a.	8.7
Rice	15.6	17.2	33.5	52.3
Tires and tubes	4.8	1.0	33.5	30.1
Electricity	4.8	15.8	23.4	14.2
Truck chassis	19.9	4.4	41.4	23.4
Iron rods	28.8	5.9	21.7	49.3
Structures and parts	44.3	3.3	8.7	8.7
Machinery components	14.6	6.2	49.6	21.2
Hardware	2.0	1.3	21.1	2.5
Passenger automobiles	2.0	2.5	4.1	6.6
Bitumen	11.3	5.2	13.3	2.5
Textiles	12.0	1.3	17.0	16.4
Other	320.8	482.7	463.1	598.4
Total imports	520.6	600.6	800.0	899.7
TRADE BALANCE	-354.4	-443.4	-530.0	-197.3

—means no trade.
n.a.—not available.
* For value of the ngultrum—see Glossary.

Source: Based on information from Bhutan, Planning Commission, Central Statistical Office,
Statistical Yearbook of Bhutan, 1989, Thimphu, May 1990, 62.

Table 29. Bhutan: Foreign Trade, Fiscal Years 1982–89
(in millions of ngultrum) [1]

Year	Exports [2]	Imports [3]	Trade Balance
1982	159.4	646.5	–487.1
1983	160.7	730.0	–569.3
1984	206.4	825.2	–618.8
1985	272.0	1,041.6	–769.6
1986	427.1	1,205.4	–778.3
1987	711.9	1,194.6	–482.7
1988	1,072.6	1,817.0	–744.4
1989	1,190.7	1,770.2	–579.5

[1] For value of the ngultrum—see Glossary.
[2] Free on board.
[3] Cost, insurance, and freight.

Source: Based on information from Bhutan, Planning Commission, Central Statistical Office, *Statistical Yearbook of Bhutan, 1989,* Thimphu, May 1990, 61; and International Monetary Fund, *International Financial Statistics,* Washington, January 1991, 124.

Table 30. Bhutan: Balance of Payments, Selected Fiscal Years, 1982–88
(in millions of ngultrum) [1]

	1982	1984	1986	1988 [2]
Exports [3]	159.4	206.4	427.1	1,072.6
Imports [4]	–646.5	–825.2	–1,205.4	–1,817.0
Trade balance	–487.1	–618.8	–778.3	–744.4
Services and transfer receipts	131.3	243.1	314.7	412.2
Services and transfer payments	–389.9	–511.4	–616.0	–635.2
Current account balance	–754.7	–887.1	–1,079.6	–967.4
Foreign aid	788.7	989.0	1,268.8	1,086.3
Other loans	n.a.	n.a.	6.3	278.3
Errors and omissions	25.9	31.9	–2.5	–48.9
Overall balance	59.9	133.8	193.0	348.3

n.a.—not available.
[1] For value of the ngultrum—see Glossary.
[2] Estimate.
[3] Free on board.
[4] Cost, insurance, and freight.

Source: Based on information from Bhutan, Planning Commission, Central Statistical Office, *Statistical Yearbook of Bhutan, 1989,* Thimphu, May 1990, 61.

Table 31. Bhutan: Diplomatic Relations with Other Nations, 1990

Nation [1]	Year [2]
Austria	1989
Bangladesh	1973
Denmark	1985
Finland	1986
India	1949
Japan	1986
Kuwait	1983
Maldives	1984
Nepal	1983
Netherlands	1985
Norway	1985
Pakistan	1988
South Korea	1987
Sri Lanka	1987
Sweden	1985
Switzerland	1985

[1] In 1988 Bhutan also recognized the State of Palestine as proclaimed by the Palestine National Council in Algiers.
[2] Date relations were established.

Table 32. Bhutan: Membership in Major International Organizations, 1990

Organization	Year [1]
Asian Development Bank	1982
Asia-Pacific Postal Union	1983
Colombo Plan for Cooperative Economic and Social Development in Asia and the Pacific	1962
Coordination Bureau of Non-Aligned Countries	1973
European Community	1985 [2]
Food and Agriculture Organization	1981
International Civil Aviation Organization	1989
International Development Association	1981
International Fund for Agricultural Development	1981
International Monetary Fund	1981
International Telecommunications Union	1988
Group of 77	1982
South Asia Co-operative Environmental Programme	1982
South Asian Association for Regional Cooperation	1983
United Nations	1971
United Nations Economic and Social Commission for Asia and the Pacific	1972
United Nations Educational, Scientific, and Cultural Organization	1982
Universal Postal Union	1969
World Bank	1981
World Health Organization	1982

[1] Date Bhutan became a member.
[2] Observer status.

Table 33. Bhutan: Ranks in the Royal Bhutan Army, 1991

Bhutanese Rank *	Translation
Goongjey	Field marshal
Maksi goong	General
Goonglon	Lieutenant
Goonglon wogma	Major general
Dozin/Wangpon	Brigadier
Maksi gom	Colonel
Maksi wom	Lieutenant colonel
Lingpon	Major
Chipon	Captain
Deda gom	Lieutenant
Deda wom	Second lieutenant
Dimpon gom	Warrant officer
Dimpon wom	Sergeant major
Pelpon	Sergeant
Peljab	Corporal
Gopa	Lance corporal
Chyuma	Private

* Not all ranks have incumbents. Royal Bhutan Police ranks are the same as those used by the Royal Bhutan Army.

Source: Based on information from Rigzin Dorji, *Forms of Address in Bhutan,* New Delhi, 1976, 14.

Bibliography

Chapter 1

Adhikari, Krishna Kant. *Nepal under Jang Bahadur, 1846-1877.* Kathmandu: Buku, 1984.

Agrawal, Hem Narayan. *Nepal: A Country Study in Constitutional Change.* New Delhi: Oxford & IBH, 1980.

Baral, Lok Raj. "Nepal in 1987: Politics Without Power," *Asian Survey,* 28, No. 2, February 1988, 172-79.

_____. "Nepal in 1986: Problems of Political Management," *Asian Survey,* 27, No. 2, February 1987, 173-80.

Dhanalaxmi, Ravuri. *British Attitude to Nepal's Relations with Tibet and China, 1814-1914.* Chandigarh, India: Bahri, 1981.

Gaige, Frederick H. *Regionalism and National Unity in Nepal.* Berkeley: University of California Press, 1975.

Goswami, Prodyot Kumar. *Indian Currency and Exchange, 1835-1940.* New Delhi: Milind, 1983.

Gurney, Gene. *Kingdoms of Asia, the Middle East, and Africa: An Illustrated Encyclopedia of Ruling Monarchs from Ancient Times to the Present.* New York: Crown, 1986.

Heck, Douglas. "Nepal in 1980: The Year of the Referendum," *Asian Survey,* 21, No. 2, February 1981, 181-87.

Jain, M.S. *Emergence of a New Aristocracy in Nepal, 1837-58.* Agra, India: Sri Ram Mehar, 1972.

Joshi, Bhuwan Lal, and Leo E. Rose. *Democratic Innovations in Nepal: A Case Study of Political Acculturation.* Berkeley: University of California Press, 1966.

Kapuria, R.S. *The Indian Rupee: A Study in Retrospect and Prospect.* Bombay: Vora, 1967.

Khadka, Narayan. "The Political Economy of the Food Crisis in Nepal," *Asian Survey,* 25, No. 9, September 1985, 943-62.

Khanal, Y.N. "Nepal in 1984: A Year of Complacence," *Asian Survey,* 25, No. 2, February 1985, 180-86.

Koirala, Niranjan. "Nepal in 1989: A Very Difficult Year," *Asian Survey,* 30, No. 2, February 1990, 136-43.

Kulke, Hermann, and Dietmar Rothermund. *A History of India.* Totowa, New Jersey: Barnes and Noble, 1986.

Kumar, Satish. *Rana Polity in Nepal: Origin and Growth.* New York: Asia, 1967.

Lévi, Sylvain. *Le Nepal: Etude historique d'un royaume hindou.* (3 vols.) Paris: E Leroux, 1905-8.

Misra, Shashi P. *B.P. Koirala: A Case Study in Third World Democratic Leadership.* Bhubaneswar, India: Konark, 1985.

Mitra, Debala. *Buddhist Monuments.* Calcutta: Sahitya Samsad, 1971.

Mojumdar, Kanchanmoy. *Anglo-Nepalese Relations in the Nineteenth Century.* Calcutta: K.L. Mukhopadhyay, 1973.

Panday, Devendra Raj. "Nepal in 1981: Stagnation Amidst Change," *Asian Survey,* 22, No. 2, February 1982, 155-62.

Parmanand. *The Nepali Congress since Its Inception: A Critical Assessment.* Delhi: B.R. Publishing, 1982.

Pemble, John. *The Invasion of Nepal: John Company at War.* Oxford: Oxford University Press, 1971.

Petech, Luciano. *Mediaeval History of Nepal (ca. 750-1480).* (2d ed.) (Serie orientale, toma 54.) Rome: Institutio Italiano per il Medio ed Estremo Oriente, 1984.

Pick's Currency Yearbook. New York: Pick, 1973.

Regmi, Dilli Raman. *Ancient Nepal.* (3d ed.) Calcutta: K.L. Mukhopadhyay, 1969.

_____. *Medieval Nepal.* (4 vols.) Calcutta: K.L. Mukhopadhyay, 1965-66.

Rose, Leo E. *Nepal: Strategy for Survival.* Berkeley: University of California Press, 1971.

Rose, Leo E., and Margaret W. Fisher. *The Politics of Nepal: Persistence and Change in an Asian Monarchy.* Ithaca: Cornell University Press, 1970.

Rose, Leo E., and John T. Scholz. *Nepal: Profile of a Himalayan Kingdom.* Boulder, Colorado: Westview Press, 1980.

Shah, Sukhdev. "Developing an Economy: Nepal's Experience," *Asian Survey,* 21, No. 10, October 1981, 1060-79.

Slusser, Mary Shephers. *Nepal Mandala: A Cultural Study of the Kathmandu Valley.* (2 vols.) Princeton: Princeton University Press, 1982.

Spear, Percival. *A History of India.* New York: Penguin Books, 1981.

Stiller, Ludwig. *The Rise of the House of Gorkha: A Study in the Unification of Nepal.* New Delhi: Manjusri, 1973.

_____. *The Silent Cry: The People of Nepal, 1816-1839.* Kathmandu: Sahayogi Prakashan 1976.

Thapar, Romila. *A History of India.* New York: Penguin, 1966.

Tucci, Giuseppe. *Nepal: The Discovery of the Malla.* (Trans., Lovett Edwards.) New York: Dutton, 1962.

Tyagi, Sushila. *Indo-Nepalese Relations, 1858-1914.* Delhi: D.K. Publishing, 1974.

Wright, Daniel (ed.). *Vamsavali: History of Nepal.* (Trans., Munshi Shew Shunker Singh and Pundi Gunanand.) Kathmandu: Nepal Antiquated Book Publishers, 1972.

Chapter 2

Bajracharya, Deepak. "Fuel, Food or Forest? Dilemmas in a Nepali Village," *World Development* [Oxford], 11, No. 12, December 1983, 1057–74.

Banister, Judith, and Shyam Thapa. *The Population Dynamics of Nepal.* (Papers of the East-West Population Institute, No. 78.) Honolulu: East-West Center, 1981.

Bishop, Barry C. *Karnali under Stress: Livelihood Strategies and Seasonal Rhythms in a Changing Nepal Himalaya.* (Geography Research Paper Nos. 228–29.) Chicago: University of Chicago, 1990.

Bista, Dor Bahadur. *Fatalism and Development: Nepal's Struggle for Modernization.* Calcutta: Orient Longman, 1991.

Blaikie, Piers M., and Harold Brookfield, with contributions by Bryant Allen. *Land Degradation and Society.* London: Methuen, 1987.

Blaikie, Piers M., John Cameron, and David Seddon. *Nepal in Crisis: Growth and Stagnation at the Periphery.* New York: Oxford University Press, 1980.

The Cambridge Encyclopedia of India, Pakistan, Bangladesh, Sri Lanka, Nepal, Bhutan and the Maldives. (Ed., Francis Robinson.) Cambridge: Cambridge University Press, 1989.

Caplan, A. Patricia. *Priests and Cobblers: A Study of Social Change in a Hindu Village in Western Nepal.* San Francisco: Chandler, 1972.

Caplan, Lionel. *Land and Social Change in East Nepal.* Berkeley: University of California Press, 1970.

_____. "From Tribe to Peasant? The Limbus and the Nepalese State." *Journal of Peasant Studies* [London], 18, No. 2, January 1991, 305–21.

Chaube, S.K. (ed.). *The Himalayas: Profiles of Modernisation and Adaptation.* New Delhi: Sterling, 1985.

Conway, Dennis, and Nanda R. Shrestha. *Causes and Consequences of Rural-to-Rural Migration in Nepal.* Bloomington: Indiana University, 1981.

_____. "Urban Growth and Urbanization in Least-Developed Countries: The Experience of Nepal," *Asian Profile* [Hong Kong], 8, No. 5, October 1980, 477–94.

Dixit, Shanta B. "Hear No AIDS, See No AIDS, Speak No AIDS," *Himal* [Lalitpur, Nepal], 3, No. 3, 1990, 26–29.

The Encyclopedia of Eastern Philosophy and Religion. (Eds., Ingrid Fischer-Schreiber, Franz-Karl Ehrhard, Kurt Friedrichs, and Michael S. Diener.) *The Encyclopedia of Eastern Philosophy and Religion.* Boston: Shambhala, 1989.

Fisher, James F. "Education and Social Change in Nepal: An Anthropologist's Assessment," *Himalayan Research Bulletin,* 10, Nos. 2–3, 1990, 30–34.

――――. *Sherpas: Reflections on Change in Himalayan Nepal.* Berkeley: University of California Press, 1990.

Furer-Haimendorf, Christoph von. "Caste in the Multi-Ethnic Society of Nepal," *Contributions to Indian Sociology* [Paris], 4, April 1960, 12–32.

――――. *Himalayan Traders: Life in Highland Nepal.* London: Murray, 1975.

Gaige, Frederick H. *Regionalism and National Unity in Nepal.* Berkeley: University of California Press, 1975.

Gurung, Harka B. *Regional Patterns of Migration in Nepal.* (Papers of the East-West Population Institute, 0732–0531, No. 113.) Honolulu: East-West Center, September 1989.

Hagen, Toni, Friedrich Traugott Wahlen, and Walter Robert Corti. *Nepal: The Kingdom in the Himalayas.* (Rev., Ewald Osers; trans., Britta M. Charleston and Toni Hagen.) Chicago: Rand McNally, 1971.

Hitchcock, John T. *Magars of Banyan Hill.* New York: Holt, Rinehart & Winston, 1966.

Holmes, Dwight R. "Education Through Radio in Nepal: Changes Within and Beyond the Classroom," *Himalayan Research Bulletin,* 10, Nos. 2–3, 1990, 24–29.

Ives, J.D. "The Theory of Himalayan Environmental Degradation: Its Validity and Application Challenged by Recent Research," *Mountain Research and Development,* 7, No. 3, August 1987, 188–99.

Ives, Jack D., and Bruno Messerli. *The Himalayan Dilemma: Reconciling Development and Conservation.* New York: The United Nations University and Routledge, 1989.

Jha, Sasinath. *Conservation for Development in Nepal.* New Delhi: National Book Organization, 1990.

Joshi, Bhuwan Lal, and Leo E. Rose. *Democratic Innovations in Nepal: A Case Study of Political Acculturation.* Berkeley: University of California Press, 1966.

Kansakar, Vidya Bir Singh. *Effectiveness of Planned Resettlement Programme in Nepal.* Kathmandu: Centre for Economic Development and Administration, Tribhuvan University, 1979.

_____. *Population Projections for Nepal, 1970–2000*. Kathmandu: Centre for Economic Development and Administration, Tribhuvan University, May 1980.

Kaplan, Paul F., and Nanda R. Shrestha. "The Sukumbasi Movement in Nepal: The Fire from Below," *Journal of Contemporary Asia* [London], 12, No. 2, April–June 1982, 75–88.

Karan, Pradyumna P. *Nepal: A Cultural and Physical Geography*. Lexington: University of Kentucky Press, 1960.

Karan, Pradyumna P., and Shigeru Iijima. "Environmental Stress in the Himalaya," *Geographical Review*, 75, No. 1, January 1985, 71–92.

Karan, Pradyumna P., and William M. Jenkins, Jr. *The Himalayan Kingdoms: Bhutan, Sikkim and Nepal*. Princeton, New Jersey: Van Nostrand, 1963.

Karan, Pradyumna P., and Cotton Mather. "Tourism and Environment in the Mount Everest Region," *Geographical Review*, 75, No. 1, January 1985, 93–95.

Kasaju, P.K., B.D. Pande, and W.M. Matheson. "Nepal: System of Education." Pages 3498–3501 in Torsten Husen and T. Neville Postlethwaite (eds.), *The International Encyclopedia of Education: Research and Studies*, 6. Oxford: Pergamon Press, 1985.

Levine, Nancy E. "Women's Work and Infant Feeding: A Case from Rural Nepal," *Ethnology*, 27, No. 3, July 1988, 231–51.

McDougal, Charles. *Village and Household Economy in Far Western Nepal*. Kathmandu: Tribhuvan University Press, 1986.

Macfarlane, Alan. *Resources and Population: A Study of the Gurungs of Nepal*. (Cambridge Studies in Social Anthropology, No. 12.) Cambridge: Cambridge University Press, 1976.

Mahat, I.B.S., D.M. Griffin, and K.R. Shepherd. "Human Impact of Some Forests of the Middle Hills of Nepal 1: Forestry in the Context of the Traditional Resources of the State," *Mountain Research and Development*, 6, No. 3, August 1986, 223–32.

Mathema, Padma. *Primary Health Care in Nepal*. Kathmandu: Vijaya Ram Mathema, 1987.

Messerschmidt, Donald A. *The Gurungs of Nepal: Conflict and Change in a Village Society*. Warminster, Wiltshire, United Kingdom: Aris and Phillips, 1976.

Metz, John J. "Conservation Practices at an Upper Elevation Village of West Nepal," *Mountain Research and Development*, 80, No. 1, February 1990, 7–15.

_____. "Forest-Product Use in Upland Nepal," *Geographical Review*, 80, No. 3, July 1990, 279–87.

Mihaly, Eugene Bramer. *Foreign Aid and Politics in Nepal*. New York: Oxford University Press, 1965.

Negi, Sharad Singh. *A Handbook of the Himalaya.* New Delhi: Indus, 1990.

Nepal. Ministry of Health and World Health Organization. *Country Health Profile: Nepal.* Kathmandu: 1988.

_____. Ministry of Planning and Development. *Draft Outline of Five-Year Plan.* Kathmandu: United States Operations Mission, International Cooperation Administration, 1953.

_____. National Planning Commission. Secretariat. Central Bureau of Statistics. *Demographic Sample Survey, 1986–87.* (First Report.) Kathmandu: 1987.

_____. National Planning Commission. Secretariat. Central Bureau of Statistics. *National Sample Census of Agriculture.* Kathmandu: 1985.

_____. National Planning Commission. Secretariat. Central Bureau of Statistics. *Population Census, 1981.* Kathmandu: 1984.

_____. National Planning Commission. Secretariat. Central Bureau of Statistics. *Population Monograph of Nepal.* Kathmandu: 1987.

_____. National Planning Commission. Secretariat. Central Bureau of Statistics. *Statistical Pocket Book: Nepal, 1988,* Kathmandu: 1988.

_____. National Planning Commission. Secretariat. Central Bureau of Statistics. *Statistical Year Book of Nepal, 1989.* Kathmandu: 1989.

_____. National Planning Commission. Secretariat. Central Bureau of Statistics. *Statistical Year Book of Nepal, 1991.* Kathmandu: 1991.

Parker, Barbara. "Moral Economy, Political Economy, and the Culture of Entrepreneurship in Highland Nepal," *Ethnology,* 27, No. 2, 1988, 181–95.

Paudel, N.B. (comp.). *Nepal Resettlement Company: An Introduction.* Pulchowk, Lalitpur: Nepal Resettlement, 1989.

Poffenberger, Mark. *Patterns of Change in the Nepal Himalaya.* Delhi: Macmillan, 1980.

Rana, Pashupati Shumshere J.B., and Kamal P. Malla (eds.). *Nepal in Perspective.* Kathmandu: Centre for Economic Development and Administration, Tribhuvan University, 1973.

Regmi, Mahesh Chandra. *An Economic History of Nepal, 1846–1901.* Banaras, India: Nath, 1988.

_____. *Landownership in Nepal.* Berkeley: University of California Press, 1976.

_____. *The State and Economic Surplus: Production, Trade, and Resource Mobilization in Early 19th Century Nepal.* Banaras, India: Nath, 1984.

_____. *A Study in Nepali Economic History, 1768–1846.* New Delhi: Manjusri, 1971.

_____. *Thatched Huts and Stucco Palaces: Peasants and Landlords in 19th Century Nepal.* New Delhi: Vikas, 1978.

Rose, Leo E., and John T. Scholz. *Nepal: Profile of a Himalayan Kingdom.* Boulder, Colorado: Westview Press, 1980.

Sebaly, Kim P. "Nepal." Pages 904–10 in George Thomas Kurian (ed.), *World Education Encyclopedia,* 2. New York: Facts on File, 1988.

Seddon, David. *Nepal: A State of Poverty.* New Delhi: Vikas, 1987.

Seddon, David. (ed.), with Piers M. Blaikie and John Cameron. *Peasants and Workers in Nepal.* Warminster, Wiltshire, United Kingdom: Aris and Phillips, 1979.

Shaha, Rishikesh. *Modern Nepal: A Political History, 1769–1955.* (2 vols.) New Delhi: Manohar, 1990.

Sharma, Gopi Nath. "The Impact of Education During the Rana Period in Nepal," *Himalayan Research Bulletin,* 10, Nos. 2–3, 1990, 3–7.

Sharma, Pitamber. *Urbanization in Nepal.* (Papers of the East-West Population Institute, No. 110.) Honolulu: East-West Center, 1989.

Shreshtha, Badri Prasad. *An Introduction to Nepalese Economy.* Kathmandu: Ratna Pustak Bhandar, 1981.

Shreshtha, Badri Prasad, and S.C. Jain. *Regional Development in Nepal: An Exercise in Reality.* New Delhi: Development, 1978.

Shrestha, Bhumin. *Evaluation of Land Reform Programme in Nepal.* Kathmandu: Centre for Economic Development and Administration, Tribhuvan University, 1978.

Shrestha, Nanda R. "Frontier Settlement and Landlessness Among Hamalayan Migrants in Nepal Tarai," *Annals of the Association of American Geographers,* 79, No. 3, 1989, 370–89.

_____. "Human Relations and Primary Health Care Delivery in Rural Nepal: The Case of Deurali," *Professional Geographer,* 40, No. 2, May 1988, 202–13.

_____. *Landlessness and Migration in Nepal.* (Westview Special Studies on Social, Political, and Economic Development.) Boulder, Colorado: Westview Press, 1990.

_____. "The Political Economy of Economic Underdevelopment and External Migration in Nepal," *Political Geography Quarterly* [Sevenoaks, Kent, United Kingdom], 4, No. 4, 1985, 289–306.

_____. "A Preliminary Report on Population and Land Resources in Nepal," *Journal of Developing Areas,* 16, No. 2, January 1982, 197–212.

Shrestha, Nanda R., and Dennis Conway. "Issues in Population

Pressure, Land Resettlement, and Development: The Case of Nepal," *Studies in Comparative International Development,* 20, No. 1, Spring 1985, 55–82.

Sill, Michael, and John Kirkby. *The Atlas of Nepal in the Modern World.* London: Earthscan, 1991.

Stone, Linda. "Cultural Crossroads of Community Participation in Development: A Case from Nepal," *Human Organization,* 48, No. 3, Fall 1989, 206–13.

Tuker, Francis Ivan Simms. *Gorkha: The Story of the Gurkhas of Nepal.* London: Constable, 1957.

United States. Department of the Interior. Division of Geography. *Preliminary NIS Gazetteer: India, I: Bhutan, French India, Jammu and Kashmir, Nepal, Portuguese India, and India A-J.* Washington: April 1952.

_____. Department of State. Bureau of International Narcotics Matters. *International Narcotics Control Strategy Report.* Washington: March 1990.

_____. Department of State. Bureau of International Narcotics Matters. *International Narcotics Control Strategy Report.* Washington: March 1991.

Wood, Hugh B., and Knall, Bruno. "Educational Planning in Nepal and Its Economic Implications." (Draft Report of the UNESCO Commission to Nepal.) Kathmandu: May 1962.

World Bank. *Nepal: Policies for Improving Growth and Alleviating Poverty.* (Report No. 7418-NEP.) Washington: 1988.

_____. *Nepal: Policies for Improving Growth and Alleviating Poverty.* (Report No. 0253-2123.) Washington: 1989.

Worth, Robert M., and Narayan K. Shah, *Nepal Health Survey, 1965-66.* Honolulu: University of Hawaii Press, 1969.

Zaman, M.A. *Evaluation of Land Reform in Nepal, Based on the Work of M.A. Zaman, Land Reform Evaluation Adviser.* Kathmandu: Ministry of Land Reform, 1973.

Zurick, David. "Resource Needs and Land Stress in Rapti Zone, Nepal," *Professional Geographer,* 40, No. 4, November 1988, 428–43.

(Various issues of the following periodical were also used in the preparation of this chapter: *Nepal Press Digest* [Kathmandu], 1989-91.)

Chapter 3

Asia Yearbook, 1988. Hong Kong: Far Eastern Economic Review, 1988.

Asia Yearbook, 1991. Hong Kong: Far Eastern Economic Review, 1991.

Blaikie, Piers M., John Cameron, and David Seddon. *Nepal in Crisis: Growth and Stagnation at the Periphery.* New York: Oxford University Press, 1980.

Europa World Year Book, 1990, 2. London: Europa, 1990.

Far East and Australasia, 1990. London: Europa, 1990.

Gaige, Frederick H. *Regionalism and National Unity in Nepal.* Berkeley: University of California Press, 1975.

Graphics Rachana. *Nepal Road Network, 1985: Existing, under Construction, Planned, and Proposed.* Kathmandu: 1985.

Hay, Keith A.J. "Aid to South Asia in the 1980s," *Journal of Developing Societies* [Leiden, Netherlands], 7, Fasc. 2, July–October 1991, 83–92.

International Monetary Fund. *Financial Statistics, 1989.* Washington: 1989.

Joshi, Bhuwan Lal, and Leo E. Rose. *Democratic Innovations in Nepal: A Case Study of Political Acculturation.* Berkeley: University of California Press, 1966.

Khadka, Narayan. "The Political Economy of the Food Crisis in Nepal," *Asian Survey,* 25, No. 9, September 1985, 943–62.

Mihaly, Eugene Bramer. *Foreign Aid and Politics in Nepal.* New York: Oxford University Press, 1965.

Nepal. Ministry of Finance. *Current Economic Situation.* (Unofficial translation.) Kathmandu: May 25, 1990.

_____. Ministry of Finance. *Economic Survey, 1987–88.* Kathmandu: 1988.

_____. Ministry of Finance. *Economic Survey, 1989–90.* Kathmandu: 1990.

_____. Ministry of Finance. *Speech by Finance Minister.* Kathmandu: 1990.

_____. National Planning Commission. Secretariat. *Basic Principles of the Seventh Plan.* Kathmandu: 1984.

_____. National Planning Commission. Secretariat. Central Bureau of Statistics. *Statistical Pocket Book: Nepal, 1990.* Kathmandu: 1990.

_____. National Planning Commission. Secretariat. Central Bureau of Statistics. *Statistical Year Book of Nepal, 1991.* Kathmandu: 1991.

Nepal Rastra Bank. Research Department. *Main Economic Indicators.* Kathmandu: February–April 1991.

Nugent, Nicholas. "Nepal." Pages 135–37 in *The Asia & Pacific Review, 1990. The Economic and Business Report.* Saffron Walden, Essex, United Kingdom: World of Information, 1990.

Pant, Yadav Prasad. *Problems in Fiscal and Monetary Policy: A Case Study of Nepal.* London: Hurst, 1970.

Regmi, Mahesh Chandra. *An Economic History of Nepal, 1846-1901.* Banaras, India: Nath, 1988.

_____. *Land Tenure and Taxation in Nepal.* Kathmandu: Ratna Pustak Bhandar, 1978.

_____. *Readings in Nepal Economic History.* Banaras, India: Kishor Vidya Niketan, 1979.

_____. *The State and Economic Surplus: Production, Trade, and Resource Mobilization in Early 19th Century Nepal.* Banaras, India: Nath, 1984.

_____. *A Study in Nepali Economic History, 1768-1846.* New Delhi: Manjusri, 1971.

Rose, Leo E. *Nepal: Strategy for Survival.* Berkeley: University of California Press, 1971.

Shaha, Rishikesh. *Nepali Politics: Restrospect and Prospect.* Delhi: Oxford University Press, 1978.

Sharma, Pitamber. *Urbanization in Nepal.* (Papers of the East-West Population Institute, No. 110.) Honolulu: East-West Center, 1989.

Shreshtha, Badri Prasad. *The Economy of Nepal.* Bombay: Vora, 1967.

_____. *Nepalese Economy in Retrospect and Prospect.* Kathmandu: Himalayan Booksellers, 1990.

Shreshtha, Chandra M., and Konstadinos A. Mattas. "Economic Growth Through Development Planning: Evidence from Nepal," *Journal of Developing Societies* [Leiden, Netherlands], 6, Fasc. 2, July–October 1990, 229–40.

Shrestha, Babu Ram. *Managing External Assistance in Nepal.* Kathmandu: Jamuna Shrestha, 1990.

Statesman's Yearbook, 1990-1991. (Ed., John Paxton.) New York: St. Martin's Press, 1990.

United States. Central Intelligence Agency. *The World Factbook, 1990.* Washington: 1990.

_____. Department of Interior. Bureau of Mines. *Mineral Industries of the Far East and South Asia, 1988.* Washington: 1988.

_____. Department of State. *Background Notes: Nepal.* Washington: August 1990.

Uppal, Joginder S. *Economic Development in South Asia.* New York: St. Martin's Press, 1977.

Wallace, Michael B. "Forest Degradation in Nepal: Institutional Context and Policy Alternatives." (Research Report Series, No. 6.) Washington: United States Agency for International Development, March 1988.

World Bank. *Trends in Developing Economies, 1990.* Washington: October 1990.

———. *World Development Report, 1989.* New York: Oxford University Press, 1989.

———. *World Development Report, 1990.* New York: Oxford University Press, 1990.

World Radio TV Handbook, 1991, 45. (Ed., Andrew G. Sennitt.) Amsterdam: Billboard A.G., 1990.

Chapter 4

Agrawal, Hem Narayan. *The Administrative System of Nepal.* New Delhi: Vikas, 1976.

Amnesty International. *Nepal: A Pattern of Human Rights Violations.* London: 1987.

Asia Watch Committee, Human Rights Watch. *Human Rights Violations in Nepal.* New York: 1989.

Asia Yearbook, 1991. Hong Kong: Far Eastern Economic Review, 1991.

Banskota, N.P. "Nepal: Toward Regional Economic Cooperation in South Asia," *Asian Survey,* 21, No. 3, March 1981, 342–54.

Baraith, Roop Singh. *Transit Politics in South Asia: A Case Study of Nepal.* Jaipur, India: Aalekh, 1989.

Baral, L.S. "Nepal and Non-Alignment," *International Studies* [New Delhi], 20, Nos. 1–2, January–June 1981, 257–72.

Baral, Lok Raj. "Nepal 1978: Year of Hopes and Confessions," *Asian Survey,* 19, No. 2, February 1979, 198–204.

———. "Nepal in 1986: Problems of Political Management," *Asian Survey,* 27, No. 2, February 1987, 173–81.

———. "Nepal in 1987: Politics Without Power," *Asian Survey,* 28, No. 2, February 1988, 172–79.

———. *Opposition Politics in Nepal.* Columbia, Missouri: South Asia Books, 1978.

———. "Party-Like Institutions in 'Partyless' Polities: The GVNC in Nepal," *Asian Survey,* 16, No. 7, July 1976, 672–81.

Baxter, Craig, Yogendra K. Malik, Charles H. Kennedy, and Robert C. Oberst. *Government and Politics in South Asia.* Boulder, Colorado: Westview Press, 1987.

Chaturvedi, Shailendra Kumar. *Indo-Nepal Relations in Linkage Perspective.* Delhi: B.R. Publishing, 1990.

Chauhan, R.S. *The Political Development in Nepal 1950–70: Conflict Between Tradition and Modernity.* New Delhi: Associated, 1971.

Das, Rabindra K. *Nepal and Its Neighbors.* Banaras, India: Konark, 1986.

Dharamdasani, M.D. "Nepal: Political Development of a Mountain Kingdom," *China Report* [Delhi], 17, No. 3, May–June 1980, 35–43.

Forum for Protection of Human Rights. *FOPHUR & Pro-Democracy Movement.* Lalitpur, Nepal: 1990.

Fukui, Haruhiro (ed.). *Political Parties of Asia and the Pacific.* (The Greenwood Historical Encyclopedia of the World's Political Parties, 2. Laos—Western Samoa.) Westport, Connecticut: Greenwood Press, 1985.

Gaige, Frederick H. *Regionalism and National Unity in Nepal.* Berkeley: University of California Press, 1975.

Ghoble, T.R. *China-Nepal Relations and India.* New Delhi: Deep and Deep, 1986.

Heck, Douglas. "Nepal in 1980: The Year of the Referendum," *Asian Survey,* 21, No. 2, February 1981, 181–87.

Jayaraman, T.K., and O.L. Shrestha. "Some Trade Problems of Landlocked Nepal," *Asian Survey,* 16, No. 12, December 1976, 1113–23.

Jha, Shankar Kumar. *Indo-Nepal Relations.* New Delhi: Archives Books, 1989.

Joshi, Nanda Lau. *Evolution of Public Administration in Nepal.* Kathmandu: Centre for Economic Development and Administration, Tribhuvan University, 1973.

Khadka, Narayan. "Crisis in Nepal's Partyless Panchayat System: The Case for More Democracy," *Pacific Affairs* [Vancouver], 59, No. 3, Fall 1986, 429–54.

Khanal, Y.N. "Nepal in 1984: A Year of Complacence," *Asian Survey,* 25, No. 2, February 1985, 180–86.

Koirala, Niranjan. "Nepal in 1989: A Very Difficult Year," *Asian Survey,* 30, No. 2, February 1990, 136–43.

_____. "Nepal in 1990: End of an Era," *Asian Survey,* 31, No. 2, February 1991, 134–39.

Lohani, Prakashe. "Nepal 1975: Not a Normal Year," *Asian Survey,* 16, No. 2, February 1976, 140–45.

Mojumdar, Kanchanmoy. *Political Relations Between India and Nepal 1877–1923.* New Delhi: Munshiram Manoharlal, 1973.

Muni, S.D. *Foreign Policy of Nepal.* New Delhi: National, 1973.

Panday, Devendra Raj. "Nepal in 1981: Stagnation Amidst Change," *Asian Survey,* 22, No. 2, February 1982, 155–62.

Parmanand. *The Nepali Congress since Its Inception: A Critical Assessment.* Delhi: B.R. Publishing, 1982.

Rahul, Ram. "Making of Modern Nepal," *International Studies,* 16, No. 1, January–March 1977, 1–15.

Ramakant. *Nepal-China and India.* New Delhi: Abhinav, 1976.

Rose, Leo E. *Nepal: Strategy for Survival.* Berkeley: University of California Press, 1971.

Rose, Leo E., and Margaret W. Fisher. *The Politics of Nepal: Persistence and Change in an Asian Monarchy.* Ithaca: Cornell University Press, 1970.

Rose, Leo E., and John T. Scholz. *Nepal: Profile of a Himalayan Kingdom.* Boulder, Colorado: Westview Press, 1980.

Scholz, John T. "Nepal in 1977: Political Discipline or Human Rights," *Asian Survey,* 18, No. 2, February 1978, 135–41.

_____. "Nepal in 1976: Problems with India Threaten Birendra's New Order," *Asian Survey,* 17, No. 2, February 1977, 201–7.

Shah, Sukhdev. "Nepal's Economic Development: Problems and Prospects," *Asian Survey,* 28, No. 9, September 1988, 945–57.

Shaha, Rishikesh. "Democracy's Second Chance in Nepal," *Commonwealth Journal of International Affairs,* No. 277, January 1980, 65–73.

_____. *Essays in the Practice of Government in Nepal.* New Delhi: Manohar, 1982.

_____. *Nepali Politics: Retrospect and Prospect.* Delhi: Oxford University Press, 1978.

_____. "The 1986 Elections in Nepal: Implications for the Future," *International Studies,* 26, No. 1, January–March 1989, 1–14.

_____. *Politics in Nepal, 1980–1990: Referendum, Stalemate, and Triumph of People Power.* New Delhi: Manohar, 1990.

_____. *Three Decades and Two Kings (1960–90): Eclipse of Nepal's Partyless Monarchic Rule.* New Delhi: Sterling, 1990.

Sharma, Kul Shekhar. "Nepal in 1983: Another Year of Confusion and Lack of Direction," *Asian Survey,* 24, No. 2, February 1984, 257–62.

Sharma, Kunjar M. "Nepal." In Albert P. Blaustein and Gisbert H. Flanz (eds.). *Constitutions of the Countries of the World,* 16. Dobbs Ferry, New York: Oceana, June 1979.

Sharma, Kunjar M., and Mark J. Plotkin, "Nepal." In Albert P. Blaustein and Gisbert H. Flanz (eds.). *Constitutions of the Countries of the World,* 12. Dobbs Ferry, New York: Oceana, February 1985.

Shrestha, Mangal Krishna. *Public Administration in Nepal.* Kathmandu: Educational Enterprise, 1975.

Tiwari, Chitra Krishna. "Domestic Determinants of Foreign Policy in South Asia: The Case of Nepal," *Journal of South Asian and Middle Eastern Studies,* 10, No. 3, Spring 1987, 62–77.

Tyagi, Sushila. *Indo-Nepalese Relations, 1858–1914.* Delhi: D.K. Publishing, 1974.

United States. Congress. 99th, 1st Session. Senate. Committee on Foreign Relations. *South Asia and U.S. Interests: A Report to the Committee on Foreign Relations, United States Senate.* Washington: GPO, 1985.

Uprety, Tulsi P. "Nepal in 1982: Panchayat Leadership in Crisis," *Asian Survey,* 23, No. 2, February 1983, 143–49.

Yearbook on International Communist Affairs. (Eds., Richard F. Staar, Milorad M. Drachkovitch, and Lewis H. Gann.) Stanford, California: Hoover Institution, 1991.

" 'Zone of Peace': Nepal's Quest for Identity," *China Report* [Delhi], 15, No. 5, September–October 1979, 13–19.

(Various issues of the following publications also were used in the preparation of this chapter: *Asian Recorder* [New Delhi], 1986–91; *Asian Survey,* 1989–91; *JPRS Report: Near East and South Asia,* 1986–91; *New York Times,* 1989–91; *Rising Nepal* [Kathmandu], 1989–91; and *Washington Post,* 1989–91.)

Chapter 5

Adshead, Robin. *Gurkha: The Legendary Solider.* Sinagpore: Asia Pacific Press, 1970.

Ahmar, Moonis. *Superpower Rivalry in the Indian Ocean since the Withdrawal of Great Britain.* Karachi: Area Study Centre for Europe, University of Karachi, 1986.

Amnesty International. *Nepal: A Pattern of Human Rights Violations.* London: 1987.

Baral, Lok Raj. *Nepal's Politics of Referendum: A Study of Groups, Personalities, and Trends.* New Delhi: Vikas, 1983.

Bhasin, A.S. (ed.). *Documents on Nepal's Relations with India and China, 1949-66.* Bombay: Academic Books, 1970.

Bishop, Edward. *Better to Die: The Story of the Gurkhas.* London: New English Library, 1976.

Caplan, Lionel. " 'Bravest of the Brave': Representations of 'The Gurkha' in British Military Writings," *Modern Asian Studies* [London], 25, No. 3, July 1991, 571-97.

Chant, Christopher. *Gurkha: The Illustrated History of an Elite Fighting Force.* Poole, Dorset, United Kingdom: Blandford, 1985.

Cohen, Stephen P. *The Indian Army: Its Contribution to the Development of a Nation.* Berkeley: University of California Press, 1971.

Cross, J.P. *In Gurkha Company: The British Army Gurkhas, 1948 to the Present.* London: Arms and Armour, 1986.

Enloe, Cynthia H. *Ethnic Soldiers: State Security in Divided Societies.* Harmondsworth, United Kingdom: Penguin, 1980.

Farwell, Byron. *The Gurkhas.* New York: Norton, 1984.

Forum for Protection of Human Rights. *FOPHUR & Pro-Democracy Movement.* Lalitpur, Nepal: 1990.

Harrison, Selig S., and K. Subrahmanyam (eds.). *Superpower Rivalry in the Indian Ocean.* New York: Oxford University Press, 1989.

Heitzman, James, and Robert L. Worden (eds.). *Bangladesh: A Country Study.* Washington: GPO, 1989.

Koirala, Niranjan. "Nepal in 1989: A Very Difficult Year," *Asian Survey,* 30, No. 2, February 1990, 136–43.

_____. "Nepal in 1990: End of an Era," *Asian Survey,* 31, No. 2, February 1991, 134–39.

Leonard, R.G. *Nepal and the Gurkhas.* London: Her Majesty's Stationery Office, 1965.

Masters, John. *Bugles and a Tiger: A Volume of Autobiography.* New York: Viking Press, 1956.

The Military Balance, 1988–1989. London: International Institute for Strategic Studies, 1988.

The Military Balance, 1989–1990. London: International Institute for Strategic Studies, 1989.

The Military Balance, 1990–1991. London: International Institute for Strategic Studies, 1990.

Mojumdar, Kanchanmoy. *Anglo-Nepalese Relations in the Nineteenth Century.* Calcutta: Firma K.L. Mukhopadhyay, 1973.

Pemble, John. *The Invasion of Nepal: John Company at War.* Oxford: Oxford University Press, 1971.

Proudfoot, C.L. *Flash of the Khukri: History of the 3rd Gorkha Rifles, 1947 to 1980.* New Delhi: Vision Books, 1984.

Rose, Leo E. *Nepal: Strategy for Survival.* Berkeley: University of California Press, 1971.

Rose, Leo E., and Margaret W. Fisher. *The Politics of Nepal: Persistence and Change in an Asian Monarchy.* Ithaca: Cornell University Press, 1970.

Sheil-Small, D. *Green Shadows: A Gurkha Story.* London: Kimber, 1982.

Tuker, Francis Ivan Simms. *Gorkha: The Story of the Gurkhas of Nepal.* London: Constable, 1957.

United States. Arms Control and Disarmament Agency. *World Military Expenditures and Arms Transfers, 1989.* Washington: GPO, October 1990.

_____. Arms Control and Disarmament Agency. *World Military Expenditures and Arms Transfers, 1990.* Washington: GPO, November 1991.

_____. Central Intelligence Agency. Directorate of Intelligence. *Handbook of Economic Statistics.* Washington: GPO, 1989.

_____. Central Intelligence Agency. Directorate of Intelligence. *Handbook of Economic Statistics.* Washington: GPO, 1990.

_____. Department of State. *Country Reports on Human Rights Practices for 1990.* (Report submitted to United States Congress, 102d, 1st Session, Senate, Committee on Foreign Relations, and House of Representatives, Committee on Foreign Affairs.) Washington: GPO, February 1991.

Woodward, David. *Armies of the World, 1854-1914.* New York: Putnam, 1978.

Yearbook on International Communist Affairs. (Eds., Richard F. Staar, Milorad M. Drachkovitch, and Lewis H. Gann.) Stanford, California: Hoover Institution, 1991.

(Various issues of the following publications also were used in the preparation of this chapter: *Asian Defence Journal* [Kuala Lumpur], 1985-91; *Asian Survey,* 1985-91; *Far Eastern Economic Review* [Hong Kong], 1985-91; *Independent* [Kathmandu], 1989-91; *Jane's Defence Weekly* [London], 1989-91; and *Rising Nepal* [Kathmandu], 1989-91.)

Chapter 6

Adams, Barbara S. *Traditional Bhutanese Textiles.* Bangkok: White Orchard Press, 1984.

Adams, Jonathan. "Bhutan: Right From the Start," *World Wildlife Fund Letter,* No. 6, 1989, 1-8.

"All the King's Men," *Asiaweek* [Hong Kong], 16, No. 46, November 16, 1990, 25.

Amnesty International Report, 1991. New York: Amnesty International, 1991.

Aris, Michael. *Bhutan: The Early History of a Himalayan Kingdom.* Warminister, Wiltshire, United Kingdom: Aris and Phillips, 1979.

Asia Yearbook, 1991. Hong Kong: Far Eastern Economic Review, 1990.

Avtar, R. "Bhutan—A Geopolitical Survey." Pages 193-200 in Gautam Sharma and K.S. Nagar (eds.), *India's Northern Security: Including China, Nepal, and Bhutan.* New Delhi: Reliance, 1986.

Awasthi, J.D. *Agricultural Development of Himalayas with Special Reference to Bhutan.* (Centre for Himalayan Studies, Special Lectures, No. 4.) Raja Rammohunpur, India: University of North Bengal, 1984.

"Bank Loans Total $750 Million in the Third Quarter." *Asian Development Bank Quarterly Review* [Manila], QR–4–90, October 1990, 14.

Bank of Bhutan. *Annual Report* (annuals 1970–84). Thimphu: 1970–84.

Baraith, Roop Singh. *Transit Politics in South Asia: A Case Study of Nepal.* Jaipur, India: Aalekh, 1989.

Bhattacharya, S.S. "Planning Strategy in Bhutan." Pages 210–28 in S.K. Chaube (ed.), *The Himalayas: Profiles of Modernization and Adaptation.* New Delhi: Sterling, 1985.

Bhattacharyya, Anima. "Human Ecology in Bhutan and Modernizing Trends." Pages 17–25 in S.K. Chaube (ed.), *The Himalayas: Profiles of Modernization and Adaptation.* New Delhi: Sterling, 1985.

Bhattacharyya, Dilip. *Bhutan: The Himalayan Paradise.* New Delhi: Oxford and IBH, 1975.

Bhutan. Department of Education. *Dzongkha Reader.* (4 vols.) Thimphu: Royal Government of Bhutan Press, 1979.

_____. Department of Education. Text Book Division. *Dzongkha Dictionary.* Thimphu: 1986.

_____. Department of Trade and Commerce. Trade Information Centre. *Bhutan, Trade and Industry Aspects: A Bibliography.* Thimphu: 1984.

_____. Ministry for Communications and Tourism. *Visitors' Guide to the Kingdom of Bhutan.* Thimpu: July 1983.

_____. Planning Commission. *Royal Government of Bhutan Fifth Plan, 1981–1987: Main Document.* Thimphu: 1982.

_____. Planning Commission. *Sixth Five-Year Plan, 1987–92.* Thimphu: 1987.

_____. Planning Commission. Central Statistical Office. *Statistical Yearbook of Bhutan, 1989.* Thimphu: May 1990.

_____. Sherubtse College. Workshop on Environmental Studies. *Bhutan and Its Natural Resources.* New Delhi: Vikas, 1991.

Bhutan Tourism Corporation. *Bhutan.* Thimpu: 1986.

Bhutan and United Nations Development Programme. *Report of the Workshop on the Evaluation and Planning of Human Resources Development, Thimphu, May 27–June 2, 1985.* Thimphu: 1985.

"Bhutan: Democracy Calls," *Asiaweek* [Hong Kong], 16, No. 37, September 14, 1990, 38.

"Bhutan Plans to Double Tourist Visas," *New York Times,* January 6, 1991, 3.

Bladen, W.A. "Patterns of Relationship Between Land and Resources and Population in Bhutan," *Asian Profile* [Hong Kong], 11, No. 4, August 1983, 411–18.

Bunting, Bruce W. "Bhutan: Kingdom in the Clouds," *National Geographic*, 179, No. 5, May 1991, 79–101.

The Cambridge Encyclopedia of India, Pakistan, Bangladesh, Sri Lanka, Nepal, Bhutan and the Maldives. (Ed., Francis Robinson.) Cambridge: Cambridge University Press, 1989.

Chakravarti, Balaram. *A Cultural History of Bhutan.* Chittaranjan, West Bengal, India: Hilltop, 1979.

_____. "The Life Style and Customs of the Bhutanese People." Pages 41–48 in S.M. Dubey, P.K. Bordoloi, and B.N. Borthakur (eds.), *Family, Marriage, and Social Change on the Indian Fringe.* New Delhi: Cosmo, 1980.

Chaube, S.K. (ed.). *The Himalayas: Profiles of Modernization and Adaptation.* New Delhi: Sterling, 1985.

Clad, James. "The King Speaks Out: Monarch Stresses Dialogue to Resolve Conflict," *Far Eastern Economic Review* [Hong Kong], 150, No. 51, December 20, 1990, 26.

_____. "The Kukri's Edge: Nepali Influx Threatens the Hermit Kingdom," *Far Eastern Economic Review* [Hong Kong], 150, No. 51, December 20, 1990, 22–26.

Das, B.S. "Bhutan." Pages 299–308 in U.S. Bajpai (ed.), *India and Its Neighborhood.* New Delhi: Lancer International in association with India International Centre, 1986.

_____. "Economic Development and Social Changes in Bhutan." Pages 82–99 in Urmila Phadnis, S.D. Muni, and Kalim Bahadur (eds.), *Domestic Conflicts in South Asia.* New Delhi: South Asian Publishers, 1986.

Das, Nirmala. *The Dragon Country: The General History of Bhutan.* Bombay: Orient Longman, 1974.

Davies, Derek. "Coups, Kings, and Castles in the Sky," *Far Eastern Economic Review* [Hong Kong], 84, No. 23, June 10, 1974, 26–27.

Dhakal, Deo Narayan S. "Hydropower Development in Bhutan: An Analytical Framework for Evaluating Prospects and Strategy." (Ph.D. dissertation.) Colorado School of Mines: 1990, DAI 51/03a.

Dogra, Ramesh C. (comp.). *Bhutan.* (World Bibliographical Series, No. 116.) Santa Barbara, California: Clio, 1991.

Dorji, Chenkhap. "Forestry in Himalayan Bhutan," *Unasylva* [Rome], 38, 1, 1986 (151), 46–51.

Dorji, Dasho Rigzon. *A Brief Religious, Cultural, and Secular History of Bhutan.* New York: Asia Society Galleries, 1990.

Dorji, Rigzin. *Forms of Address in Bhutan.* New Delhi: Royal Bhutan Mission, 1976.

Dowman, Keith, and Sonam Paljor (trans.). *The Divine Madman: The Sublime Life and Songs of Drukpa Kunley.* London: Rider, 1980.

Drukpa, Jamba Tsheten. "The Colombo Plan and Bhutan," *Druk Losel* [Thimphu], 2, Nos. 2-3, August-November 1980, 4-8.

------. "Pisciculture in Bhutan," *Druk Losel* [Thimphu], 2, No. 4, February 1981 and 3, No. 1, May 1981, 12-13.

Dutt, Srikant. "Bhutan's International Position," *International Studies* [Delhi], 20, Nos. 3-4, July-December 1981, 601-23.

------. "Scholarship on Bhutan," *China Report* [Delhi], 17, No. 5, September-October 1981, 58-62.

Elahi, Mahmood-i. "From Confrontation to Cooperation: Emerging Regionalism in South Asia," *Asian Profile* [Hong Kong], 14, No. 6, December 1986, 541-56.

Encyclopedia of Asian History (4 vols.). (Ed., Ainslee T. Embree.) New York: Scribner's, 1988.

The Encyclopedia of Eastern Philosophy and Religion. (Eds., Ingrid Fischer-Schreiber, Frans-Karl Ehrhard, Kurt Friedrichs, and Michael S. Diener.) Boston: Shambhala, 1989.

Europa World Year Book, 1990. London: Europa, 1990.

The Far East and Australasia, 1990. (21st. ed.) London: Europa, 1989.

Fischer, Fritz. *Bhutan: The Importance of the Forests for a Continuous Development of Human Ecology in High Mountain Conditions.* (Trans., A. Huber.) Zurich: Forest Consult, 1976.

Frey, Kathleen. "Studies in Bhutanese History Dealing with the Structural Organization of the Bhutanese Theocracy," *Tibetan Review* [New Delhi], 18, No. 5, May 1983, 15-22.

Gansser, Augusto. *Geology of the Bhutan Himalayas.* Basel, Switzerland: Birkhauser Verlag, 1983.

Ghosh, Udipto. *Bhutan's Economic Development: Objects, Strategies and Problems.* (Centre for Himalayan Studies, Special Lectures, No. 3.) Raja Rammohunpur, India: University of North Bengal, 1984.

Gupta, Shantiswarup. *British Relations with Bhutan.* Jaipur, India: Panchsheel Prakashan, 1974.

Gurney, Gene. *Kingdoms of Asia, the Middle East, and Africa: An Illustrated Encyclopedia of Ruling Monarchs from Ancient Times to the Present.* New York: Crown, 1986.

Hasrat, Bikrama Jit. *History of Bhutan: Land of the Peaceful Dragon.* Thimphu: Education Department, Royal Government of Bhutan, 1980.

"India's Aid to Bhutan," *South Asian Studies* [Jaipur, India], 18, No. 1, January-June 1983, 75-84.

India. Botanical Survey of India. *Records of the Botanical Survey of India: Materials for the Flora of Bhutan,* 20, No. 2. Calcutta: 1973.

International Labour Organisation. *Bhutan: Project Findings and Recommendations: Royal Bhutan Polytechnic, Deothang.* (BHU/72/003.)

Geneva: United Nations Development Programme and International Labour Organisation, 1980.

International Monetary Fund. *Annual Report on Exchange Arrangements and Exchange Restrictions, 1990.* Washington: 1990.

Janus. "Bhutan in the Bahamas!" *Philatelic Magazine* [London], 75, No. 3 (1344), February 3, 1967, 88, 103.

Javed, Musarrat (ed.). *Bhutan.* (Country Information Series, No. 7.) Lahore: Centre for South Asian Studies, University of the Punjab, 1981.

Joshi, S.C. *Forestry Handbook of Bhutan.* Dehra Dun, India: International Book Distributors, 1986.

Karan, Pradyumna P. *Bhutan: A Physical and Cultural Geography.* Lexington: University of Kentucky Press, 1967.

_____. *Bhutan: Development Amid Environmental and Cultural Preservation.* (Monumenta Serindica, No. 17.) Tokyo: Institute for the Study of Languages and Cultures of Asia and Africa, Tokyo University of Foreign Studies, 1987.

Katwal, D.N. "Postal Services in the Country," *Druk Losel* [Thimphu], 1, No. 1, May 1979, 27–29.

Khalid, Zulfikar A. "Bhutan—The Dragon Kingdom," *Asian Defence Journal* [Kuala Lumpur], December 1982, 30–31.

"Kingdom of Bhutan," *Current World Leaders,* 33, No. 1, February 1990, 16.

"Kingdom of Bhutan," *Current World Leaders,* 34, No. 1, February 1991, 17–18.

Kohli, Manorama. "Bhutan's Strategic Environment: Changing Perceptions." *India Quarterly* [New Delhi], 42, No. 1, January–March 1986, 142–53.

_____. "Chinese Interest in Bhutan: Evolution of the British Indian Perspective," *China Report* [Delhi], 19, No. 4, July–August 1983, 37–45.

_____. "Dragon Kingdom's Urge for an International Role." *India Quarterly* [New Delhi], 37, No. 1, January–March 1981, 228–40.

_____. *India and Bhutan: A Study in Interrelations, 1772–1910.* New Delhi: Munshiram Manoharlal, 1982.

_____. "Portrayal of Bhutan in the British Himalayan Policy—Curzon Years." Pages 375–87 in N.R. Ray (ed.), *Himalaya Frontier in Historical Perspective.* Calcutta: Institute of Historical Studies, 1986.

Kurian, George Thomas. *Encyclopedia of the Third World,* 1. New York: Facts On File, 1987.

Labh, Kapileshwar. "The Himalaya Frontier: A Case Study of the Bhutanese Part of the Frontier." Pages 388–99 in N.R. Ray (ed.), *Himalaya Frontier in Historical Perspective.* Calcutta: Institute of Historical Studies, 1986.

————. "The Himalayan Kingdom of Bhutan: Issues and Trends." Pages 138–49 in M.D. Dharmadasani (ed.), *Contemporary South Asia.* Banaras, India: Shalimar, 1985.

————. *India and Bhutan.* (Studies in Asian History and Politics.) Delhi: Sindhu, 1974.

————. "Monarchical System of Bhutan: Challenges in Modernization." Pages 182–94 in Urmila Phadnis, S.D. Muni, and Kalim Bahadur (eds.), *Domestic Conflicts in South Asia.* New Delhi: South Asian, 1986.

Lamitare, Devi Bhakat. *Murder of Democracy in Himalayan Kingdom.* New Delhi: Amarko, 1978.

Lopeln Nado. "Buddhism in Bhutan." Pages 348–49 in P.N. Chopra and Tokan Sumi (eds.), *Contribution of Buddhism to World Civilization and Culture.* New Delhi: Chand, 1983.

Mehra, G.N. *Bhutan: Land of the Peaceful Dragon.* New Delhi: Vikas, 1974.

Misquitta, Michelle. "Bhutan." Pages 46–47 in World of Information (ed.), *Asia and Pacific Review: 1990.* Saffron Walden, Essex, United Kingdom: World of Information, 1990.

Misra, H.N. *Bhutan: Problems and Policies.* New Delhi: Heritage, 1988.

Misra, R.C. "Institutional Achievements and the Process of Nation-Building in Bhutan." Pages 185–95 in S.K. Chaube (ed.), *The Himalayas: Profiles of Modernization and Adaptation.* New Delhi: Sterling, 1985.

Musée d'ethnographie. *Collection du Bhoutan, Catalogue.* Neuchatel, Switzerland: 1982.

Nado, Lopon. "The Development of Language in a Buddhist Kingdom," *Druk Losel* [Thimphu], 4, No. 2, August 1982, 4–8.

Naidu, A.G. "Bhutan Looks Outwards: Its Search for Identity," *Indian Journal of Political Science* [Calcutta], 47, No. 4, October–December 1986, 533–45.

Negi, Sharad Singh. *Forest Types of India, Nepal, and Bhutan.* Delhi: Periodical Expert Book Agency, 1989.

————. *A Handbook of the Himalaya.* New Delhi: Indus, 1990.

Nepal. National Planning Commission. Secretariat. Central Bureau of Statistics. *Statistical Pocket Book: Nepal, 1988.* Kathmandu: 1988.

Norbu, Thinley. *Account of the Great Chaitya of Thimbu.* Thimphu: 1974.

Official Airlines Guide. (Worldwide ed.) Oakbrook, Illinois: September 1990.

Olschak, Blanche Christin. *The Dragon Kingdom: Images of Bhutan.* (Trans., Michael H. Kohn.) Boston: Shambhala, 1988.

Pemala, Lonpon. "A Short History of Buddhism in Bhutan," *Druk Losel* [Thimphu], 6, No. 1, May 1984, 5–10.

Pemberton, Robert B. *Report on Bootan.* (Indian Studies: Past and Present.) Calcutta: Bengal Military Orphan Press, 1839. Reprint. Calcutta: K.L. Mukhopadhyaya, 1961.

"Portfolio: On the Road," *Life,* 11, No. 3, March 1988, 86–95.

Rahul, Ram. *Royal Bhutan.* New Delhi: ABC, 1983.

Rennie, David Field. *Bhotan and the Story of the Dooar War.* London: John Murray, 1866.

Rinchhen, N. "Bhutan: System of Education." Pages 479–81 in Torsten Husen and T. Neville Postlethwaite (eds.), *The International Encyclopedia of Education: Research and Studies,* 1. Oxford: Pergamon Press, 1985.

_____. "The Last Shangri La," *History Today* [London], 36, December 1986, 7–8.

Rose, Leo E. *The Politics of Bhutan.* Ithaca: Cornell University Press, 1977.

"Royal Bhutan Police," *Druk Losel* [Thimphu], 1, No. 1, May 1979, 20.

Roychoudhury, Tapash K. "Indian's Settlement in Bhutan." Pages 125–35 in I.J. Bahadur Singh (ed.), *Indians in South Asia.* New Delhi: Sterling, 1984.

Rustomji, Nari. *Bhutan: The Dragon Kingdom in Crisis.* Delhi: Oxford University Press, 1978.

Samarasinghe, S.W.R. de A. "The Bhutanese Economy in Transition," *Asian Survey,* 30, No. 6, June 1990, 560–75.

Saran, Hari. "Bhutan—Historical Survey." Pages 201–16 in Gautam Sharma and K.S. Nagar (eds.), *India's Northern Security: Including China, Nepal, and Bhutan.* New Delhi: Reliance, 1986.

Shah, Sukhdev. "Developing Bhutan's Economy: Limited Options, Sensible Choices," *Asian Survey,* 29, No. 9, August 1989, 816–31.

Sharma, Gautam, and K.S. Nagar (eds.). *India's Northern Security: Including China, Nepal and Bhutan.* New Delhi: Reliance, 1986.

Shaw, Brian C. "Bhutan." Pages 250–63 in *The Far East and Australasia, 1990.* (21st ed.) London: Europa, 1989.

Shaw, Brian C., and Leo E. Rose. "Bhutan." In Albert P. Blaustein and Gisbert H. Flanz (eds.), *Constitutions of the Countries of the World,* 2. Dobbs Ferry, New York: Oceana, June 1989.

Shaw, Felicity M. "The National Library of Bhutan: Preserving the Nation's Heritage," *HKLA Journal* [Hong Kong], No. 9, 1985, 39–58.

Singh, Amar Kaur Jasbir. *A Guide to Source Materials in the India Office Library and Records for the History of Tibet, Sikkim, and Bhutan, 1765-1950.* London: British Library, 1988.

_____. *Himalayan Triangle: A Historical Survey of British India's Relations with Tibet, Sikkim, and Bhutan, 1765-1950.* London: British Library, 1988.

Singh, Kedar Man. "Bhutan: Distant Thunder, Growing Unrest Among Nepalese Community," *Far Eastern Economic Review* [Hong Kong], 150, No. 41, October 11, 1990, 25.

Singh, Laxman. *The Changing Bhutan.* New Delhi: Jain, 1974.

Singh, Nagendra. *Bhutan: A Kingdom in the Himalayas. A Study of the Land, Its People, and Their Government.* New Delhi: S. Chand, 1985.

Sinha, A.C. *Bhutan: Ethnic Indentity and National Dilemma.* (Sociological Publications in Honour of K. Ishwaran Series, No. 10.) New Delhi: Reliance, 1991.

Statesman's Yearbook, 1990-91. (Ed., John Paxton.) New York: St. Martin's Press, 1990.

Strydonck, Guy van. *Bhutan: A Kingdom of the Eastern Himalayas.* (Trans., Ian Noble.) Boston: Shambhala, 1985.

Surdam, Wayne (ed.). *Bibliography of Asian Studies, 1983.* Ann Arbor, Michigan: Association for Asian Studies, 1988.

_____. *Bibliography of Asian Studies, 1984.* Ann Arbor, Michigan: Association for Asian Studies, 1989.

_____. *Bibliography of Asian Studies, 1985.* Ann Arbor, Michigan: Association for Asian Studies, 1990.

_____. *Bibliography of Asian Studies, 1986.* Ann Arbor, Michigan: Association for Asian Studies, 1991.

Thapar, O.D. (ed.). *Seminar on Science, Technology, and Society.* (Proceedings, February 25-27, 1986.) Thimphu: Directorate of Science and Technology, Royal Government of Bhutan, 1986.

"The Disinherited: A Dossier on the Thirty-one Least Developed Countries," *The UNESCO Courier* [Paris], 34, October 1981, 15-27.

Thinley, Jigme. "The Role of the DYT," *Druk Losel* [Thimphu], 4, No. 2, August 1982, 17-18.

Tobgeyl, Kunzang, and Mani Dorji. *280 Folk Songs of Bhutan.* Thimphu: Department of Education, Royal Government of Bhutan, 1985.

Yearbook of International Organizations, 1990-91, 2: Countries. (Ed., Union of International Associations.) Munich: K.G. Sauer, 1990.

United Nations. Department of International Economic and Social Affairs. Statistical Office. *1987 Statistical Yearbook.* New York: 1990.

_____. Department of International Economic and Social Affairs. *World Population at the Turn of the Century.* (Population Studies, No. 111, SESSER. A/111.) New York: 1989.

_____. Department of International Economic and Social Affairs. *World Population Monitoring 1989: Special Report: The Population Situation in the Least Developed Countries.* (Population Studies, No. 113, SESSER. A/113.) New York: 1990.

United Nations Development Programme. Secretariat. *Report on the Round Table Conference for Bhutan Held in Geneva, April 24, 1986.* New York: June 1986.

_____. *Bhutan-United Nations Development Programme (UNDP): A Profile of Technical Co-operation.* Thimphu: Department of Information and Broadcasting, August 1985.

_____. *Development Co-operation: Bhutan, 1988 Report.* Thimphu: August 1989.

_____. *Development Co-operation: Bhutan, 1989 Report.* Thimphu: September 1990.

United States. Bureau of Mines. Division of International Minerals. *Mineral Industries of the Far East and South Asia.* Washington, 1988.

_____. Central Intelligence Agency. *The World Fact Book, 1991.* Washington: 1991.

_____. Central Intelligence Agency. Directorate of Intelligence. *Reference Aid: Chiefs of State and Cabinet Members of Foreign Governments.* (LDA CS 91-002.) Washington: March–April 1991.

_____. Congress, 99th, 1st Session. Senate. Committee on Foreign Relations. *South Asia and U.S. Interests.* Washington: GPO, 1985.

_____. Congress, 100th, 2d Session. House of Representatives. Committee on Foreign Affairs. Subcommittee on Human Rights and International Organizations and Subcommittee on Asian and Pacific Affairs. *Human Rights in South Asia.* (Hearings, July 18, 1990.) Washington: GPO, 1991.

_____. Department of the Interior. Division of Geography. *Preliminary NIS Gazetteer: India, I. Bhutan, French India, Jammu and Kashmir, Nepal, Portuguese India, and India A-J.* Washington: April 1952.

_____. Department of State. Bureau of Public Affairs. *Background Notes: Bhutan.* (Background Notes Series, No. 8334.) Washington: November 1987.

_____. Department of State. *Country Reports on Human Rights Practices for 1989.* (Report submitted to United States Congress, 101st, 2d Session. House of Representatives, Committee on Foreign

Affairs, and Senate, Committee on Foreign Relations.) Washington: GPO, February 1990.

Upadhyaya, G.S. "Social Change in Bhutan." *Druk Losel* [Thimphu], 1, No. 2, August 1979, 26-27.

Vas, E.A. *The Dragon Kingdom: Journeys Through Bhutan.* New Delhi: Lancer International, 1986.

Verma, Ravi. *India's Role in the Emergence of Contemporary Bhutan.* Delhi: Capital, 1988.

Weintraub, Richard M. "Bhutan's King to Marry 4 Sisters," *Washington Post,* October 31, 1988, A14.

World Bank. *Bhutan: Development in a Himalayan Kingdom.* (A World Bank Country Study.) Washington: 1984.

———. *Bhutan: Development Planning in a Unique Environment.* (A World Bank Country Study.) Washington: 1989.

World Radio TV Handbook, 1991, 45. (Ed., Andrew G. Sennitt.) Amsterdam: Billboard A.G., 1990.

World Wildlife Fund. "Bhutan Fact Sheet." Washington: March 1991, 2 pp.

———. "Bhutan, WWF, UNDP Endowment Trust Fund for Environmental Conservation." March 6, 1991, 3 pp.

Young, Lincoln J. "Agricultural Changes in Bhutan: Some Environmental Questions," *Geographical Journal* [London], 157, No. 2, July 1991, 172-78.

(Various issues of the following publications also were used in the preparation of this chapter: Foreign Broadcast Information Service, *Daily Report: Near East and South Asia,* 1990-91; International Monetary Fund, *International Financial Statistics,* 1990-91; and *Kuensel* [Thimphu], 1975-90.)

Glossary

Asian Development Bank—Established in 1966, the Asian Development Bank assists developing member countries in economic development and promotes growth and cooperation. Membership includes both developed countries and developing countries in Asia, and developed countries in the West. Nepal joined the bank in 1966, Bhutan in 1982. The bank is headquartered in Manila.

birta—Nepalese tax-free land tenure granted by the government primarily as a pension or as a reward to political supporters and family members, important especially during the Rana period; abolished 1959.

Colombo Plan for Cooperative, Economic, and Social Development in Asia and the Pacific (Colombo Plan)—Founded in 1951, originally under a slightly different name, to coordinate and aid development among newly independent countries. Members include nations throughout the Asia-Pacific region (Nepal joined in 1952; Bhutan, in 1962). Donor countries include Australia, Britain, Canada, India, Japan, New Zealand, and the United States. The organization's headquarters are in Colombo, Sri Lanka.

dzong—Bhutanese combined administrative and religious complex; a fortified monastery and often the seat of government for the local jurisdiction.

fiscal year (FY)—In Nepal: July 16 to July 15. In Bhutan: July 1 through June 30 after July 1, 1988. Prior to March 31, 1987, the fiscal year was from April 1 through March 31. The period from April 1, 1987 to June 30, 1988 was used for FY 1988. The text of this book uses FY 1990, for example, when referring to 1989–90.

Gorkha—A principality west of Kathmandu and the ancestral home of the Shah kings, which became the House of Gorkha.

gross domestic product (GDP)—A value measure of the flow of domestic goods and services produced by an economy over a period of time, such as a year. Only output values of goods for final consumption and investment are included because the values of primary and intermediate production are assumed to be included in final prices. GDP is sometimes aggregated and shown at market prices, meaning that indirect taxes and subsidies are included; when these have been eliminated, the result is GDP at factor cost. The word *gross* indicates that deductions for depreciation of physical assets have not been made. *See also* gross national product.

gross national product (GNP)—Gross domestic product (*q.v.*) plus the net income or loss stemming from transactions with foreign countries. GNP is the broadest measure of the output of goods and services of an economy. It can be calculated at market prices, which include indirect taxes and subsidies. Because indirect taxes and subsidies are only transfer payments, GNP is often calculated at factor cost by removing indirect taxes and subsidies.

Gurkha—The British derivative of Gorkha evolved from the name Gorkha (*q.v.*), which originally was applied to the soldiers of that region. The Gurkha soldiers of Nepal, who became famous for their service in the British and Indian armies in the nineteenth and twentieth centuries, principally were composed of members of the Magar, Gurung, Limbu, and Rai tribes, and were not a single ethnic group, tribe, clan, or caste.

International Monetary Fund (IMF)—Established along with the World Bank (*q.v.*) in 1945, the IMF is a specialized agency affiliated with the United Nations and is responsible for stabilizing international exchange loans to its members (including industrialized and developing countries) when they experience balance of payments difficulties. These loans frequently carry conditions that require substantial international economic adjustments by the recipients, most of which are developing countries.

jagir—A type of land tenure in Nepal granted primarily to military personnel, allowing them tax-free access to produce from the land in return for military service. This tenure was a basic feature of military service in northern India and in Nepal during late medieval times, and disappeared in Nepal only in the twentieth century.

Khasa—A term applied to the peoples and languages in the western parts of Nepal, closely related to the cultures of northern India.

Kirata—A Tibeto-Burman ethnic group inhabiting eastern Nepal since before the Licchavi Dynasty, just prior to and during the early years of the Christian era.

ngultrum—Bhutan's unit of currency adopted in 1974. In November 1990, the official exchange rate was US$1 equals ngultrum (Nu) 17.95 and at par with the Indian rupee (Nu1 = Rs1). There are 100 chetrum (Ch) in one ngultrum. There are 5, 10, 25, and 50 chetrum cupro-nickel coins and a 1 ngultrum bronze coin, and 1, 2, 5, 10, 20, 50, and 100 ngultrum notes. Large ngultrum amounts are counted using the Sanskrit terms *lakh* (100,000) and *crore* (10 million); thus Nu1 lakh = Nu 100,000 and Nu 1 crore = Nu10 million). The term is derived from the Dzongkha *ngul,* meaning silver, and *trum,* probably a Hindi word, meaning money. Before 1957 Indian and Bhutanese coins circulated in nondecimal paisa and rupee denominations (1 rupee = 64 paisa); after the decimal system was adopted in 1957, paisa, rupee, and sertum circulated (1 sertum = 100 rupees; 1 rupee = 100 paisa).

nibbana—More commonly known in Western literature as nirvana. The goal of the path, the extinction of desire, hate, and the illusion of selfhood. A state of mystical union with the absolute one world soul (*brahman*), not an individual soul that attains it (as in Hinduism). For the Hindu, a state of liberation or illumination. For the Buddhist, there are no immortal particular souls, only the world soul, in which all beings, both animate and inanimate, are participants. The goal of spiritual practice in all branches of Buddhism. Enlightenment is the realization of the identity of the self with the absolute. The release from the cycle of rebirths and the annihilation of the individual being that occurs on achievement of perfect spiritual understanding.

official development assistance (ODA)—Those flows to developing countries and multilateral institutions provided by official agencies, including state and local governments, or by their executive agencies, each transaction of which meets the following criteria: it is administered with the promotion of the economic development and welfare of developing countries as its main objective; and it is concessional in character and contains a grant element of at least 25 percent.

panchayat—In ancient times, a Nepalese public assembly, ideally comprised of the five (*pancha*) most important caste or occupational groups in the village. A *pancha* is a member of a *panchayat.* From 1962 until the 1990 constitution took effect, assemblies modeled on this ancient system formed the backbone of political structure in Nepal, at the village and district levels, and at the top in the National Panchayat, or Rashtriya Panchayat.

Rana—Term, used as an honorific personal name, signified strength in battle in late medieval north India. It was adopted as a title by Jang Bahadur Kunwar in the 1850s, and by his heirs after him, and became the standard name used for this Nepalese dynasty of prime ministers and their families.

rupee—(Rs) or Nepalese rupee (NRs), the unit of currency, universal since the late 1960s. The Nepalese rupee is linked to the

Indian rupee and is fully convertible although restrictions were imposed during the 1989–90 trade and transit dispute. The equivalency rate used in Chapter 1 is Rs2.1 = US$1 in 1919. By 1973 the official exchange rate was Rs6.55 = US$1; in 1991, Rs30.80 = US$1. One Nepalese rupee = 100 paisa.

samuha—Interest group within a *pancha* (*q.v.*). The term is derogatory when used by someone who does not belong to a *pancha*.

soft loan—A loan bearing either no rate of interest, or an interest rate below the true cost of the capital lent. The International Development Association, an affiliate of the International Bank for Reconstruction (see World Bank, *q.v.*), grants soft loans to developing countries for long-term capital projects.

South Asian Association for Regional Cooperation (SAARC)—Comprises the seven nations of South Asia: Bangladesh, Bhutan, India, Maldives, Nepal, Pakistan, and Sri Lanka; headquartered in Kathmandu. Founded as South Asia Regional Cooperation (SARC) organization at a meeting for foreign ministers in New Delhi on August 1–2, 1983; a second organizational meeting of foreign ministers was held in Thimphu in May 1985; inaugural meeting of heads of state and government in Dhaka on December 7–8, 1986. The goal is to effect economic, technical, and cultural cooperation, and to provide a forum for discussions of South Asia's political problems.

United States Export-Import Bank (Eximbank)—An independent corporate agency of the United States government, founded in 1934 to stimulate foreign trade during the Great Depression. The Eximbank facilitates export financing of United States goods and services by neutralizing the effect of export credit subsidies from other governments and by absorbing reasonable credit risks beyond the reach of the private sector.

World Bank—Informal name used to designate a group of four affiliated international institutions: the International Bank for Reconstruction and Development (IBRD), the International Development Association (IDA), the International Finance Corporation (IFC), and the Multilateral Investment Guarantee Agency (MIGA). The IBRD, established in 1945, has as its primary purpose the provision of loans to developing countries for productive projects. The IDA, a legally separate loan fund but administered by the staff of the IBRD, was set up in 1960 to furnish credits to the poorest developing countries on much easier terms than those of conventional IBRD loans. The IFC, founded in 1956, supplements the activities of the IBRD through loans and assistance designed specifically to encourage the growth of productive private enterprises in the less-developed countries. The MIGA, founded in 1988, insures private foreign investment in developing countries against various noncommercial risks. The president and certain senior officers of the IBRD hold the same positions in the IFC. The four institutions are owned by the governments of the countries that subscribe their capital. To participate in the World Bank group, member states must first belong to the Intentional Monetary Fund (IMF—*q.v.*).

Index

401

Hillary, Sir Edmond, 138
Hill Region, 57, 59–60, 66, 69; agriculture in, 123; elite class in, 163; food shortage in, 59, 100; migration from, 59, 70; migration to, 59; underemployment in, 122; unemployment in, 122
Himalayas, xv, 57, 269; and defense strategy, 212; role of, in precipitation, 61
Hindi, 76, 274, 276; publications in, 178
Hinduism, 10, 76, 90–91, 284; and Buddhism, 88; as official religion, xix, 88, 152, 190
Hindus: geographical distribution of, 90
Hindustan Times, 178
hippies, 82
Hodgson, Brian, 25
hotels, 138
House of Representatives, 43, 148, 157; women in, 174
housing
    Bhutan: 280–81, 289
    Nepal: 112
human rights
    Bhutan: xxvii, 325
    Nepal: 146, 164, 227
Hutton, Michael, xxvii, xxviii
hydroelectric production
    Bhutan: 304–5
    Nepal: 129, 132; foreign aid for, 119, 120, 190; river system as source for, 65; Tanakpur project, xx

IMF. *See* International Monetary Fund
immigrants, illegal, xxii, xxvi
imports
    Bhutan: 297, 298
    Nepal: auction system for, 118; of consumer goods, 116; control of, 115; earnings from, 119; to exports ratio, 140; increase in, 118, 119; from India, 116; of petroleum, 132
IMTRAT. *See* Indian Military Training Team
income: from agriculture, 42; distribution, 140; per capita, 107, 209; taxes, 113, 114
Index on Censorship, xxvii
India: aid to Bhutan by, 265, 290, 291, 292, 295, 304, 330; aid to Royal Bhutan Army by, 335, 337; border issues,

179; Bhutanese students in, 287; Bhutan's debt to, 297; ideas imported into Bhutan from, 324; influence on Nepal of, 6; migration from, 59; Nepalese opposition to, 233; Nepalese political agitation in, 238, 327; as protector of Bhutan, 335; reaction of, to Nepal's zone of peace initiative, 182; reaction of, to prodemocracy movement, 146, 182–83; trade agreement with Bhutan, 331; trade with Bhutan, 297
India-Bhutan relations, xxiv, 330–31; annual subsidy, 263; border issues in, 331; influences on, 330; military, 335
India-Nepal relations, xx, 180–83, 185, 232–36; arms supplies from, 215; financial aid from, 119, 133, 146, 181; military, 180, 220, 232–36; military training in, 216, 221; Nepalese demonstrations against, 51; during Sino-Indian border war, 44; and trade and transit treaty, 43, 51, 115, 139, 235; technical assistance from, 133; threat by, 212; trade with, 107, 116, 118
Indian Air Force, 338
Indian Army: cooperation of, with Royal Nepal Army, 233–34; Gurkha soldiers in, xviii, 79, 176, 197, 198, 203, 205, 224, 338
Indian Border Roads Organization, 207
Indian College of Combat, 338
Indian Military Academy, 337, 338, 339
Indian Military Liaison Group, 220
Indian Military Mission, 220, 233
Indian Military Training and Advisory Group, 220
Indian Military Training Team (IMTRAT), 335, 337
Indian National Congress, 36–37; Nepalese collaboration with, 37
Indian National Defence Academy, 337
Indian Police Academy, 340
Indian School Certificate Council, 285
Indo-Aryan people, 79
Indo-Nepalese people, xix, 74–76, 77
Indo-Pakistani War, 181, 331
Indo-Soviet Treaty of Peace, Friendship, and Cooperation (1971), 181
Indo-Sri Lankan Peace Agreement (1987), 184
Indrawati River, 65
Industrial Enterprises Act (1974), 128
Industrial Policy of Nepal, 121

industry
  Bhutan: 303
  Nepal: 66, 109, 110, 119, 126–29, 189
inflation: in 1980s, 51
Inner Himalayas, 269
Integrated Fisheries Development Project, 300
Intelsat. *See* International Telecommunications Satellite Organization
Interim Government of Nepal Act (1951), 147
internal security
  Bhutan: xxviii, 325–26, 336, 339–40
  Nepal: 213–14, 237–39; as mission of Royal Nepal Army, 197–98
International Civil Aviation Organization, 191
International Committee of the Red Cross, xxviii, 191
International Covenant on Civil and Political Rights, 228
International Development Association, 120
International Human Rights Commission, 326
International Labour Organisation, 287, 306
International Lumbini Development Project, 190
International Military Education Training (IMET) program, 221
International Monetary Fund (IMF)
  Bhutan: 334
  Nepal: 119, 191
International Telecommunications Satellite Organization (Intelsat), 311
irrigation
  Bhutan: 300
  Nepal: 112, 122, 123; under First Five-Year Plan, 109; foreign aid for, 119, 120; under Second Five-Year Plan, 109; sources for, 62, 65; Tanakpur project, xx
Islam, 284

Jackson, Michael, 55
jagir, 23, 201
Jaldhaka hydroelectric plant, 304
Janadoot, 178

Janakpur Railway, 135
Janata (The People), 36
Janata Dal, 165
Jan Morcha, 238
Japan: aid to Bhutan by, 295, 296; aid to Nepal by, 119, 121, 132, 146; Bhutanese students in, 287; imports from, 118; reaction of, to prodemocracy movement, 146; tourists to Bhutan from, 313; volunteer programs, 296
identification cards, 328
IMET. *See* International Military Education Training
Jayajyotirmalla (king), 12
Jayaprakasa of Kathmandu (king), 18
Jayasthitimalla, 12
Je Khenpo, 257, 258, 282, 315
Jesuit missionaries, 256
jhankri, 100, 101
Joshi, Bhuwan Lal, 74, 75
jotishi, 101
Judicial Council, 158; duties of, 230; established, 230; members of, 230
Judicial Service Commission, 158–59
judicial system
  Bhutan: xxi, 264, 321, 341
  Nepal: 157–59, 228–31

kaji, 28
Kali Gandaki Valley, 57
Kali River, 65
Kami caste, 83
Kanjur (Collection of the Words of the Buddha), 282
Kantavati, 19
Karnali River, 60, 65, 132
Kathmandu, 8, 59, 69; elite class in, 163; Gorkha conquest of, 17–18; origins of, 11; population of, 68; rainfall in, 61; in Three Kingdoms period, 13, 15; united with Patan, 13
Kathmandu Valley, 55, 59; ethnic groups in, 76; urban population in, 69
Kharbandi Technical School, 287
Khasa kings, 11
Khasa people, 5
Khas bhasha (Khasa language), 13
Khoprn, 8
Khoprngrama. *See* Khoprn
Khulekhani I, 132
Khulekhani II, 132
Khulekhani III, 132

Published Country Studies

(Area Handbook Series)

550-65	Afghanistan		550-87	Greece
550-98	Albania		550-78	Guatemala
550-44	Algeria		550-174	Guinea
550-59	Angola		550-82	Guyana and Belize
550-73	Argentina		550-151	Honduras
550-169	Australia		550-165	Hungary
550-176	Austria		550-21	India
550-175	Bangladesh		550-154	Indian Ocean
550-170	Belgium		550-39	Indonesia
550-66	Bolivia		550-68	Iran
550-20	Brazil		550-31	Iraq
550-168	Bulgaria		550-25	Israel
550-61	Burma		550-182	Italy
550-50	Cambodia		550-30	Japan
550-166	Cameroon		550-34	Jordan
550-159	Chad		550-56	Kenya
550-77	Chile		550-81	Korea, North
550-60	China		550-41	Korea, South
550-26	Colombia		550-58	Laos
550-33	Commonwealth Caribbean, Islands of the		550-24	Lebanon
550-91	Congo		550-38	Liberia
550-90	Costa Rica		550-85	Libya
550-69	Côte d'Ivoire (Ivory Coast)		550-172	Malawi
550-152	Cuba		550-45	Malaysia
550-22	Cyprus		550-161	Mauritania
550-158	Czechoslovakia		550-79	Mexico
550-36	Dominican Republic and Haiti		550-76	Mongolia
550-52	Ecuador		550-49	Morocco
550-43	Egypt		550-64	Mozambique
550-150	El Salvador		550-35	Nepal and Bhutan
550-28	Ethiopia		550-88	Nicaragua
550-167	Finland		550-157	Nigeria
550-155	Germany, East		550-94	Oceania
550-173	Germany, Fed. Rep. of		550-48	Pakistan
550-153	Ghana		550-46	Panama